PARTICIPATORY
Biblical Exegesis

READING THE SCRIPTURES

Gary A. Anderson, Matthew Levering, and Robert Louis Wilken

series editors

PARTICIPATORY
Biblical Exegesis

A Theology of Biblical Interpretation

MATTHEW LEVERING

University of Notre Dame Press
Notre Dame, Indiana

Designed by Wendy McMillen
Set in 10.6/14 Monotype Bell by Four Star Books
Printed on 60# Nature's Natural by Sheridan Books

Library of Congress Cataloging-in-Publication Data

Levering, Matthew, 1971-
    Participatory Biblical exegesis : a theology of Biblical interpretation /
Matthew Levering.
        p.   cm. (Reading the Scriptures)
    Includes bibliographical references and index.
    ISBN-13: 978-0-268-03406-1 (cloth : alk. paper)
    ISBN-10: 0-268-03406-0 (cloth : alk. paper)
    ISBN-13: 978-0-268-03408-5 (pbk. : alk. paper)
    ISBN-10: 0-268-03408-7 (pbk. : alk. paper)
    1. Bible—Hermeneutics.   2. History—Religious aspects—
Catholic Church.   3. Bible—Criticism, interpretation, etc.—History.
4. History—Religious aspects—Catholic Church—History of doctrines.
I. Title.
    BS476.L49   2008
    220.601—dc22
                                                      2007051041

To Michael Dauphinais

CONTENTS

ACKNOWLEDGMENTS

This study had its beginnings in four invitations: from Thomas Weinandy, O.F.M. Cap., Daniel Keating, and John Yocum to contribute an essay on Aquinas's *Commentary on John* for their book *Aquinas on Scripture*; from Robert Jenson (and Reinhard Hütter) to contribute an essay to *Pro Ecclesia* for a symposium on the Pontifical Biblical Commission's "The Jewish People and Their Sacred Scriptures in the Christian Bible"; from Frederick Christian Bauerschmidt and Jim Fodor to contribute a response to an essay by Catherine Pickstock for a symposium in *Modern Theology*; and from Stephen Fowl to speak to his session at the Society for Biblical Literature. I am deeply grateful to all these scholars for their generosity. Thanks also to Joseph Torchia, O.P. of *The Thomist*, who kindly accepted for publication an earlier version of chapter 5.

Various conversations laid the groundwork for this study. The insights of Michael Dauphinais, Fr. Matthew Lamb, and Fr. Francis Martin are visible, I think, on almost every page. As dean of faculty, Michael Dauphinais helped me find time to write the first draft of the manuscript in the spring of 2005. During that semester, Larry Goeckner, an undergraduate theology major at Ave Maria University, provided valuable assistance in obtaining secondary sources.

During the early stages of the manuscript, Bernhard Blankenhorn, O.P. offered criticisms that enabled me to realize what it was that I wanted to say. Jörgen Vijgen read the manuscript with his usual care and eye for bibliographical resources. Another cherished friend, Andrew Hofer, O.P. also offered keen criticisms, as did

Stephen Ryan, O.P. Jeremy Holmes both offered excellent criticisms and helped me obtain crucial late-medieval and early-modern texts. As the manuscript began to take somewhat readable shape, Guy Mansini, O.S.B. applied his brilliant insight to it, as did William Kurz, S.J. and Matthew Gerlach. David Yeago kindly read a draft of the introduction and encouraged further labor. Encouragement of various kinds from John Webster, Kavin Rowe, Darren Sarisky, Jared Staudt, Daniel Treier, Robert Ashworth, Rusty Reno, and Christopher Seitz, also deserve grateful acknowledgment. A crucial labor was performed by Philip McCosker, who both offered his own insightful criticisms and suggested that I send the manuscript to his friend Michael Tait, who deserves much credit for any clarity the book possesses. Louise Mitchell graciously prepared the bibliography and corrected the endnotes. Chuck van Hof of the University of Notre Dame Press strongly supported and guided the manuscript to publication; many thanks to him and to the anonymous readers.

David Solomon's Center for Ethics and Culture at the University of Notre Dame awarded me the Myser Fellowship for the 2006–7 academic year, which provided the time to complete the final revisions of the manuscript. The many good works of David Solomon and his colleagues Elizabeth Kirk and Daniel McInerny have been inspiring. Gary Anderson, David Burrell, C.S.C., Tremayne and Regina Cates, John Cavadini, Karen Chan, Patrick and Jennifer Clark, David Fagerberg, Fred Freddoso, Raymond Hain, Fr. Michael Heintz, Mary Hirschfeld, Andrew Hofer, Jim Lee, Daria Lucas, Ralph McInerny, Austin Murphy, O.S.B., John O'Callaghan, Cyril O'Regan, Drew Rosato, Thomas and Susan Scheck, and others welcomed me and my family to South Bend for the year. Brian Daley, S.J. kindly allowed me to audit his superb course on the Cappadocians.

In addition to those named above, many other friends have sustained me through the writing of this manuscript. I wish particularly to thank Romanus Cessario, O.P., David Dalin, Gilles Emery, O.P., Diane Eriksen, Reinhard Hütter, Fergus Kerr, O.P., Steven Long, Bruce Marshall, Graham McAleer, Charles Morerod, O.P., Roger Nutt, Joseph Pearce, Richard Schenk, O.P., Michael Sherwin, O.P., and Thomas Weinandy, O.F.M. Cap. I thank my parents, in-laws, brother, and extended family for their support and love. To my children, David, Andrew, Irene, John, and Daniel, and to my amazing wife Joy, words cannot express the gift that God has given me in you.

This book is dedicated to a dear friend whose labor, intelligence, and love of Christ have made so many things possible: to Michael Dauphinais, in thanksgiving for your constant friendship. May God "supply every need of yours according to his riches in glory in Christ Jesus" (Phil 4:19).

INTRODUCTION

The chapters of this book advance the proposal that Christian biblical exegesis, in accord with the Christian and biblical understanding of reality, should envision history not only as a linear unfolding of individual moments, but also as an ongoing participation in God's active providence, both metaphysically and Christologically-pneumatologically.[1]

What are the implications of this proposal? While it must await a full spelling-out in the chapters themselves, some implications can be identified here. In agreement with historical-critical exegesis, I affirm that the Bible should be studied in its original ancient contexts. Yet what I call "participatory" biblical exegesis also holds that these original contexts never stand on their own. While temporal reality is a "linear" unfolding of moments, it is so precisely as participating in the triune God. Moment follows moment in succession, and yet these moments are not atomistic, but rather constitute an organic web of interrelation. This is so because the intimate "vertical" presence of the Trinity's creative and redemptive action suffuses the "linear" or "horizontal" succession of moments. This metaphysical and Christological-pneumatological participation in God joins past, present, and future realities in a unified whole, so that through God's presence each moment is related intrinsically, not merely extrinsically, to every other moment.[2] It follows that one properly understands historical-temporal reality by integrating its linear and participatory dimensions. In short, my thesis is that to enter into the realities taught in the biblical texts requires not only linear-historical tools (archeology, philology, and so forth), but also, and indeed primarily, participatory tools—doctrines and practices—by which the exegete enters fully into the biblical world.[3]

The problematic situation I seek to address is well captured by the biblical scholar Walter Moberly, who eloquently and accurately describes the current disjunction between biblical interpretation and systematic theology:

For most Christians there are also [in addition to the creeds] various post-patristic formulations and confessions which are also normative. On the other hand, none of these doctrinal confessions were formulated by the biblical writers, nor (in all likelihood) even envisaged by them. Although the biblical writers provide a content for which the Fathers and others have sought to provide appropriate means of articulation and appropriation, such formulations are always technically anachronistic with regard to any particular biblical text in its likely original context. It is common knowledge that modern biblical criticism only became a recognizable discipline through the process of explicit severing of the Bible from classic theological formulations. The basis for this was the belief that only so could the Bible be respected and heard in its own right, untrammeled by preconceptions which supposed that the answers were already known even before the questions were asked, or by anachronistic impositions of the conceptualities and assumptions of subsequent ages. The fruitfulness of the severance, in terms of a clearer sense of practical and conceptual differences both within the Bible and between the Bible and post-biblical formulations, is well known. Moreover, the approach has been justified theologically, at least by Protestants, in terms of the need for the authentic voice of scripture to critique the always provisional formulations of post-biblical theology. This has led to a curious situation. To be a Christian means, at least in part, the acceptance and appropriation of certain theological doctrines and patterns of living. Yet the task of reading the Bible "critically" has regularly been defined precisely in terms of the exclusion of these doctrines and patterns of living from the interpretative process.[4]

This "curious situation" has led theologians and biblical scholars increasingly to recognize the need for a deeper philosophical and theological understanding of historical realities.[5] As Adrian Walker remarks with regard to the dominant "scientific" philosophy of history, "The question is simply what counts as science—and, so, whether or not the paradigm of 'scientific' exegesis that dominates Scriptural interpretation today is indeed sufficiently scientific. Ultimately, this question hinges on the nature of *history*."[6] In this book I suggest that a fully historical biblical exegesis depends on reinstating the participatory dimension of historical realities. One way to recover a fuller account of historical realities is to seek insight into why history became understood as solely linear or horizontal in the first place. Let me briefly introduce this approach, which I take up again in much more detail in chapters 1 and 2.

Linear and Participatory History

Numerous scholars have argued that fourteenth-century metaphysical nominalism led, in a gradual fashion as its implications were developed, to the modern understanding of history. While nominalism began in the twelfth century as a debate over the metaphysical status of such universals as "man," later fourteenth-century "nominalist" thinkers advanced a powerful critique of the patristic-medieval account of the relationship between human beings and God.[7] The standard patristic-medieval account explained creatures in terms of finite participation in divine being, and grace as a radical Christological-pneumatological deepening of this participation. As Norris Clarke comments with regard to Thomas Aquinas's approach to reality:

This key metaphysical doctrine of St. Thomas—reconciling the One and the Many in the universe as diverse participations of all beings in the central perfection of existence through limiting essence—if properly understood, opens up a magnificent synoptic vision that can easily deepen into a religious or mystical vision of the whole universe of real beings as a single great community of existents, with a deep "kinship" of similarity running through them all, which turns out when fully analyzed to imply that all are in some way *images of God*, their Source, each in its own unique but limited (imperfect) way.[8]

By contrast, for various reasons, the fourteenth-century nominalist approach to conceiving the relationship between creatures and God radicalized the patristic-medieval account of God's freedom and creaturely contingency, so that "Creation itself became a discontinuous act to be renewed at each moment of a creature's existence."[9] If I might summarize here the arguments of chapter 1, a new conception of the creature–Creator relationship emerged that, by breaking the participatory relationship of creatures to God, appears to have encouraged the modern understanding of temporal reality as a strictly linear or horizontal continuum rather than a participation in God (except when conceived extrinsically as a function of God's will). Once the "historical" is understood as a solely linear temporal continuum, then a separation of historical exegesis from patristic-medieval exegesis becomes inevitable. As we will see in chapter 2, the former comes to provide historical/conceptual insights, the latter at best "merely" mystical meanings.

The participatory structure of the life of grace finds support in Scripture's teaching that Christians "share Christ's suffering" (1 Pet 4:13) so that they might "partake in the glory that is to be revealed" (cf. 1 Pet 5:1) and "become partakers of the divine nature" (2 Pet 1:4).[10] What happens, however, if the order of grace is recognized as participatory while the order of creation is not? As I propose in chapter 1, late-medieval nominalist metaphysics brings about this situation, and the resulting account of reality, inclusive of time and history, is not theologically satisfying. Colin Gunton has put the problem well: "All historical action takes place with some relation to God," a relation contextualized "within the created order established by divine action" and marked by human "intentional and purposive activity" in time.[11]

Recovering this participatory way of understanding human and divine action assists in uniting traditional historical-critical biblical scholarship (which generally sees history as a linear continuum to be reconstructed) with patristic-medieval biblical scholarship (which sees history in relation to the triune God in whom we participate). As I should emphasize at the outset, there need be no dichotomy between the two approaches; they are not mutually exclusive.[12]

Yet, in proposing this understanding of historical reality—linear and participatory, the horizontal participating in the vertical—one cannot help but raise the concerns about "eisegesis" mentioned by Moberly. At stake is the biblical texts' historical character. For participatory biblical exegesis, it is not just that the words of Scripture point beyond themselves despite their very human historical composition and transmission. Rather, it is precisely in their humanness that the biblical texts are participatory. The texts and their human authors are already historically caught up in a participatory relationship, however obscure, with the trans-temporal realities of faith (Israel as God's covenantal people, Jesus Christ, the Mystical Body, the sacraments, and so forth).[13] Can exegesis that proceeds along these lines be sensitive to the "messiness" of the human composition and transmission of Scripture?

It seems to me that the answer is "yes." For one thing, such problems as the apparent discrepancies in the Pentateuch or between the gospels no longer loom as large as they do when truth claims in biblical interpretation stand or fall entirely on history as *solely* linear. Second, the patristic-medieval tendency to suppose that the realities depicted by the biblical authors are truly penetrated by the Church's later theological and metaphysical explanatory categories is not so much a condoning of eisegesis as it would seem to be from a perspective that understands historical realities as solely linear. Since historical realities are richer than a solely linear or atomistic understanding of time might suggest, the Church's theological and metaphysical "reading into" biblical texts may largely be expected to *illumine* the realities described in Scripture rather than to obscure them.[14] While I discuss this point more fully in chapters 3–5, I should note that here I am agreeing with numerous contemporary historical-critical biblical scholars. Richard Hays, for instance, has recently challenged biblical scholars to read the gospel narratives with eyes illumined by the reality that Christ has risen from the dead.[15]

Indeed, participatory biblical exegesis is already being done by numerous contemporary Protestant and Catholic biblical exegetes, as well as by theologians, preachers, and persons in the pew in their efforts to understand and proclaim biblical revelation. Participatory biblical exegesis locates the linear-historical details within a participatory-historical frame, a frame established by God's creative and redemptive work in history. Such exegesis is ongoing whenever people presume that a biblical text about Jesus is about the Jesus whom they worship in the Church, or whenever people suppose that the local churches founded by St. Paul have a real analogue today. It is ongoing whenever people pray, receive the sacraments, or ask forgiveness in the context of the reading and teaching of Scripture. It involves an understanding of historical realities, of our place in the history of salvation, that comes naturally to the believer. Yet it is one whose justification has largely been lost and needs reclaiming.

This book seeks to contribute to that task. The modern (metaphysical) understanding of history as a solely linear continuum, insofar as this understanding has taken hold in biblical scholarship, is incapable of accounting for the theological and metaphysical reality of human history. *History* cannot be confined to what can be known by linear historical modes, important as those modes are; the historical includes a participation in realities known by faith.

While Catholics and Protestants differ somewhat as to what those realities are, they agree much more than they disagree. Inaccessible to solely linear history, realities such as the Trinity, creation, original sin, Israel, divine Revelation, Christ crucified and risen, the grace of the Holy Spirit, the mission of the Church to proclaim the gospel and celebrate the sacraments, the forgiveness of sins, divine Providence, and final judgment largely unite Protestant and Catholic understandings of the participatory dimensions of human history.

Interpretation of the Bible thus requires, as Joseph Ratzinger puts it, examination of the biblical text's "proper historical context" in light of a Christological-pneumatological understanding of reality: "the mechanical principle must be balanced by the teleological principle."[16] The realities recognized by linear historical-critical research are thus illumined also by the participatory understanding of reality, which flows both from faith (the order of grace) and from metaphysical reflection (the order of creation). Indeed paradoxically, the insistence on the validity of the participatory aspect of historical realities upholds history's *linear* dimension against postmodernism, by affirming the existence of an intelligible continuum.[17]

I should note that my proposal in this book should not be confused with the function that David Williams gives to the spiritual sense of Scripture—namely, to be "a bridge between past intention and present situation."[18] As traditionally understood, the spiritual sense of Scripture serves to go deeper into the infinitely rich dimensions of the biblical realities. Williams is right, therefore, to say that the spiritual sense is not "a privileged or alternative understanding of the witness itself."[19] But my proposal is different insofar as I hold that the literal sense itself possesses the resources for bridging past and present, because of the literal sense's conjoined linear and participatory dimensions. The literal sense of the divinely ordained realities present and active in linear history (for instance, covenantal Israel, Jesus Christ, the Holy Spirit, the Eucharist, the Church) possesses a participatory-historical dimension, since these diachronic realities expose how human time, already metaphysically participatory in God, shares ever more deeply in the infinite wisdom and love of divine action. The "bridge" then is another direction suggested by Williams, that of more fully drawing together divine and human agency so as to understand history more deeply.[20] I propose doing this through exploration of the inseparability of the linear and participatory dimensions of reality.

Admittedly, however, it is quite risky to broaden the concept of historical reality to an extent that most non-Christian, and many Christian, historians would find hard to accept.[21] I am aware that all the talk of metaphysics (participatory and nominalist) and its exegetical implications may put off both biblical scholars and theologians, for whom such discourse may be an undiscovered country or an outmoded theory. It might seem preferable to lay the standard linear-historical exegetical approach (with its hermeneutical variants) alongside other more "theological" exegetical approaches, as others have done. The most important example of such a strategy, of course, is that of Brevard Childs. This introduction requires here, therefore, a brief assessment of his work before I develop my approach in the chapters of this book.[22]

The Contribution of Brevard Childs

How does the project of participatory biblical exegesis relate to Brevard Childs's canonical approach? Throughout his impressive corpus, Childs's main concern has been how to relate theology and history.[23] In a relatively early essay he notes that when the patristic-medieval integration of history and theology broke down, the Reformers faced the problem that "to restrict biblical interpretation to a strictly grammatical reading seemed to threaten the whole theological dimension of the Bible as it related both to teaching and practice."[24] While he suggests that the Reformers reunited history and theology under the aegis of the literal sense, he finds that this unity too quickly collapsed due to the dissolution not (as previously) of theology but of history. Similarly in his most recent work, *The Struggle to Understand Isaiah as Christian Scripture*, he notes that "the heirs of the Enlightenment, indebted to but differing from the Protestant Reformers," responded to the patristic-medieval exegetical tradition by arguing "that serious biblical interpretation required a rigorous separation between the author's historical interpretation and all subsequent theological reflection."[25] The early Childs called for the restoration of the unity of history and theology in the literal sense of Scripture, but although he advanced the canon as a norm, he had not yet fully articulated how to achieve this unity. Childs's mature account of his canonical approach enables him to affirm that the separation between history and theology is both methodologically valuable and fundamentally bridgeable.[26]

He grants that the biblical texts contain a multilayered history that must be distinguished from later exegetical-theological framing, both intrabiblical and extrabiblical. The recovery of this multilayered history serves as a "constraining force" that, when functioning properly, keeps theology biblical. As Childs affirms in this regard, "The central hermeneutical issue turns on the question of whether there is indeed coercion from the biblical text in terms of its subject matter to serve as a constraining force."[27] Distinctly historical research into the authorship and redaction of biblical texts thus increases theological understanding of the Bible by acquainting theologians with the constraining pattern of God's historical activity. In this regard he agrees "with von Rad's position that no stage in the Old Testament's long history of growth is obsolete, and that something of each phase has been conserved until its final form. . . . The hermeneutical issue at stake does not lie in an alleged contrast between historical process and scripture's final form."[28] As might be expected, then, the problem for exegesis, in Childs's view, ultimately lies not with history, but with theology: God's action "cannot be fused with empirical history, nor can it be separated."[29] In other words, how are we to understand God's action so as to bridge the distance between God's action and history in Scripture's literal sense?

For Childs, as *God's* action, this history must be understood theologically; as God's action *in history* through historical agents, it must be understood historically. Childs concludes that the bridge between the two is the final form of God's canonical revelation. He explains that "[t]o speak of the privileged state of the canonical form is not to disregard Israel's past history. However, it refuses to fuse the canonical process of the shaping of the *witness* of the prophets and apostles with an allegedly objective scientific reconstruction that uses a critical filter to eliminate those very features that constitute its witness, namely, the presence of God in the history of Israel and the church."[30] The canon provides the link that enables the interpreter to appreciate historical research critically from a theological perspective, making it possible for Childs to see a broad continuity between his canonical exegesis and patristic-medieval forms of exegesis as regards biblical authority, the literal and spiritual senses of Scripture, the relationship of the two Testaments, the relationship of the divine and human authors, the unity of Scripture, the Bible's Christological content, and what he calls the "dialectical" understanding of history.[31]

All this is very well, but does Childs avoid a disjunction between the "canon" and "history" by making the former serve as the theological guide for evaluating the latter? In other words, in his effort to articulate their relationship as dialectical, does history lose too much of its theological depth and instead become a linear substratum on which theology, through its canonical principle, works?[32] In Childs's view, as noted above, non-theological readings of the "history" within the canon serve theological purposes by exposing the workings of God in history. But the danger, to which Childs is well attuned, is that the unresolved issue of the nature of history (theological or non-theological?) threatens even in canonical exegesis to "eliminate those very features that constitute its [canonical] witness, namely, the presence of God in the history of Israel and the church."[33] Given this danger, he argues for a strict distinction between study of the Bible as "the sacred scriptures of the church" and "the study of the Bible in history-of-religions categories," and yet he affirms that the former cannot cut itself off from the latter: "There is a subtle interrelationship that must be maintained."[34] Without this relationship, the "historical nature" of the Church's "confessional stance toward its scriptures" would falter.[35]

To what degree does Childs equate this "historical nature" with the presuppositions of "history-of-religions categories"? Describing Aquinas's practice of "intertextual" reading,[36] Childs comments on the expansion of the literal meaning and the value of the movement from the literal to the spiritual sense of Scripture:

The sophistication of his use of intertextual reference emerges especially when Thomas moves from the literal sense to a figurative level of interpretation. For example, in chapter 1 [of Isaiah], Thomas summarizes at the outset the intention of the main body of the text: the advent of Christ and the calling of the Gentiles. However, what exactly he understands by these two rubrics is revealed by close attention to the verses that follow. Ps. 25:10 begins his interpretation: "All the paths of the Lord are mercy and truth." This is followed by Luke 2:34: "This child is set for the fall and rising of many in Israel." Next the Apostle Paul provides a transition to the Gentiles in Rom. 11:25: "a hardening has come upon part of Israel until the full number of the gentiles come in and so all Israel will be saved." In sum, lest we think that Thomas is only concerned with the advent of Christ and the inclusion of the nations, the intertextual references show that he interpreted the biblical context to address the ultimate joining of the "Old Testament saints" with "those hardened within Israel," who together with the Gentiles comprise the salvation of all of Israel.

Another form of Thomas's application of intertextuality is the addition of *notandum super illo verbo,* which are set editorially usually at the end of a section. Usually this rubric consists of theological reflections focused on a single word or concept that he joins together on the basis of content. This is to say, Thomas makes the association according to his understanding of a resemblance of subject matter that extends to both testaments (cf. chapter 9 on the attributes of the Savior). This procedure, like the *dicta probantia,* consists of a catena of verses without commentary that nevertheless prompts the reader to reflect on the nature of the reality undergirding these different witnesses. To name this ontological interpretation is probably a terminological anachronism, but it does touch on an essential feature of Thomas's theological approach to the substance of scripture.[37]

Childs recognizes the central importance for Aquinas of interpretive reflection "on the nature of the reality undergirding these different witnesses." As Childs suggests, this "ontological interpretation" involves expanding the "literal sense" through parallel biblical passages (and, he could have added, patristic commentary and metaphysical reflection) and inspires interpretive deepening through the spiritual senses.[38] He also appreciatively notes "Thomas's careful attention to the ontological force exerted by the subject matter itself (its *res*)."[39]

Yet Childs is unwilling to go quite as far as Aquinas. His hesitancy stems from the fact that "it remains hermeneutically significant to understand the range of questions that are in accord with the intention of the biblical author and those that are only indirectly related to the writer's concerns."[40] Aquinas, Childs thinks, affirms this in principle (through the affirmation of the value of the literal sense), but in practice conflates questions about the literal sense with questions, such as the quality of prophetic knowledge, that do not pertain to the literal sense understood as the author's intended meaning. In Childs's canonical approach, such philosophical/theological questioning is kept carefully separated from research into the text's original meaning. This separation limits the literal sense to a historical meaning that includes only the linear aspect of history, the province of "history-of-religions categories."[41] Can these categories do justice even to the linear aspect of history? Childs seems to assume that in a certain sense they can, even while denying that "there is nothing intrinsically Christian about the Old Testament."[42]

Yet, one might ask, what would happen if one insisted on a historical engagement that *includes* the knowledge of faith, or even a minimal belief in a Creator? Would theological and metaphysical convictions swallow the diversity and messiness of linear history, and thereby swallow the distinct voices of the scriptural texts in their historical contexts? So long as the historical task is properly understood, the answer is surely "no." N. T. Wright has described the historical method as one of "hypothesis and verification"[43] where one seeks to explain the historical data as simply as possible, taking into account the society's worldview, as evidenced by its symbols, characteristic behavior, and literature, along with what one knows about the aims, intentions, motivations, and mindsets of the historical agents.[44] In connecting the data in this context and developing an account of "what happened," the historian has to "tell a story."[45] But, as Childs is well aware, in order to tell the story—any story—one must already accept a framing narrative of what is historically possible and thus of what is presently ongoing. It is here that the (metaphysical and theological) question of whether history is *strictly* linear or both linear and participatory must be decided.[46] As Hans Urs von Balthasar puts it, one cannot neutrally describe, for instance, the development of ancient Israel's religion: "the essential question concerns *what* is here developing."[47] This "what," namely the reality, can be properly known, even as regards historical methodology, only in its metaphysical and teleological participation in God's providential plan. There is no "original context" whose integrity requires, even temporarily, exegetical neutrality as regards the fullness of the participatory dimensions.

This point only enhances the value of linear-historical research into the Old and New Testaments. The process of hypothesis and verification, and the new hypotheses generated by this process, deepen and challenge our understanding of the particular realities the biblical authors attempt to describe. Von Balthasar also observes (following Karl Barth) that the "gap" between the portraits arrived at by historical-

critical scholarship and the reality known in faith—"between the testimony and that to which it points"—serves to make clear that the
words of Scripture are themselves not the realities sought; rather interpreters must seek in and through Scripture the realities to which Scripture points.[48] Yet these realities can only be sought in and through the
words of Scripture, in and through the messiness of human history, into
which linear-historical research can attain such valuable insight. For its
full flourishing, participatory biblical exegesis thus requires not merely
theological and metaphysical insights into God's work of creation and
redemption, but also the historical-critical procedure of hypothesis and
verification, as well as literary analysis. These approaches give insight
into the full fabric of the texts' richly *human* aspects, which are both
participatory- and linear-historical. The integrity of linear-historical
research does not require bracketing the participatory reality of God's
presence and action in history.[49]

In short, historical reconstruction that recognizes that historical
reality is not solely linear, but rather is both linear and participatory
(in the triune God's creative and redemptive work), will be illumined
both by linear-historical data and by participatory-historical ecclesial
judgments about the divine realities involved.[50] Granted the need for
historical biblical interpretation open to both the linear and participatory dimensions of the realities of faith, exegetical work requires, as
Childs has suggested, the canonical text of the Bible as the inspired
communication, in the Church, of the triune God's saving work. In canonical Scripture the Holy Spirit, through the human authors and the
diverse literary-historical modes, makes manifest a "history" possessed
of participatory dimensions that exceed what can be garnered from
solely linear reconstruction of historical realities. But neither can these
participatory dimensions be understood outside of the messiness of
"linear" human history; the participatory indwells the linear.

Plan of the Work

In engaging with Childs's position, then, we have seen that participatory biblical exegesis relies on a delicate interpretive balance, in which

linear and participatory exploration of Scripture must go hand-in-hand without negating either dimension of history. For various reasons, good and bad, this proper balance of participatory and linear was lost in the modern period, and it is not clear that Childs, despite his profound contributions, has fully recovered it. In the situation in which we find ourselves, the participatory dimension no longer counts as "historical" and "history" signifies a realm of human autonomy to which theological realities are extrinsic. Exploring the patristic-medieval participatory understanding of reality, and its gradual displacement from biblical exegesis after the high Middle Ages, is thus the task of chapters 1 and 2.

When the participatory dimension of reality is lacking, either anthropocentric readings of Scripture or, conversely, theocentric readings that deny the human dimension altogether, take over. By contrast, in participatory biblical exegesis one can integrate conceptually divine and human agency. On the one hand, everything comes from the triune God, the one in whom all finite things participate (metaphysically and Christologically-pneumatologically). For biblical exegesis, this means that the Bible is not ultimately about human beings, but rather about the triune God. Interpreting the texts of the Bible in faith means to encounter, in a radically theocentric fashion, "God teaching." This is the argument in chapter 3.

On the other hand, the participatory relationship means that God's action and human action are not in competition.[51] In Scripture, the centrality of God's teaching does not displace the human writing, editing, transmission, and interpretation of biblical texts, that is, the human aspects of the text. These human aspects, of course, are not solely linear-historical. The task of appreciating the linear-historical "messiness" of the biblical texts requires engaging the human aspects in their participatory-historical dimensions. So chapter 4 shows—by means of dialogue with contemporary Jewish biblical exegesis—that participating in "God teaching" comes about most fruitfully from within the practices that God has ordained for his people. "Historical" and "critical" engagement with the biblical texts thus includes both historical-critical research into the linear past and participatory "wisdom-practices" (liturgical, moral, and doctrinal) that conform the divinely ordained interpretive community, and individual exegetes within it, to the realities expressed in God's teaching as scripturally mediated.[52]

The central tasks of the first four chapters—namely, (1) renewing our Christological and metaphysical awareness of historical reality as "participatory," and thereby (2) perceiving God the Teacher in Scripture *(sacra doctrina)* and (3) identifying the role of the community, in Christ and the Holy Spirit, in receiving/teaching this scriptural *sacra doctrina*—go a significant way, I think, toward reclaiming for contemporary exegesis the strengths of patristic-medieval exegetical practice (which is exemplified in this book largely by Aquinas's exegesis of the Gospel of John). Chapter 5 then addresses the question of whether God's teaching and human ecclesial teaching can be reunited without biblical exegesis appearing to be an exercise of arbitrary power rather than wisdom. This final chapter takes up the modern inheritance in terms of biblical interpretation's relationship to ecclesial authority, and thus ultimately of the relationship of truth to power. An important reason for contemporary critics not wanting to relinquish any of the "objectivity" established by history understood as *solely* linear is the suspicion that ecclesial tradition and authority lead down a corruptive path in which the Church's authority threatens either human freedom or (by constricting God) divine freedom. On this view, biblical interpretation of the traditional historical-critical kind functions as an independent doctrinal corrective.[53]

Without overlooking such concerns, this book seeks to assist in the development of a biblical interpretation that understands itself as an ongoing ecclesial participation in God's historical *sacra doctrina*, and so engages once again with the full dimensions of "history" that the Bible itself envisions. While more is needed that cannot be done in this book, including a full-scale account of revelation and inspiration (and thus ultimately of ecclesiology),[54] the book's proposed exegetical practice recommends itself by its capacity to unite historical-critical research with what otherwise would seem anachronistic or eisegetical readings of the literal sense—readings informed by metaphysical and theological understandings that belong to and are developments from (in Newman's sense)[55] the realities depicted in the biblical text. The literal sense is thereby expanded to include fuller and richer exposition of the realities present in the text. One can then see more clearly how the spiritual senses of Scripture flow intrinsically from the effort to probe and illumine the literal sense.[56]

Once one understands reality as participatory-historical (providential and Christological-pneumatological) as well as linear-historical, what aspects of patristic-medieval biblical exegesis might once again be found valuable within contemporary biblical exegesis? Let this question stand as an overarching concern of the present book.

CHAPTER ONE

Late-Medieval Nominalism and Participatory Biblical Exegesis

The first section of this chapter draws on recent scholarship to provide a more detailed account of the fourteenth-century shift to a nonparticipatory metaphysical understanding of the creature–Creator relationship, as well as the possible implications of this shift for biblical exegesis.[1] The second section of the chapter turns to an example of biblical exegesis before the fourteenth-century shift, namely Thomas Aquinas's exegesis of John 3:27–36.[2] These two steps should provide the resources necessary for the work undertaken in chapter 2, which treats in comparative fashion exegesis of John 3:27–36 from the fourteenth through the twentieth centuries.

At the outset, let me say that neither this chapter nor the next one can prove a directly causal or necessary link between the shift away from the metaphysics of participation, the decadence in biblical exegesis during the same period, and the later rise of Enlightenment exegetical modes. However, as Charles Taylor observes with regard to historical explanation, when "a very clear and plausible diachronic-causal story" cannot be given, scholars may turn to "a second, less ambitious question. It is an interpretive one. Answering it involves giving an account of the new identity which makes clear what its appeal was. What drew people to it? Indeed, what draws them today?"[3] Taylor admits that such questions cannot be entirely isolated from the "diachronic-causal" questions, and I have found that to be the case as well. Yet, at the heart of these first two chapters is the question why one form of biblical exegesis lost its appeal and another form became appealing. Taken together, I hope that the two chapters give strong reasons for considering a connection between biblical exegesis and metaphysical presuppositions regarding historical reality.

The Fourteenth-Century Metaphysical Shift

The Catholic exegete and theologian Francis Martin has shown that biblical interpretation requires an account of historical reality informed by a scriptural metaphysics rooted in the relation of "participation" that is creation.[4] This is so because exegesis (including much contemporary exegesis) that participates doctrinally and spiritually in the realities depicted by Scripture, and thus reads Scripture not merely as a record of something strictly in the past, requires the sense that all human time participates metaphysically (order of creation) and Christologically-pneumatologically (order of grace) in God's eternal Providence and therefore that no historical text or event can be studied strictly "on its own terms."[5] Conversely, certain metaphysical presuppositions are inadequate to Christian biblical interpretation.[6] It seems to me that Catherine Pickstock describes just such a set of presuppositions in recounting the impact of Duns Scotus's thought:

As a "proto-modern" thinker, Scotus's contributions had implications for the alliance between theology and the metaphysical (in the broad sense of pre-Scotist Platonic-Aristotelian philosophical realism, not in the sense of onto-theology). For within the prevailing theologico-metaphysical discourse of participated-in perfections, there was a ready continuity between reason and revelation: reason itself was drawn upwards by divine light, while, inversely, revelation involved the conjunction of radiant being and further illuminated mind. Here, as we have seen, to rise to the Good, before as well as within faith, was to rise to God. But once the perceived relationship to the transcendentals has undergone the shift described above, to abstract to the Good tells us nothing concerning the divine nature. To know the latter, we wait far more upon a positive revelation of something that has for us the impact of a contingent fact rather than a metaphysical necessity. One can interpret the latter outcome as modern misfortune: the loss of an integrally conceptual and mystical path.[7]

Although the positions of the theological movement in which Pickstock is a prime mover have been criticized for historical sloppiness,[8] her central claims here—that the fourteenth century marks a shift away from the patristic-medieval understanding of "participated-in perfections," and that Scotus, although not a nominalist in the twelfth-century sense, plays a crucial role in this development—find broad scholarly agreement among experts on late-medieval thought.[9]

Olivier Boulnois, the preeminent contemporary interpreter of Scotus's work, refers to "the Scotist rupture."[10] The human will for Scotus mirrors the freedom of the divine will,[11] and Scotus denies that the will is an appetite that seeks its fulfillment or perfection. Scotus also rejects the teleological framework of "final causality" as "a flight into fantasy *(fugiendo finguntur viae mirabiles)."*[12] The patristic-medieval tradition prior to Scotus interpreted reality in terms of participation (Platonic) and teleological nature (Aristotelian). In contrast to Aquinas, who unites these two approaches through a metaphysics of creation, Scotus brings about "a strange fragmentation" in which goodness no longer has its Platonic participatory character.[13] For Scotus, too, God does not know creatures in knowing himself (the strong sense of participation), but rather knows creatures as a conceptual object of the divine mind.[14] While participation remains in Scotus, it does so in a deracinated form: representation rather than exemplarity. Lacking a rich account of participation and analogy, reality is "desymbolized": human time is no longer understood as caught up in a participatory relationship with God, and history becomes a strictly linear, horizontal, intratemporal series of moments. After Scotus, human freedom may submit to the divine will, but thereafter on the grounds of God's obligating power rather than on participatory-teleological grounds.[15]

Does the shift toward understanding human freedom and history as a non-participatory reality—the "rupture" identified by Boulnois—begin, therefore, with Duns Scotus? That question must be left to medievalists, but it does seem that we can identify in his work certain metaphysical patterns that remain influential today. The question for us is how to assess the theological effects of these patterns.[16] Evaluating the fourteenth-century shift positively, the historian Anthony Levi describes the autonomous humanism that emerges once participation theories are displaced:

Renaissance and reformation were connected because they were each forms taken by the restatements of the view that human perfection, even religious perfection, is intrinsic to human moral elevation as judged against norms based on rational human nature itself. However surprising it may sound to say so today, the history of the renaissance and the reformation seems not only to have a moral, but a moral that gives grounds for optimism, although not for complacency. However far it may still have to go, however patchy and sporadic success may so far have been, and however compromised by the modern technology of repression, in the end it looks as if, in the best possible environmental circumstances which Rabelais, borrowing from Erasmus, envisaged for Thélème, human nature tends in the long term to construct human societies according to increasingly humanitarian ethical norms.[17]

For Levi, denial that the human path toward perfection involves teleological participation in God (and thus participation in God's wise and loving Trinitarian *ordo*)[18] allows human beings to reason out their own paths and thereby to achieve greater success in finding truly "humanitarian" ethical norms. Levi is joined in his positive evaluation by ethicists who find in the autonomous agent's blind leap of obedience a noble and exalted "charity" that does not dare to "know" and thereby does not onto-theologically lay claim to the radically free "God," as well as by ethicists who do not believe in God.[19]

A very different assessment is offered by Matthew Lamb, among others.[20] Lamb argues that the nominalist shift produces an inability to conceive of the self or of history as marked by either divine presence or human judgments that participate in transcendental truth and goodness. Instead, what remains, as Lamb shows by means of a comparison between Augustine's and Rousseau's *Confessions*, are the brute facts of dates and places, which reveal nothing but the ego confined within a strictly linear (horizontal) space-time horizon.[21] In the logistic matrix described by Lamb, human beings stand over against the "God" (presuming his existence) whose agency is now seen as imposing limits on human agency, rather than as a participatory framework that establishes freedom. Lamb elsewhere recounts this relationship of opposition between time and divine eternity:

> Nominalism paved the way for the Enlightenment to set eternal life in opposition to history, so that those seeking eternal life were despising the good life on earth. . . . From this loss of a grasp of the simultaneous totality of time in God's presence, there was a dissolution of time itself into a continuum of isolated moments. The present was set in opposition to the past. Memory and tradition were disparaged; the apocalyptic expectation that awaited the advent of the kingdom of God was emptied into what Metz calls a softened evolutionary eschatology.[22]

By the seventeenth century, the participatory understanding of historical reality was on its last legs among intellectuals, although the overall unity of the onward-marching linear-historical moments was still presumed.[23]

Hans Frei finds a similar logistic conceptualism in Enlightenment biblical hermeneutics, although unlike Lamb he does not, so far as I know, draw the connection to late-medieval thought. Discussing the "supernaturalist" position on the Bible offered—within the context of the emergence of historical criticism—by the eighteenth-century Lutheran theologian Sigmund Jakob Baumgarten, Frei notes that for Baumgarten the accuracy of biblical history "'can be brought to the highest degree of probability or the greatest possible moral certainty in accordance with all the logical rules of a historical proof.'"[24] By the eighteenth century, logical rules of historiography took priority over the Bible's narrative as the ground on which Christians could understand themselves.[25] These rules envisioned God's action as radically "external" to human action, and thus extrinsic to historical accounts of Scripture's genesis and meaning. In patristic and medieval hermeneutics, by contrast, not logical rules of historiography, but faith in a providential God grounded the assumption that the books of the Bible displayed the divine pattern of salvation.[26] This faith nourishes and is nourished by the Church's biblical reading, understood as a set of embodied and liturgical practices constituting the Church's *conversatio Dei*.

As Frei no doubt knew, he could have traced his insight into the ascendancy of historiography further back than the eighteenth century. Joseph Levine remarks:

> By the end of the eighteenth century, theology had become dependent on history, and religion was justified by an appeal to "matter of fact." Even such mysteries as the doctrine of the Trinity, which had eluded the reason of St. Thomas and the schoolmen and had remained dependent on the dictates of church councils from Chalcedon to Trent, had come now to depend in some fashion on the evidence of Scripture considered as history. At the same time, the removal of final causes from the narrative of human events threatened to leave it—with every other Christian doctrine and event— to the arbitrament of ordinary scholarship.[27]

We have already encountered in Scotus this "removal of final causes," which Levine finds so crucial to modern understanding of history. Levine traces the shift, embodied in the eighteenth century by the historian Edward Gibbon, to Desiderius Erasmus and John Colet. Levine argues that Erasmus "began to think of the Bible principally as a record of history, rather than as an arsenal of theological texts, above all as the story of Christ on earth—Christ as the supreme exemplar to be followed and imitated."[28] Behind Erasmus, Levine finds the mid-fifteenth-century humanist Lorenzo Valla: "For Valla, grammar was the supreme science, or at least the indispensable preliminary that was required for understanding any writing, and hence any doctrine. . . . In these crucial matters, the philologist was above the theologian."[29]

What happens, then, when Scripture is seen *primarily* as a linear-historical record of dates and places rather than as a providentially governed (revelatory) conversation with God in which the reader, within the doctrinal and sacramental matrix of the Church, is situated?[30] John Webster points to the disjunction that appears between "history" and "theology" and remarks on "the complex legacy of dualism and nominalism in Western Christian theology, through which the sensible and intelligible realms, history and eternity, were thrust away from each other, and creaturely forms (language, action, institutions) denied any capacity to indicate the presence and activity of the transcendent God."[31] Similarly, Lamb contrasts the signs or concepts that can be grasped by modern exegetical methods with the moral and intellectual virtues that are required for a true participatory knowledge and love of the realities expressed by the signs or concepts. Lacking the framework of participatory knowledge and love, biblical exegesis is reduced to what Lamb calls "a 'comparative textology' à la Spinoza."[32] Only participatory knowledge and love, which both ground and flow from the reading practices of the Church, can really attain the biblical realities. As Joseph Ratzinger thus observes, the meaning of Scripture is constituted when

> the human word and God's word work together in the singularity of historical events and the eternity of the everlasting Word which is contemporary in every age. The biblical word comes from a real past. It comes not only from the past, however, but at the same time from the eternity of God and it leads us into God's eternity, but again along the way through time, to which the past, the present and the future belong."[33]

This Christological theology of history, which depends on a metaphysics of participation inscribed in creation, provides the necessary frame for apprehending the true meaning of biblical texts.[34]

In short, for the patristic-medieval tradition and for those attuned to it today, history (inclusive of the work of historiography) is an individual and communal conversation with the triune God who creates and redeems history—and the Bible situates us in history thus understood.[35]

Participatory spiritual exercises constitute the very possibility for reading Scripture with an adequate appreciation for the realities it describes, a "sapiential" history that goes far beyond the fragmentary, atomistic dates and places (instantiations of divine and human willing) possible within a non-participatory metaphysics. Webster depicts the impact of the nominalist loss of a Trinitarian understanding of creation and redemption: God's "action comes to be understood as external, interruptive, and bearing no real relations to creaturely realities. God, in effect, becomes causal will, intervening in creaturely reality from outside but unconnected to the creation."[36]

The intrinsic relationship of participatory metaphysics to biblical interpretation (and thus to Christian doctrine) has perhaps been most richly articulated, among recent theologians, by the Eastern Orthodox theologian David Bentley Hart. In a crucial passage from his exploration of evil and suffering, *The Doors of the Sea*, Hart argues:

> Not only are the speculative concerns of developed Christian philosophy already substantially present in the Hellenistic metaphysical motifs and assumptions that permeate the New Testament (deny these though some might), but classical Christian metaphysics, as elaborated from the patristic through the high medieval periods, is a logically necessary consequence of the gospel: both insofar as it unfolds the inevitable ontological implications of Christian doctrines concerning the Trinity and creation *ex nihilo;* and insofar also as Christianity's evangelical vocation requires believers to be able to articulate the inherent rationality of their faith . . . "God is light, and in him is no darkness at all" (1 John 1:5); and as he is the source of all things, the fountainhead of being, everything that exists partakes of his goodness and is therefore, in its essence, entirely good.[37]

Such exegetically imperative participatory metaphysics, Hart shows, requires a rejection of Heidegger's critique of "being" and "participation" as onto-theological attempts to grasp the ungraspable.[38] Similarly Hart's "dogmatica minora," comprising the bulk of his *The Beauty of the Infinite*, moves through the biblical and theological warrants of the

Christian creed, from the Trinity through creation, the *imago Dei*, salvation in Christ, the economy of "peace" (the Church), and eschatology. At each step, Hart shows how participation is carried through in a unity both philosophical and theological, thereby exhibiting how tightly participatory metaphysics is bound to the Church's reading of Scripture.

Aquinas on John 3:27–36

The above sketch of the origins and implications of the fourteenth-century metaphysical shift needs to be filled out by concrete examples of exegesis. The remainder of this chapter thus offers Aquinas's commentary on John 3:27–36 as a benchmark. As the last great representative of patristic-medieval exegesis, Aquinas's exegetical practice provides insight into the possibilities of an exegesis governed by the participatory metaphysics of creation, providence, and salvation. This second section of the chapter thus both looks back on the preceding arguments regarding what is lost for exegesis after the metaphysical shift, and looks forward to the next chapter's discussion of representative commentaries on John 3:27–36 from the fourteenth through the twentieth centuries. Recalling Pickstock's description of the "modern misfortune" as "the loss of an integrally conceptual and mystical path,"[39] I examine Aquinas's interpretation of John 3:27–36 with the particular goal of illumining the understanding of historical reality that belongs to a participatory theological and metaphysical exposition of the biblical text.[40]

John 3:27–36 reads:

27 John [the Baptist] answered, "No one can receive anything except what is given him from heaven. 28 You yourselves bear me witness, that I said, I am not the Christ, but I have been sent before him. 29 He who has the bride is the bridegroom; the friend of the bridegroom, who stands and hears him, rejoices greatly at the bridegroom's voice; therefore this joy of mine is now full. 30 He must increase, but I must decrease." 31 He who comes from above is above all; he who is of the earth belongs to the earth, and of the earth he

speaks; he who comes from heaven is above all. 32 He bears witness
to what he has seen and heard, yet no one receives his testimony;
33 he who receives his testimony sets his seal to this, that God is
true. 34 For he whom God has sent utters the words of God, for it
is not by measure that he gives the Spirit; 35 the Father loves the
Son, and has given all things into his hand. 36 He who believes in
the Son has eternal life; he who does not obey the Son shall not see
life, but the wrath of God rests upon him.[41]

Interpreting this passage, Aquinas employs a radically participatory
understanding of reality that draws together Trinitarian theology, Christology, the Church's hierarchical structure, the transformative movement of deification, and eschatology. He provides, in other words, a portrait of the biblical realities of creation and redemption into which the
lives of believers are already incorporated (both metaphysically as creatures and Christologically-pneumatologically) and must be more fully
incorporated until "the riches of his glorious inheritance in the saints"
(Eph 1:18) have been fully manifested.[42] He returns continually to the
themes of participation, gifting, mediation, receptivity, and transformation.[43] He begins by discussing the origin of the "offices" of John the
Baptist and Jesus. Following St. John Chrysostom, he affirms John
the Baptist's appreciation of providence, which he metaphysically identifies as "the order of perfection and goodness" (§515).[44] One can share
in this order only through God's gift, and therefore it is fruitless to try
to usurp what God has not given one. All offices or missions are thus
God's gift and are participations in God's perfection and goodness.

Christ's office, Aquinas states, "is to judge and to preside" (§516).
It might seem, then, that Christ's office stands aloof in the manner of
a courtroom judge. But the very opposite is the case. Following the
text of John 3:27–29, Aquinas notes that the unique office of Christ
in fact constitutes the source of a continuous stream of mediations of
divine gifts. This mediation occurs through our relationship to Christ.
As *friends* of Christ, believers participate in bringing the "bride" (the
Church) to the "groom" (Christ), and receiving from Christ the consummation of truth and love. Believers refer all things to Christ: John the
Baptist "did not keep the bride, i.e., the faithful, for himself, but brought

them to the groom, that is, to Christ" (§519). To be brought to the groom means receiving and nourishing the gift of obedient faith.

This account of office in terms of receptivity and participation has ecclesiological resonance, as Aquinas recognizes. Christ's office is the source of all, and believers rejoice in Christ's gifts. Aquinas observes, "if it made me [John the Baptist, but also Aquinas himself and every Christian] sad that Christ, who is the true groom, preaches to the bride, i.e., the Church, I would not be a friend of the groom; but I am not sad" (§520). Believers cannot and should not be jealous of Christ as the source; Christ employs his office as source to enable believers to share in his perfections. Nonetheless, as Aquinas recognizes, some who have office in the Church do in fact become jealous and attempt to usurp Christ's role. They set themselves up as autonomous sources: "This is in opposition to those evil prelates who do not follow Christ's command in governing the Church" (§520). In so doing, they both cut themselves off from the source and also lead astray the faithful who seek the "groom."

John the Baptist, in contrast, exemplifies the proper office of a shepherd in the Church, who "decreases" (John 3:30)—that is, who directs "esteem and reverence" to the source (Christ)—and so enables Christ to "increase" (John 3:30) as his members share increasingly in his perfections. Christ, Aquinas notes, increases "not in himself, but in relation to others, in the sense that his power becomes more and more known" through his holy members (§523).

This relation between spiritual decrease and increase belongs to the pattern of our deification.[45] Interpreting John 3:30 "[i]n the moral sense," Aquinas says that for us to decrease means for Christ to increase in us by our participating in his perfections more deeply. Our decrease is actually an increase in perfection, but it is one that occurs by our coming to participate more in God (Christ's increase in us) and to rely less on ourselves (our decrease). The more we deepen our wisdom and love, the more Christ increases in us, because Christ is wisdom and love. Aquinas observes:

> Christ must increase in you, i.e., you should grow in the knowledge and love of Christ, because the more you are able to grasp him by knowledge and love, the more Christ increases in you; just as the

more one improves in seeing one and the same light, the more that light seems to increase. Consequently, as men advance in this way, their self-esteem decreases; because the more one knows of the divine greatness, the less he thinks of his human smallness. (§524)

Here the themes of mediation and participation are clear: Christ's office, as the mediator, is to share the divine gifts (wisdom and love) with us, and our sharing depends on the grace of humility, through which we recognize God, rather than ourselves, to be the source. In sharing in Christ, we are transformed and increase even as we decrease. In this participatory framework, the path of increasing is decreasing.

Aquinas therefore divides the text somewhat differently than do modern commentators, most of whom view John 3:31–36 as a later addition in which the voice is no longer John the Baptist's.[46] Aquinas treats John 3:27–32 (through "He bears witness to what he has seen and heard") as a unit depicting the source of our deifying participation. Christ is "above all" (John 3:31) both because of his origin and because of his teaching. On both counts, Aquinas is concerned to interpret "above all" not in terms of an aloof power, but in terms of gifting, mediation, and participation. Thus as regards his origin, not only is Christ God and therefore the fundamental source, but also his human nature is "above all" in that it is perfectly constituted to mediate the divine gifts as the Head of the Church (§§526–29). This emphasis on mediation continues with Aquinas's description of Christ's teaching as "above all." Aquinas affirms that "the quality of a teaching or doctrine is considered according to the quality of its origin" (§531). John the Baptist's teaching is therefore inferior to Christ's, even though John's is also divine teaching. Drawing on Augustine, Aquinas explains that "we can consider what any person has of himself and what he has received of another" (§532). When John teaches divinely revealed realities, he does so by participation. In contrast, when Christ teaches of divine realities, Christ as man testifies to himself as God, and thereby teaches not merely as one who participates, but indeed as the source of all participation.

John 3:32 enables Aquinas to explore the Trinitarian dimension of the source. Christ's "seeing" and "hearing" of divine realities pertain, Aquinas suggests, to God's unity and Trinity. Hearing differs from seeing in that sight provides immediate knowledge, whereas the knowing that arises from hearing involves an act of understanding. Aquinas thus links seeing with the divine unity (act of being) and hearing with the procession of the Word in the divine Trinity (act of understanding). It follows that "in the Son, to see and to hear are the same thing," since the divine Person is the same as the divine essence (§534). Yet, Christ's "hearing" of the divine realities expresses Christ's identity as the Word—and it is *our* hearing of the Word, which is none other than the divine essence, that enables us to participate in God by being deified.

If for Aquinas John 3:27–32a forms a unit in which the author of the Gospel describes the *source* of our deification, John 3:32b–36 (beginning with "no one receives his testimony") constitutes a second unit that depicts those who participate, or fail to participate, in the source. In verse 32 we read that no one accepts Christ, while in verse 33 we read that some do. While suggesting that this apparent divergence may simply be a manner of speech, Aquinas also applies to the difference between the verses his understanding of causality and participation. No one, he notes, "receives" Christ's testimony on his or her own; rather such receptivity to the Word of God is always a gift of grace (§537). God's gift of grace, he goes on to say, fits with his gift of the incarnate Son, and the former gift enables one to affirm the latter. To affirm the gift of the incarnate Son is to participate in the expression of the Father: Christ "expressed verbally nothing but the Father and the words of the Father, because he has been sent by the Father, and because he is the Word of the Father. Hence, he [Christ] says that he even bespeaks the Father" (§540). In short, the economy of gift brings about nothing less than deifying participation in Trinitarian life.

Moving from verse 33 to verse 34, Aquinas remarks that Christ, who as God possesses the Holy Spirit perfectly (in that the Father spirates the Spirit through the Son), is able as man to express the Father perfectly because of his perfect anointing with the Spirit. Unlike the prophets, Christ the true Prophet never speaks except in the fullness of the Spirit (§541). In perfectly expressing the Father's Word in the Spirit, Christ as man mediates the gift of the Spirit to all human beings. Christ sanctifies his members by giving them his Holy Spirit. This participatory economy of gift requires Aquinas to analyze Christ's grace in the course of his commentary. He first points out that the hypostatic union itself is a grace, as an unmerited gift that elevates Christ's holy humanity at the instant of its conception to perfect union with the divine nature in the Person of the Word. As a result of that perfect union, Christ as man receives the full influence of the Holy Spirit on his soul, filling his soul with the charity and wisdom that befit such a union. Given his uniqueness, Christ in his holy humanity receives a graced participation in God's life that includes "everything that could pertain to the nature of grace" (§544). Created nature cannot receive a higher participation in the divine life than that received in Christ's soul, as befits the union, at the instant of his conception.

Yet, this perfection is not for Christ alone. On the contrary, his perfect participation as man in God is intended, as the goal of the Incarnation, to enable others to share by grace in God's own life. Thus Christ's grace also makes him "head" of the Church: "For from the fact that he possessed that from which the gifts of the Spirit could flow out without measure, he received the power to pour them out without measure, so that the grace of Christ is sufficient not merely for the salvation of some men, but for all the people of the entire world" and indeed for all worlds (§544). The dignity of Christ and his office as source is grounded in radical gift. His human participation, while higher than ours, is ordered to our own.

Commenting on the next verse, "the Father loves the Son, and has given all things into his hand" (John 3:35), Aquinas distinguishes its significance regarding Christ's divinity and humanity. If one takes the verse as referring to the Son in his divinity, then one must be careful not to make the Son himself a participated "god." The Son is not loved into being, even eternal being, by the Father. This would make the Son the product of the Father's will, which would mean that "the Father generated the Son by will, and not by nature; and this is the Arian heresy" (§545). Moreover, the Father's love is the Holy Spirit. As Aquinas notes, "if the love of the Father for the Son were the reason why the Father put everything into his hands, it would follow that the Holy Spirit would be the principle of the generation of the Son," whereas in fact the Father is the principle (§545). Instead, on the divine level, this verse means that the Father gives everything to the Son, a communication of goodness that is signaled by the Father's love for the Son (§545).

This level of intra-Trinitarian gift undergirds what Aquinas has to say about the other way of taking the verse, namely as referring to the Son in his humanity. Here the aspect of participation—participation in the Trinitarian gifting—stands out once again as the key. Creatures come into existence when God wills to create finite participations in God's infinite existence, and thus it is true to say that God loves all creatures into existence. In willing the greatest possible participation in God for Christ's humanity (union in the Person of the Son), God loves Christ above all else, because he gives Christ's humanity the greatest possible created degree of sharing in God's perfection, goodness, and existence (§545). This greatest sharing grounds the gift of all "authority" to Christ, who possesses the "kingdom" as the "beloved Son" (Aquinas cites Matthew 3:17 and 28:18, as well as Colossians 1:13, in support of John 3:35). In short, we see in this discourse from the Gospel of John, interpreted in the patristic-medieval participatory mode, what Pickstock calls "the prevailing theologico-metaphysical discourse of participated-in perfections" that sustains, in both method and content, "a ready continuity between reason and revelation."[47]

The discourse concludes with the fruit of faith and the consequences of unbelief. Faith, when enlivened by charity, enables us to share in Christ's own participation in the divine life. Aquinas emphasizes that faith gives an intimate spiritual contact or unity with Christ. He states, "Whoever believes in the Son has that toward which he tends, that is, the Son, in whom he believes" (§547). To possess the Son is to possess the Son's life, which is eternal life. This state of being is a sharing in the intra-Trinitarian giving: "For if the Father has given everything he has to the Son, and the Father has eternal life, then he has given to the Son to be eternal life" (§547). We come to share in the Father's gift, the eternal life of the Son, by receiving Christ in the economy of gift and participation. By contrast, however, the reverse of this participatory transformation is to lack a sharing in true life. If one rejects God's saving gift through unbelief, one cannot come to share in the love and knowledge that is God, what Aquinas calls "the sweetness of eternal life" (§548). Refusing in pride to be caught up into the participatory economy of gift, one stays rooted in one's own selfishness. To be bound forever by selfishness is to experience the "wrath of God," both as loss of the eternal communication of wisdom and love for which one was created, and as the punishment incumbent on such selfish wickedness.[48] And yet the logic of gift, even here, cannot be avoided: only the gift of faith frees us from the selfishness that we inherit by birth, as members of a disordered human race descending from Adam. In sum, as St. Paul puts it, "Then what becomes of our boasting? It is excluded" (Rom 3:27).

Conclusion

Aquinas's probing of the realities set forth in John 3:27–36 invites us to share in the mystical-metaphysical dynamisms inscribed in the Gospel of John, thereby instancing the "discourse of participated-in perfections" and "ready continuity between reason and revelation" that Pickstock seeks to retrieve. Most modern exegetes, however, would find that his interpretation *eisegetically* imposes theological and metaphysical claims not present in the text. How else to explain Aquinas's account of hearing and seeing (John 3:32, "He bears witness to what he has seen and heard") as referring to the divine unity and the Word's procession, or to explain Aquinas's understanding of the reception of testimony (John 3:32–33, "yet no one receives his testimony; he who receives his testimony sets his seal to this, that God is true") as a reference to the necessity of grace to receive God's Word? Before determining what constitutes eisegesis, however, one must apprehend the patristic-medieval understanding of reality. Since reality includes the triune God, creatures cannot be fully understood by attending solely to their linear historicity. Rather, creatures, in their historicity, bear a participatory relation to God metaphysically and Christologically-pneumatologically.

In bearing participatory reference to divine and created realities, the words of the Gospel refer to both the linear and participatory historical dimensions of these realities—to the creative and redemptive work of the Son and Holy Spirit that make creatures' metaphysical participation and their deeper participation of grace possible. As regards the linear historical past, historical-critical interpretation may show that the evangelist John—let alone John the Baptist, in the places where he is the one speaking—did not have "grace" conceptually in mind when discussing the reception of Christ's testimony, and did not intend to gesture toward "God's unity and Trinity" in describing the witness of "he who comes from heaven."[49] Yet as regards the participatory historical aspect of the realities depicted by the Gospel, Aquinas's interpretation of John 3:27–36 captures a dimension of the text that remains closed to linear historical-critical research. Surveying Aquinas's verse-by-verse interpretation makes this clear. For Aquinas verse 27 points to the reality of creaturely receptivity; verse 28 to vocation; verse 29 to Christ's primacy; verse 30 to the humility that glorifies Christ; verse 31 to Christ's divinity and theandric humanity; verse 32 to Christ's manifestation of the triune God; verse 33 to faith and grace; verse 34 to Christ's relationship to the Father and Holy Spirit; verse 35 to Christ's authority as mediator; verse 36 to faith and eschatology. As regards human creatures, we see the theological and metaphysical aspects of receptivity, vocation, humility, grace, faith, and eschatological life. As regards Jesus, we see the aspects of his primacy, grace, headship in the Church, glorification in his members, manifestation of the Trinity, relationship to the Father and Holy Spirit, and authority as mediator. These elements belong at the heart of Aquinas's participatory understanding of reality.

When history is understood as a participation in God, the words and deeds depicted in John's Gospel take on what for Christians is recognizable as their true and deepest meaning. Jesus Christ constitutes the center of linear and participatory history as the incarnate Word, the one Mediator, in whom human beings receive the Holy Spirit and are led to the Father. Such Johannine phrases as "no one can receive anything except what is given him from heaven," "I have been sent," "the friend of the bridegroom," "he must increase," "he who comes from heaven is above all," "what he has seen and heard," "he who receives his testimony," "it is not by measure that he gives the Spirit," "the Father loves the Son," and "he who believes in the Son has eternal life"—all possess a "participatory" historical meaning along with their "linear" historical meaning. John the Baptist and/or the inspired author certainly may not have known many of the theological and metaphysical implications that Aquinas draws from the biblical words. This is the linear-historical dimension. But the linear aspect does not say all, because these words possess, equally historically, a participatory dimension expressed by Aquinas's theological and metaphysical language. Jesus Christ, the sacraments, the Church—these realities, active and present in linear history, cannot be confined to linear history, which they transcend by their ongoing mediation of the divine life of the Trinity in which human beings participate.

Receptivity belongs (metaphysically and theologically) to the historical reality of John the Baptist and/or the evangelist, because of the realities of creation, vocation, grace, inclusion in Christ, and so on. Thus John the Baptist's and/or the evangelist's attempts to express the reality of "Christ" as well as the reality of the "Father, Son, and Spirit"—all named in John 3:27–36—participate likewise, historically and not merely by a later eisegetical projection, in the fullness of truth about these realities. Historical criticism itself can often identify these participatory dimensions within John's text, since the evangelist so clearly has them in mind. These (metaphysical and theological) realities are not projected into the biblical text, but rather are actively present therein, just as their presence marks all of human history. Human history is never separate from these divine and divinity-mediating realities, which are constitutive of human history. This point applies even more to the biblical texts, which are caught up uniquely in the historical revelation of these realities. In approaching John's Gospel not only as linear history, but also as participatory history, Aquinas, despite his relative lack of linear historical-critical tools, penetrates profoundly the true *historical* dimensions of the realities depicted in the text. The reference of the words of John's Gospel has a richness that goes deeper than warranted solely by its linear-historical reference.

Christian biblical interpretation, then, must avoid an interpretive historicism that defines "history" solely as linear.[50] In faith we affirm that Christ is the Word of God. Thus what he has "seen and heard" pertains to the life of the Trinity: "No one has ever seen God; the only Son, who is in the bosom of the Father, he has made him known" (John 1:18). In faith we know that grace alone enables us to receive what Christ has "seen and heard." Such knowledge, which belongs to the biblical witness as taught in the Church, "reads into" John's Gospel in a manner that affirms the continuity of the realities there taught with the same realities as taught in the ongoing Church.[51] Robert Jenson makes clear that this understanding of continuity conforms with the biblical understanding of time: "time, in any construal adequate to the gospel, does not in fact march in this wooden [strictly linear] fashion. Time, as we see it framing biblical narrative, is neither linear nor cyclical but perhaps more like a helix, and what it spirals around is the risen Christ."[52] Time or history as understood biblically, as Christologically and metaphysically participatory, challenges the modern understanding of eisegesis by understanding biblical realities from within their ongoing historical "conversation" with God.[53] In the next chapter, I survey the gradual decline, though not extinction, of this exegetical practice.

CHAPTER TWO

From Aquinas to Raymond Brown

The previous chapter suggested that once historical reality came to be understood as metaphysically non-participatory, one could hardly expect exegetical practice to remain unaffected. To make this argument more concrete, I set forth Thomas Aquinas's exegesis of John 3:27–36 as a benchmark of the kinds of truth claims one finds in "participatory" biblical exegesis. Building on this work, the present chapter takes some further steps, admittedly tentative, toward appreciating how the understanding of history develops and changes in Catholic biblical exegesis from the fourteenth century to the twentieth.

Often such narratives begin with seventeenth-century exegetes such as Richard Simon, and locate the significant shift largely in the eighteenth and especially nineteenth centuries. Taking my cue however from Henri de Lubac—who showed that Catholic biblical exegesis, especially as regards the spiritual senses, had already undergone a significant shift by the fifteenth century[1]—I discuss ten examples of Catholic biblical exegesis of John 3:27–36 from the fourteenth through the twentieth century.[2] The ten figures include Meister Eckhart, O.P. (Germany, 1260–1328), Nicholas of Lyra, O.F.M. (France, 1270–1349), Denys the Carthusian (Belgium and Holland, 1402–71), Erasmus (Holland, 1466–1536), Tommaso de Vio, O.P. (Cajetan) (Italy, 1469–1534), Francisco de Toledo, S.J. (Spain, 1532–96), Juan de Maldonado, S.J. (Spain, 1534–83), Alexander Natalis, O.P. (France, 1639–1724), Marie-Joseph Lagrange, O.P. (1855–1938), and Raymond Brown, S.S. (1928–1998).[3] It seems to me that these figures illumine, however partially, the gradual stages by which a new understanding of history influenced Catholic biblical exegesis. This development does not displace all at once the participatory dimensions of history; these dimensions remain but grow increasingly tangential. Catholic biblical exegesis very gradually takes account of this change, which accelerates in the late-nineteenth and twentieth centuries. By the twentieth century the difference between Aquinas's exegesis and contemporary mainstream exegesis is striking. This difference certainly does not mean that contemporary mainstream exegesis lacks value and insight. But contemporary mainstream exegesis does understand history in a restricted way that, in my view, limits interpretative options and should not go unchallenged.

I have chosen these ten figures because of their importance in their day, but the ten hardly constitute an exhaustive historical survey, a task that I hope others will take up. In what follows I arrange them into three time periods: fourteenth and fifteenth centuries; sixteenth century; seventeenth through twentieth centuries. For each of the three periods, after describing their exegesis of John 3:27–36, I offer a brief summary of how the understanding of historical realities appears to be shifting during the period. What we will find, through patient examination because the transition is at first so gradual, are signs of increasing disjunction of the literal and the spiritual senses, along with an increasing display of linear-historical apparatus.

Meister Eckhart, Nicholas of Lyra, Denys the Carthusian: Late-Medieval Options

Aquinas belonged to the last generation of high-medieval theologians. After the deaths of Aquinas and Bonaventure in 1274, and Albert the Great six years later, theological rationalisms gained ascendancy in the late-medieval universities. As a result, whereas before 1274 the leading theologians had all commented on the Bible, afterward this practice became rare.[4] Describing this situation, Hans Urs von Balthasar comments:

> Particularly in the universities, Averroism, quite independently of the "spirituals," had accorded pride of place to *ratio* over *fides*, thus profoundly upsetting the entire clerical world of learning; in doing so, it had also pushed the latter toward the contrary movement, an irrational mysticism that was no less dangerous to faith in the incarnate Word, or toward a voluntaristic Nominalism that was partly to blame for the break that took place in the Reformation.[5]

It is telling that the greatest theological minds of the period, Scotus and Ockham, did not write commentaries on the Bible, and their formal theological writings relatively infrequently appeal to Scripture or the Fathers.[6] During this period, biblical interpretation became increasingly the province not of the "masters," but of "mystically" inclined theologians, generally outside the universities. I will discuss three examples of theologians from this period who wrote commentaries on John 3:27–36: Meister Eckhart, Nicholas of Lyra, and Denys the Carthusian. All were university trained, and yet none had much influence on the dominant nominalist theology that prevailed in academic theology up to the Protestant Reformation.

The Dominican theologian Meister Eckhart continues to receive attention today as both a speculative and a mystical theologian. His training accentuated the Dionysian stream in Albert the Great's thought that also influenced Aquinas. Eckhart's *expositio* on John consists in short discourses, generally highly philosophical in character, on particular verses of the Gospel. While his commentary is quite lengthy, he does not treat every verse. As regards John 3:27–36, he treats only 3:31–34, with a passing mention of verse 35.[7]

Discussing Christ's truthful speaking of heavenly matters (verses 31–33), Eckhart refers the reader to two verses from the Gospel of Matthew, two from the Wisdom literature (Ecclesiastes and Sirach), and a text from Seneca. He then turns to a much more extended analysis of verse 34, "For he whom God has sent utters the words of God, for it is not by measure that he gives the Spirit." His commentary on this passage takes the form of a meditation on Trinitarian theology. Eckhart begins by listing eight points of Trinitarian faith: the Trinity is three Persons; these three are one essence (neither masculine nor feminine); there is only one Father, one Son, and one Holy Spirit; the Father communicates himself totally to the Son and totally to the Holy Spirit; the three Persons are coequal and coeternal; the Father is the principle without principle, whereas the Son is the principle from the principle and the Holy Spirit proceeds from both; the Trinity acts as one *ad extra* because the Persons are distinct solely by relation to each other, even while leaving room for appropriation of particular acts to particular Persons; and, finally, the Son and the Spirit are sent (missions).

Eckhart argues that these eight points are contained in John 3:34, when properly read according to the highest light of reason as part of the work of faith seeking understanding. In arguing for this position, he notes four premises of reason that shed light on the meaning of John 3:34: nothing can beget or produce itself, and yet substance can be communicated (in God most perfectly), and thus it is not irrational to say that God is both three and one; love follows upon knowledge, as in the relationship of "the words of God" and "the Spirit" suggested by verse 34; a perfect self-communication is being described by "it is not by measure that he gives the Spirit" (3:34); and the notion of "mission" ("he whom God has sent," 3:34) comes directly from "procession."

Eckhart concludes that God is "the same in nature, while differing in mode of being." He holds that this presentation suffices for exegeting the first half of 3:34, and he adds a few more remarks on "it is not by measure that he gives the Spirit" (3:34). He notes that the *Glossa Ordinaria* indicates that the giver of the Spirit here is Christ the Son of God.[8] He explains that as regards the divine giver, the Spirit is not measured, whereas the Spirit is measured as regards the created recipient. Eckhart here cites 1 Corinthians 12 and Matthew 25, as well as the *Liber de causis* and Plato. It is "most beautiful" *(fortassis pulchrius)*, he notes, to observe that the Spirit and every divine gift are both "immense" and "within measure." He quotes Psalm 147:5, "his understanding is not numbered," and similarly St. Bernard who holds that "the mode of loving God is a 'mode without mode.'" Finally, citing the *De sententiis Prosperi*, attributed to Augustine, he affirms that perfect love always grows.

Eckhart, a German Dominican, leaves to the side historical details as he ascends philosophically and theologically toward speculative truth. The result is a richly theological commentary that nonetheless risks an ahistorical rationalism, no longer rooted sufficiently in the incarnate Christ. Nicholas of Lyra, by contrast, does not exhibit the theological and philosophical range of an Eckhart. A French Franciscan and schoolfellow of Scotus, Nicholas wrote only a few minor theological works, displaying an affinity with Scotus's philosophy. Otherwise, he devoted his career to writing biblical commentaries. As late as the mid-sixteenth century these commentaries were published along with the *Glossa Ordinaria*.[9] Nicholas organizes his commentary on John 3:27–36 by first treating the literal sense and secondly the moral sense.[10] His commentary is not far from what we found in Aquinas.

Exploring the literal sense, Nicholas holds that the disciples of John the Baptist think that Jesus is usurping John's "office" *(officium)*. John thus teaches that Jesus is not usurping his office. Rather, all such distinction of office comes from God. John the Baptist only received authority from God to baptize in order to prepare people for the coming of Christ. As John the Bapist says in verse 28 — "You yourselves bear me witness" — he never usurped the "alien office" of Christ. This "office of Christ," that is to say the "office of the bridegroom," is to baptize so as to generate spiritual children for the Church, his bride. The friend of the bridegroom rejoices and congratulates the bridegroom on his spiritually begotten children. Were John the Baptist to try to usurp Christ's office, he would be an enemy and "adulterer," rather than a true begetter of spiritual children. Thus John the Baptist is teaching his disciples that they ought to rejoice, and not complain, when they find that Christ is baptizing.

Nicholas considers it noteworthy that John the Baptist here calls Christ his "friend," in contrast to his earlier statement that he was unworthy to untie Christ's shoes. The reason, Nicholas suggests, is that whereas earlier (verse 27) John the Baptist wished to reprove his disciples for their jealousy, he now wishes to emphasize the relationship of love. Treating verse 30, "He must increase, but I must decrease," Nicholas holds that John the Baptist means that Christ's fame will justly increase because of Christ's divine origin (verse 31) that leads to faith in Christ and gives Christ the highest authority and dignity, whereas John the Baptist's fame will decrease just as the rising of the sun obscures the morning star. It is because of Christ's divinity, and the knowledge that he possesses in his human nature due to the beatific vision, that we receive Christ's teaching with complete certitude. A mere man, in contrast, could speak with authority solely of earthly realities. Even a prophet such as John the Baptist, who speaks of heavenly realities by divine prophetic illumination, cannot compare with Christ who knows directly of what he speaks because he "hears" God the Father. Even so, few of the Jews believe (verse 32).

Commenting on verses 33–35, Nicholas treats a number of technical theological topics. As the one whom God has sent, Christ fulfills the words of the prophets. He shows that God is true by the excellence of his teaching ("the words of God"), and from his plenitude of grace his members receive grace. Christ's grace is the grace of headship of his body, the Church. This does not mean, however, that his habitual grace is infinite. He has the highest degree of grace possible, and in this sense he receives the grace of the Holy Spirit "not by measure" because he is the measure. Furthermore, he receives the Spirit from the Father not by adoptive participation, as even the highest angel must, but as the only begotten Son. In loving the Son (verse 35), the Father communicates to the Son the divine essence and power. However, the Father's love does not, Nicholas points out, cause the generation of the Son, because the begetting of the Son is not a voluntary act on the part of the Father. The Father's love is a "sign," not the cause, of the Son's eternal generation. This divine love is the cause of every gift made through the humanity of Christ. The grace of the Holy Spirit that believers receive from Christ is the seed of beatitude. Thus for Nicholas, John the Baptist, as the precursor of Christ, has as the goal of his discourse in John 3:27–36 the persuasion of his disciples to believe in Christ and receive this divinizing grace. The punishment of sin, for those who reject the grace of reconciliation, is to lack the beatific vision. Nicholas adds at the end of his discussion of the literal sense of John

3:27–36 a relatively lengthy discourse on the relationship of John's baptism and Christian baptism, quoting Chrysostom and Augustine.

Reading John 3:27–36 in the moral sense, Nicholas sees the discourse between John the Baptist and his disciples as an important lesson in how to understand the proper relationship of students to a teacher. Teachers such as John the Baptist have no concern for worldly fame and honors, but prefer truth. In contrast, suggests Nicholas, many theologians and members of religious orders adhere more to the doctrines of the revered masters of their religious order than to truth. Teachers should take John the Baptist as an exemplar, and students should take John's disciples as a warning.

If Eckhart's commentary is rather abstracted from the biblical world, Nicholas's largely traditional commentary presents the opposite risk, as the work of an exegete who eschewed theological scholarship. By contrast, Denys the Carthusian, known as the Ecstatic Doctor, aimed at reuniting the roles of theologian and exegete. He earned a master of arts from the university at Cologne in his early twenties and entered the Carthusian monastery in Roermond (in modern Holland) after completing his degree. Thenceforth he devoted his life to prayer and writing, leaving the monastery only twice—in 1451 with Cardinal Nicholas of Cusa to assist in the renewal of parishes and religious communities, and in 1465 to assist in founding a new monastery in Bois le Duc.[11] As Terence O'Reilly observes, Denys "deplored the theology of his own day, especially the currents associated with John Duns Scotus (1265–1308) and William of Ockham (1285–1347)," and also disliked the biblical commentaries of Nicholas of Lyra.[12] He sought to retrieve the theology and exegesis of Aquinas and the earlier patristic-medieval tradition. Denys Turner remarks poignantly of Denys the Carthusian: "he wrote at a point very late in the Middle Ages where it was possible to perceive rather clearly what was happening; but it was both too late to prevent it, too early to see that preventing it was no longer possible."[13]

Discussing 3:27, "No one can receive anything except what is given him from heaven," Denys observes that all good, whether of nature or of grace, comes "mediately or immediately" from God.[14] He quotes key texts to the same effect from St. Paul, 1 Corinthians 4:7 and 2 Corinthians 3:5, as well as Hosea 13:9. He explains that in the context of John the Baptist's discourse to his disciples, the meaning is that only God gives the authority and power to baptize. Discussing 3:28, he explains that John the Baptist is here testifying that he is only an "adopted son," a servant, lacking the grace possessed by the Savior. Citing Matthew 3:14, Denys notes that John the Baptist is profoundly aware of "the great distance and difference between Christ and himself." He continues in the vein of John the Baptist's, and the Church's, participation in Christ in his description of verse 29. For Denys, it is clear that while the bridegroom is Christ, the bride is the Church; he points also to Ephesians 5, the book of Revelation, and the Song of Songs. Christ weds the Church in his Incarnation, baptism, and Passion, and Christ incorporates the Church into himself by grace, begetting spiritual children. Denys then discusses at some length how Christ is the bridegroom in different ways: to the universal Church and to particular churches, to each holy soul, and to the blessed Virgin. Despite sinful "adulteries" on the part of her members, the whole Church, as "the bride of her Creator," is "impregnated" with the seed of the Word, in the light of grace, and made fruitful by the Holy Spirit. These fruits are the seven fruits of the Spirit listed in Galatians 5.

Denys affirms strongly that John the Baptist, as Christ's friend, is in Christ perfectly through ardent love, and so his joy is now full (3:29). John the Baptist is not only Christ's friend, but also a kind of matchmaker *(paranymphus)* who makes the spiritual marriage between Christ and his Church. This affirmation leads Denys to pause on the question of why John the Baptist is not among the disciples, in light of the Manichean view that John the Baptist would have been damned because the Spirit had not yet come (cf. John 16:7). Denys holds that what Christ means in John 16:7 has to do with loving Christ according to the Spirit rather than according to the flesh; here he cites 2 Corinthians 5:16 to make the point: "even though we once regarded Christ from a human point of view, we regard him thus no longer." By nature the Baptist is not worthy to tie Christ's shoes (John 1:27), but by the grace of the Holy Spirit he is Christ's friend, as one who loves Christ. Denys then ponders how Christ can be said to "increase" (3:30), since he is already perfect. Christ increases in popular estimation, while John decreases in popularity. He also cites Augustine's interpretation about their respective manners of death, and compares their numbers of disciples.

In commenting on verse 31, "He who comes from above is above all," Denys points out that Christ is "above all" by his eternal generation and by the direct formation of his human body by the Holy Spirit, and he is also "above all" as regards his wisdom and teaching. Christ is able to teach divine realities because his human knowledge participates in his divine knowledge. The generation of the divine Word can also be understood as a "hearing" of the Father who speaks the Word: thus Christ "bears witness to what he has seen and heard" (3:32). The end of verse 32 poses a problem: how can John the Baptist say that "no one" has accepted Christ's teaching? Citing Philippians 2:21 and Micah 7:2, Denys explains that John the Baptist means that few of the Jews would accept Christ's teaching. Christ's teaching vindicates the claim "that God is true" (3:33) because in Christ, God fulfills the prophets' words. Denys both distinguishes Christ from the prophets and unites them to him. He explains that the Word of God is sent by the Father perfectly, in contrast to other prophets or teachers who speak God's words; but nonetheless John the Baptist, the Apostles, and all the holy preachers share according to their mode in Christ's preaching of the words of God. This sharing comes from Christ, because he receives the grace of the Holy Spirit "not by measure" (3:34).

This point leads Denys into a short theological discourse on the modes of Christ's grace: the grace of the hypostatic union is infinite, whereas Christ's habitual grace is not infinite in its essence, but can be said to be infinite, in a certain sense, in other ways such as with regard to its effects, with regard to Christ's absolute fullness of grace, and with regard to the unceasing pouring forth of grace from Christ to others. Here he quotes Ephesians 4:7, "grace was given to each of us according to the measure of Christ's gift."

Interpreting John 3:35, "The Father loves the Son, and has given all things into his hand," Denys states that the first clause refers to the incomparable divine love and does not mean that the Father's love is the cause of the Son's being begotten. Rather, the point is the same as Paul makes in Colossians 1:13–14: "He has delivered us from the dominion of darkness and transferred us to the kingdom of his beloved Son, in whom we have redemption, the forgiveness of sins." Denys then explains what the Father gives the Son in his divinity, in comparison with what he gives the Son as man. Drawing on Matthew 28:18, Denys observes that the Father has given all things to the incarnate Son, although as Hebrews 2:8 indicates, the revelation of Christ's full power awaits the Day of Judgment. The gift of all things to the incarnate Son accounts for the next verse, "He who believes in the Son has eternal life; he who does not obey the Son shall not see life, but the wrath of God rests upon him" (John 3:36). After suggesting that the phrase "see life" indicates the beatific vision, the intellectual seeing of God — the lack of which is the punishment of those who persist in their sins (Revelation 21:8) — Denys emphasizes that the discourse's end lies in its beginning: "No one can receive anything except what is given him from heaven" (John 3:27). The greatest gift, he concludes, is the gift of the incarnate Son of God, who teaches us God's Word, what he has "seen and heard." We are called to receive this extraordinary gift.

To summarize this section: Eckhart's commentary engages almost entirely in theological speculation, whereas Nicholas comments on Scripture while leaving to others the composition of speculative theological works. The two early fourteenth-century theologians thus suggest emerging problems in the relationship between biblical-historical and speculative-theological reflection. Similarly, in the fifteenth century near the height of Renaissance humanism, Denys the Carthusian is not sufficiently attuned to the humanists' new understanding of history to be able to respond to it.[15] While the exegesis of these three figures is not in marked discontinuity with their predecessors, their significance for our narrative consists in the increasingly peripheral character of such biblical exegesis to the nominalist and humanist currents of the universities. These currents — opposed to each other but rooted in similar understandings of history — were leading to the autonomy of history from theology and thus to a problematic situation for theological exegesis.

Erasmus, Cajetan, Maldonado, Toledo: Responses to Renaissance Humanism

Not surprisingly, biblical interpretation in the sixteenth century — Catholic and Protestant — continued to be deeply indebted to the medieval exegetical tradition.[16] Even so, while knowledgeable in the Fathers through critical editions, the Renaissance exegetes differ from the Fathers and medievals' simple acceptance of participatory dimensions of history.[17] Commenting on this development, James Barr observes that "[a] certain space is created between the literary and historical questions on the one side and the ultimate theological decisions on the other."[18] He connects this separation to a "reduction of confidence in a scholastic universe in which text, interpretation, and metaphysic were understood to interpenetrate each other."[19]

The leading Catholic humanist and biblical scholar during this period was Erasmus, born not far from Denys the Carthusian's monastery. Erasmus devoted much of his intellectual labor to the production of critical editions of Scripture and of the Fathers' biblical commentaries. For him, the Fathers' exegesis offered an antidote to nominalist theology's abstraction from Scripture. He admired the Fathers' attention to the literal sense and their use of the spiritual sense to understand difficult Old Testament passages.[20] Erasmus's humanist effort to recover the original texts of Scripture and the Fathers exhibits his linear-historical sense.[21]

Erasmus's 1523 commentary on John 3:27–36 has the primary aim of achieving a linear-historical rendering of the biblical text. His method in his short commentaries, or "paraphrases" as he called them, which he composed on all the gospels and epistles, reflects interpretative rules for which he credits the Fathers: in Louis Bouyer's words he "never take[s] a quotation out of its context, nor out of the general way of thought of its author, nor yet out of the thought of the Scriptures as a whole."[22] The commentaries do not draw significantly on the Fathers, because what Erasmus seeks, says Bouyer, is "a perfectly objective summary of the content of the epistles and Gospels" attentive to "the questions of the place, the moment, the occasion, the intention, and the tone of the work being studied."[23] In praising Erasmus as a forebear of twentieth-century *ressourcement*, Bouyer notes that Erasmus "is at least as much an innovator in his sense of history and in his attachment to the human content of biblical theology as in his conception of critical philology and his use of it as the basis of all biblical research."[24]

Commenting on John 3:27–36, Erasmus interprets John the Baptist's reply to his disciples as the words of a man whose accomplishments have attained the fullness of his talents. He considers John the

Baptist to be saying, "Are you asking that I make myself out to be greater than I am? No one can receive anything except what is given to him from heaven. These things are not done with human resources, but at God's direction. The task that he had assigned to me according to my ability I have faithfully completed."[25] This task was to prepare for the coming of Christ. Now that Christ has come, John the Baptist expects his disciples and others to follow Christ, in whom is salvation; John the Baptist will therefore decrease in public attention, and Christ will increase. Since Christ is greater than a mere human, he rightly supersedes John the Baptist. As the Son of God, his words should be taken as God's words. Only the Son has received the fullness of God's Spirit, in contrast to human prophets who receive a limited share of the Spirit. Out of love the Father has given the fullness of power over the whole universe to the Son, and all the Father's gifts to humankind—above all eternal life—are mediated through the Son. The Son has promised to give us this gift of eternal life, and if we refuse or disbelieve this offer, then we are insulting the Father's veracity. Unbelievers remain in their sins and thus subject themselves to the full punishment of sin, everlasting death rather than eternal life.

Very different from Erasmus's work is the commentary on John composed five years later by the Dominican theologian (and eventual Master General of the Order) Thomas de Vio, Cardinal Cajetan, whose commentary on Aquinas's *Summa theologiae*, along with his debates with Martin Luther, make him well known to this day. Cajetan's method is to raise numerous philosophical and theological questions in commenting on the meaning of the biblical text.

Interpreting John 3:27, "No one can receive anything except what is given him from heaven," Cajetan describes the "offices, titles, dignities, grades" that one finds among human beings.[26] Understanding the work proper to one's "officium" should guide one's actions. The key is recognizing oneself as occupying an "inferior grade" in comparison to Jesus. John the Baptist recognizes in humility that he is less than Jesus, but John's disciples do not recognize this divine dispensation. Thus John, in this discourse, must teach them what Jesus is owed and must explain for them the true nature of his own "office," in which he relates to Jesus as a friend of the bridegroom relates to the bridegroom. John has baptized as the friend of the bridegroom; Jesus baptizes as the bridegroom, begetting spiritual children for his virginal bride the Church. John the Baptist's love for Jesus is the "love of friendship," distinguished from other kinds of friendship by its rejoicing in the friend's good without desiring anything for itself. This kind of friendship, Cajetan points out, is metaphorically well symbolized by the image of a friend of the bridegroom. Such a friend joyfully "hears" the bridegroom's voice, in other words the manifestation of Jesus by Jesus' preaching.

Cajetan's commentary on verse 30, "He must increase, but I must decrease," further exemplifies the role of philosophical-theological questioning. In light of late-medieval interest in divine freedom and kinds of necessity, Cajetan clarifies that the "must" that characterizes the "increase" and "decrease" signifes a "necessity of divine determination" *(necessitatem divinae definitionis)*. Like Nicholas, he compares the increasing/decreasing to the dimming of the stars when the sun rises. He notes that historically the reference is to John the Baptist's upcoming imprisonment and the attraction of the crowds to Christ's public ministry.

Commenting on John 3:31–32, Cajetan suggests that verse 32's claim that "no one receives his testimony" is an example of the literary trope of hyperbole, or else an indication that those going to Christ (John 3:26) do not yet have full faith in his divinity. His knowledge of the Greek text enables him to correct "super" (as Aquinas and Denys had it) with "supra," noting that this signifies eminence rather than merely an entity in the order of entities.[27] He explains that Christ is above all because, as verse 35 states, the Father has given everything to him. In this regard, he compares the earthly person/hypostasis with a heavenly or divine Person/hypostasis. Earthly human understanding, including the prophets' understanding, always begins with the senses, whereas Christ knows everything and has power over everything by means of the grace of the hypostatic union. Cajetan interprets the reference to what the Son has "seen" and "heard" (John 3:32) also in epistemological fashion: vision signifies understanding, while hearing signifies the order of origin. For Cajetan, the verses' emphasis that Christ is above everything ensures that no one imagines that the friendship described between John the Baptist and Christ in verse 29 is a friendship between equals or kin, as in Aristotle's understanding of the requirements of true friendship. Rather, Christ is a *divine* Person.

Cajetan similarly brings philosophical and theological clarification to bear on the remaining verses. Regarding verse 33, he observes that faith in Jesus has a twofold fruit, one relative to God who is known as true, and the other relative to the person who confesses God as true. Faith in Jesus has these effects because, as verse 34 indicates, Jesus is "absolutely" and "simply" to speak the words of God, in contrast to the prophets who only occasionally speak in God's name. Whereas others receive in various degrees one or more of the gifts of the Spirit, Jesus, by the grace of union, receives the Spirit without measure. The love by which the Father loves the Son is the reason why the incarnate Son receives everything, but is not the reason for the eternal generation of the Son, as if the Father begot by free will. Although the Father has given everything into the hands of the incarnate Son, there is a difference between possession and use, and the full use of the Son's power is still to come. Likewise, the believer has the seed of eternal life, because the grace of God is the gift of eternal life. In contrast, the nonbeliever does not have eternal life but instead bears the punishment of sins. Citing Luke 16, Cajetan proposes that in Hell the damned, unlike human beings on earth, cannot divert their attention from their afflictions.

Informed by humanist text-critical research and largely lacking the spiritual sense developed by the Fathers, Cajetan's commentary responds to the growing linear understanding of history by seeking to reclaim Scripture as a text for theological and philosophical speculation. From Cajetan to the later sixteenth century manifests a further shift. The biblical scholarship of the Counter-Reformation was spearheaded by Spanish Jesuits. As F. J. Crehan states: "The Golden Age of Spain was marked by a great florescence of Scripture studies in that land, the Spanish exegetes of the period from 1560 to 1630 surpassing those of other lands."[28] At the forefront were Juan de Maldonado and Cardinal Francisco de Toledo, the former known also for his work on a critical edition of the Septuagint and on the Jesuit *Ratio studiorum*, the latter also the author of a commentary on the *Summa theologiae*.[29] The biblical commentaries of Toledo and Maldonado were published thanks to the support of the General of the Jesuits, Claudius Aquaviva, and they also benefited from the Polyglot Bible (Syriac, Greek, Hebrew, Latin) sponsored by Philip II and put together by Benito Arias between 1568 and 1572. The demand for Jesuit commentaries on Scripture flowed in part from the Constitutions of the Society of Jesus, pt. IV, chap. 14, which contains the instruction that there should be professors and courses devoted to the study of the Bible and of Hebrew and Greek.[30]

I will briefly summarize Maldonado's treatment of John 3:27–36.[31] His exegetical approach, rooted in erudition, appears in his advice to theology students to "spend the first hour of the morning in reading the New Testament in Greek and the first hour of the evening in reading the Old Testament in Hebrew."[32] He thoroughly interweaves theological questions, biblical parallels (here he demonstrates a knowledge of the Greek text), and the Fathers' teachings into his commentary. Yet, his frequent appeals to the Fathers take the form of lists in which he adduces as many as possible of the authorities for the various positions. In these lists, he combines Chrysostom, Augustine, Cyril, Gregory the Great, Ambrose, Origen, and Bede with lesser known exegetes such as Ethymius, Theophylact the Bulgarian, Strabo, Rupert, Ammonius, Phoebadius, and Eucherius. To use an anachronistic term, Maldonado's exegesis thus has a rather "encyclopedic" flavor. Evincing his linear-historical orientation, in his commentary on verse 30 he finds it necessary to offer an explicit *apologia* for his use of patristic readings that expose the spiritual sense. The historically erudite listing of the Fathers' opinions, rather than the deep appropriation of their insights, marks Maldonado's exegetical work and suggests his response to the humanist understanding of history. His historical erudition displays his linear-historical credentials while enabling him also to insert the Fathers' participatory insights.

Toledo, writing shortly after Maldonado, separates linear-historical commentary on the biblical text (in which he occasionally includes "historical" remarks from the Fathers) from annotations that display his patristic erudition and advert to the other senses.[33] Thus, commenting on John 3:27, "No one can receive anything except what is given him from heaven," Toledo notes that John the Baptist is warning against taking an office that God has not given—as for example the false prophets.[34] He supports this reading with two parallel biblical texts, Romans 12 and John 19, and then moves to his *annotatio* in which he surveys the readings of Chrysostom and Cyril that apply the saying to Christ. Toledo follows a similar method in his commentary on John 3:28–29 and his appended *annotatio* on these verses. In his literal commentary, he observes that John the Baptist explains that he cannot exceed the "measure" that God has given him, which is to be precursor. He explains the difference between a bridegroom and a friend of the bridegroom: the friend does not aspire to be the bridegroom, but rather rejoices when the bridegroom, Christ, unites his bride the Church to himself. Hearing the "voice" of the bridegroom (verse 29) signifies the witnessing of Christ's miracles and preaching. In his *annotatio*, Toledo cites 1 Corinthians 12, Matthew 25, Hosea 2, Ephesians 5, and the Song of Songs, along with Gregory the Great and Chrysostom. He discusses the two ways in which the marriage of God and humankind took place: in the womb of the Blessed Virgin, and in the union of Christ and his Church. The profundity of this marriage is symbolized by St. Paul's discussion of the Mystical Body. Many people are united to Christ in the Church, and yet all become one eucharistically.

Toledo's discussions of the remaining verses follow this same pattern of separating the literal commentary or historical-conceptual narration from the mystical *annotatio* and of including the great majority of the parallel biblical texts, patristic citations, and theological reflections in the *annotatio*. While common also in patristic-medieval exegesis, this separation here threatens to become a disjunction: the integral connection of the patristic *annotatio* to the linear-historical study is less evident, even though Toledo himself holds to the connection.

Examining verses 30–31a, Toledo finds that John the Baptist is attempting to persuade his disciples to follow Christ. Having preached the coming of the Christ, John's task now is to direct his disciples toward Christ. The "increase" and "decrease" occur in popular opinion, as the crowds move from John the Baptist to Christ. In contrast, the *annotatio* to this passage delves into Cyril's controversy against the Arians, as well as Chrysostom, and treats Trinitarian theology. Commenting on verses 31b–34a he finds that the literal sense includes the Son's procession from the Father, since the passage is about Christ's origins;

but he leaves full exposition of this aspect for the *annotatio*, where he draws on Cyril and Ambrose.

In addition to showing his independence from the Fathers by largely separating their exegesis from his own, Toledo offers innovative interpretations of verses 34b–36a, "It is not by measure that he gives the Spirit; the Father loves the Son, and has given all things into his hand. He who believes in the Son has eternal life." In his *annotatio* to verse 34b, he shows that the Fathers—he cites Cyril and Chrysostom— interpret "he gives the Spirit" as primarily the Father to the Son, both in eternity in the Father's self-communication and in time to the incarnate Son. Toledo insists by contrast that since the verse reads "gives the Spirit" rather than "gives him the Spirit" it means simply that God has offered salvation to all people, instead of merely to some. Likewise, in his *annotatio* to verse 35, he argues (again against Cyril in particular) that the meaning is that all human beings are given by the Father to Christ. In other words, Toledo steadfastly holds that the meaning of these two verses is strictly soteriological rather than also referring to Christ in himself. Regarding verse 36a, "He who believes in the Son has eternal life," he rules out the view that grace gives an inchoate possession of eternal life; rather the verse, he thinks, refers to the future meritorious effect of faith.

To summarize this section: Erasmus emphasizes history by organizing his commentary as a historical synopsis, although this history contains a significant amount of theology.[35] Cajetan goes in the opposite direction, focusing on speculative philosophical and theological reflection, which he considers to be the true literal meaning. Cajetan does not cite the Fathers in his commentary on John 3:27–36 and only very rarely includes "parallel" biblical texts; nor does he include the spiritual senses. Maldonado responds to the growing historical erudition of the period by developing encyclopedic lists of the opinions of patristic commentators. Toledo separates his historical interpretation of the text (still filled with theological meanings) from *annotationes* that contain the spiritual and more evidently theological meanings derived largely from the Fathers. In different ways, then, these authors evince that history has become exegetically problematic. Their commentaries do not blend history and theology in the easy way—often by means of the spiritual senses—that we find in patristic-medieval commentary.

Natalis, Lagrange, Brown: The Rise of
the Historical-Critical Method

The exegetical work of Alexander Natalis deepens the separation of the spiritual meaning from the historical meaning, the latter now encapsulated largely in lists of the opinions of patristic authorities (demonstrating the critical apparatus of historical recovery) and standard questions and answers culled from the tradition of exegesis.[36] Natalis's life reflects the turbulent theological times of the Enlightenment period. After earning his doctorate in theology from the Sorbonne at the age of 36, he published over a period of ten years a multivolume history of the Church. Its Gallican sympathies, beginning with its treatment of the eleventh century, led to the work's being formally condemned by the pope three times between 1684 and 1687. Later Natalis wrote a major treatise in dogmatic and moral theology, and polemicized in other smaller works against the Jesuits, thereby once again falling afoul of ecclesial authorities on suspicion of Jansenism. He devoted his sixties to writing biblical commentaries.

Natalis's method is first to offer a brief overview of the literal sense of all the verses of the particular chapter, and then to provide a more extensive and profound exploration of the moral sense of certain of the key verses. His exegesis aims principally at inflaming the heart rather than enlightening the mind. Toledo moved patristic references (and biblical parallels) largely to annotations so as to engage critically the Fathers' insights separately from his literal reflection on the biblical text; similarly, Natalis moves the Fathers' insights regarding our participation in the divine realities exposed in Scripture into a separate section for the purposes of stimulating pious morality. Again the separation threatens to become a disjunction.

Regarding the literal sense of John 3:27–36, Natalis devotes a short paragraph to every two or three verses, in which he summarizes their meaning.[37] John the Baptist is the precursor who teaches that one must not arrogate authority, power, or office not given to one by God. Jesus is the bridegroom who makes worthy the bride, the Church. The friend of the bridegroom rejoices to hear the bridegroom's words to the bride; John the Baptist is like a matchmaker *(paranymphus)*. His office ceases, without envy on his part, once the marriage has taken place. Jesus Christ, who is God and man, is above all, even the prophets. Jesus reveals the divine mysteries that he has known in the bosom of the Father from eternity. Although few receive his testimony, those who believe recognize that God in Christ has proven himself to be truthful to his promises. Jesus teaches nothing but the words of God. The Father gives his Spirit to the Son not by measure, but infinitely and totally; and the Son has the Spirit not by participation, but by his eternal generation (here Natalis cites biblical and patristic texts). He who believes that Jesus is the divine Son, and believes what the Church proposes for the faithful to believe about him, has eternal life. He who does not believe remains in his sins and falls under the "wrath" of God as St. Paul describes in Ephesians 2:3, "Among these we all once lived in the passions of our flesh, following the desires of body and mind, and so we were by nature children of wrath, like the rest of mankind."

Turning, in the second part of his commentary on John 3:27–36, to the moral sense, Natalis finds in John the Baptist's disciples an example of the danger of jealousies and contention in seminary formation, among congregations and religious orders, and among devout persons. He urges his readers to imitate John the Baptist's humbling of himself before Jesus. He includes a text from Augustine's commentary emphasizing that every good thing comes from God, not our own powers. Christian humility, Natalis proposes, is the key. Likewise, discussing the relationship of the bridegroom Christ to the bride the Church (3:29 f.), he notes that not particular human pastors, but Jesus Christ himself is the bridegroom of the Church. He warns against the desire for honors and the desire to dominate rather than to serve, and again cites a text from Augustine's commentary. Natalis compares the virginal purity of the Church with the sinfulness of her members. Pointing to a parallel biblical text, 1 Corinthians 3:7, he begs that pastors and teachers will hear the words of the Apostle Paul: "So neither he who plants nor he who waters is anything, but only God who gives the growth." Thus one should rejoice solely in God; those who rejoice in themselves will be sad, as Augustine says in his commentary. Discussing how God grows in us when we humble ourselves (verse 30), he includes a lengthy text from Augustine, also cited, as we have seen, by Aquinas. By faith, Christ dwells in our hearts and gives life to our souls, which become his temple.

Such faith is already the germ of eternal life. In contrast, unbelievers remain in their sins, as a text from Augustine's *Enchiridion* serves to explain.[38]

The next step in Protestant biblical exegesis after pietism is the introduction of a more strictly linear-historical method; so too with Catholic exegesis. The Catholic Church's reaction to the Enlightenment, however, meant that Catholic biblical studies found itself a generation or two behind in this regard. In the late nineteenth and early twentieth centuries German historical criticism caused a crisis for both Protestant and Catholic churches. During this time Marie-Joseph Lagrange, the founder of the École Biblique in Jerusalem and a leading contributor to the new journal *Revue biblique,* provided a devoutly Catholic counterpoint to scholars such as Albert Loisy who renounced the Catholic Church due to the apparently devastating findings of historical-critical scholarship.[39] During the modernist crisis and afterward, Lagrange's scholarly integrity and productivity, deep faith, and ecumenical range led the way toward the Catholic Church's growing acceptance of historical-critical methodologies in biblical interpretation.[40]

Lagrange's reading of John 3:27–36 is instructive as regards his blending of historical-critical approaches with awareness of the positions of patristic exegetes. Employing the Greek text of the New Testament, he places his critical commentary in footnotes rather than within the line-by-line reading of the text itself.[41] In his footnote to verse 27, Lagrange begins with Chrysostom's reading that John the Baptist is attempting to show his disciples that Jesus' success is a gift of God. Modern commentators—Lagrange cites Schanz, Loisy, Calmes, Zahn, and Tillmann among others—situate the concern of John the Baptist's disciples about Jesus' success (verse 26) in the context of later efforts to explain why Jesus is greater than John the Baptist. Noting that he is agreeing with Augustine and Cyril, as well as with Belser, Lagrange remarks that the key is that Jesus comes from heaven. After a word study, reviewing translations from the Greek proposed by Loisy and Calmes, Lagrange turns to verse 28, which he reads as an "ad hominem" argument. He agrees with Chrysostom that John the Baptist is not brusque with his disciples. Rather he hopes to lead his disciples from sadness over his "decrease" to joy over Christ's coming.

Regarding verse 29, Lagrange's question is "Who is the bride?" The community of Israel? Humanity as a whole? Lagrange holds that in the Gospel "the Church is still not in view." He quotes parallel biblical texts that employ this image of bridegroom and bride: Song of Songs 3:11, Mark 2:19 and parallels. He cites Augustine approvingly on the relationship between John the Baptist and Christ. Discussing verse 30, he observes that self-humbling leads to elevation of the soul. He also picks up on Augustine's observation about the time of birth of John the Baptist and Christ (John when the length of day was decreasing, Christ when it was increasing), but remarks that it does not seem that the symbolism of verse 30 in fact influenced the Church's liturgical choice of feast days for the two births.

Two points are of particular importance thus far in Lagrange: first, his careful mix of modern and patristic commentators, with his clear effort to show that he is not dismissing the latter, even though the modern (historical-critical) commentators' views are determinative; and second, the relativizing of patristic-medieval participatory exegesis, indicated by his ruling out the idea that the Church could be the bride— what John the Baptist is referring to in his historical context could not be what we, in a very different historical context, experience. With regard to verses 31–36 he attributes these verses to the inspired evangelist rather than to John the Baptist as the speaker. Lagrange's central reason for this attribution is that verses 31–36 parallel 3:16–21, and both passages indicate a later date after the crisis caused by the revelation of the Son of God; the implication is that otherwise one would have to suppose that John the Baptist already possessed a fully articulated faith.

After defending his position that verses 31–36 represent the later voice of the evangelist, Lagrange returns to Greek word study, textual criticism (following Tischendorf), and raising questions from the text. For instance, he asks whether it should be assumed that John the Baptist is "he who is of the earth" in contrast to Christ who "comes from above." Lagrange remarks that if John the Baptist himself were speaking, as the patristic-medieval commentators thought, then one could understand this as humility. But if it is the evangelist speaking, it would seem that John the Baptist, as the one who bears witness to Christ, does not speak "of the earth" but rather speaks of heavenly things. Lagrange answers that the evangelist is referring to John the Baptist's disciples and people such as Nicodemus who do not comprehend Christ's origin. In the same vein, he reads verse 32 as an echo of verse 11, in which Jesus complains of Nicodemus's unbelief. Regarding that text and others, Lagrange asks whether Jesus, who always has the vision of God, knows what words to reveal at different moments.

Lagrange begins his footnote on verse 33 with a quotation from Aquinas's commentary on this verse. Agreeing with Aquinas about the basic meaning of the text, he nonetheless disagrees that the "seal" referred to should be interpreted as sealed (baptismally) on the hearts of believers. It is rather a metaphor, drawn from ancient Babylonian contracts, that indicates the truth that he who believes God must believe Christ who reveals God. He compares verse 34 to Syrian manuscripts and discusses a debate over textual criticism that involves the question of whether it is God or Christ who "gives the Spirit" without measure; and he also asks whether the gift of the Spirit refers to the eternal generation of the Son or to the moment of baptism of the incarnate Son. Lagrange concludes by celebrating the gift of the Spirit, which Christ both gave and taught. Following Origen and Cyril, he considers Christ to be the source of the Spirit. If so, then verse 35, "the Father loves the Son, and has given all things into his hand," shows the dignity of Christ who is the sole source of salvation. Here he treats texts from Maldonado, Augustine, and Thomas Aquinas, including Aquinas's point that the Father's love is the sign, not the cause, of the Son's eternal generation. Lagrange is thus not adverse to making a technical theological point. Finally verse 36, like John 17:2 (and Lagrange also cites Romans 1:18), seems to Lagrange to indicate simply our position vis-à-vis God.

Lagrange prepares the way for the flowering of historical-critical scholarship among Catholics during the twentieth century. Raymond Brown, the leading English-speaking Catholic biblical scholar of that century, belonged to the first generation of Catholic exegetes to work entirely under the aegis of the Church's full acceptance of historical-critical methods, although he frequently endured painful criticism from Catholics outside the exegetical guild.[42] In his doctoral dissertation

Brown remains close to Lagrange by advocating a *sensus plenior* understood as the meaning intended by the divine Author, a meaning that becomes clear in later stages of revelation and of the development of doctrine.[43] Even at this early stage in his career, however, Brown holds that this *sensus plenior* does not belong to the "literal sense" of the Bible.[44]

In his mature work, the task of biblical exegesis per se does not include this *sensus plenior*, which is handed over to theologians. Brown articulates the guiding principle of his mature exegesis in the preface to his highly regarded two-volume commentary on the Gospel of John:

> Fortunately we live at a time when a considerable degree of objectivity has been reached in biblical scholarship, so that a commentator can profit from the serious work of scholars of all religious communions. What has contributed most in this direction has been the establishment of the clear difference between the thoughts of the various biblical authors (which are the concern of the biblical scholar) and the subsequent use and development of those thoughts in divergent theologies (which are the concern of the theologian). The second point is important, for the majority of those who read Scripture are believers for whom the Bible is more than an interesting witness to past religious phenomena. Nor can it be neglected by the biblical scholar without peril of religious schizophrenia. Nevertheless, as we have come to realize, sincere confessional commitment to a theological position is perfectly consonant with a stubborn refusal to make a biblical text say more than its author meant it to say. There is no reason why scholars of different denominations cannot agree on the literal meaning of Scripture, even though they may disagree on the import of certain passages in the evolution of theology.[45]

The biblical text has a historical meaning, a concept or set of concepts, that can be confined to history as the linear past. On this view, history, for the purposes of biblical exegesis, is a linear continuum. Biblical interpretation has as its proper task to reconstruct this past "literal meaning." Given this strictly linear-historical meaning, the theologian then is able to map "the subsequent use and development of those thoughts in divergent theologies" over the course of "the evolution of theology."[46] The connection of this evolution to the realities depicted in the Bible is inevitably tenuous, requiring bridging a chasm between strictly linear history and participatory theology.

True to this methodological principle, in his bibliographical entries Brown includes work that dates back to the 1920s but not earlier; his exegesis of John 3:27–36 cites only four articles published earlier than 1956 (a decade before the publication of his volume), the earliest being 1938. In the text of his commentary on John 3:27–36, he mentions Augustine as capturing "with epigrammatic flair" the "Johannine contrast between John the Baptist and Jesus,"[47] and he cites Origen and John Chrysostom as regards the question of whether verse 31 refers to Jesus and John the Baptist. He does not, however, draw significantly on these Fathers, and otherwise he mentions only modern commentators: Taylor, Boismard, Bauer, Barrett, Black, Bernard, Bultmann, Dodd, Lagrange, Schnackenburg, Cullmann, and Thüsing.

Brown finds that the theological meaning of John 3:27–30 is that faith is God's gift—put another way, that "The believer is God's gift to Jesus."[48] In Brown's view, John the Baptist happily accepts his role as the one who prepares for Jesus. He hypothesizes that John the Baptist's last words in the Gospel of John were included "by way of answer to the sectarians of John the Baptist."[49] Regarding John 3:31–36, Brown first argues against fellow scholars such as Bauer and Barrett who hold that John the Baptist remains the speaker. In Brown's view, "what was once an isolated discourse of Jesus . . . has been attached to the scenes of ch. iii as an interpretation of those scenes. Many problems about the interpretation of individual verses in 31–36 can be solved if we recognize two levels of meaning corresponding to the two stages in the history of this discourse."[50] Theologically, Brown concludes that the verses belong to the Johannine editor's polemic against the ongoing sect of John the Baptist. The text's purpose is to make clear that only Jesus' baptism, not John the Baptist's, is related to the Spirit. Brown here indicates the importance of understanding verses 31–36 as an insertion: "Once again we stress that such a reference relating Jesus' baptism to the giving of the Spirit stems from the context in which vss. 31–36 have been placed; it does not imply at all that in Johannine thought Jesus' early ministry of baptizing actually communicated the Spirit."[51] He notes that the final verses show that the Father gives the Spirit, but only through Jesus; that the Father has given to the Son all things; and that the Johannine editor conceives of a "dualistic reaction to Jesus," resulting in either eternal life or condemnation. For Brown, the polemical context holds the key to the discourse, and the theological meaning follows from that context.[52]

To summarize this section: In Natalis, we find a strong distinction between history and piety, an emphasis that indicates a further shift in the understanding of history. During the same period, his contemporaries Isaac de la Peyrère, Baruch Spinoza, and Richard Simon were developing the lineaments of what came to be known as the historical-critical method.[53] As a Catholic expositor of this method, Lagrange no longer depends on the Fathers for his historical exposition of Scripture. Rather, he blends them with contemporary historical-critical scholars and carefully distinguishes between how theological realities would have been understood by John the Baptist, by the inspired evangelist, and by twentieth-century persons. What counts as history thus becomes more linear. Raymond Brown's conviction that the literal meaning can be limited to a set of concepts located within the first-century A.D. context, and that further meaning belongs not to biblical interpretation proper but to the "use and development" of biblical texts in "the evolution of theology," goes beyond Lagrange.

For Brown, the set of concepts established by biblical interpretation is an objective set of data that best explains what we know about the text and its context. For the patristic-medieval tradition, in contrast, the concepts cannot be confined in this way. The biblical interpreter continually encounters realities that both are historical and break the boundaries of linear history: the biblical "present" is greater and more capacious than our understanding of it. As we will see more fully in the next two chapters, in order to interpret such realities, the interpreter, and his methods, must enter and be open to these participatory depths. This task involves seeking in biblical texts God the teacher, and understanding biblical exegesis as primarily an ecclesial practice.[54] Such an exegetical approach does not invalidate historical approaches of the kind that Brown takes. On the contrary, linear-historical research, at its best, enables the realities depicted in the biblical text to be seen in their linear-historical past. Yet theological reading of the biblical text is no mere add-on that indicates the evolution of postbiblical thinking.[55] Rather, theological reading explores the historical in its participatory dimensions.[56]

Conclusion

By gradual stages, biblical exegesis moved away from the patristic-medieval understanding of history that we saw in Aquinas, and that was present also in Nicholas of Lyra and Denys the Carthusian. This development is no cause for dismay. The increase in historical knowledge on the basis of the new linear-historical tools made available by post-nominalist humanism required a period of centuries in which participatory exegesis would, at best, be in flux. Today, however, evaluation of the fruits of linear-historical research has made clear to many scholars that for biblical interpretation to be truly "historical" and "critical" in its practice, a philosophical/theological understanding of history adequate to the claims of the Bible's texts is needed. As Robert Wilken puts it:

[M]uch of what one learns through historical study is introductory, propadeutic. It is a necessary first step but it can only carry us so far. Interpretation requires context, a framework of meaning created by the events, persons, ideas, and experiences to which one relates the text. In which context is the Bible to be interpreted? The classical Christian commentators believed that the context was provided by the church, its creeds and conciliar decrees, its worship and sacraments, by Christian history and experience.[57]

Can biblical scholars and theologians integrate the insights of historical study and the insights of ecclesial teaching and practice? If so, then attention will have to be paid first to what it means to read the Bible's words "historically" and "critically." What would it mean for the exegete no longer to claim "history" as autonomous (metaphysically and/or Christologically-pneumatologically) from the triune God revealed in Christ Jesus and known in the Church? The chapters that follow seek to set forth the parameters of just such an exegetical practice, in which the insights of historical-critical and patristic-medieval exegesis (both of which contain within themselves a wide variety of perspectives) illumine each other.

CHAPTER THREE

Participatory Biblical Exegesis
and God the Teacher

The previous chapter sought to document the shift in the understanding of history. This shift corresponds to another one, namely
with respect to the goal of exegesis. Whereas modern exegetes, with
notable exceptions, tend to focus on the *biblical texts*—the origins
of their composition, what seems to have been consciously known
and intended by the authors/redactors, and so forth[1]—the patristic-
medieval tradition of exegesis reads the texts with a focus on
the *divine Teacher*. In this tradition, the texts are read primarily
in order to learn from and to come to know the Teacher, a knowledge that uncovers the deepest meaning of the texts themselves.
Such biblical interpretation, R. R. Reno has noted, is a conversation with God mediated by the texts' *participatory* historicity that
unites "hermeneutical discipline" with "spiritual discipline."[2] Understood in this way, exegesis is primarily a participation in the
Teacher, Jesus Christ, in and through participation in the realities
that Christ, by the Holy Spirit, communicates to his Church. As
Alister McGrath states, "Scripture is read in order to encounter
Christ."[3]

However, is this understanding of *sacra scriptura* as God's *sacra
doctrina*, whose purpose it is to mediate our participation in Christ

the Teacher, possible today? Can humanly authored texts, written in particular historical contexts by authors whose understanding of reality did not possess comprehensiveness, communicate the Wisdom that is God's providential Love? If the human authors/redactors of biblical texts teach in human genres and from a particular historical context, will not the human authors/redactors' limited knowledge and purposes restrict the possibility of readers encountering the divine Teacher?[4]

The standard way of engaging such concerns is to probe ever further, by means of linear-historical tools, into the texts as historically constituted documents. By contrast, I am proposing that linear-historical tools alone will not suffice; instead the participatory-historical quest must be restored to its proper position. Linear-historical tools should be taken up from within the participatory-historical frame rather than seeking to validate (an unending and never-fulfilled task) the participatory-historical frame by means of linear-historical tools, which, as we have seen, are incapable of reaching beyond themselves to establish truth claims about *divine* being and action.

Does this approach open up the biblical texts to true exegesis by drawing exegetes into the realities described by the Bible, or does it, on the contrary, make of the biblical texts a mere screen on which to project, eisegetically, our ideas about God and his action in the world? In order to shed light both on the primacy of God the Teacher in exegesis and on the potential of this exegetical mode for contemporary exegesis, this chapter places two patristic-medieval expositions of biblical exegesis—Augustine's *De doctrina christiana* and Aquinas's Inaugural Sermon "Commendation of and Division of Sacred Scripture"—in dialogue with two efforts to unite patristic-medieval and modern exegesis, namely Luke Timothy Johnson and William Kurz, S.J.'s *The Future of Catholic Biblical Scholarship* and the Second Vatican Council's Dogmatic Constitution on Divine Revelation, *Dei Verbum*.[5] I hope to show that renewing the tradition that sees biblical exegesis as a deifying participation in God the Teacher (*sacra scriptura* as *sacra doctrina*) offers believers precisely the theocentric model of biblical interpretation that is needed for exegesis rather than anthropocentric (and thus, from the Bible's perspective, idolatrous) eisegesis.[6]

St. Augustine, Scriptural Teaching, and the Divine Teacher

In his *De doctrina christiana*, begun in 396 and completed in 427, Augustine[7] sets forth "certain precepts for treating the Scriptures," grounded in his reading of Matthew 22:34–40 in which Jesus teaches that on the two commandments of love of God and love of neighbor "depend all the law and the prophets" (22:40). In this way Augustine seeks to assist students in their efforts to teach Scripture.[8]

After granting that the unlearned can understand Scripture by the Holy Spirit, and that the learned can fail to understand Scripture, Augustine emphasizes the importance of mediation, of learning from others. Even Paul, he points out, though taught directly by a divine voice, "was nevertheless sent to a man that he might receive the sacraments and be joined to the church."[9] Given that most people learn from others, he inquires into how the process of teaching occurs, and finds that teaching *(doctrina)* "concerns either things *(res)* or signs"; all signs are things, but not all things signify something else. If, therefore, all teaching is about *res*, realities, then in order to understand true teaching one must learn how to judge the relative importance of various *res*, so as to be able to get to the heart of the teaching.[10]

Having thus placed teaching at the heart of his analysis of how to interpret Scripture, Augustine introduces his distinction between enjoyment *(frui)* and use *(usus)*. Only divine *res*—the Father, Son, and Holy Spirit, one God—can rightly be "enjoyed," in the sense of "to cling to it with love for its own sake."[11] Clearly, clinging to created realities, loving them without reference to their Creator, is a doomed enterprise; not only is this world passing away, but also created things cannot truly be loved except *as* created, that is, with reference to God as their cause, sustainer, and ultimate end. However, humankind finds itself precisely in the situation of cleaving to created realities rather than to the true God. Augustine compares us to wanderers who, provided with the means of reaching our true eternal home, came to love the means above the end. In this state of sin, we are lost and cannot return to God; we have lost that which we were created to embrace in knowing and loving. Only recognizing the true Teacher by faith will enable us to understand his teaching in Scripture.

Many people, Augustine knows, think they worship God but do not yet know the true Teacher. Before proceeding with his investigation of Christian teaching, therefore, Augustine makes the case that such teaching is necessary and desirable. Everyone who worships a "god," he argues, "seeks to attain something than which there is nothing better or more sublime."[12] Otherwise the worshipper would turn to something better. Similarly, no worshipper of a "god" imagines the god as not alive. All value living things above nonliving things, and of living things all value intelligent living things most of all. Since one can change from living to not living, and understanding to not understanding, it follows that intelligent living things that could not change in this way, because already possessed of perfection, would be superior—in terms of degree of "life"—to things that do change for better or worse. Yet, an unchanging foolish living thing would not be very impressive, and so in aiming to worship that than which there is no better, worshippers would aim at an unchanging intelligent living thing. Once the meaning of the terms is understood, it is clear to all what kind of *res* would deserve worship.

It follows that the *res* that is to be enjoyed is not a pagan god, a limited entity, but "God the Trinity, the Author and Founder of the universe."[13] Yet, given our prideful tendency to cleave to created things, how can we attain this true enjoyment? Augustine's answer is that God, "Wisdom Himself," has taught us how—a transformative teaching, not merely abstract knowledge—in the humility of Christ Jesus, who is both the "end" and the "Way."[14] The invisible has become visible, so as to humble the proud and lead them back to the invisible by means of the visible. This teaching, Augustine recognizes with St. Paul, sounds like "foolishness," even though it proclaims the supreme Wisdom of the true Teacher.[15] When one accepts in faith and love the realities proclaimed by the teaching, one enters into the Church, Christ's body and bride. In the Church, we receive from Christ what we need to complete the journey to union with the Trinity. Among these necessities, Augustine points out, is the teaching of the future life, either of blessedness or punishment.[16] Without the hope of the future life, we could not cleave properly to God above the created things of this world, and we would remain in injustice.[17]

If this is so, then the way for human beings truly to love themselves is to love God the Trinity above all things, a love made possible by faith in Christ who teaches us both that God is triune Love and that we are called to attain union with this God by imitating his self-giving love. Before continuing, Augustine addresses an axiomatic objection: "no one hates himself."[18] We would prefer good for our souls and bodies, rather than harm. It would seem, therefore, that we hardly need to be taught how to love ourselves, since we already do. But Augustine points out that while Scripture indeed includes no precept commanding us to love ourselves, Scripture makes clear that love of self must be rightly ordered, since the self is always in relationship to God and to other human beings. Rightly estimating our true good requires rightly ordered loves. For instance, we must love God more than bodily health, and we must love all human beings, including our enemies, because they too are the "image of God," called like us, by God's sheer generosity, to share God's life.[19] Augustine states, "The sum of all we have said since we began to speak of things [res] thus comes to this: it is to be understood that the plenitude and the end of the Law and of all the sacred Scriptures is the love of a Being which is to be enjoyed and of a being that can share that enjoyment with us."[20]

Because, after sin, our natural inclination to love God and our neighbor has been darkened, God must *teach* us to do so. God teaches us in Christ, who brings to a radical fulfillment God's teaching in Israel. Christ is the true Teacher. Yet, Christ, as well as the Trinity and all realities of our salvation, must be taught to us in human words; and this is the task of Scripture. In and through Scripture, according to Augustine, God teaches us the "thing" to be loved, namely God himself. Thus understanding the texts of Scripture in themselves is not, in itself, the purpose of reading Scripture. Instead, understanding the texts has as its purpose the encounter with Love—none other than incarnate Wisdom, Jesus Christ—teaching through them, so that we might be caught up into Love's wise pattern for our lives. This proper reading and hearing involves us in Christ's communion, the Church, in which we are configured to the heavenly image that Christ teaches us.[21]

Interpreting Scripture, a task that at its best is a participation in God's own teaching, thus is only fully possible within Christ's Body.

The process of scriptural interpretation necessarily involves a tradition of ecclesial interpreters. In a first sense, these are readers who, having recognized Scripture as Love's teaching (and thereby having become incorporated in his Body), recognize that such teaching, in its true meaning, always aims at building up love of God and neighbor in ecclesial communion. In a sentence that provides the key to his exegetical practice, Augustine affirms, "Whoever, therefore, thinks he understands the divine Scriptures or any part of them so that it does not build the double love of God and of our neighbor does not understand it at all."[22] Since Scripture is Love's teaching and mediates (by teaching and stimulating faith, hope, and love) the encounter with Love, every passage in Scripture aims at the transformative teaching of true love of God and neighbor. In a second sense, those who read Scripture properly will be "ecclesial" readers because, as configured to Christ in his Body, they will recognize humility as a norm of scriptural reading, rather than, when perplexed by a difficulty in Scripture, becoming "angrier with the Scriptures" than with oneself and ending by asserting one's own teaching, one's own authority, over that of the Scripture.[23]

Far from valuing the understanding of the texts as an end in itself, then, Augustine argues that persons may and do live without the books of Scripture in faith, hope, and love, and that a person who firmly possesses faith, hope, and love "does not need the Scriptures except for the instruction of others."[24] This is so because Scripture is about *res*, ultimately the divine Trinity who teaches through Scripture (as well as through other ways). The faith-filled interpreter of Scripture, reading literally and spiritually, will discern even in difficult passages the mark of the Love who is this *res* and who calls us, in Christ and the Holy Spirit, to love him and our neighbors. The encounter with God teaching is the purpose of the texts. It follows that no understanding of the texts that fails to rise up to God teaching, but remains instead solely at the level of the words, can be adequate to the teaching that the words contain.[25]

How does Augustine apply this understanding of exegesis to actual texts of Scripture?[26] He understands that Scripture possesses "many and varied obscurities and ambiguities."[27] The complexity of Scripture is increased, he points out, by the fact that some things can be signs of other things, in other words can express a spiritual meaning rather than solely the meaning that would appear on the surface. As an example, Augustine gives Song of Songs 4:2, "Thy teeth are as flocks of sheep, that are shorn, which come up from the washing, all with twins, and there is none barren among them," which he interprets in terms of the saints or in terms of the baptized bearing holy fruit. Without insisting on this interpretation, which he recognizes as playful, he insists that however one wishes to interpret the *res* of the Song of Songs, or any other biblical text, one's interpretation must conform with the end or goal of God's teaching, namely our conversion in love. Such a reader of the biblical texts, "having found nothing else in them except" love of God and love of neighbor in God, will be converted by God's teaching because he will recognize in the narratives of Scripture his own sinful narrative. As Augustine says, "Then it follows that the student first will discover in the Scriptures that he has been enmeshed in the love of this world, or of temporal things, a love far remote from the kind of love of God and of our neighbor which Scripture itself prescribes."[28] Encountering Christ the Teacher in all the texts of Scripture, readers are enabled to walk the path of the Sermon on the Mount's beatitudes, a path from conversion to the peace that is holiness.[29]

As befits the great scholar and preacher that Augustine was, the remaining three books of his *De doctrina christiana* are filled with practical advice on how to acquire the canonical, linguistic, historical, grammatical, and rhetorical gifts useful for discerning and teaching persuasively the true meaning of Scripture. Augustine's most important contribution, however, comes in the first book, which we have explored above, since it is here that he makes clear that proper interpretation of Scripture requires expanding our notion of the "hermeneutical" task to include at its heart "existential" participation: to read Scripture properly means to encounter God teaching and to have one's loves re-ordered. For the purposes of this chapter, namely to think about how to reengage the pre-historical-critical ecclesial tradition of scriptural interpretation, Augustine's position has particular significance for two reasons.

First, Augustine reverses our contemporary expectations of what we should learn from the study of Scripture, although many contemporary exegetes would agree with Augustine. Gaining knowledge of the texts of Scripture means primarily, according to Augustine, gaining a transformative participation in the divine Persons, God teaching. Second, Augustine places the entire content of Scripture, with its various genres and styles, under the rubric of "teaching."[30] It seems to me that this rubric enables us to contemplate more richly the conjunction of God's teaching, the human author's teaching, and the interpretive teaching of the doctrinal tradition of the Church as well as that of the tradition of ecclesial exegesis. In the light of this interpersonal context of teaching, the conjunction, in a canonical collection of human books, of divine and human teaching seems more intelligible: God the Teacher may teach more through the human teachers' words than the human teachers know, and so God's teaching is not in conflict with the "messiness" of human teaching.

The great variety of the forms of human teaching in the biblical texts thus enters into and enriches the encounter with God the Teacher. Exegetes who would teach the Bible well have to learn how to interpret the various literary genres in which human teachers, mediating God's teaching, communicated truth—what Nicholas Wolterstorff calls their "unfamiliar illocutionary stance."[31] Likewise, exegetes need to be connaturalized to the realities of faith taught in the biblical texts, so as to share truly in the work of teaching as receptive "students" of the divine Teacher.[32] On this view biblical interpretation, far from a neutral engagement with texts, achieves an increasingly profound encounter with the divine Teacher in and through the human teachings of the Bible (and thus in and through the Church as the community of human teachers who participate in the divine Teacher). Here we see again how biblical exegesis in the Church is a participation in the teaching of the triune God—where "the teaching of the triune God" is, because of the action of the Holy Spirit, *both* the triune God's teaching and human teachings about the triune God.[33]

Aquinas as an Augustinian Reader of Scripture

In his Inaugural Sermon "Commendation of and Division of Sacred Scripture," his inaugural lecture at the University of Paris, Aquinas begins in two ways. First, he takes as his scriptural text Baruch 4:1, "This is the book of the commandments of God, and the law that is for ever. All that keep it shall come to life: but they that have forsaken it, to death." Here we find the affirmation of Scripture as transformative *sacra doctrina*. Second, in his first sentence he recalls Augustine's portrait of the Christian teacher in *De doctrina christiana*.[34] Aquinas writes, "According to Augustine in *On Christian Doctrine* 4.12, one skilled in speech should so speak as to teach, to delight and to change; that is, to teach the ignorant, to delight the bored and to change the lazy. The speech of Sacred Scripture does these three things in the fullest manner."[35]

Drawing on Augustine means, for Aquinas, inscribing his own reading of Scripture within the traditional focus on God the Teacher.[36] He selects three biblical verses to show how "the speech of Sacred Scripture" accomplishes the three Augustinian requirements for teaching. In each of the selected biblical texts, he shifts the attention from the scriptural texts themselves to God the Teacher, without reducing the value of the scriptural texts, since they are the words of God. Thus, for Aquinas, Scripture teaches the ignorant because it teaches eternal truth, as confirmed in Psalm 119:89, "Thy word, O Lord, stands firm for ever in heaven." Likewise Scripture delights the bored because, as Psalm 119:103 says, "How sweet are thy words to my mouth!" And Scripture changes the lazy because of its efficacious authority, as witnessed by Jeremiah 23:29, "Are not my words as a fire, saith the Lord?" Each of these scriptural texts, which together affirm the transformative, delightful, and efficacious power of the words of Scripture, draws attention primarily not to the words themselves but to God teaching. The words of Scripture continually point beyond themselves toward the encounter with their divine source; the transformative power of the words is known in their ability to direct the reader or hearer to the divine Teacher.[37]

Jeremiah 23:29, one of the texts Aquinas cites, is part of a memorable instance of God's revelation of his power. The entirety of this portion of Jeremiah is presented as God speaking directly. Vowing "[w]oe to the shepherds who destroy and scatter the sheep of my pasture!" (Jer 23:1), God warns those who have presumed to rule and speak for God in unjust ways, bringing about the destruction of God's people. God promises the coming of the Davidic Messiah, who will establish righteousness for the "remnant" whom God will restore: "Behold, the days are coming, says the Lord, when I will raise up for David a righteous Branch, and he shall reign as king and deal wisely, and shall execute justice and righteousness in the land. In his days Judah will be saved, and Israel will dwell securely. And this is the name by which he will be called: 'The Lord is our righteousness'" (Jer 23:5–6). God then condemns the false prophets who are leading Judah to believe itself impregnable. As if amazed that the false prophets would not hear his voice, God inquires, "Am I a God at hand, says the Lord, and not a God afar off? Can a man hide himself in secret places so that I cannot see him? says the Lord. Do I not fill heaven and earth? says the Lord" (Jer 23:23–24).

Similarly, Psalm 119, from which Aquinas cites verses 89 and 103, is a series of highly personal testimonies of praise to God for the gift of his law. The law is here no abstract teaching, but rather a life-giving encounter with God teaching. The psalm contains cries to God throughout beseeching him for such an encounter: "The earth, O Lord, is full of thy steadfast love; teach me thy statutes!" (119:64); "Thou art good and doest good; teach me thy statutes" (119:68); "Let thy mercy come to me, that I may live; for thy law is my delight" (119:77); "My soul languishes for thy salvation; I hope in thy word" (119:81). In the segment from which Aquinas takes verse 89, the psalmist begs, "I am thine, save me; for I have sought thy precepts" (119:94). Likewise, in the passage containing verse 103 we find, "I have more understanding than all my teachers, for thy testimonies are my meditation" (119:99). The words of the law, of Scripture, are holy and good, precisely because they mediate the encounter with the saving God, the efficaciously transformative Teacher, for which the psalm begs. Far from idolizing the words of the law as such, the psalmist focuses attention on the saving, living God who teaches, just as in Jeremiah the point of God's words being "as a fire" is that they mediate encounter with the God who is not "afar off," whose presence fills heaven and earth, and who is acting to save the remnant through the coming Davidic Messiah.

Interpreting Baruch 4:1, the text on which he is preaching, Aquinas makes the same point about the need for the interpretation of the words of Scripture to be grounded in a focus on the living God who is teaching. According to Baruch, Aquinas says, Scripture has efficacious divine authority, teaches eternal truth, and draws the reader or hearer into the divine life. All three facets of Scripture describe God's saving action, since only God has such authority, only God is Truth, and only God can draw us, through transformative knowledge, into his life. Aquinas explains God's action, never separated, of course, from human response, as the key to Scripture in commenting further on each of the scriptural facets—efficacious authority, eternal truth, and transformative power.

As regards Scripture's efficacious authority, Aquinas points to three aspects that explain why Scripture, unlike other texts, commands and obtains the response of faith. The first aspect is that "God is its origin."[38] When one recognizes that in and through Scripture God is teaching, one must believe Scripture's teachings. God is truth, perfect wisdom, and his words are not merely offered to us. Rather, in Scripture, his words demand or command our response of faith. This demand or command is the second aspect of Scripture's efficacious authority. Faith, for Aquinas, is assent to God by assenting to what God has revealed; faith's assent constitutes a relationship with God, rather than being merely a conceptual grasp of propositions. Scripture's commanding aspect brings about faith, "inform[s] the affections with love" and "induce[s] to action."[39] In other words, encountering God teaching in and through Scripture goes beyond the mere reception of abstract knowledge. God, teaching in and through Scripture, renews and transforms the entire person by directing the person to relationship with God.

Furthermore, God's teaching in and through Scripture has in view consistently the goal of bringing about human relationship with God in faith, hope, and love. Here then is the third aspect: Scripture's efficacious authority derives from its *unity.* In Scripture Aquinas sees a collection of texts that teach consistently the same goal, the restoration and perfection of human relationship with God. The entire Bible reveals the working of "one teacher," manifested in his pupils' "one spirit" and "one love from above."[40] Like Augustine, then, Aquinas does not hesitate to say that "all who teach the sacred doctrine [in Scripture] teach the same thing."[41] This same thing is divine Wisdom and Love, ultimately the Teacher himself, in which the scriptural authors are, in the historical unfolding of God's work of salvation, participating by their teaching.

Aquinas similarly describes Scripture's eternal truth. Just as Scripture's efficacious authority comes primarily from its source, God teaching, so also Scripture's eternal truth flows from "the power of the lawgiver," the immutable God whose wise decree is true. No one can gainsay or change God's law, because God is unchanging Wisdom, whose knowledge cannot be contradicted. God's law, expressed most fully in and by Christ, is love; and this law is faithful, steadfast, and enduring, as Aquinas makes clear with selected quotations from Scripture. To make the point that God's law will be eternally accomplished, because it is eternally true, Aquinas cites Luke 21:33, "Heaven and earth will pass away but my words shall not pass away." This verse, belonging to Jesus' discourse about the end of the world and the establishment of the eternal kingdom of God, makes clear that God's law, or true teaching, is again not presented here as a merely abstract decree. Rather God's law is the establishment of Love as all in all; this law is true, and cannot change. God's eternal truth, his teaching, is his accomplishment of salvation. Once again it is not simply the texts of Scripture in themselves, but God's action (the manifestation of his eternal law, his Wisdom and Love), that provides the *focus* of Aquinas's interpretation of the texts of Scripture.

Turning lastly in this section of his Inaugural Sermon to Scripture's transformative power, its ability to draw people to union with God, Aquinas likewise grounds this power in God the Teacher: "'I am the Lord thy God that teach thee profitable things.'"[42] Aquinas explains that the "life" set forth in Scripture, and toward which Scripture disposes, leads, and directs, is threefold. The first, the life of grace, makes possible the second, "the life of justice consisting in works."[43] This active charity, flowing from grace, is consummated in the life of glory. Quoting John 6:69, "Lord, to whom shall we go? Thou hast the words of everlasting life," Aquinas emphasizes that Christ's teaching, as the expression of the Word of God, is the ultimate source of the knowledge that deifies.

In a brief compass of the entire Scriptures, Aquinas next examines how God, in teaching through the words and deeds recorded in Scripture, draws distinctions that assist in human learning of God's teaching, *sacra doctrina*. Thus, for instance, he treats the differences of the Old and New Testaments. Regarding the Old Testament, he indicates why

God included the various kinds of literature contained therein, specifically the law (the Old Testament's first five books), the prophets (including historical books such as Samuel), the wisdom literature, and the deuterocanonical books. He suggests how the distinctions between books, such as the division between Exodus, Leviticus, and Numbers, serve to enhance the clarity and order of God's teaching. He describes the special teaching entrusted particularly to each of the major prophets, Isaiah, Jeremiah, and Ezekiel.

Regarding the New Testament, he observes that the gospels describe the origin of grace, the Pauline epistles the power of grace, and the remainder the historical enactment of the power of grace in the life of the virtues and gifts that constitute the Christian community, culminating in the eschatological glory depicted in Revelation. Similarly, he proposes that the four gospels are distinguished among themselves on the basis of how they present the origin of grace, Jesus Christ. John teaches primarily of Christ's divine nature, while the other gospels teach primarily of Christ's human nature. In accord with the threefold dignity of Christ's human nature, Matthew emphasizes Christ's kingly office, Mark emphasizes Christ's prophetic office, and Luke emphasizes Christ's priestly office.

In short, Aquinas's Inaugural Sermon reads the scriptural texts in the broader context of God's teaching. Scripture, he affirms, is not a random hodgepodge of ancient devotional, historical, and theological documentation. Instead, Scripture has an inner unity and order that human reason (illumined by faith) can discern and explore, and that displays the pedagogical presence of a wise and loving teacher. Once one has by faith discerned the Teacher, the deifying patterns in Scripture become intelligible. The Teacher's authority explains why Scripture itself commands the response of faith, rather than being a mere repository of facts and ideas. The one Teacher ensures that all Scripture teaches the same teaching that, when received in the Holy Spirit, binds human beings together into a communion of love. The divine Teacher guarantees the truth of Scripture's teaching and directs his pupils in the transformative attainment of true life, the life of grace that is enacted in the virtues and consummated in glory. Like any good teacher, God employs distinct kinds of teaching, and diverse approaches to the same reality, in the words and deeds recorded in Scripture. Thus awareness of the divine Teacher does not require one to deny that God is teaching through human, historical modes that diversely express, in the messiness of human history, the Wisdom and Love of God's plan for human creatures.

As Aquinas recognized, this account of Scripture as mediating a participatory encounter with the divine Teacher belongs to the Christian East as well. John Damascene marvelously describes biblical reading:

> So let us knock at the very beautiful paradise of the Scriptures, the fragrant, most sweet and lovely paradise which fills our ears with the varied songs of inspired spiritual birds, which touches our heart, comforting it when grieving, calming it when angry, and filling it with everlasting joy, and which lifts our mind onto the back of the sacred dove, gleaming with gold and most brilliant, who bears us with his most bright wings to the only begotten Son and heir of the Husbandman of the spiritual vineyard and through Him on to the Father of lights.[44]

Damascene urges that readers of Scripture not become disheartened by trouble in understanding Scripture's meaning. Instead, readers should "knock" ever harder, and trust that God and the Church's "elders," the tradition of ecclesial interpretation, will unlock the meaning. Scripture itself, he observes, assures that the reading of Scripture conduces to the encounter with the divine Teacher. Jesus tells his audience at the temple, "Search the scriptures: for these give testimony of me" (John 5:39); and Hebrews opens with the affirmation, "God, who, at sundry times and in diverse manners, spoke in times past to the fathers by prophets, last of all, in these days, hath spoken to us by his Son" (Hebrews 1:1–2).

God the Teacher and Contemporary Biblical Interpretation

In arguing that to understand the authors / redactors of Scripture (Israelites and early Christians) one needs to join them in their encounter with the living God, I have moved some distance away from the position that linear-historical tools must first be employed as a "neutral" means of validating the participatory-historical claims. As we have seen, for Augustine and Aquinas, reading Scripture as primarily a quest for God the Teacher comes about through a participatory understanding of reality (creation and grace). Their participatory biblical exegesis requires receptivity to the realities of grace, ongoing in human history through God's action, and to the wisdom inscribed in the created order. Admittedly, from a modern perspective, distanced from the view of scriptural reading as a mode of participation in *sacra doctrina*, Augustine's and Aquinas's exegetical practices seem to be inevitably eisegetical. But from a perspective that in faith centers on the divine Teacher and the dynamics of mediated divine teaching, their approach is required to account for even the linear-historical complexity of the biblical texts. God is alive and historical realities cannot be understood outside of human relationships with him—relationships that God, not human beings, sets in motion according to his plan for our salvation.

We must ask again, however: can an exegesis that *focuses* on the divine Teacher rather than simply on the texts really be justified in practice? Are not the messy historical provenance and intrabiblical divergences thereby ignored, flattening the historical reality of the biblical texts and fitting them into preconceived boxes? Luke Timothy Johnson's "Imagining the World That Scripture Imagines" helps us understand why and how the focus on the divine Teacher works without destroying the linear-historical dimensions.[45] Johnson proposes that "Scripture as a whole and in all of its parts imagines a world, and by imagining a world, it reveals it to readers."[46] The world "imagined" by Scripture is a world of *sacra doctrina*, of God the Teacher and the human and angelic mediations of his transformative, healing, and deifying teaching. As Johnson says, "By imagining the world as essentially and always related to a God who creates, sustains, judges, saves, and sanctifies, Scripture at the same time reveals that world and reveals this God."[47] The world described by Johnson has the redemptive work of the Trinity—God the Teacher in the sense of "teaching" as an activity that is not merely conveying ideas but healing, transforming, and deifying— at its graced center. That same world as described by Johnson is metaphysically rich: it is a world "essentially and always related to a God who creates." Lastly the world described by Johnson is communally/ ecclesially related to God, since God is always the one who is judging, saving, and sanctifying.[48] Johnson does not limit his retrieval to the task of "imagining," although at times he overemphasizes the centrality of the imagination. He rightly affirms in a later section of the book, "It is appropriate as well to think philosophically about the text and readers. Philosophy includes metaphysics. The lack of any sense of ontology se- verely limits contemporary scholars reading Scripture."[49]

In searching for a point of integration, Johnson conceives of patristic-medieval interpretation as *sapientia* and historical-critical in- terpretation as *scientia*.[50] By *scientia* he denotes the contemporary wealth of historical and archeological data, the "mind" as it were, whereas by *sapientia* he denotes insight into what makes Scripture tick, the "heart."[51] In his view, "The church must . . . somehow discover again how mind and heart can be united in the study of God's word. Chief among these resources is a tradition of reading Scripture as a form of wisdom rather than simply a science, a tradition that extended across the first 1600 years of the church's life."[52] The competing claims of *scientia* and *sapi- entia* suggest for Johnson that exegesis requires uniting fundamentally disparate elements, the scientific data and the possible spiritual mean- ings (wisdom). On what basis could such a union not appear fatally extrinsic?

Johnson attempts to resolve this dilemma by arguing that the *sci- entia* of historical researches into the gospel narratives and the figure of Jesus needs to be complemented and normed by the *sapientia* that is the Church's multifaceted experiential witness—set down normatively in the narratives of the four gospels—to the living Jesus (the Jesus who, as risen, lives today).[53] In Johnson's emphasis on the "living Jesus" we find a parallel with the patristic-medieval tradition's emphasis on union with the divine Teacher. Learning the Teacher is learning the living Jesus. To be inserted into the ongoing risen life of the living Jesus re- quires participating in the truth and transformative power of the triune God's teaching *(sacra doctrina)* by means of various modes of knowl- edge. Such Trinitarian insertion into Jesus' teaching, by the Holy Spirit, would require the modes of human *scientia* as well as the deeper order- ing and insight of human *sapientia*, an ordering that requires metaphysical and ecclesial teaching. Scripture as God's teaching requires of interpreters that they understand their own scriptural teaching as a participation in that of the Teacher, a participation that clearly must go beyond, while including, the acquisition of linear-historical data.

For Johnson, believers know the living Jesus through a dialectical relationship between Scripture and tradition: "The Creed lives out of Scripture and expresses the truth of Scripture in propositional form, but it does not come close to capturing the rich ambiguity of the person of Jesus as presented by John's Gospel."[54] Johnson's perspective needs deepening here: the Creed *strengthens* the "rich ambiguity of the person of Jesus" in that through the Creed we come face-to-face with the extraordinary mystery of the reality of Jesus' Godmanhood and are instructed to read the gospels (to learn Christ the Teacher) in this light—a light that adds mystery, or "rich ambiguity," just as much as clarity.[55] By focusing on the living Jesus, however, Johnson is able to show that *scientia* and *sapientia* are not in competition, because the knowledge of faith engages the key task of scriptural interpretation, to learn—in a Trinitarian manner—the Teacher. Since what is sought is actually a "who," one must begin with the more interpersonal perspective of *sapientia*, and the tools of *scientia* then have their place within the task of deepening encounter with the living God revealed in history.[56] The emphasis on scriptural interpretation as seeking union with a Person (the triune Teacher) makes intelligible the claim that the real Jesus, taught in the Scriptures, is not obscured by the development of the Church's teaching.[57] Rather the Church's teaching, as a participation in the revealed *sacra doctrina* that is Scripture and tradition, illumines more deeply the Teacher narrated in Scripture.[58]

But have we not here brought to an end Scripture's "otherness" and erased the discontinuity that persists within the participatory continuity, what Johnson calls "the negative pole of the dialectic, which is the way in which Scripture also must challenge the tradition so that tradition does not seek to constrain and control the power of Scripture through its normative readings"?[59] By emphasizing the participatory unity of God's *sacra doctrina*, how can one account for differences within this *doctrina* in its diverse modes (in creation, Israel, the Church, and Scripture)? Granting that the divine "authorial intention" possesses the

unity proper to a good Teacher, can one say that the diverse *human* authorial intentions possess such a unity, let alone a continuity with the
Church's later teachings?[60]

It should first be said that a historical mode of teaching, in diverse
human contexts and with the multiplicity of human intentions and authors, inevitably includes the unsystematic portraiture and presentation that characterizes human authorship. Without this unsystematic
historical portraiture, the radicality of God's presence (the true "otherness") as teaching precisely in the history of Israel and the Church
would not be made fully manifest. From this perspective, for example,
the evangelist Mark's historical embeddedness reflects the historical
embeddedness of the triune God's work in Israel and in Christ Jesus.
Certainly Mark, in teaching Jesus, participates in Jesus' own *doctrina*,
which has depths far beyond Mark's knowledge.[61] Mark need not, in his
conscious understanding, know all aspects of this Trinitarian *doctrina*,
which faith recognizes to include the doctrinal formulations of Chal-
cedon. Aquinas observes in this regard: "even if commentators adapt
certain truths to the sacred text that were not understood by the author, without doubt the Holy Spirit understood them, since he is the
principal author of Scripture."[62] Mark's teaching conveys the aspects of
the salvific reality that the triune God, knowing the reality more fully,
intends to teach. As David Steinmetz points out with Christian exegesis of Isaiah in mind: "It is not anachronistic to believe such added dimensions of meaning exist. It is only good exegesis."[63]

An exegetical focus on the living God who teaches allows, therefore,
for differences, divergences, and development. It does not require suggesting that all biblical authors / redactors, working in various genres,
are saying and intending the same thing or that God the Teacher is easy
to recognize in all biblical passages. It simply requires that Scripture's
human authorial teachings and intentions be recognized as belonging
to the participatory framework—divine revelation and inspiration—of
the Trinitarian *doctrina*.

Such reading is "historical" in the sense that the human authors'
doctrina in Scripture is seen to belong within the broader historical
pattern of the triune God's teaching—a historical context that spans
not only Israel but also the metaphysical and theological realities that

characterize human history in its entirety, and that thereby belong to any adequately historical exegesis. Such reading is also "critical" because it requires a non-reductivist analysis of the realities (God, Christ, and so forth) expressed in Scripture: no exegesis can be critical if it misapprehends the very realities with which it deals. Finally, such reading displays the challenge that Scripture presents to the Church, the challenge of Christ's call to non-idolatrous holiness in the Holy Spirit. This challenge, as given by Christ through the gift of the Holy Spirit, is also an exegetical one directed not merely at individuals but at the Church, built up by the Holy Spirit as Christ's Body.[64]

It is thus not the difficult passages that provide the critical norm for biblical interpretation. Rather, the entire *doctrina* governs interpretation of the difficult passages not by making their problematic aspects any less difficult, but by receiving them, despite their difficulty, as belonging to the transformative divine *doctrina*.[65] For example, pondering a possible contradictory statement in Genesis 1:8, the story of creation, Aquinas applies Augustinian (and broadly patristic) principles: "In discussing questions of this kind two rules are to be observed, as Augustine teaches (*Gen. ad lit.* i. 18). The first is, to hold the truth of Scripture without wavering. The second is that since Holy Scripture can be explained in a multiplicity of senses, one should adhere to a particular explanation, only in such measure as to be ready to abandon it, if it be proved with certainty to be false; lest Holy Scripture be exposed to the ridicule of unbelievers, and obstacles be placed to their believing."[66] Is such an allowance for multiple potential meanings a relativistic hermeneutic, a mere escape hatch from troublesome passages? No, because it is grounded metaphysically and theologically by Love, to whom Scripture witnesses. As Augustine explains in *De doctrina christiana*:

> The sum of all we have said since we began to speak of *res* thus comes to this: it is to be understood that the plenitude and end of the Law and of all the sacred Scriptures is the love of a Being which is to be enjoyed and of a being that can share that enjoyment with us. . . . That we might know this and have the means to implement it, the whole temporal dispensation was made by divine Providence for our salvation. . . . Whoever, therefore, thinks that he understands

the divine Scriptures or any part of them so that it does not build the double love of God and of our neighbor does not understand it at all.[67]

This biblical exegesis flows from participation, in the fullest sense, in Trinitarian *doctrina*. It calls for a rich understanding of the linear-historical portraiture—whose dimensions historical-critical and literary exegesis fleshes out in important ways—within the framework of the participatory-historical dimensions, illumined in the Holy Spirit not merely by the individual exegete's perspicacity but by the Church's historical doctrinal-theological reflection. What is required, then, is most certainly not a "return" to a biblical exegesis uninformed by contemporary linear-historical scholarship. Rather than choosing faith over history, and thereby constricting God's historical teaching that is ongoing in the Church's contemporary appropriation of Scripture, participatory biblical exegesis seeks to integrate linear-historical and participatory-historical modes into an interpretive, ecclesial, and performative pattern of engagement with *sacra doctrina*, in which the goal is learning the triune Teacher—learning the Love of the Word of the Father.

Dei Verbum and Patristic-Medieval Exegesis

If Johnson and Kurz's book helps us see why the participatory-historical framework needs recovering, it also leads us to *Dei Verbum*, the Dogmatic Constitution on Divine Revelation promulgated by the Second Vatican Council. William Kurz in particular draws attention to the second half of §12 of *Dei Verbum*.[68] This second half of §12 reads:

But since sacred Scripture must be read and interpreted in the same Spirit in which it was written, no less attention must be devoted to the content and unity of the whole of Scripture, taking into account the Tradition of the entire Church and the analogy of faith, if we are to derive their true meaning from the sacred texts. It is the task of exegetes to work, according to these rules, towards a better understanding and explanation of the meaning of sacred Scripture in order that their research may help the Church to form a firmer judgment. For, of course, all that has been said about the manner of interpreting Scripture is ultimately subject to the judgment of the Church which exercises the divinely confirmed commission and ministry of watching over and interpreting the Word of God.[69]

Kurz finds in this text several of the five "premises" of patristic-medieval exegesis that Johnson identifies in chapter 2 of *The Future of Catholic Biblical Scholarship*. These five premises are: (1) the single divine author unifies the Old and New Testaments; (2) therefore Scripture speaks harmoniously; (3) as God's Word the Bible is authoritative; (4) Scripture speaks in various ways and levels; and (5) Scripture requires a hermeneutics of charity.[70] Johnson's first premise, Kurz points out, corresponds to §12's reference to the Holy Spirit who ensures the "unity of the whole of Scripture."[71] The second premise regarding harmony, as Kurz notes, flows from Scripture's unity. Both premises depend on seeking, and discerning, the triune Teacher. Following §12's directive to "[take] into account the Tradition of the entire Church and the analogy of faith," interpreters discern Scripture's harmony when interpretation seeks union with the triune Teacher who grounds, in scriptural and ecclesial teaching, our communion with the realities of faith.[72]

The third premise of patristic-medieval exegesis set forth by Johnson—the Bible as the authoritative Word of God—again focuses on God the Teacher, and is alluded to at the end of the passage that Kurz quotes from §12. This third premise finds full expression in §11, which commences *Dei Verbum*'s account of the inspiration and interpretation of Scripture by articulating the key themes of the patristic-medieval understanding of Scripture as God's teaching. Section 11 grounds biblical interpretation in the foundation of God teaching. It begins, "The divinely revealed realities, which are contained and presented in the text of sacred Scripture, have been written down under the inspiration of the Holy Spirit. . . . [T]hey have God as their author, and have been handed on as such to the Church herself."[73] Since Scripture is God teaching, biblical interpretation seeks salvific truth: "Since, therefore, all that the inspired authors, or sacred writers, affirm should be regarded as affirmed by the Holy Spirit, we must acknowledge that the books of Scripture, firmly, faithfully and without error, teach that truth which God, for the sake of our salvation, wished to see confided to the sacred Scriptures."[74] For the sake of our salvation, God teaches saving truth through Scripture. Section 11 makes the transformative aspect clear by concluding with 2 Timothy 3:16–17, "all Scripture is inspired by God, and profitable for teaching, for reproof, for correction and for training in righteousness, so that the man of God may be complete, equipped for every good work." In order to interpret Scripture's truth correctly, we must participate, through conversion and Trinitarian communion, in the Trinity's active and transforming *doctrina*.[75]

The fourth premise of patristic-medieval exegesis noted by Johnson, namely that Scripture speaks in many ways and levels, follows from the point, made at the outset of §12, that "God speaks through men in human fashion." This reality of mediation—the triune God teaching divine realities through human language and human teachers—illumines, as §13 notes, "the marvelous 'condescension' of eternal wisdom" in a manner analogous to the Incarnation, in which God reveals himself through the historical particularity and finite limitations of a man.[76] Kurz points out that in its treatment of the Old Testament, for instance, *Dei Verbum* suggests the many ways and levels, the multiple senses, in which God teaches in Scripture. Thus §15, on the Old Testament, remarks that "[t]hese books, even though they contain matters imperfect and provisional, nevertheless show us authentic divine teaching."[77] With regard to the depth of meaning in Scripture, §16 likewise notes that "God, the inspirer and author of the books of both Testaments, in his wisdom has so brought it about that the New should be hidden in the Old and that the Old should be made manifest in the new."[78]

Lastly, Kurz observes that Johnson's fifth premise of patristic-medieval exegesis, the hermeneutics of charity, can be found in §12's statement that "sacred Scripture must be read and interpreted in the same Spirit in which it was written." The Holy Spirit is Love. This point, of course, is Augustine's, and affirms once again the centrality of God the Teacher—both for patristic-medieval exegesis and for *Dei Verbum*. Thus by tracing each of Johnson's five premises in *Dei Verbum* (and the *Catechism of the Catholic Church*), Kurz shows that Vatican II's reflection on exegesis articulates the key themes of the tradition of ecclesial biblical interpretation. "Rejoining the long conversation" (Johnson's wonderful phrase) thus not only remains possible, but indeed is mandated by the Council's Dogmatic Constitution.

By contrast, Kurz finds the first half of §12, the section that has received the most scholarly attention and appreciation in contemporary Catholic biblical scholarship, to be in certain respects dated:

> Seeing that, in sacred Scripture, God speaks through men in human fashion, it follows that the interpreter of sacred Scriptures, if he is to ascertain what God has wished to communicate to us, should carefully search out the meaning which the sacred writers really had in mind, that meaning which God had thought well to manifest through the medium of their words. In determining the intention of the sacred writers, attention must be paid, inter alia, to "literary forms for the fact is that truth is differently presented and expressed in the various types of historical writing, in prophetical and poetical texts," and in other forms of literary expression. Hence the exegete must look for that meaning which the sacred writer, in a determined situation and given the circumstances of his time and culture, intended to express and did in fact express, through the medium of a contemporary literary form. Rightly to understand what the sacred author wanted to affirm in his work, due attention must be paid both to the customary and characteristic patterns of perception, speech and narrative which prevailed at the age of the sacred writer, and to the conventions which the people of his time followed in their dealings with one another.[79]

Kurz points out that the emphasis on authorial intention, common at the time of the Council, has since been called into question by hermeneutical theorists.[80] On the other hand, he thinks that it is historically valuable to examine "[t]he historical meaning of words, phrases, idioms, genres, etc., in the time and culture of the original writing."[81] I would suggest that "authorial intention" is neither so perspicuous as perhaps was then thought nor so hidden as some may think. Rather the search for "authorial intention," as described by *Dei Verbum*, signals an effort to learn what, in the time that the biblical authors were writing, their writings communicated. In this regard Stephen Fowl's distinction (following Mark Brett and Quentin Skinner) between "authorial motives," which cannot be uncovered, and "an author's communicative intentions," which can, is particularly helpful. Communicative intentions—"what an author is trying to say"—belong to the intelligibility of human discourse, and are recoverable, even if not perhaps fully so, by linear-historical modes aided by participatory-historical ones.[82]

The Council's injunction in the first part of §12 has to do primarily with the linear aspect of history, whereas the second part pertains to the participatory aspect. It is the second part that, in *Dei Verbum*, possesses the normative role; but the Council makes clear that the participatory aspect, while normative, does not negate the linear aspect. Historical-critical retrieval of the author's communicative intentions, as regards their linear-historical aspect, takes us much farther in certain respects than the patristic-medieval tradition of exegesis was able to go. For instance, Luke Timothy Johnson's knowledge of the Maccabean revolt, of the genre of historical biography in the ancient world, and so forth significantly expands our understanding of biblical teaching. Thus, when combined with participatory-historical retrieval of the theological and metaphysical realities whose active presence unites us to the realities depicted in the text, such linear-historical retrieval makes possible a more full engagement with the communicative intentions of the human and divine authors.[83]

In accord with Augustine and Aquinas's approach, *Dei Verbum* places biblical interpretation in the primary light of the Trinity's teaching (cf. §§2–6). It is within this context that *Dei Verbum* includes discussion of the role of linear historical-critical study of the *doctrina* of biblical authors. If to some degree *Dei Verbum* has been neglected by biblical scholars and theologians, it has been, at least in part, because it seems to occupy a no-man's land between partisans of historical-critical scholarship and partisans of other interpretive modes. It can therefore be hoped that recovering the linear and participatory dimensions of history makes possible, among other things, the recovery of the significance of the Dogmatic Constitution for biblical scholarship that places God teaching at the center.[84]

Conclusion

Having traversed the distance from Augustine's *De doctrina christiana* to the Second Vatican Council's *Dei Verbum* together with the more recent exploratory study of Luke Timothy Johnson and William Kurz, let us recall the goal of biblical interpretation. The opening sentence of *Dei Verbum* quotes the first letter of John: "We proclaim to you the eternal life which was with the Father and was made manifest to us—that which we have seen and heard we proclaim also to you, so that you may have fellowship with us, and that our fellowship may be with the Father and with his Son Jesus Christ" (1 John 1:2–3). By opening with this biblical quotation, *Dei Verbum* makes clear that understanding biblical "proclamation" cannot prescind from the "fellowship" that provides the proclamation's context—the fellowship of the Church, which is the first fruits of the communion with the Trinity that the blessed in heaven enjoy eternally.[85] This "fellowship" involves the entire scope of God's *sacra doctrina*, including the "created realities" that testify to God as well as the "plan to open up the way of heavenly salvation" whose fullness John proclaims.[86]

As *Dei Verbum* suggests, then, the interpretation of *sacra doctrina* must include intrinsically integrated historical, theological, and metaphysical modes in order to attain the full depth of the realities taught in creation and redemption.[87] The Trinitarian constitution of the ecclesial "fellowship" provides the locus in which interpretation attains its object, God the Father, Son, and Holy Spirit. For *Dei Verbum*, as for the first letter of John, participation in the ecclesial fellowship (in Christ through the Spirit) provides a set of interpretive practices, above all *charity*, that mediate fuller understanding of the triune God's teaching. *Dei Verbum* thus both recognizes that valuable partial understanding of biblical realities is available to interpreters outside this fellowship, and that the meanings available to interpreters are in important ways shaped by the communities in which interpreters seek meaning— a point that applies especially to the fellowship of the Holy Spirit who illumines biblical realities.[88] As William Babcock states, interpreting Augustine's *De doctrina christiana*: "it is precisely by knowing what Scripture signifies [by ecclesial faith and charity] that we put ourselves in a position to discern how it signifies what it signifies."[89] The depths of human history, as revealed in Scripture, are opened to faith and charity. Historical research cannot rightly interpret the linear-historical realities without attending to the participatory-historical aspects of these realities[90]; and these participatory aspects are known, in faith and charity, in the ecclesial/communal context in which the realities possess a providential (Christological) continuity with the past and future. God's scriptural *sacra doctrina* cannot ultimately be separated from the ecclesial Trinitarian fellowship from which it flows and whose growth it seeks to foster.

Again, does this claim endanger the "otherness" of the biblical texts that enables them to challenge the Church? Johnson worries about what he sees as failures in ecclesial interpretation of Scripture, largely having to do with sexual teachings.[91] Yet both Johnson and Kurz affirm strongly that what Johnson elsewhere calls the norm of "church, canon, and creed"[92] works. It does so because Scripture is not an esoteric manual, but is instead *sacra doctrina* (as I would put it) that in the hands of ecclesial interpreters, using all the contemporary tools and resources of *doctrina*, provides "a means of strengthening authentic faith, of transforming minds into the mind of Christ, and of building up the church in love."[93]

This argument, it will be seen, falls back on the claim, found in the first letter of John, that Trinitarian "fellowship" is intrinsic to the teaching of Scripture. Since the principle of the Church's fellowship is love, Augustine's interpretive rule retains its force in separating exegesis from eisegesis: "Whoever thinks that he understands the divine Scriptures or any part of them so that it does not build the double love of God and of our neighbor does not understand it at all." Since the Church's faith makes claims about the reality of this world,[94] the interpreter can abide, within the *regula fidei*, by Aquinas's dictum: "since Holy Scripture can be explained in a multiplicity of senses, one should adhere to a particular explanation, only in such measure as to be ready to abandon it, if it be proved with certainty to be false; lest Holy Scripture be exposed to the ridicule of unbelievers, and obstacles be placed to their believing."[95] To do otherwise would be to love one's own opinions above truth, and thereby manifest cupidity rather than Trinitarian *caritas*.

In short, Scripture challenges false teaching by recalling us to God the Teacher's holiness, the holiness God teaches in Scripture. In order to read and proclaim Scripture we need love, but Scripture reminds us that we lack love. It thus fuels our relationship with the living Lord, Jesus Christ, who is "the righteousness of God" (Rom 3:22), a relationship that is worked out by the Father, Son, and Holy Spirit in the Church. For Augustine (and Aquinas), as Babcock states, "any socially constructed alternate scheme of signification must rest on a flawed social order. Any prevailing set of social customs that does not conform to *caritas* must express *cupiditas*."[96] The practice of Trinitarian love—the love that seeks not self but, empowered by the Holy Spirit, seeks "Truth in Person"[97] in scriptural teaching—shapes ecclesial interpretation of the *sacra doctrina* in which we meet the living divine Truth and Love who heals and transforms us.[98]

We have reached, then, a point of transition. This chapter has focused on the centrality of God the Teacher, in whose teaching exegetes participate. But because learning this Teacher comes about in the fellowship of God, the next chapter examines, in the context of Jewish–Christian dialogue, participatory biblical exegesis as the work of God's people.

CHAPTER FOUR

Participatory Biblical Exegesis and Human Teachers

Building on our examination of the centrality of the *divine Teacher* in participatory biblical exegesis, this chapter explores participatory biblical exegesis in light of the *divinely ordained fellowship* in which context exegesis proceeds.[1] In this regard, some Christians have expressed hope that historical-critical exegesis can overcome the divisions that more participatory forms of exegesis seem to foster due to their emphasis on particular communal faith commitments. In light of such concerns about participatory forms of exegesis, the chapter takes up its inquiry from within the framework of Jewish–Christian dialogue.[2] If participatory biblical exegesis highlights the particularity of divinely ordained interpretive communities in the quest for truth, does this emphasis undercut dialogue with those, such as (for Christians) our Jewish "elder brothers," who read some of the same texts as scriptural?[3] At the heart of this question is an even more fundamental question: what happens to the texts of Scripture when read through the lens of the synagogue or the Church, rather than solely through the perspectives of the academy?[4]

This chapter explores these questions about the proper locus for biblical exegesis by proceeding in two steps. First, I examine responses to the Pontifical Biblical Commission's recent document "The Jewish People and Their Sacred Scriptures in the Christian Bible," which is marked by a strong commitment to historical-critical exegesis at the risk of attenuating the participatory aspects of Jewish and Christian biblical exegesis.[5] As a second step, I survey the approaches to biblical exegesis put forward by the Jewish scholars Jon D. Levenson, Peter Ochs, and Michael Fishbane. Much Jewish biblical exegesis, like the Christian exegesis explored in previous chapters, strongly affirms the participatory and communal framework of biblical exegesis.[6] On the basis of this investigation, I seek to show why ecclesial biblical exegesis is the most fertile ground on which Christians can extend and develop, in a dialogic fashion, their exegetical encounter with God the Teacher.

Responses to the Pontifical Biblical Commission: Positive and Negative

As a prelude to his summary, Henry Wansbrough points out that John Paul II personally requested that the Pontifical Biblical Commission take up the topic. In the context of John Paul's consistent understanding of "relations with Judaism as being an internal rather than an external element in the Church,"[7] Wansbrough explains the purposes of the three sections of the document. The first section explores the role given in the New Testament to the Old Testament, and the range of "similar attitudes and ideas" found "in Judaism and in the New Testament."[8] The document also finds similar "techniques of presentation," exegetical methods, understandings of the relationship of Scripture and oral tradition, and processes in the formation of a canon.[9] These similarities enable one to see that the community in which the New Testament was written was deeply Jewish in many respects and accepted the authority of the Old Testament.

The second section of the document probes in detail how Old Testament themes are taken up in the New. This section defends the notion of fulfillment and affirms the validity of a Christological reading of the Old Testament, according to which Christ fulfills and confers an unanticipated (in the document's view) fullness on the themes of the

Old Testament. Wansbrough states that this section of the document notably proposes that "[t]he advance and focus of Old Testament ideas in the New Testament does not imply that the Christian should hold a Jewish reading of the Bible to be illegitimate. Each way of reading the Bible is valid."[10] With regard to patristic and medieval allegorical reading of the Old Testament, the document holds that because "such teaching was not based on the commentated text" but rather was "superimposed on it," it follows that "[i]t was inevitable, therefore, that at the moment of its greatest success, it went into irreversible decline."[11] The document credits Thomas Aquinas for initiating this inevitable process of "irreversible decline." According to the document:

> Thomas Aquinas saw clearly what underpinned allegorical exegesis: the commentator can only discover in a text what he already knows, and in order to know it, he had to find it in the literal sense of another text. From this Thomas Aquinas drew the conclusion: a valid argument cannot be constructed from the allegorical sense, it can only be done from the literal sense. Starting from the Middle Ages, the literal sense has been restored to a place of honour and has not ceased to prove its value. The critical study of the Old Testament has progressed steadily in that direction culminating in the supremacy of the historical-critical method.[12]

The document here also warns against a contemporary tendency to reject all patristic exegesis, and encourages reclaiming Christological readings of the Old Testament in modes that "avoid arbitrariness and respect the original meaning."[13] It seeks to contribute to such efforts by identifying "shared fundamental themes"[14] that the New Testament "prolongs" from the Old Testament and, by means of the proclamation of Christ, "deepens."[15]

After briefly sketching these themes, Wansbrough turns to the third section, which he describes as "an examination, book by book, of the charge of anti-Semitism (or, more accurately, anti-Judaism) in the New Testament."[16] Here, Wansbrough notes, the document focuses on two points: the context in which the New Testament was written, in which polemical language in intra- and extra-Jewish debate was commonplace; and the New Testament authors' recognition of and love for the Jewish context of their faith.

By means of these three steps — (1) identification, in light of the New Testament's conscious unity with the Old, of Jewish modes of discourse, argument, and interpretation both within the New Testament and in the Church's understanding of the New Testament; (2) discussion of how the New Testament draws on key themes from the Old, in light of the concept of fulfillment in Christ, but rejecting allegorical readings that spiritualize away the specificity of the Old; and (3) contextualization of New Testament passages that might seem to be anti-Jewish — the document seeks to assist in the post-Holocaust reconciliation of Christians and Jews. Suggesting that the document's even-handed and forward-looking analysis works better than do general apologies for past sins, Wansbrough holds that the document establishes a true basis for dialogue: "It puts on a firm footing a steady and well-reasoned relationship between members of the same family who in the past have been sometimes violently estranged from each other. It shows respect for the traditions and thinking of the other party and acknowledges the riches received by the authors' branch of the family from the other tradition."[17]

Does the Pontifical Biblical Commission's document achieve what Wansbrough thinks it does? Denis Farkasfalvy and Roch Kereszty suggest not. Farkasfalvy critiques the document on several fronts. He begins with the issue of the Holy Spirit's activity in the inspiration of the Scriptures and the formation of the canon, an activity that can be recognized by the Christian as unique (as opposed to the writing and formation of other religious texts) solely on the basis of faith, which is always faith in Christ.[18] The Holy Spirit's activity produces a profound unity, rather than a mere continuity or prolongation, of the Old Testament and the New.[19]

At stake, Farkasfalvy thinks, is the "spiritual sense" of Scripture recovered by the *Ressourcement* theologians (de Lubac, Balthasar, Daniélou, among others) of the past century, but rejected in the document's narration of the history of exegesis. Following de Lubac, Farkasfalvy challenges the document's depiction of Aquinas's role in the ascendancy of the literal sense.[20] He argues that the belief that Christ fulfills the themes of the Old Testament, and the belief in the unity of Scripture as inspired by the Holy Spirit, cannot do without the spiritual sense of

Scripture. Lacking the spiritual sense, one would have to read Scripture simply as a historical unfolding to which the "Divine Perspective" would be extrinsic.[21] He asks, "Is the historical-critical method up to the task of deciphering God's point of view, which makes the biblical text point beyond its merely human perspective? Is God's point of view detectable by the tools of biblical criticism and historical investigation?"[22]

For Farkasfalvy, the document thus ignores how the Christian community identifies the divine meaning of Scripture, a meaning that often clearly goes beyond the original meaning known to the author and yet nonetheless truly is the meaning of the scriptural text. As he points out, such meaning is not an "additional" meaning that could be added to what the historical-critical scholar knows. Rather, such meaning is the true interior meaning that is known when the Bible is interpreted as it was written, namely under the guidance of the Holy Spirit in the community of faith, a community that was, in the divine perspective, centered on Christ from the beginning.

This refusal to engage the interrelated theological questions of inspiration and interpretation also mars, in Farkasfalvy's view, the final section on anti-Judaism. He remarks that from the document "we never learn if the problem [anti-Judaism] we are dealing with is ultimately historical or theological. Therefore, the problems discussed in this section are not really solved, only 'dissolved' in alternating positive and negative observations and hypothetical historical reconstructions."[23] Some of what seems in the New Testament to be anti-Judaism and is therefore explained away in the document might in fact belong to the core of what differentiates theologically Christianity from Judaism.

For his part, Kereszty begins by identifying what he considers to be the positive contributions of the document. Among these he lists the document's conviction that understanding the New Testament depends on understanding its Old Testament roots; its affirmation that the covenants with Israel have not been revoked; its recognition of the similarity between messianic expectation in Judaism and Christian expectation of Jesus' Second Coming; and its finding that the texts of the New Testament are not anti-Jewish or anti-Semitic.[24] However, Kereszty agrees with the thrust of Farkasfalvy's critique. By ignoring the Holy Spirit's role in the inspiration and interpretation of Scripture in the community of faith, and instead promoting a neutral comparison of texts on the basis of historical-critical analysis (§20), the document distorts the dialogue between Jews and Christians, in Kereszty's view, into a dialogue between historians (qua historians) rather than between believers. Like Farkasfalvy, he writes:

> With this [historical-critical] method one can establish historical facts and uncover a certain continuity and discontinuity between the themes of both Testaments; but one cannot accept the reference of the texts to the one divine plan of salvation, the stages of the divine pedagogy that God has gradually implemented and fulfilled in Christ. . . . Only if one reads the documents of the Old and New Testaments in faith, can both Jews and Christians proclaim the "eternal Israel" in differing yet interdependent ways.[25]

Kereszty argues that the literal sense must be complemented, if not by the allegorical sense, then at least by the "moral" and "anagogical" senses that enable one to interpret Scripture in light of God's work of sanctification and the ordering of all things to God's plan of eschatological fulfillment, respectively.

Jews and Christians, Kereszty affirms, share these two spiritual senses despite their division over Jesus Christ, a division that is itself bridged by the reality that the Jesus whom Christians anticipate in the Second Coming is none other than the "perfect eschatological Israel."[26] The Messiah embodies Israel's communal life both in suffering and in glorious fulfillment. Given this understanding of the Messiah, Kereszty urges that the document should state more clearly in §22, which evaluates the Jewish reading of the Bible, that Judaism and Christianity are (in Kereszty's words) not "two parallel ways of salvation."[27] Rather, Jesus is the promised Messiah of the Jews in whom Jews and Gentiles are united in God's one covenantal plan of salvation through the life, death, and resurrection of his Son. Through his Son, who unites all humankind in his life-giving Body, God achieves the salvation of the entire world, even though individuals may freely reject God's saving love.

Thus far the document's Catholic supporters and critics. I agree with Wansbrough that the Pontifical Biblical Commission's document does a good job in its comparative work. It judiciously weighs evidence of the New Testament's regard for the Old and the influence of Jewish modes of composition and exegesis on Christian writings and interpretive practices (section I), the notion of fulfillment and shared themes in the Old and New Testaments (section II), and the absence in the New Testament itself of the kind of anti-Jewish rhetoric that later emerged (section III). To this extent, perhaps the document will serve as a basis for dialogue and reconciliation between Jews and Christians. Furthermore, the document's affirmation of Jesus' messianic claim to fulfill Israel's covenants is particularly valuable, given the denial by some recent Christian authors of this basic tenet of Christian soteriology.[28]

Even so, Farkasfalvy and Kereszty rightly find the document inadequate in its brief narration (§§19–22) of the history and prospects of biblical exegesis. The document focuses mistakenly on excluding the spiritual senses in the name of Thomas Aquinas.[29] Moreover, as both Cistercians point out, without a sustained and significant account of the inspiration and interpretation of the Scriptures in the Church, the document cannot but fall into what Matthew Lamb, identifying the weakness of historical-critical methodology, terms "comparative textology." For Christians, biblical interpretation, under the guidance of the Holy Spirit, belongs to the Church's ongoing receptive participation in Christ the Teacher.[30] By methodologically excluding the sapiential practices (liturgical-sacramental, moral, and doctrinal) that flow from understanding the exegetical task in this way, the document cannot account for how and why the biblical texts are more than ancient texts. That this presumption of a solely linear-historical model is as troubling to many Jews as it is to many Christians can be seen from the remarks of Yosef Hayim Yerushalmi in his study *Zakhor: Jewish History and Jewish Memory*:

There is an inherent tension in modern Jewish historiography even though most often it is not felt on the surface nor even acknowledged. To the degree that this historiography is indeed "modern" and demands to be taken seriously, it must at least functionally repudiate premises that were basic to all Jewish conceptions of history in the past. In effect, it must stand in sharp opposition to its own subject matter, not on this or that detail, but concerning the vital core: the belief that divine providence is not only an ultimate but an active causal factor in Jewish history, and the related belief in the uniqueness of Jewish history itself.[31]

In short, the weakness of the Pontifical Biblical Commission's document, like that of modern historiography (Christian and Jewish), is that it insufficiently allows for the participatory dimension of historical reality, what Yerushalmi describes as "the belief that divine providence is not only an ultimate but an active causal factor." Without this dimension of history, biblical exegesis is flattened, its realities unattainable.

In order to display participatory biblical exegesis in the Jewish context, as previous chapters have done for the Christian exegesis, I turn to three contemporary Jewish scholars, Jon D. Levenson, Peter Ochs, and Michael Fishbane. Their exegetical approaches, I suggest, manifest the intrabiblical and postbiblical practices of communal interpretation, rooted in an awareness of the participatory dimensions of linear history, that characterize the particular (and universal) salvation that "is from the Jews" (John 4:22).[32]

Jewish Biblical Interpretation: Jon D. Levenson, Peter Ochs, and Michael Fishbane

Jon D. Levenson opens his collection of essays on biblical interpretation, *The Hebrew Bible, the Old Testament, and Historical Criticism: Jews and Christians in Biblical Studies*, by remarking on the university locus of much of contemporary exegesis: "those eager to adapt biblical studies to the modern university now find their own discipline plunging into the crisis that has engulfed the entire university. At the heart of that crisis lie the loss of a transcendent goal for learning and the weakening of the communities and practices that can sustain the faith and belief upon which all learning—and not only biblical studies—depends."[33] Clearly this "loss of a transcendent goal" affects biblical studies even more deeply than other disciplines, since biblical interpretation, as practiced by Jews and Christians in response to God's call, aims at participating (in a deifying fashion) in God's own wisdom. Neither Levenson nor I advocate a renunciation of historical-critical research; as Levenson puts it, what is needed is a "reengagement" of historical-critical research and traditional interpretation "on new terms."[34]

Levenson compares, for instance, Exodus 12:15 and Deuteronomy 16:8, the former of which mandates the eating of unleavened bread during Passover for seven days while the latter only for six. Talmudic exegesis resolved the problem by postulating that if the seventh day appeared to be optional (as not included in Deuteronomy 16:8) then all the days were optional except for the first which is commanded in Exodus 12:18. Levenson writes, "The assumption of the rabbis here is that the Deuteronomic law is not independent of that given in Exodus. On the contrary, the operative law is to be discovered by taking *both* passages into account. The unity of the Mosaic Torah requires that *all* its data be considered."[35] Both laws are holy and exist eternally in the mind of God; true participation in the mind of God, in his plan for Israel's holiness, requires reading Deuteronomy in light of Exodus and reading history in light of God's presence in history.

The alternative, according to Levenson, is to excise God's presence in and through the text, as Spinoza requires. For Levenson, however, "Jews and Christians can participate equally in the Spinozan agenda only because its naturalistic presuppositions negate the theological foundations of *both* Judaism and Christianity."[36] Such negation, practiced by Wellhausen in his historicist condemnation of the written Torah as the ossification of the original religious impulses of Israel,[37] removes communal participation in divine wisdom from biblical interpretation. If in the academy "what unites Jews and Christians in biblical studies is a common commitment to a nonsupernaturalistic approach to the text," Levenson observes that this "historicization of biblical studies" places a greater strain on Christian scholars since (secular) Jewish scholars can find identity in the secular history of ancient Israel without adverting to the supernatural.[38] Yet he is clear that both Jewish and Christian communities cannot long sustain their practices in the "grip of historicism."[39]

Indeed, communal participatory appropriation of *sacra doctrina* means that God's teaching, as understood by Jews and Christians, is not fully separable from the ongoing teaching, inspired by God as a participation in his wisdom, of the people of God. Since the divine realities depicted in the biblical text are operative in diverse historical contexts, the effort to rid biblical interpretation of these contexts undermines both the biblical text—itself a product of these diverse historical contexts[40]—and the interpretive community as a locus of the *sacra doctrina*. As Levenson says, therefore, "the 'personal stance' of a faithful contemporary Jew does not allow for the *isolation* of the Jewish Bible (Tanakh) from the larger tradition,"[41] including the oral Torah and medieval rabbinic interpretations. This larger tradition belongs to living Judaism as a locus of historical participation in the divine *doctrina* of Scripture.[42]

The attempt to rid biblical interpretation of the tradition of communal interpretation belongs not only to the Protestant Reformation and its *sola scriptura*, Levenson observes, but also to an eighth-century Jewish sect, the Karaites: "For the Karaites, there is only one Torah, the Pentateuch, whereas for the rabbis (from whom they separated) Torah was twofold, written and oral, and it is this oral Torah that eventually found written expression in the Mishnah, the Talmuds, the midrashic collections, and their medieval and modern descendants."[43] The Karaite position ultimately gained few followers, because it could not make sense of the community's role in the appropriation of God's Torah. Surely the people of God should participate in the ongoing interpretive appropriation of God's teaching.[44] The question then is not whether communal interpretation remains necessary, but instead whether the promised Messiah has come and reconstituted the interpretive community and its practices around himself as its fulfillment.[45] To this question Levenson thinks, certainly, that the answer is "no." (It should be noted that fulfillment accounts themselves, as participatory in structure, by no means negate the Judaism of those who continue to seek to participate in the coming fulfillment without, obviously for many reasons, recognizing its messianic arrival.[46])

Levenson holds that one cannot "be well-equipped for exegesis without knowledge of the medieval Jewish commentaries."[47] Such knowledge represents more than an additional set of information about the Bible. Rather, it represents and enacts a way of reading the Bible from within the living Jewish community as a locus of the mediation of *sacra doctrina*. Receiving the medieval commentaries as a necessary tool for understanding the Bible requires receiving the Bible as *sacra doctrina* participated within the community that is witnessed to by the Bible and is formed through the reading and practice of scriptural *sacra doctrina*. The Bible does not stand on its own as a historical text from the past to be excavated for meaning; rather the Bible's meaning, as *sacra doctrina*, cannot be apprehended apart from the tradition of reading that includes moral, doctrinal, and liturgical formation and that participates today in the history depicted in the Bible, as displayed in the Talmud, the medieval commentaries, and so forth.

Thus, while strongly supportive of historical-critical research, Levenson warns that in academic biblical studies, even among practicing Jews and Christians, "it is the past-tense sense of scripture that still predominates." This "historicism," as Levenson sees it, turns both Judaism and Christianity into "historical contingencies" rather than loci of divine revelation, *sacra doctrina*.[48] The Bible is relegated to the past, and with the Bible, Jews (and Christians) as the people of God become a defunct or past reality. As Levenson points out in this regard, "A particularly curious and chilling example is Martin Noth's *History of Israel*, which ends after the defeat of the bar Kosiba rebellion in 135 C.E. Noth's last sentence is this: 'Thus ended the ghastly epilogue of Israel's history.'"[49] Noth, a German scholar writing just after the Holocaust, could not see—even illumined by the Holocaust—Israel's history as ongoing. In Levenson's view, reclaiming the multiple senses of Scripture may thus have a role in recovering the people of God as a present reality in biblical interpretation. As he writes, "It may be time to reexamine how different senses of the text once coexisted in minds that had not surrendered to the nihilistic notion of total semantic indeterminancy."[50]

Thus Levenson. The Jewish philosopher Peter Ochs's approach to biblical interpretation, summarized in his "An Introduction to Postcritical Scriptural Interpretation," likewise resonates with the view that biblical exegesis is human communal participation in God's teaching. In addition to his debts to David Weiss Halivni and Max Kadushin, Ochs draws from C. S. Peirce's triadic semiotics, from Hans Frei's hermeneutics, and from George Lindbeck's theory of the three ways of understanding religions.[51]

Ochs finds that modern biblical scholarship assumes only two possibilities for scriptural meaning: either referential, directly describing realities outside the text, or nonreferential, that is, metaphorical or obscure. These two possibilities, Ochs argues, leave out the community's participation, the meaning that arises from within communal biblical exegesis. He states that "scriptural texts may have pragmatic reference: that is . . . they may represent claims about the inadequacy of certain inherited rules of meaning and about ways of transforming those rules or adjusting them to new conditions of life. To the degree that they refer pragmatically, scriptural texts will not disclose their meanings to modern methods of study."[52] In seeking to elucidate this "pragmatic" reference, Ochs is indebted to Peirce's concept of symbol. Symbols, for Peirce, elude the opposition of either direct reference or mere metaphor; symbols belong within "communal traditions of meaning," which symbols shape and within which symbols develop.

Ochs thus observes, "The simultaneously conservative and reformatory activity of interpreting a symbol is what we call pragmatic inquiry."[53] Such inquiry, it is clear, can only be undertaken within a community whose practices shape readers to be able to understand the "tradition of meaning" within which the symbol functions. "Pragmatic" inquiry recognizes how the "activities of mediation" of a community of readers flow from their communal practices of reading the biblical text; it is precisely their shared reading of the biblical text that teaches them how it is to be interpreted and applied.[54] The biblical text possesses a meaning, then, that neither refers to something outside it nor is mere metaphor but arises from the reading practices themselves. The dialogic relationship of the community of readers and the biblical text, over time, hands on and further develops shared meanings of Scripture that cannot be found by historical-critical research alone but that belong deeply to Scripture as a lived text.

In his presentation of what he terms this "postcritical" understanding of scriptural meaning, Ochs owes much to Peirce, Frei, and Lindbeck for the conceptual frame; but he credits the intuition behind his work to his teacher Max Kadushin.[55] As Ochs describes Kadushin's project: "His method was to identify the collection of rabbinic exegetes as a community of interpreters whose work provided the context in which scriptural texts had meaning for the Jewish people. He argued that this meaning was embodied in the practice of rabbinic exegesis itself and that the rules which informed this practice represented the conceptual order of rabbinic Judaism."[56] Within the communal practice of biblical exegesis certain virtues or "value-concepts" (in Ochs's term "symbols")[57] are received and developed, and these interpretive virtues constitute the meaning of Scripture. Meaning emerges within the community's exegetical task that, once again, could not be identified by historical-critical research but is recognized by the rabbinic tradition as the truth of Scripture. To know what Scripture "means" is to see the rabbis at work and to learn how to participate in such work. Although Ochs affirms that historical-critical research can uncover an aspect of Scripture's meaning, he emphasizes with Kadushin the meaning that is found in the practical symbols or values that both constitute, and are renewed and reformed within, the communal practices of reading the Bible.

Like Levenson, in other words, Ochs holds that biblical interpretation has participatory dimensions that require the living community and its tradition of sharing in God the Teacher. The point is that there are realities in Scripture that cannot be known solely through historical research because they are embedded within the very practices of exegetical teaching. Where Augustine places the practice of love manifested by Christ and the saints, Ochs and Kadushin place the virtues manifested by the rabbinic exegetes; and it is clear that Christ's status as the "Teacher" and the "Word" who interprets the Scriptures by the supreme love of his Pasch draws Augustine's position close, in certain respects, to that of Ochs and Kadushin. Learning the interpretive practices of the Teacher and those who follow him most closely, we learn how to interpret Scripture in its various levels of meaning. In sum, communal intellectual, moral, and liturgical practices—which arise out of the tradition of interpretation and which are continually renewed within this ongoing tradition as guided by God—give proper form to the task of teaching Scripture, and indeed embody Scripture's meanings.

A third Jewish scholar who stands out for his contributions to understanding Jewish biblical interpretation is Michael Fishbane, best known for his studies of the practice of biblical interpretation *within* the Bible. Fishbane remarks regarding the impossibility of escaping communal exegesis: "So much, it seems, is derivation—as opposed to radical innovation—a central ingredient of the human religious condition, that Gautama Buddha set his whole revolution of consciousness deliberately against it, only to have his followers turn him into a transcendent source of wisdom and his works into the subject-matter of exegesis."[58] Such interpretive "derivation," in the Buddha's case vis-à-vis the Upanishads and Brahmanic orthodoxy, belongs as Fishbane shows to the biblical texts themselves: later biblical writings extended and adjusted earlier biblical writings within what came to be the Hebrew Scriptures. This intrabiblical tradition, in which human interpretation (as would be expected) takes its place within the fully human mediation of divine revelation, shapes the postbiblical rabbinic understanding of their exegetical work. The early rabbis, Fishbane points out, considered exegesis so much a participation in God's wisdom that they "actually portrayed their God midrashically as a scholar of his own Torah and as subordinate to the decisions made by the disciples of the wise."[59] The interpretation of God's wisdom for creatures (Torah) is itself, as the supreme act of human reason and love, so closely bound with God's wisdom that he shares, with his chosen exegetes, responsibility for declaring his law.

Fishbane's work thus emphasizes the continuity between intrabiblical and postbiblical exegesis. As he describes intrabiblical exegesis, "our received traditions are complex blends of *traditum* and *traditio* in dynamic interaction, dynamic interpenetration, and dynamic interdependence. They are, in sum, the exegetical voices of many teachers and tradents, from different circles and times, responding to real and theoretical considerations as perceived and as anticipated."[60] There is no biblical text, in other words, that comes to us unmediated by communal practices of interpretation; divine Revelation contains in itself, as a constitutive element, communal interpretation. Postbiblical exegesis is therefore not a foreign amalgam in relation to Scripture understood as Revelation. Rather, "the inner-Jewish cultivation of preexistent native traditions of interpretation" requires attention to how communal meaning in biblical Revelation is related to the communal modes of exegesis practiced in biblical times and beyond.[61]

In short, these three contemporary Jewish approaches expose how membership in the "fellowship" constituted by God—a fellowship that has to do both with creation (as human beings) and grace (as members of God's covenanted people)—extends the range of meanings one can learn from God's teaching.[62] While these meanings differ for Jews and Christians—differences that have sometimes shamefully provided Christians (and post-Christians) an excuse for anti-Semitic violence that manifests a sinful failure to appropriate what should have been exegetically received—nonetheless to ignore the role of communal interpretation in discerning Scripture's realities would be a grave mistake.[63] Jewish biblical exegesis, like the patristic-medieval biblical exegesis that we have explored in previous chapters, depends on acceptance of the rationality of participatory biblical exegesis.[64]

Concluding Reflections

In its General Conclusion to "The Jewish People and Their Sacred Scriptures in the Christian Bible," the Pontifical Biblical Commission remarks that "it is especially in studying the great themes of the Old Testament and their continuation in the New which accounts for the impressive symbiosis that unites the two parts of the Christian Bible and, at the same time, the vigorous spiritual ties that unite the Church of Christ to the Jewish people."[65] This statement is certainly true, but, as I have tried to show, the Commission does not sufficiently appreciate the "vigorous spiritual ties" constituted by the ongoing practice of participatory biblical exegesis. As Marcel Dubois observes with regard to Aquinas:

[W]e have to pay attention to another dimension of his [Aquinas's] approach which I would call a subjective one, more precisely a way of sharing the Jewish subjectivity before God and his word. Thomas has emphasized the similarity between the Jewish and the Christian dependence on the gift of a revealing God, and on the way of receiving the Revelation. . . . And so, there must be a similarity in our attitude and in our way of listening to the word of God. In other words, the Jewish people have given us the Word, which they have heard and which has called them to life; but they have also shown us how to be attentive, to listen, to receive, to keep and to live according to this message. *Shema Israel.* Listen, Hear Israel. We have inherited from the people of the Covenant this invitation and the relation with God which it implies. Without any doubt, this is the deepest way, for a Christian, in his approach to the Bible, to share the *hebraica veritas.*[66]

It would seem a shame to acknowledge, as the Commission so rightly does, "the patrimony they [Jews and Christians] share and . . . the links that bind them,"[67] without exploring the most fundamental link of all, namely a shared understanding of the Sacred Scriptures of the Jewish people as requiring not solely linear-historical approaches, but also a participatory understanding of historical reality, in which the interpretation of Scripture constitutes one mode among others by which the community formed by God seeks, over the course of history, to hear and practice the wisdom and righteousness of God.

We see this difficulty in other spheres too. In criticizing the approach to Jewish–Christian dialogue undertaken by the distinguished authors and signers (including Peter Ochs) of *Dabru Emet*—a statement that seeks to emphasize what Jews hold in common with Christians—Jon Levenson challenges *Dabru Emet*'s statement that "Jews and Christians seek authority from the same book, the Bible (what Jews call 'Tanakh' and Christians call the 'Old Testament')":

> In its paragraph about the Bible, *Dabru Emet* also passed up an opportunity to correct one of the most common Christian misconceptions about Judaism, that its sole authority is the Old Testament. Had the statement taken a different and more accurate tack, however, pointing to the importance of the Oral Torah (i.e., Mishnaic and subsequent Rabbinic teaching), it would have undermined its claim that the two communities have "the same book," from which they "take away similar lessons."[68]

Levenson goes on to say that the question is "who is now the 'Israel'" in which reading of the Tanakh/Old Testament authoritatively takes place.[69] But I would suggest that had *Dabru Emet* emphasized "the importance of the Oral Torah," it would have exposed, not first and foremost a difference, but rather above all a point of commonality. If Jews insist on reading the Bible from within an authoritative communal tradition of exegesis, then this insistence recalls Christians to what is required for worshipping the God of Israel who teaches salvifically through his Word.[70] Biblical research unformed by the wise patterns of love for God that God has taught the people of God, cannot suffice for exegeting in words and deeds the participatory realities that God has made known to Jews and Christians. Jewish modes of communal exegesis thus invite Christians to the full dimensions of the exegetical task, namely the task to allow exegesis to draw us into union with God the Teacher, and to appreciate that without this learning-in-love, a communal task, human interpretation of the Bible cannot apprehend the biblical realities.

CHAPTER FIVE

Participatory Biblical Exegesis and Ecclesial Authority

This final chapter draws together the account in the first and second chapters of the shift away from God in biblical interpretation, with the exploration in the third and fourth chapters of God the Teacher and exegetical participation in God's wisdom and love. If participatory biblical exegesis is to bear fruit, it will have to manifest charitable wisdom. Yet, as we have had occasion to observe, it seems to some that participatory biblical exegesis does the very opposite, by fostering a kind of sectarianism.

One such allegedly sectarian text occurs in the Gospel of John, where Jesus teaches, "If you love me, you will keep my commandments. And I will pray the Father, and he will give you another Counselor, to be with you for ever, even the Spirit of truth, whom the world cannot receive, because it neither sees him nor knows him; you know him, for he dwells with you, and will be in you" (Jn 14:15–17). Jesus thus connects love—the love that inspires us interiorly to keep his commandments in holiness—and truth, the indwelling "Spirit of truth." As Aquinas interprets this passage, Jesus teaches that "[a]s long as they [human beings] love the world they cannot receive the Holy Spirit, for he is the love of God. And no one can love, as his destination, both God and the world."[1]

If interpreters possessed of "truth" will hate the "world," then does not such participatory biblical exegesis foster division and (whether or not intentionally) violence?

This is the challenge classically posed to participatory biblical exegesis by Thomas Hobbes and Baruch Spinoza in the midst of the religious warfare of the seventeenth century. They argue that Christianity (and the Judaism that excommunicated Spinoza) leads to a violent exegesis, and therefore that neutral parties must take over the exegetical task. The present chapter thus begins by setting forth in some detail their challenge. Second, I examine a leading contemporary effort to overcome that challenge, namely the work of Stephen Fowl. Finally, I propose that Fowl's work be augmented by the interpretations of John 14:15–17 offered by Thomas Aquinas, so as to provide an account of the Church's doctrinal authority in biblical exegesis that more fully meets the challenge posed by Hobbes and Spinoza.

Hobbes and Spinoza

Hobbes's goal is to sever exegetical authority from the Church and give it to the king.[2] He begins with an account of the history of philosophy. So long as philosophy was free to make its own inquiries unbounded by Christian faith, Hobbes thinks, philosophy was of value. Although he has a largely negative view of Plato and Aristotle, nonetheless at least "[n]o one was forced to swear by the words of Aristotle."[3] For Hobbes Christianity then introduced the principle of power: "Those [doctrines] they condemned, they called *heresies;* those they confirmed, they called *the Catholic faith.*"[4] In the medieval period, the Schoolmen mixed together Aristotle and Scripture within universities governed by, and in service to, the authority of the pope. By Hobbes's accounting, the result was that philosophy too was destroyed.

According to Hobbes, Aristotle provided the perfect philosophical master for the pope's effort to seize power, since "Aristotle was not so much concerned with *things* as with *words,*"[5] in particular with the word "being." For Aristotle, Hobbes holds, "being" is actually a reality, as is "essence," when in fact these are mere words. Hobbes connects this metaphysics to the false wisdom that Scripture condemns: "An essence, therefore, is not a thing, either created or uncreated, but only a name feigned out of guile. It is only Aristotle who has given birth to new, bastard and empty *beings* of this kind, the first principles of a philosophy which St. Paul calls empty deceit [Col 2:8]."[6] From Aristotle follow faulty philosophical doctrines to which the Roman Church requires assent, for instance that God has no size and that the soul is wholly in each part of the body and wholly in the whole of the body.[7] Only in a few cases, such as transubstantiation, does the Church diverge from Aristotle in order to uphold still more unlikely doctrines.[8]

Hobbes draws the conclusion that this subservience to Aristotle, necessary to prop up papal power, is the cause of Christians' abandoning Scripture's teaching that subjects should obey their kings (cf. Rom 13). Having abandoned this scriptural teaching in favor of false philosophy, Christians have become embroiled in religious wars: "What, then, is the origin of those civil wars concerning religion in Germany, France, and England, if not the ethical and political philosophy of Aristotle and of those Romans who have followed Aristotle?"[9] Thus briefly commenting on Cromwell's revolution, the execution of Charles II, and the Restoration (*Leviathan* was originally published in 1651 with the Latin edition appearing in 1668), Hobbes blames the mess on a bad combination of Scripture and metaphysics, brought about by human will to power. If Scripture's voice had been allowed by the Roman Church to override Aristotle's, Christians would have known about the requirement of obedience to the king, a requirement obscured in order to promote the pope's power.

If in Hobbes's narrative the popes and their scholastic universities were responsible for obscuring (by the admixture of philosophical errors) central truths of Christianity from ordinary Christians, thereby causing Christians to fail in their proper love for their king, what does Hobbes consider the remedy to be? The remedy that Hobbes advocates is a proper reading of Scripture. Right reading of Scripture, he argues, requires governance of the teaching of Scripture. Turning to the history of Israel, Hobbes holds on exegetical grounds that "every sovereign, before Christianity, had the power of teaching, and ordaining teachers."[10] The popes claimed to take away this power from Christian kings, but the popes' claim, contradicted by Scripture, was illegitimate. The king, then, should have the final say in who teaches Scripture, and therefore what is taught. Comparing the king to a father of a family, Hobbes reasons that the king, far more than a foreign pope, will have the true good of his children-subjects in mind and will not twist Scripture philosophically so as to further his own power. Since the king will govern the Church's teaching, Christians will be taught to love their king, in accord with the true word of Scripture.

The role of the king in Hobbes's understanding of Christian teaching becomes more clear when one grasps what it is, for Hobbes, that Christianity teaches beyond what can be known through philosophizing. The purpose of Christ's coming was to die so that he might be raised and assist in the recovery of God's kingdom. God willed Christ's sacrifice "for the reduction of his elect to their former covenanted obedience," which had been lost when Israel, rejecting God's kingship, elected Saul.[11] Christ represents God (called, after Christ's coming, "the Father") and Christ's kingship is "subordinate or vicegerent of God the Father."[12] The goal of Christ's kingship was to return the kingship to God that the Israelites at the time of Saul had taken from God. Yet, before Christ's second coming, "Christ's kingdom is not of this world; therefore, neither can his ministers (unless they be kings) require obedience in his name."[13] Neither Christ nor his Church, founded on the apostles, can compel obedience. Since Christ's kingdom is not of this world, furthermore, Christ does not take away temporal kings' power to wield the sword and compel obedience over all their subjects, including subjects who hold ecclesial office. Faith is solely an interior obedience that no king's commands can take away.

The obedience of faith contains an element of knowledge: it assures believers of eternal life in God the Father's otherworldly kingdom.[14] Other than belief in the Resurrection, however, faith does not add any knowledge not knowable otherwise. For Hobbes, Christology is reduced to the practical doctrine of life after death; the "kingdom" of God that Christ's first coming proclaims will come about. Similarly the doctrine of the Trinity is reduced to a practical history of his representatives on earth: "God, who is always one and the same, was the person represented by Moses [the "Father"]; the person represented by his Son incarnate [the "Son"]; and the person represented by the apostles [the "Holy Spirit"]."[15] In sum, the teaching of Christianity, when Scripture is properly understood, amounts to life after death and the one God who has been represented variously in history.[16]

Hobbes argues that kings effectively preserve the simplicity of this doctrine, since they have no vested interest in complicating it in order to augment their power over their subjects, in contrast to the interests of ecclesial authorities. He recounts the history of Christianity as a history of a fall from grace. The apostles possessed a pure kind of "power," consisting in "wisdom, humility, sincerity, and other virtues."[17] This power moved people to convert without compelling them. At this pure, early stage, the apostles' spiritual power did not conflict with, but rather submitted to, the temporal power of kings. The first Christians' "consciences were free, and their words and actions subject to none but the civil power."[18] They believed in a life after death (the "kingdom of God") and in God. But as Hobbes argues, since fear of invisible things is the root of "religion," true religion tends to decline into superstition, as human beings "nourish, dress, and form it ["religion" or its natural "seed"] into laws, and to add to it, of their own invention, any opinion of the causes of future events by which they thought they should best be able to govern others, and make unto themselves the greatest use of their powers."[19] Soon "presbyters," assembling in council, decreed that nothing opposed to their teaching should be taught or believed by Christians on pain of excommunication; and still later these presbyters acquired the title "bishops," eventually leading to the Bishop of Rome, largely because of the authority of the emperors, declaring and enforcing his primacy over all other bishops. In this way, Christian liberty came to an end. The English Reformation restored Christian liberty, first by deposing the pope, second by deposing the bishops (the presbyterians under Cromwell), and third by deposing the presbyterians and giving back the king's authority. The key liberative move, Hobbes thinks, was the denial that the Church is the kingdom of God. Rather, Christ proclaimed God's kingdom, to be brought about in the life after death, until which temporal kingdoms should fully govern their subjects; the Church then distorted this teaching in the interests of its own aggrandizement.[20]

Spinoza's view arrives at similar results regarding interpretive authority. He holds that the authority that Christ gave to his disciples "was a unique occurrence" and remarks, "As for the arguments by which my opponents seek to separate religious right from civil right, maintaining that only the latter is vested in the sovereign while the former is vested in the universal church, these are of no account, being so trivial as not even to merit refutation."[21] For Spinoza, as for Hobbes, the external elements of religion must be entirely under the control of the sovereign. Spinoza likewise contrasts this position explicitly with that of the papacy. He blames the allegedly overreaching doctrinal claims of the Catholic Church on an unholy mixture of Scripture and metaphysics: "if you enquire into the nature of the mysteries which they see lurking in Scripture, you will certainly find nothing but the notions of an Aristotle or a Plato or the like, which often seem to suggest the fantasies of any uneducated person rather than the findings of an accomplished biblical scholar."[22] Like Hobbes, Spinoza argues that Scripture when read properly meshes with sound philosophical teaching. If anything, Spinoza goes further in this direction than does Hobbes, because Spinoza reduces Scripture's content even more than Hobbes. Despite his placement of power at the center of all reality, including intellectual life, Hobbes still assumes that Christianity has something to teach and therefore the king should be in charge of the teaching of it. Spinoza, while agreeing about the role of the king, reduces the "teaching" of Christianity to a command to the will.

Spinoza envisions Scripture as teaching, in essence, solely two doctrines, which were then, he says, complicated by theologians. Far from attempting to teach "scientific knowledge," Scripture teaches solely that human beings must obey God by loving their neighbor, and that God is worthy of such obedience because he is justice and charity. No other knowledge about God or about reality is taught authoritatively in Scripture: "Other philosophic questions which do not directly tend to this end, whether they be concerned with knowledge of God or with knowledge of Nature, have nothing to do with Scripture, and should therefore be dissociated from revealed religion."[23] Spinoza proceeds to demonstrate this claim exegetically through analysis of biblical texts. Extending his argument, he proposes that Scripture requires "faith" not as new knowledge but simply as obedience. Interpreting 1 John 4:13, among other biblical texts, he notes that "since nobody has seen God he [John] concludes therefrom that it is only through love of one's neighbour that one can perceive or be conscious of God, and thus no one can discover any other attribute of God except this love, insofar as we participate therein."[24] Christianity is not a matter of true doctrine, therefore, but simply pious teachings that "move the heart to obedience."[25] So long as this obedience happens (with the assistance of the pious teachings that "strengthen the will to love one's neighbour"), it does not matter what falsehoods are believed about God and reality: "Each man's faith, then, is to be regarded as pious or impious not in respect of its truth or falsity, but as it is conducive to obedience or obstinacy."[26]

Yet, this position might seem to suggest that all religions are equal, so long as love of neighbor occurs. In fact, all religions are not equal, because some religions put stumbling blocks, in the form of dogmas, in the way of obedient love of neighbor. Wars are fought over dogmatic controversies, which is quite a ridiculous and terrible situation given that all that Scripture teaches is the command to love one's neighbor. For this reason Spinoza takes as a principle for evaluating true interpretation of Scripture, and true religion, that "a catholic or universal faith must not contain any dogmas that good men may regard as controversial."[27] Instead, a "universal faith" such as Spinoza thinks Scripture teaches must limit itself to the propositions that God is justice and love and that human beings must love their neighbor. Even though from these two key propositions seven other ones (and no more) follow— that a just God exists, is one, knows everything, is supreme, requires love of neighbor, saves those who obey him, and forgives sin—these propositions need solely produce pious action, rather than being measured by whether they are true or not.[28] Every other theological proposition, including inquiries into the intelligibility of the ones that he allows, is dismissed by Spinoza as idle speculation, not only useless for the goal of love of neighbor, but potentially and often practically destructive of it. As he concludes, such theological inquiries, by aiming at truth, mistake the nature of the faith called for by St. John and the entire Scriptures: "faith demands piety rather than truth; faith is pious and saving only by reason of the obedience it inspires, and consequently nobody is faithful except by reason of his obedience."[29] Theology should aim at obedience, leaving the seeking of truth to philosophy.

Much of Scripture, Spinoza affirms, makes no sense philosophically, nor should it be expected to do so. Scripture was not written by or for philosophers, but for the common people who lack sophisticated understanding of truth. When theologians (Spinoza gives Maimonides as an example) attempt to read these passages as if they expressed philosophical truth, theologians go astray and end up in complicating the simple and pious message of Scripture, just as when philosophers allow Scripture to govern philosophy they go astray by importing false notions (intended for simple readers) into the complex realm of philosophical truth.[30] Similarly, liturgical practices such as the ceremonies of Israel or the sacraments of the Church, while useful in Israel to uphold and distinguish the state and useful in Christianity to unify the ecclesial society, must not be mistaken for the true worship required by God, which consists solely in the love of neighbor.[31] The value of the teachings of Scripture is found not in complex teachings or practices, but rather in Scripture's ability to communicate pious obedience to a wide audience. Belief in the teachings of Scripture is therefore necessary for "the common people who lack the ability to perceive things clearly and distinctly."[32] In contrast, by "the natural light" the few enlightened members of society may know, without knowing Scripture, what Scripture contains, which is reducible to love of neighbor as commanded by "God." If these enlightened persons love their neighbor, then they are "blessed" just as are the piously obedient common people who are reliant on the key passages of Scripture.[33]

Yet, as Spinoza sees it, the salvation of these common people is seriously impeded by the nonsense taught by theologians. As Spinoza argues, with much evidence on his side, "people in general seem to make no attempt whatsoever to live according to the Bible's teachings. We see that nearly all men parade their own ideas as God's Word, their chief aim being to compel others to think as they do, while using religion as a pretext. We see, I say, that the chief concern of theologians on the whole has been to extort from Holy Scripture their own arbitrarily invented ideas, for which they claim divine authority."[34] Theologians not only do not live piously, loving their neighbor, but moreover their work, motivated by greed and lust for power, simply fosters controversies that result in the common people equally displaying hatred of neighbor. In their passion to be believed and followed, theologians claim that "the most profound mysteries lie hidden in the Bible, and they exhaust themselves in unravelling these absurdities while ignoring other things of value."[35] Having invented these fake complexities in the Bible, theologians insist that others must follow their ideas, and "the bitterest hatred" and contention results among the common people. In light of the peril faced by the common people, Spinoza seeks to outline better principles for interpreting "what the Bible or the Holy Spirit intends to teach."[36]

Spinoza's key principle corresponds, in a certain way, to the parallel that the medieval (and some patristic) theologians had drawn between "the book of Nature" and "the book of Scripture." He argues that one must interpret nature and Scripture by using the same methods. Just as one must analyze empirical data and draw explanatory conclusions about natural phenomena, so also one must analyze scriptural material (understood as a historical product) in order to draw conclusions about Scripture. Spinoza points out that the material of Scripture, describing moral doctrines, miraculous occurrences, and divine revelations, cannot "be deduced from principles known by the natural light" (that is, philosophy).[37] The determination of what Scripture teaches can only be achieved through study of Scripture in itself: interpreters must work "against the undue influence, not only of our own prejudices, but of our faculty of reason insofar as that is based on the principles of natural cognition."[38] Separated from metaphysical judgment, Scripture can be evaluated on its own terms. The difference with patristic-medieval interpretation thus begins with a different understanding of "nature": for the patristic-medieval tradition, nature is a created participatory reality that signifies its Creator and possesses a teleological order; for Spinoza nature simply yields empirical data within the linear time-space continuum. It is not that the medievals rejected empirical study of nature; rather the difference is that Spinoza's "nature" is metaphysically thin.

In order to determine exactly what Scripture says, Spinoza proposes three rules for scriptural study that is non-philosophical but yet open to all who possess "the natural light of reason," whether Jew,

Christian, or other: (1) painstaking linguistic analysis of each passage, made difficult by the obscurity of many Hebrew words in Scripture[39]; (2) concordance-style comparison of all the teachings in each book; (3) a historical quest for origins (whose problematic character Spinoza fully recognizes),[40] that is, questions of authorship, date, context, redaction, variant texts, authenticity, and the formation of the canon.[41] Having ruled out metaphysical judgments implying participation in realities depicted in Scripture, each concept can be compared with every other concept, and the strictly this-worldly investigation of the origins of each concept can proceed through linguistic and historical efforts. The lack of a participatory metaphysical account is crucial: since scriptural teachings are not to be studied as if they had existence anywhere other than on the pages of Scripture, they cannot be studied in a participatory manner, as realities in which we (faith-filled readers) participate. Thus cut off from "realities" and our sharing in these realities, Scripture becomes a set of distinct concepts each of which finds its meaning solely in the linear time-space continuum marked out by the time period of the composition and redaction of the texts. It will be clear that in displacing the metaphysical stance from which the patristic-medieval tradition read Scripture, Spinoza has substituted another (inevitably "metaphysical") account of what kind of realities scriptural teachings are: they are concepts strictly embedded in history understood as a linear time-space continuum.

Spinoza also proposes that just as in the study of nature one identifies first certain "universal and common" phenomena, so also in the study of Scripture the universal and foundational teachings should be first sought. This inquiry, Spinoza suggests, will lead the interpreter to Spinoza's basic doctrines, which we have enumerated above. The inquiry into these universal and foundational teachings is all the more necessary because, in his view, attempts to provide an authoritative basis for doctrine in tradition (whether Jewish tradition or the Catholic Magisterium) have failed.[42] Furthermore, beyond these "universal and common" teachings, few or no teachings can be firmly established as defined in Scripture, due to the problems arising from the present-day obscurity of ancient Hebrew (the first rule: linguistic study) and from the redactional obscurities endemic to numerous biblical books (the third rule:

historical study). Spinoza anticipates opposition to his approach from those who hold that Scripture can be understood only through a "supernatural light," a reading guided by the Holy Spirit.[43] He responds that the prophets and apostles intended, by their teaching and preaching, to convert "unbelievers and the impious," and so it would be odd to claim that their words were unintelligible to those lacking the "supernatural light." Besides, he adds, the interpretations allegedly produced by the "supernatural light" bear all the marks of interpretations produced by the natural light. He concludes that interpreters who proclaim the necessity of a "supernatural light" not only lack such a gift themselves, but fall short too as regards the natural light of reason.[44]

Spinoza holds ultimately that since theologians and authoritative communal readings (Jewish and Christian) have so thoroughly misled common people away from the core scriptural truth of love of neighbor, the only solution is to distinguish religious opinion (belonging to "private right") carefully from civil law ("public right"). Obviously, he notes, "If every man were free to interpret the civil laws as he chose, no state could survive."[45] There must be authoritative communal enforcement of civil law. But religion ultimately involves love rather than truth— or, if truth, then the truth of love. As Spinoza states, "Since it [religion] consists in honesty and sincerity of heart rather than in outward actions, it does not pertain to the sphere of public law and authority."[46] No state can compel or enforce interior love of neighbor. Therefore each individual has the right to interpret "religion," as a matter of the will, for himself (or herself). For Spinoza, the "natural light" of reason suffices for scriptural interpretation precisely because religion is an individual, not a communal, matter: the religious truth of love of neighbor, which is the central teaching of Scripture (despite the sectarian claims of the Jewish and Christian theologians), calls each individual to obedience of will.[47]

In both Hobbes and Spinoza, in sum, we find a thoroughgoing critique of the ability of religious communities authoritatively to teach truth that leads to rightly ordered love. Hobbes argues that because of the human desire for self-aggrandizement, religious communities inevitably distort Scripture's teaching by means of metaphysical admixtures so as to claim absolute power, including power over the king.

Such claims embroil the state in sectarian conflict, as citizens take different sides in religious controversies. Thus in order to preserve the peace the sovereign, usually a king, must have power over religious teaching. Hobbes shows exegetically that this role of the king in fact accords with both Israel's political structure and Jesus' preaching of the kingdom that will come about in the life after death. He concludes that only the king can rightly order loves, and that the king does so as the authoritative teacher of truth, including religious truth (which boils down, as a practical matter, to God's existence and life after death). Scripture requires obedience to the king in this life and to God as King in the life to come; the former is a training for the latter.

Similarly, as we have seen, Spinoza holds that Jewish and Christian religious communities, both claiming supernatural authority to interpret Scripture definitively, have radically distorted both Scripture and (thereby) the religion of the common people. Scripture's teaching can be summed up as God's command to love one's neighbor; any further doctrine comes not from Scripture itself (understood as a historical document), but from self-aggrandizing theologians. Losing sight of the key truth of love of neighbor, the common people have become embroiled in violence caused by interpretive controversies. Such violence, the very opposite of religion, mandates that the content of "religion" be left to individual interpretation understood as constituted solely by linguistic and historical exegetical study. As a private matter of interior love rather than of specific external acts, "religion" thereby avoids public controversies and is restored to the common people in accord with Scripture's command to pious obedience. Thus understood, true religion involves not public truth but instead private obedience of will. Like Hobbes, Spinoza affirms that "religion" in its public and external manifestations must be governed entirely by the Sovereign.

Stephen Fowl

Stephen Fowl's *Engaging Scripture* stands as a preeminent contemporary response to Hobbes's and Spinoza's rejection of the Church's authority to interpret Scripture.[48] In the introduction to *Engaging Scrip-*

ture,[49] Fowl contrasts his approach with Brevard Childs's groundbreaking work.[50] With appropriate appreciation, Fowl remarks that without Childs's efforts, very little scholarly space would presently be open for theological exegesis by biblical scholars. He also agrees with Childs's canonical principle for Christian biblical interpretation.[51] He disagrees, however, with Childs's methodological distinguishing of historical-critical discussions of the Old and New Testament from "Biblical Theology."[52] He thereby pinpoints the aspect of Childs's approach that is most problematic for efforts to overcome non-participatory exegesis. In Childs's approach, surveying the results of historical-critical research intends to allow the particular voices of each Testament to be heard, before undertaking the more synthetic, canonical evaluation of the Bible's meaning under the rubric of "Biblical Theology." Fowl questions why the "voices" of the Old and New Testament should be those set forth by historical-critical research. Why should one assume that historical-critical methodology gives a privileged access to the voices of the two Testaments? What if historical-critical research leaves out, methodologically, key realities that belong to both Testaments' voices?[53] Fowl questions, for example, whether the historical-critical effort to locate the particular voices of the Old Testament on its own, without any reference to the New Testament, does not result in a distortion (from a Christian perspective) of the voices of the Old Testament, which Christians understand to be profoundly caught up already in God's Christological and pneumatological action made manifest in the New Testament.[54]

Fowl finds especially troubling Childs's rejection of allegory. He notes that the practice of allegorical reading in fact belongs to what Childs might call the "voice" of the New Testament, at least the letters of Paul.[55] He therefore denies that historical-critical research, the quest for the original voices of the Testaments, can act as a "control" over allegorical reading that otherwise could become more and more eisegetically distant from the meanings in the biblical texts themselves.[56] For Fowl, Childs's use of his historical-critical summaries indicates the view that ecclesial reading must be at a fundamental level normed by historical-critical reading, so that ecclesial reading does not become eisegetical. Put another way, Childs grants that historical-critical reading, as relatively neutral, should provide the norm for theological (or canonical and ecclesial) reading, although he also obviously considers historical-critical reading insufficient. Because Childs does not want non-biblical realities read back into the biblical texts, historical-critical analysis plays for him the role of curtailing the Christian tendency to read contemporary realities and concerns back into Scripture. Whereas Childs's concern about such bad reading leads him to set in place historical-critical reconstructions as the rock on which Christian canonical readings must be tested, Fowl suggests that historical-critical reconstructions, while potentially valuable and informative, cannot play that role for Christians, because historical-critical readings are incapable of engaging the *realities* most deeply at play in Scripture.

If I understand Fowl correctly, he is saying that historical-critical readings can apprehend competing concepts and warring factions within the biblical texts, but cannot apprehend historically the theologically known realities that, Christians believe, inform the texts qua Scripture.[57] It follows that, as I have argued above, only by learning within the gathered community both of the Triune God and the practices of sapientially appropriating and participating in God's saving *doctrina* can one adequately read the Scriptures that describe these very realities. Such well-formed readers will be able to recognize the interpretations, including of course historical-critical ones, that adequately illumine the reality described in Scripture.[58]

Fowl holds that the norm for what counts as a good reading of scriptural texts must be "communal judgments about whether such interpretations will issue forth in faithful life and worship that both retain Christians' continuity with the faith and practice of previous generations and extend that faith into the very specific contexts in which contemporary Christians find themselves."[59] Given this position that formation of ecclesial readers (whom I would describe as participants in *sacra doctrina*) rather than historical-critical judgments should be the ultimate test of adequacy in biblical exegesis, Fowl affirms that "Christians need to be more intentional about forming their members to be certain types of readers, readers who, by virtue of their single-minded attention to God, are well versed in the practices of forgiveness, repentance, and reconciliation."[60] Otherwise, the interpretation of Scripture will miss the point by being unable to apprehend the very realities about which God teaches in Scripture. This inability produces the worst kind of eisegesis by importing into the interpretation of the texts precisely the blindness and deafness to God's active Presence that the divine and human authors of the scriptural texts warn against.

It should be emphasized that Fowl is well aware of the distinction between Scripture and theology that Childs, by his use of historical-critical exegetical summaries, is attempting to uphold as regards eisegesis. Fowl too wishes to avoid eisegesis. As he remarks in comparing theological texts and scriptural texts, "Christians theoretically could ignore or diverge sharply from the views of texts from the tradition," while "Christians could not ignore or diverge sharply from scriptural texts in this way."[61] The key question of course is how to read Scripture so as to avoid diverging sharply from its texts.

For Fowl, the answer is found not in grounding ecclesial reading on the historical-critical method's efforts to retrieve the original meanings of the texts, valuable though this may be, but in grounding ecclesial reading on the formation of readers attuned to the realities in the texts, and thus remaining open to multiple possible meanings (given the interweaving realities) within one text. This decision identifies the authority of Scripture as a canonical reality operative within the community of the Church: "The authority of scripture, then, is not so much an invariant property of the biblical texts, as a way of ordering a set of textual relationships. To call scripture authoritative also establishes a particular relationship between that text and those people and communities who treat it as authoritative."[62] Scripture's authority does not subsist apart from the community of readers formed authoritatively by God teaching through Scripture. Fowl affirms that the saints are the true interpreters of Scripture because their lives and teachings conform to the pattern of salvation that Scripture, as divine *doctrina*, teaches.[63] On this view, the Church's interpretation of Scripture need not follow one particular method, but may apply different methods at different times in order to illumine the realities at stake in a given interpretive decision. Fowl describes this practice as "underdetermined interpretation," which he defines as recognizing "a plurality of interpretive practices and results without necessarily granting epistemological priority to any one of these."[64]

Fowl can thereby argue that identification of "eisegesis" in the interpretation of Scripture must include not only the text but also the community. Interpretations of Christian Scripture that are not formed pneumatologically and Christologically by the wisdom-practices of the Church, itself shaped by the divine *doctrina* that is Scripture, will necessarily lack connection with the realities active in the *doctrina* that Scripture is. Fowl states it this way: "Christians will find that interpretations of scripture have already shaped convictions, practices, and dispositions which have, in turn, shaped the ways in which scripture is interpreted. Not only is it impossible to undo this process, it is not clear how one would ever know that one had done so."[65] He points to the "rule of faith" advanced by Irenaeus as an example of this necessarily ecclesial interpretation. The task of not diverging from Scripture thus cannot be accomplished by historical reconstructions of original meanings. Rather, not diverging from Scripture is an ecclesial task that requires the "practical reasoning" of believers formed by the Church's ongoing sapiential (receptive) practice of *doctrina*, and that may include, but has often not included (for instance in the Church's early councils), historical-critical analysis.[66]

Fowl's effort to identify a mode of theological exegesis thus concentrates on identifying "the ways in which scriptural interpretation might shape and be shaped by specific Christian convictions, practices, and concerns."[67] Given this goal, he names his effort "theological interpretation" rather than "biblical theology," because the latter's largely historical retrieval of the Bible's meanings does not give sufficient weight to the ongoing (theological) ecclesial mediation of divine *doctrina* by "pathic" and "poietic" participation—to use Reinhard Hütter's terms.[68] Theological interpretation involves readers in a circular movement of receiving God's *doctrina*, as Fowl shows with the example of the claim that Scripture is a unity. He points out that this claim, which accords with God's unity of will, "presumes a doctrine of God (which is itself shaped by scripture) and God's providence."[69] Furthermore, interpreting Scripture as a unity not only requires doctrinal presuppositions, but also, as Fowl immediately adds, ecclesial presuppositions about the unity of God's action in forming a people. The claim that Scripture is a unity "is confirmed by the presence of a contemporary community which both testifies to God's continuing action in its midst and presents itself as the continuation of God's actions beginning with Adam and Eve through Abraham and Sarah, Moses and Miriam, and the prophets, reaching its climax in Jesus, moving on through Paul and Priscilla, down to the present, and looking expectantly towards the new Jerusalem."[70] Fowl also makes clear that this ongoing circular activity of ecclesial interpretation, guided by the Holy Spirit as receptive participation in God's *doctrina*, profoundly challenges the Church because of the difficulty of living in ways that make true interpretation possible.[71]

It is at this point—the question of distinguishing well-formed ecclesial interpretation from eisegetical imposition—that Fowl's project, with which in general I am obviously in agreement, encounters difficulties. To his credit he recognizes these difficulties without seeking to resolve them in a facile manner. I will first summarize the points that he makes with regard to ecclesial authority in the conclusion to his book, and then examine these points in light of his account earlier in the book of the ecclesial embodiment of Paul's interpretive practices.

In the book's conclusion, Fowl specifies four questions about the relationship of biblical exegesis and ecclesial authority that his book has necessarily raised, without answering, in its effort "to show the integral connections between Christian scriptural interpretation, Christian doctrine and practices, and Christians' abilities to form and sustain a certain type of common life."[72] First, given the value of figural or allegorical exegesis aiming at providing Christ-focused readings, who decides which figural readings are appropriate and helpful? Second, assuming that there could be "occasions when attempts to extend a tradition into the present actually break the tradition," who would make such determinations? Third, assuming that the Spirit-filled Church comes to surprising judgments that extend without breaking the tradition, how are such judgments to be instantiated as normative for Christians? Fourth, if as Fowl proposes the formation or character of Christian readers is central for exegetical judgments that Christians make, how can the Church ensure that those who hold office and authority possess such well-formed character?

Instead of offering a direct answer to each of these questions, which would require addressing a set of issues that lie outside the scope of his book, Fowl proposes some basic "rules" (my word, not his) for testing possible answers. First, he affirms that biblical authority depends on some notion of ecclesial authority: "authority is not something that has been inserted into the Bible which can then later be found, abstracted, analyzed, and either followed or ignored. Rather, scriptural authority must be spoken of in connection with the ecclesial communities who struggle to interpret scripture and embody their interpretations in the specific contexts in which they find themselves."[73] The first rule thus indicates that the question of ecclesial authority's relationship to biblical interpretation cannot be simply bypassed, as it largely is even by Childs. The second and third rules then set in place basic norms, drawn from Scripture, for ecclesial authority: such authority must recognize the Holy Spirit's ongoing work, and must bear the cruciform mark of the body of Christ.

In light of these rules, Fowl rejects certain accounts of ecclesial authority. First, ecclesial decisionmaking must not follow a consumerist model, in which the goal would be to please the customer (the person in the pew) with efficiency and flexibility. This would be to deny the divine guidance of the Holy Spirit and would ignore Christ's command that his followers take up their cross and follow him. Second, ecclesial authority cannot be authoritarian in regard to theological and interpretive discussion and debate, because such authority would not be cruciform and would stifle the freedom of the Holy Spirit's work. Third, ecclesial authority must operate with the goal of speaking to all Christians (the one and "catholic" Church) rather than in a purely congregationalist fashion. Fourth, ecclesial authority, and theories of ecclesial authority, must be ecumenically responsive to the divisions among Christians and assist in their healing.

Clearly, some tensions arise in these four negative positions regarding how to attain these goals and how one would recognize when they were met. If ecclesial decisionmaking is not geared toward the religious "consumer" in the pew, then ecclesial authority will necessarily challenge, make uncomfortable, and provoke disagreement among the persons in the pew. Only in this way will sinners be configured to Christ's cruciform *imago* in graced repentance and prayerful discipleship. But ecclesial authority that challenges believers, thus provoking public disagreement and debate (fueled also by the media with its divergent narrative of ecclesial authority), will likely be seen as authoritarian if it attempts to govern theological (interpretive) discussion in such a way as to make clear to all believers the difference between paths that constitute true following of Christ and paths that do not.[74] Moreover, an ecclesial authority that seeks to uphold the Church's unity and catholicity will almost inevitably speak in ways that, by claiming to speak for all Christians, do not seem fully to appreciate ecclesial divisions. This situation—the perception of the ecclesial authority as authoritarian and unecumenical—will be exacerbated if the ecclesial authority teaches as normative for all Christians an interpretive position that conflicts directly with what many other Christians communities, as well as with what Christians within the ecclesial authority's own communion, believe and practice. In short, there is the question of whether the points proposed by Fowl can hold together or whether they cancel each other out.

Perhaps the key question, however, is from where, for Fowl, the ecclesial authority derives its justification. Both in proclaiming as normative certain interpretive positions not adhered to by all Christian communities and not popular within its own communion, and in insisting for the good of believers that this position is theologically definitive, an ecclesial authority may be seen as authoritarian and unecumenical.[75] Yet, as Fowl is well aware, such an ecclesial authority may in reality be embodying, guided by the Holy Spirit, the cruciformity that is marked, after all, by the experience of popular opposition. How are we to know when an ecclesial authority is interpreting Scripture in a scripturally well-formed way, and when an ecclesial authority has authority to do so for all Christians?

Fowl proposes an answer, but before sketching it I should make clear my concerns. Fowl's proposal—whose tentative character should be emphasized—is deficient, I think, in two areas. First, Fowl, surprisingly given his methodological emphases, may not give sufficient weight to the embeddedness of Scripture historically within particular sacramental modes of ecclesial authority. Can Scripture be separated from these modes, which developed historically within a clearly demarcated ecclesial community, without becoming something entirely different in the lives of Christians? Indeed, it could be suggested that Fowl's own approach is an effort to reinsert Scripture and scriptural interpretation into these ecclesial, communal modes from which it was extracted when the sacramental understanding of the Church's authority was severely challenged during the Reformation. Second, I think that Fowl's proposal may not fully account for the cruciformity, and thus obedient receptivity, required for the Christian freedom of believers, a particular cruciform freedom that should characterize all Christian biblical interpretation.

Fowl addresses the issue of the Church's authority most directly in the context of exegeting certain passages of St. Paul. On the basis of his reading of Galatians 3–4, he finds that "[t]he authority which generates and underwrites the counter-conventional interpretation on which Christians will need to rely arises out of friendships."[76] This position, he notes, is similar to that of Stanley Hauerwas, who "reads *Watership Down* to display the relationships between an authority that arises out of friendships and authority based on a coercive use of power."[77] Fowl summarizes and agrees with Hauerwas's view that "if the church is to maintain its peaceable identity then it will have to base its authority on such friendships."[78] Ecclesial authority that arises out of friendship, Fowl argues, need not deny that all Christians, not only a privileged few such as the apostles (or their successors), are enabled by the Holy Spirit to interpret Scripture proficiently. Paul's creative exegesis (in his case, of the Scriptures of Israel) is a model for all Christians; the apostle does not have a special claim to interpretive proficiency.[79] The task for each Christian is to learn how to follow Paul's example and interpret Scripture in a well-formed fashion.[80] Fowl points out, however, that the fact that each Christian is called like Paul to interpret Scripture does not mean that Christians can interpret Scripture adequately outside a well-formed interpretive community. Paul's own example suggests the contrary.

As Paul's exegesis makes clear, "certain communal habits and practices" belong to and sustain Christian reading. With Richard Hays, Fowl affirms, "To learn to read scripture like Paul means learning to read ecclesiocentrically."[81] It follows that precisely in attaining their dignity as Spirit-inspired interpreters of Scripture, Christians will learn that such interpretation is ecclesial and communal, and is made possible and sustained by ecclesial and communal practices. Christian interpretive practice thus must balance each Christian's interpretive freedom and authority with the fact that this freedom and authority flows from the Christian's ecclesial practices. In other words, in order to read in community and thereby instantiate Christian reading, Christians must in friendship (friendships formed *in Christ*) learn how "to grant one another interpretive authority."[82] Fowl recognizes that because the very venture of following Christ is at stake, it will be difficult for persons to know *how* and *when* to take the risk of granting such authority to others. He states, "There is no risk-free way of doing this. The only real way for Christians to proceed in this regard is to begin the process of forming and maintaining friendships with each other so that they will know each other sufficiently well to be able to grant one another a measure of authority to interpret in counter-conventional ways on occasions."[83] In relationships of friendship, this position implies, there will be sufficient interpersonal trust to allow for both the limitation of personal freedom and the risks that others might lead one astray, that are involved in granting (even only to a degree) to others' interpretive authority for oneself and for the community.

Yet, does the concept of freedom at work here privilege a neutral "freedom from" over deifying and participatory "freedom for"? Fowl indicates that only in relationships of friendship can the Christian trust another so much as to grant real interpretive authority. No doubt Fowl principally has in view the "hard cases" where some members of the community dissent from the established communal teaching and thereby, if granted authority, shift the community's perspective on a point of dogmatic or moral interpretation. But the two alternatives, other than sheer eclectic individualism, that he gives to the friendship-constituted granting of authority are "Christians either credulously handing themselves over to anyone claiming to speak with the voice of God or reducing interpretive authority to a form of coercion exercised by powerful individuals or groups."[84] If the granting of interpretive authority is not friendship-based, grounded on personal (individual) "judgments about character,"[85] Fowl seems to suggest that interpretive authority reduces simply to power of various kinds, whether that of a cult persona or that of an authoritarian group.

There seems to me to be another alternative, one that finds support in Fowl's account of exegesis. Why should interpretive freedom be primarily understood in terms of an individual who then "grants," in the context of friendship, others to exercise authority over his or her interpretation? Am I, as a Christian, in a position to grant interpretive authority? Or rather am I not the one to whom things are granted— in other words, a person defined by receiving all from Christ my Lord and my friend? Is not this profoundly receptive friendship, communion in his Body, precisely also my Christian "freedom," the freedom for which Christ has set me free? Would it not be usurpation, a falling away from the communion that is Christ's friendship, for me to grant someone else the authority that *Christ* grants sacramentally in his mystical Body's interpretation of his Word in the Holy Spirit?[86]

Not surprisingly, given the insights that we have summarized above, Fowl understands and agrees with this point. He writes, "By claiming that it is no longer he that lives, but Christ who lives in him, Paul has not obliterated a previously autonomous self. Rather, he has re-situated his life in a different story, the story of Christ. Paul's account of his character testifies to the power of God's grace to reconstitute a self under the lordship of Christ."[87] Autonomy was never a possibility for Paul; rather the issue was solely in what way to serve God. Fowl could not be more clear in rejecting the "modern self," which he recognizes to be misleadingly characterized "by presumptions of autonomy, individualism, unencumbered rationality, essential stability, and an absence of historical and social contingency."[88] Yet if the Christian self is ultimately a "grantor" of authority, within friendships that the self chooses and evaluates, then I do not see how this differs from the "modern self" that Fowl rejects.

Indeed, in rejecting autonomy Fowl calls into doubt the idea that the Christian can "grant" interpretive authority as regards the Word of God. In rejecting "unencumbered rationality" Fowl might, then, ask more rigorously whether Christian interpretation is not already constituted within a friendship-based community that Christians have not chosen but that is entirely the result of God's love, God's friendship in Christ. In rejecting "an absence of historical and social contingency," similarly, Fowl might explore more fully what it means to say that the

Christian friendship-based community, and its interpretive practices, are inextricable from the historical and social matrix.

Three points, in other words, follow from Fowl's own principles, in my view. First, interpretive authority in the Christian community is not based on our granting or on our love or on our friendships; rather it is based on Christ's granting and Christ's love and Christ's friendship, as befits Fowl's Christological principle. Second, in accord with Fowl's principle of cruciformity, we are "free," and exercise Christian "interpretive freedom,"[89] not *before* we grant others' interpretive authority, but rather when we, by God's grace, receive and thereby grant Christ's interpretive authority over ourselves. Third, this cruciformity means that the Church cannot be an idea or a chosen set of friendships. Rather, the Church is Christ's gift through the Holy Spirit.

This gift, as Fowl would not deny, is sacramental. It comes through baptism and through the Eucharist. These sacramental ministries are inseparable from the historical ministry of orders, and from the historical Church as a received reality that is constituted by Christ. Far from the state or the community of believers (in an Enlightenment social compact) granting the Church interpretive authority, Christ establishes the Church in human history as a reality of inseparably related word and sacrament. Thus it is not authoritarian power if the Church's ordained ministers exercise ultimate interpretive authority. Rather their ministry of ultimate interpretive authority, a historical reality to which Ignatius of Antioch and indeed Paul himself already bear witness, derives not from arbitrary power but from the wisdom of the living Christ. In his wisdom Christ thereby ensures the cruciform and receptive character of interpretation in the Church. The Church's sacramental authority — which is received, historical, contingent on Christ and the Holy Spirit's ongoing gift — frees each Christian to exercise, in liberative and creative obedience, a lived-out interpretive authority that remains united with Christ's interpreting of the entire *humanum* in the Holy Spirit. As Reinhard Hütter has evocatively put it, we are "bound to be free."[90]

I expect that Fowl would be sympathetic with much, if not all, of this. It is clear that his emphasis on "grant[ing] one another interpretive authority"[91] stems largely from his concern over "ways in which

Christians (and clergy in particular) abuse those entrusted to their care," which leads him to combine his rejection of Enlightenment theories of human autonomy with sympathy for a posture of "suspicion of anyone who might seek to have us view their voice as converging with God's voice."[92] The issue is whether ecclesial mediation of Christ's word has proven trustworthy. While affirming that "God's providential care often operates through human agents," and thereby affirming mediation in general, he also states that in discerning claims to authoritative interpretation Christians must exercise "great wisdom and even suspicion."[93] He has particularly in view such areas as slavery and the moral status of homosexual acts. As regards the former, he is well aware of justifications of racial slavery arising from the interpretation of Ham in Genesis 9:18–27. As regards the latter, he suggests that there is a need for "counter-conventional interpretations,"[94] to which he devotes a chapter arguing that "Spirit-inspired interpretation" indicates the need for reinterpreting, at least in a preliminary fashion, same-sex sexual contact in light of the experience of homosexual friendships in the Church.[95]

In light of such issues, Fowl suggests that the choices are either "grant[ing] one another a measure of authority to interpret in counter-conventional ways on occasions," or "credulously handing [ourselves] over to anyone claiming to speak with the voice of God," or "reducing interpretive authority to a form of coercion exercised by powerful individuals or groups," or eclectic individualism. If so, then the choices are inevitably rooted in power, and nominalism's account of the centrality of the arbitrary will is correct, despite all.[96]

Such a conclusion, which goes against Fowl's own concern for communal interpretation, suggests a twofold problem in his account of how Christians participate in God's *doctrina*. First, Fowl cannot identify any actual Christian communion that possesses, without individual believers granting it (more or less temporary) authority, the ability to read Scripture authoritatively as a Church. Second, Fowl so emphasizes the meaning-generating role of the interpretive community that he at times risks disjoining "meaning" from the biblical texts. On both counts, the first of which is the key sticking point, Fowl could benefit from a fuller account of the mediation of God's *doctrina*. Regarding the latter count, the biblical texts possess in themselves salvific meaning because God gives them such meaning. As Fowl rightly affirms, they do not stand autonomously; on the contrary, they participate in or mediate God's *doctrina*. In so mediating, however, they actually possess (in participatory fashion) what they mediate.[97] Put another way, God's revelatory *doctrina* succeeds in expressing itself in and through the texts composed by the inspired authors, in the Holy Spirit, of Scripture. These texts possess that meaning in themselves, but not on their own, since they always participate in and mediate God the Trinity's teaching.

As I hope to have shown, Fowl's approach recognizes Scripture's place within the context of divine *doctrina* and thus fosters the recovery of a more adequate understanding of the "historical." Nevertheless, Fowl's account of the role of ecclesial authority in the interpretive handing on of divine revelation, like Brevard Childs's, runs into (I think) ecclesiological problems.[98] Fowl fears that, given the potential for abuse, ecclesial authority limits human freedom, and thus must be cautiously granted by individuals.[99]

St. Thomas Aquinas

Hobbes and Spinoza, in the context of violence stemming in part from controversies over the ecclesial interpretation of Scripture, rule out Jewish and Christian authoritative communal interpretation of Scripture. In contrast, Fowl insists on communal interpretation, but with caveats that expose a continuing unease and that seem to grant certain assumptions about the inability of human structures to mediate (in participatory fashion) divine *doctrina*. For the good of religious communities, must individuals — and even nation-states — claim the power of granting (and withholding) interpretive authority to religious communities? I think that the answer is "no" and that Fowl's arguments, which seek to move beyond the conclusions of Hobbes and Spinoza, find completion within an account of the Church that accepts more fully the Church's sacramental and receptive participation in Christ's *sacra doctrina*, manifested historically in the Church's teaching office.

By way of setting forth this position, I explore Aquinas's interpretation of John 14:15–17, which seems to exacerbate the questions raised by Hobbes and Spinoza. In this passage Jesus teaches that the disciples' love, their ability to obey his commandments, will be sustained by his and his Father's gift of the indwelling "Spirit of truth" (Jn 14:16). In John 14:15−17, truth and love depend on each other, and both clearly depend on the supernatural gift of the Holy Spirit, who gives a graced sharing in the Trinitarian communion of Father, Son, and Holy Spirit. Jesus teaches in verse 17 that those who, by the indwelling of the Holy Spirit, embody this union of truth and love will differ from "the world," because "the world . . . neither sees him [the Spirit of truth] nor knows him." What does it mean for biblical interpretation to embody the claims of Jesus' community in the Spirit as set apart from "the world"?[100] Is biblical interpretation stuck in a cycle of sectarian violence that spirals from the unity of "love" with "truth"?

I argue that Aquinas locates a unity of love and truth that grounds the nonviolent biblical interpretation which Fowl seeks. Aquinas does so by illumining biblical interpretation within the Church as an exercise of wisdom (participation in the *sacra doctrina* of the Cross) rather than of power. In giving Aquinas a role in resolving this tension, I can appeal to Fowl's own practice. Concerned like Francis Watson and Richard Hays about the institutionalized theological fragmentation that one finds in the contemporary academy, Fowl suggests that Aquinas's understanding of exegesis is in some respects an exemplar for his own:

> Thomas Aquinas, as well as his contemporaries, would have recognized that in writing his commentary on John's gospel he was engaged in a different sort of task than in writing his *Summa Theologiae*. Thomas, and his contemporaries, however, would have been puzzled by the notion that in writing one he was acting like a biblical scholar and in writing the other he was working as a systematic theologian. These tasks were all seen as parts of a more or less unified theological program of articulating, shaping, and embodying convictions about God, humanity, and the world.[101]

Recall the text of John 14:15−17: "If you love me, you will keep my commandments. And I will pray the Father, and he will give you another Counselor [Paraclete], to be with you for ever, even the Spirit of truth, whom the world cannot receive, because it neither sees him nor knows him; you know him, for he dwells with you, and will be in you." Aquinas comments on this text by observing first the work of Christ the Teacher, preparing his disciples for the fullness of the Holy Spirit.[102] This preparation involves two elements: (interior) love and (exterior) obedience. Without love of Christ and obedience to him, one cannot receive the Holy Spirit; the Spirit is not separated from the incarnate Son. On the other hand, as Aquinas points out, it seems that this is a vicious circle, because without the indwelling Holy Spirit, one cannot love Christ and obey him.

Aquinas thus indicates that the pattern that Jesus is describing to his disciples—the relationship between loving Christ by keeping his commandments, and the gift of the Holy Spirit—cannot be understood without reflection on the mystery of grace. As part of the exegetical task, assuming that Jesus knows of what he speaks, Aquinas ponders the reality of grace. What is at stake is the very order of grace.[103] Drawing on 1 John 4:10 and Matthew 25:24 (the parable of the talents), which remind us that all that human beings possess is a gift of God, Aquinas affirms that this gift-character is preeminently true of the ability to love God in Christ: "No one can love God unless he has the Holy Spirit: because we do not act before we receive God's grace, rather, the grace comes first" (§1909). Yet, one must cooperate with grace. The disciples must "make good use, by their love and obedience, of this first gift of the Holy Spirit in order to receive the Spirit more fully" (§1909). It is not a vicious circle, but rather a circle of gift, in which we come to participate more and more fully.

This circle of gift depends on Christ the mediator; the universal gift of grace cannot elide the particularity of Christ's mediation. It is for this reason, Aquinas suggests, that Christ says at this point, "And I will pray the Father" (Jn 14:16). For Aquinas, quoting Ephesians 4:8 ("When he ascended on high he led a host of captives and he gave gifts to men"), Christ's "very leaving is the reason they [the disciples] can now receive the Holy Spirit" (§1910). This is so because while on earth Christ teaches the truth in his public ministry, by returning to the Father in his Paschal Mystery the crucified and risen Christ intercedes for us and gives the (ecclesial-sacramental) gifts that give and strengthen the presence of Christ's Spirit in us.[104] As the mediator, Christ intercedes as man and gives the Holy Spirit as the Son of God. In making us his members as the Church, he enables us to share in, as the measure of our interpretation, the Trinitarian communion of gift.

The Holy Spirit enables the achievement in us of the Son's work. Citing Galatians 5:22, "The fruit of the Spirit is love, joy," and Romans 8:26, "We do not know how to pray as we ought, but the Spirit himself intercedes for us with sighs too deep for words," Aquinas shows that the mystery of grace depicted by Jesus in John 14:15–17 unites the missions of the Son and the Holy Spirit, both of whom draw us into the Trinitarian communion. However, at this juncture Aquinas raises an exegetical and theological difficulty. When Jesus in John 14:16 says "he [the Father] will give you another Paraclete," does this phrase separate the actions of the Son and Spirit in a way that would destroy their unity as God (and thereby break the unity of Trinitarian communion)? In answer, Aquinas adverts to the tradition of Trinitarian theology, according to which the unity of the Persons is consonant with their distinct personal mode in the Trinitarian order of origin. Thus, the Son consoles according to his eternal mode of giving the Spirit, whereas the Spirit consoles according to his eternal mode as the love given; these distinct modes do not divide the unity of the divine Act, even though human beings share differently in them. Although more would need to be said—and Aquinas says more elsewhere—the key point is that what Jesus teaches is the disciples' entrance into the perfect unity of the Trinitarian communion. This point elevates the discourse beyond the level of the formation of one more competing community among other this-worldly communities.[105] Were exegetical reflection to lack this insight into the order of grace and the reality of the Trinity, it would inevitably misunderstand the nature of Jesus' promise of the gift of the Spirit to his disciples.

Commenting on the next phrase—"to be with you forever, even the Spirit of truth" (Jn 14:16–17)—Aquinas focuses first on the word "forever." Were the Spirit only a temporary gift to human beings, then we would not possess a real participation in the eternal life of the Trinity. In fact, the Spirit is only "truly given" to the disciples because he remains forever, in this life (the order of grace) and eschatologically in the life to come (the order of glory) (§1914). While the Spirit does not remain forever in all persons, as shown by the sin of Judas, nonetheless he does remain forever as a gift to be participated. Following Chrysostom, Aquinas remarks that "the Holy Spirit is said to remain in us by his gifts. Certain gifts of the Holy Spirit are necessary for salvation; these are found in all the saints and always remain in us, as charity, which never leaves (1 Cor 13:8), since it will continue in the future" (§1915). Jesus differs from the saints in that he always possesses the fullness of the Spirit's gifts, including gifts such as prophecy that are not lasting in the saints. However, while we do not possess the Spirit in the fullest way that Jesus does, we receive from him the gift of participating in the Trinitarian life as he preeminently does. This gift describes a communion infinitely greater than any possible this-worldly communion.

Owing to the greatness of this gift, Aquinas finds it valuable to explore why Jesus calls the Paraclete "the Spirit of truth" (Jn 14:17). Why "Spirit," and why "of truth"? In seeking to understand what it means to receive the gift that the Father and the Son give us, we can remark that the word "spirit" indicates a reality that is "undiscoverable and invisible" (unlike the incarnate Son) and that impels or moves us, like a wind (§1916). Against presumption, it is not we who can determine and control the Spirit's presence in us, but rather the Spirit works in us to enable us to love as sons in the Son (Aquinas quotes Romans 8:14 and Psalm 143:10). Does the Spirit then impel us arbitrarily, as arbitrary power? No, because the Spirit is the "Spirit of truth." The Spirit is the impulse of Love that flows from knowing Truth. Our sharing in the Spirit thus is a Trinitarian communion, rather than an experience of power or merely human love. In the circumcession of the divine Persons, Love flows from the Father's Word and leads to the Word: "in God, Love proceeds from the conceived Truth, which is the Son. And just as Love proceeds from the Truth, so Love leads to knowledge of the Truth: 'He [the Holy Spirit] will glorify me because he will receive what is mine and declare it to you' (Jn 16:14)" (§1916). Every truth is "from the Holy Spirit" because all truth reflects the Word, and the Holy Spirit opens the human heart to the truth-filled Word. Insofar as we possess truth, such possession evidences the Holy Spirit's call to us to become friends of the Word, and as friends, to come to share in the fullness of Truth. John 14:15–17 is thus ultimately about the unthinkable grace of *friendship* with the Trinity. As Aquinas puts it, citing 1 Corinthians 12:3, Job 36:33, and John 15:26, "It is a characteristic of the Holy Spirit to reveal the truth because it is love which impels one to reveal his secrets: 'I have called you friends, for all that I have heard from my Father I have made known to you' (Jn 15:15)" (§1916).

What then are we to make of the claims of John 14:17 about "the Spirit of truth, whom the world cannot receive because it neither sees him nor knows him; you know him, for he dwells with you, and will be in you"? Aquinas argues, following Augustine's insight into the two cities, that Christ "is here calling those who love the world, the 'world.' As long as they love the world they cannot receive the Holy Spirit, for he is the love of God" (§1918). To love self over God is to live a violent lie, because God is infinite Good, the Creator and sustainer of all finite realities.[106] The Church, despite all the sins of her members that wound her, is Christ's Body, filled with the Spirit, the communion of friendship between human persons and the divine Persons who are God. Non-sacramental structures of governance cannot attain, even though they can and should serve and reflect, the end or goal of Trinitarian communion to which all human beings are called. Aquinas comments that "no one can love, as his destination, both God and the world: 'If anyone loves the world, love for the Father is not in him' (1 Jn 2:15)" (§1918). He then spells this out by means of a quotation from Gregory the Great: "'The Holy Spirit inflames everything he fills with a desire for invisible things. And because worldly hearts love only visible things, the world does not receive him, because it does not rise to the love of what is invisible. For worldly minds, the more they widen themselves with their desires, the more they narrow the core of their hearts to the Spirit' (*Moralia* V)" (§1918). Far from being able to be privatized as pious obedience or to be confined to the governance of the king, the union of love and truth accomplished by the Holy Spirit, the gift of the Father and Son, opens the Church and her members to the widest possible purview, as opposed to the narrowness brought about by mere worldly desires.

By means of the interpretive wisdom accomplished through the Christological and pneumatological union of love and truth, human beings are enabled to break through the confines of self-aggrandizement and power so as to love others in God. All human realities, including the human social order, are called to learn to judge particular finite goods rightly by means of knowing the true "common good" that is divine filiation or the communion of friendship with God. Yet, why is it that violence, rather than the Holy Spirit's interpretive wisdom, appears to continue to dominate the world? Aquinas, commenting on why the "world . . . neither sees him [the Holy Spirit] nor knows him" (Jn 14:17), remarks that worldly persons both do not want to see the Holy Spirit and spiritual realities, and are not capable of (even if they wanted it) such seeing because of the blindness imposed by worldly desires. He follows Augustine's reading: "As Augustine says: 'Worldly love does not have invisible eyes which alone can see the invisible Holy Spirit.' 'The sensual person does not perceive those things pertaining to the Spirit of God' (1 Cor 2:14)" (§1919). We are too often interested solely in the goods of this world. Christ, however, is risen—and we are called, in the Holy Spirit, to die to the world and thereby to rise with Christ (and so to receive the world anew in new creation).

In interpreting John 14:15–17, then, Aquinas, with Augustine and Chrysostom, draws heavily on themes elucidated by St. Paul in 1 Corinthians: "'Now we have received not the spirit of the world, but the Spirit which is from God' (1 Cor 2:12). This is because you scorn the world: 'We look not to the things that are seen but to the things that are unseen'" (§1920). The intimate indwelling of the Holy Spirit in the human person is marked by a real detachment, not in the sense of lack of concern but in the sense of knowing how to seek first enduring and ultimate goods rather than the finite ends of this world and this life.[107] This indwelling both opens up the human person to the glorious fullness of reality and enables the person to judge finite goods in accord with their proper order. Since peace is not possible when the human person knows and loves only finite goods, the Holy Spirit, exegeting Christ crucified and risen to glory, provides a Truth that orders our loves. Our "interpretation" of reality thereby becomes "biblical," and we are enabled, in the Holy Spirit, to interpret the Bible truthfully.[108]

Thus whereas Hobbes and Spinoza assume that peace will be brought about only when such divine Truth is effectively minimized (placed under the authority of the king, whose responsibility peace is, and diluted to a love of neighbor defined by the king's authority), in fact peace comes about only through Spirit-filled interpretation: that is to say, through rightly ordered love guided by knowledge of the ultimate good for human beings. Biblical interpretation in the Holy Spirit, uniting love and truth, brings true peace by enabling human beings to participate in the *sacra doctrina* of the crucified and risen Lord.[109] This participation in God's wisdom is not a human exegetical achievement, but a gift of participating in the Spirit's "exegesis" of the Son, through the Spirit's indwelling. As Aquinas concludes, "Note, first, the familiarity of the Holy Spirit with the apostles, 'for he will dwell with you,' that is, for your benefit: 'Let your good spirit lead me on a level path!' (Ps 143:10); 'O, how good is your spirit, O Lord, in all things' (Wis 12:1). Secondly, note how intimate his indwelling is, for 'he will be in you,' that is, in the depths of your heart: 'I will put a new Spirit within them' (Ez 11:19)" (§1920).

This intimate indwelling of Christ's Spirit, accomplishing our sharing in Christ's Cross, is peace. This peace — the very opposite of the *libido dominandi* that is violence — is both the fruit and the cause, in the practices of the Spirit-constituted Church, of truly ecclesial biblical interpretation. Aquinas, well aware of the terrible failures of priests and laity in the Church, nonetheless trusts in the Holy Spirit to mediate Christ's Wisdom to Christ's Body.[110] Such faith in the work of Christ and the Spirit, drawing human beings to the Father in accord with God's plan of salvation, ultimately provides the grounds for undertaking the task of biblical interpretation in the Church, a task whose aim is salvation. For this reason, in discussing the relationship of theology, exegesis, and the Church's Magisterium, Jean-Luc Marion points out the centrality of cruciform *holiness*.[111] Receptivity to Christ in the Church, for Marion, belongs to faithful exegetical practice, whose central task is to challenge the Church to live up to her vocation to be radically configured to the obedient pattern of Jesus Christ's Cross and Resurrection.

In suggesting that this account of the Church's interpretive authority (resting on Christ's gifts) makes possible the biblical interpretation Fowl seeks, I remain close to Fowl's position. Writing with L. Gregory Jones, Fowl observes that "the discontinuities that arise from historical divergences are not nearly as important for faithful interpretation as are the discontinuities that arise from our contemporary failure to embody faithful living in ongoing Christian communities. That is, the discontinuities are not so much historical as moral and theological."[112] This challenge to "embody faithful living" goes beyond biblical interpretation's alleged task of challenging the Church's teachings. In affirming with Marion the office of the Church's Magisterium (participating in *sacra doctrina*) in sacramentally interpreting Christ's liberative truth, I affirm that the exegetical disputations between Arius and Athanasius, for example, need not be fought anew by each succeeding generation, even if the underlying difficult biblical texts inevitably and fruitfully reemerge—and thereby in that sense once again challenge the Church by their apparent dissonance.[113] Biblical interpretation, when configured by cruciform ecclesial authority and receptivity, continually opens the Church to God's call in Scripture, and thereby nourishes the Church in the challenge of learning the mysteries of the divine Wisdom and enacting the depths of the divine Love.

Conclusion

In agreement with Hobbes and Spinoza, we can deplore the violence fomented in part by exegetical controversies.[114] The solution offered by Hobbes and Spinoza, however, does not lead to peace. Rather, the Church's embodied interpretation of Christ, guided by the Spirit and by the risen Lord, is ever more necessary so as to proclaim the cruciform truth and love of Christ to the world. Experience since the Enlightenment has shown once and for all that to repress or to govern by state sovereignty the truth taught by the Church is not to achieve the peace of love of neighbor that Hobbes and Spinoza sought. It is not peace that results, but a loss of the true common good, a loss that affects all but whose greatest suffering falls on the poor and the physically weak and dependent.

Despite the failures of believers, the missions of the Son and the Holy Spirit enable the Church to participate in and mediate God's salvific *sacra doctrina* for the whole world. In contrast to the Hobbesian idea that individuals grant the community its authority, the Church, as Christ's Bride, receives interpretive authority by sharing in Christ's Spirit. Both the Church and divinely inspired Scripture in the Church are thus "sacramental" realities whose purpose is the salvation of the human race. In the Holy Spirit, Christ the Teacher gives his authority to the mediations—the interrelated offices, charisms, and vocations that form his visible Body—in and through which he is efficaciously embodied and proclaimed in the world. Christ has won historically the victory over the principalities and powers; through his *doctrina*, the wisdom that is kenotic love, he frees human beings from the principalities and powers. Exegetes are called to this freedom. It is precisely the Christological and pneumatological authority of the Church that allows individual exegetes the freedom of self-dispossession, the confidence that the grace of the Holy Spirit is in charge of the exegesis of the Son.

It should not surprise, then, that Aquinas throughout his exegesis of John 14:15–17 focuses on the reality of the salvific order of the grace of the Holy Spirit. He probes this reality exegetically not simply by a narrative account of John 14:15–17—although he does offer a coherent narrative account of the passage—but also by drawing in numerous scriptural passages that address the same theme, by attending to the theological problems it raises for human action, by illuming the Trinitarian missions, and by probing our graced participation in the Trinity through the Father's and Son's gift of the indwelling Spirit. This exegetical practice makes clear that Jesus' teachings are meant to be participated in and to be embodied as realities known through faith. Our sharing in the peace of Christ depends on our embodied love for spiritual realities in the world, rather than violent lust for the goods of this world as (illusory) ends in themselves. To enter into this peace, we must participate as cruciform members of Christ's Church in his scriptural pedagogy, by which our loves are reordered by the Spirit of truth given by faith in Christ.[115]

With the saints, we come to participate exegetically in the cruciform peace, won by Christ's suffering as the supreme manifestation of love and truth, of God's scriptural *sacra doctrina*. As the Polish theologian Waclaw Swierzawski has put it, "witness of the truth is connected with a participation in the truth; one cannot bear witness to truth without participating in it—which in fact means that only he who knows God's truth bears witness to it. The height of this knowledge is the witness of the martyrs."[116]

CONCLUSION

Reinhard Hütter has described "the quandary of how to relate premodern and postcritical exegesis on the one hand with historical-critical exegesis on the other."[1] He positions himself "between those who reject any theologically constituted hermeneutical horizon for historical-critical exegesis and those who argue for the superiority of premodern or postcritical exegesis."[2] Like most theologians and biblical scholars, however, he is unsure what such a position, in its practical lineaments, would look like. Even were one to present a proposal, as this book does, one would have to reckon with the fact that, as Brevard Childs points out, "[t]he field of biblical studies for the last two hundred years has been strewn with countless examples of attempts to recover serious theological exegesis which have not succeeded."[3] One recalls Samuel Johnson's dictum regarding the hopes of authors: "No place affords a more striking conviction of the vanity of human hopes than a public library."[4] Without pretending to have escaped the logic of this dictum, what can I hope to have accomplished in this book?

One way of answering this question is to recall the contrasting approaches to biblical exegesis taken by Karl Rahner and Henri de Lubac during the period between World War II and the Second Vatican Council.[5] Like de Lubac, Rahner recognizes that "Catholic exegesis is a science of faith, not merely philology and history of religions" or "profane history," and therefore that Catholic biblical exegesis must employ doctrinal norms as "a positive intrinsic principle guiding research."[6] Catholic biblical exegetes, says Rahner, are

Catholic theologians and "must therefore observe all the rules which are . . . proper to Catholic theology."[7] He emphasizes that while remaining "inexorably critical," Catholic biblical exegetes have an obligation to assist the Church in squaring the results of biblical interpretation with Church doctrine properly understood.[8] In this vein, he notes that were Catholic biblical exegetes better versed in "scholastic" modes of theology, they would be able to understand better how theological themes flow from biblical modes of expression. He urges further study of the meaning of biblical "inerrancy" as regards not taking a passage out of its historical and literary context, and he warns against favoring Protestant exegesis (on the assumption that Catholic exegesis is biased) and against teaching biblical scholarship in seminaries in such a way that seminarians, rather than being prepared to preach the Gospel, are instead diverted into the quicksands of difficult exegetical problems.

Yet, when it comes down to how to understand the proper task of biblical interpretation, Rahner returns to "history" understood as a non-participatory reality. He writes about the Catholic biblical exegete: "Having granted all that we said about the theological nature of his exegesis, he is obliged to work on the New Testament as a historian, concerned with the foundations of the faith."[9] The key is that this historical concern must "prescind, methodologically, from the inspiration and inerrancy of Scripture."[10] Prescinding from the inspiration of Scripture makes inevitable that the biblical exegete must prescind, in his or her historical task, from engaging the nature and depth of the realities depicted in the Bible, and must instead focus on analyzing and sorting through the biblical concepts in their empirically retrievable linear-historical context. The theologian's task vis-à-vis biblical interpretation then turns out to be filling these concepts with theological life and dogmatic persuasiveness. And the central way that the theologian performs this task is by seeking to give as wide a leeway as possible to biblical interpretations that deviate from strict literalism. In other words, not only does the biblical exegete's task become one of juggling and balancing concepts, but so does the theologian's task.

Although Rahner seeks to call exegetes and theologians to the work of asking and answering difficult questions,[11] by beginning with the assumption that historical research must prescind from the reality (known in faith) of inspiration—and thereby prescind from all realities in Scripture for the knowledge of which faith is required—Rahner ensures that both exegetes and theologians will end up engaging sets of biblical concepts, with the exegetes discerning and analyzing the concepts, and the theologians seeking to give the concepts dogmatic space.[12] Within this understanding of the requirements of the historical task, neither exegetes nor theologians can arrive at the heart of biblical interpretation, namely participating (ecclesially) in the realities, revealed historically in Scripture, that burst the limits of a solely linear account of history. These realities of Scripture are understood only as we share in them, in the ecclesial "present" that looks always both backward and (eschatologically) forward from within the Christological plan of human salvation, under the guidance of the Holy Spirit.

Henri de Lubac, like Jean Daniélou and Hans Urs von Balthasar, saw this clearly. As de Lubac writes in his essay "On an Old Distich: The Doctrine of the 'Fourfold Sense' in Scripture," which anticipates the key themes of his multivolume *Exégèse médiévale*, the believer's "view is basically synthetic. The Bible brings him a history that is the history of salvation. . . . This mysterious history is completely imbued with a profound significance, which is its spiritual or mystical meaning, in turn, allegorical, moral and anagogical."[13] Moreover, the believer "receives Scripture from the Tradition and reads it within the context of the Church, because it was given to the Church, it was written within it, under the inspiration of the Spirit."[14] These two points—that history as understood biblically is saturated with the divine realities of salvation and requires interpretation that can gain purchase on such realities, and that biblical interpretation is a sharing in the Church's reception of inspired Scripture—push de Lubac's understanding of what it means to read the Bible "historically" beyond the non-participatory barriers largely accepted, whether consciously or not, by Rahner.[15] Exegesis, if it is to attain "critically" to what the Bible understands by "historical," cannot prescind from faith. The realities revealed in Scripture are actively present, in various modes, throughout salvation history, and faith illumines the full historicity of these realities sought by "historical" exegesis.

Thus the "literal" or "historical" interpretation of Scripture actually requires practices that enable the exegete to participate ecclesially in transhistorical dimensions of the realities taught in Scripture. As de Lubac states, citing Aquinas, "The mystery to be believed is never exhausted or even, to tell the truth, tapped by the materiality of the fact that incarnates it: the mystery of the death and Resurrection of the Savior, for example, goes infinitely beyond what an exegete, assuming that he is both perspicacious and firm in his unbelief, would be able to learn about the death and resurrection of the man Jesus."[16] This fact does not by any means imply a rejection of what biblical scholars think of when they describe the "literal sense." On the contrary, what can be learned about the ancient Near East, the transmission of the texts, and so forth belongs to the historicity of salvation. The difference is simply that such historical work cannot, in the case of biblical interpretation, exhaust the meaning of the "historical," because we know in faith other realities operating in history—among them, for example, the triune God's creation of the world, the providential shaping of God's people Israel, the working of the Holy Spirit, the divinity of Jesus, the Church as Christ's mystical Body, the spiritual mediation accomplished by the sacraments, and the eschatological promise of divinization. Without negating historical research into the biblical texts, it is these realities that guide interpretation of the historical meaning of Scripture, since these realities enable us to understand the historical aspects in their fullness and with proper perspective.

De Lubac observes, then, that the patristic-medieval practice of the spiritual senses does not override history: "It remains history, but it is a history that is not only recorded but 'understood': it is the 'truth', the 'reality' of the history whose hidden significance it can unveil. It reveals its 'strength' and 'reason.'"[17] De Lubac argues that it is necessary to recover this understanding of the spiritual senses rather than the practice of the spiritual senses themselves. The key is to be aware that "history" cannot be reduced to sets of concepts about the past. History continually opens on past, present, and future, because of the teleological pattern of history as shaped by divine realities and our participation in them. The exegete who seeks Scripture's full "historical sense" must be attuned to spiritual realities known in faith and present and active in history.[18]

De Lubac is not requiring biblical scholars to master the spiritual senses, but he is calling for the recovery of a participatory understanding of history that will, he hopes, enable future students of Scripture to renew exegesis through the integrated use of the four senses of Scripture.[19] To put it in Blondel's words: "Real history is composed of human lives; and human life is metaphysics in act. To claim to constitute the science of history without any speculative preoccupation, or even to suppose that the humblest details of history could be, in the strict sense of the word, a simple matter of observation, is to be influenced by prejudices on the pretext of attaining to an impossible neutrality."[20] Theologians, too, must for de Lubac rededicate themselves to the *sacra doctrina* that is *sacra scriptura*. As de Lubac remarks, Aquinas, in treating both Scripture and theology under the heading "doctrina sacra," made clear that his *scientia* of theology would "be completely dedicated to deepening the understanding of Scripture, an understanding that, in human history, will never be complete."[21] From both sides of the disciplinary divide, therefore, there are compelling reasons for the renewal of a participatory biblical exegesis.

In light of the contrasting approaches of Rahner and de Lubac, let us survey once again this book's five chapters. Chapter 1 argued that the divide between historical-critical and patristic-medieval exegesis took shape from within the rejection of a participatory understanding of the human person (and history) in relation to God. The loss of a participatory framework cuts off the literal/historical sense from the spiritual sense and makes it increasingly difficult to see in the literal/historical sense anything but a set of immanently enclosed concepts. For this reason, biblical interpretation now needs to retrieve an understanding of history as not a strictly linear (enclosed) continuum but rather a providentially ordered participation in the triune God who creates and redeems. Chapter 2 then traced the gradual but noticeable shift away from participatory exegesis in Catholic biblical scholarship after the thirteenth century, by treating briefly the approaches to John 3:27–36 of ten exegetes, from the rise of fourteenth-century nominalist theology through the full-scale development of Catholic historical-critical biblical scholarship in the twentieth century.

Critiquing the presumption that history is an enclosed linear continuum marked by a disjunction between human beings and God paved the way for the constructive account of exegetical practice developed in chapters 3 and 4. Absent the participatory relationship between human beings and God, an impasse between "vertical" and "horizontal" exegesis develops because, lacking participation, no account of their integration is possible. Participatory biblical exegesis resolves this impasse. As set forth in chapter 3, a participatory metaphysics allows for a *theocentric* understanding of biblical interpretation, in which the ultimate goal is learning God the Teacher. The centrality and priority of God the Teacher upholds rather than destroys true human participation in divine teaching, *sacra doctrina*.

Chapter 4 explored human exegetical participation in God the Teacher and God's *sacra doctrina*. To reach the heart of "what happened" in biblical Israel and the New Testament Church one must enter into the work that God was doing in and through his people. In dialogue with the Pontifical Biblical Commission's "The Jewish People and Their Sacred Scriptures in the Christian Bible" as well as with leading contemporary Jewish scholars, the chapter proposed that this entering into God's work in history requires communal, liturgical, and metaphysical practices that configure the interpreter's mind and heart to God's ongoing historical work. Since "what happened" is not a neutral substratum to which the practicing community formed by God is then added (for example, at the level of canon), neither Israel nor the Church stands outside the exegetical act. The meanings of the biblical texts, both in history and in the canon, have depths that require participation in the wisdom-practices by which God forms his people. Historical-critical reconstruction that, without a priori confessional claims, builds a historical case for the activity of God in Israel and in Christ Jesus has undeniable value, but cannot attain the necessary integration: the presence of divine realities remains on the margins, outside the linear-historical bounds.[22]

The first four chapters suggested why and how biblical interpretation must overcome the presumption that history is *solely* linear. Chapter 5 then investigated the challenge regarding interpretive authority that faces participatory biblical exegesis in the modern period. Working within the context of the Enlightenment, Thomas Hobbes and Baruch Spinoza influentially claim that religious communities cannot be trusted with biblical interpretation. Hobbes and Spinoza see religious communities as exercises of autonomous human will that merely imagine themselves to be expressions of divine wisdom. On this view such communities inevitably wield "truth" as an instrument of oppressive power that destroys any possibility of uniting human persons in community. After reviewing Hobbes's and Spinoza's approaches to biblical interpretation, as well as Stephen Fowl's groundbreaking work, the chapter suggested that the beginnings of an adequate Trinitarian ecclesiology of biblical exegesis may be found in Aquinas's interpretation of John 14:15–17, which emphasizes the relationship of truth to the right ordering of our loves.

In sum, it may be said that the saints can see more deeply into even the "historical" dimension of Scripture, once "history" is properly understood, than can interpreters possessed *solely* of historical-critical tools. Thus Christians need not reject patristic-medieval exegesis for "reading into" the biblical texts the realities known in faith by the later Church. On the contrary, it is just such participatory reading that apprehends the true nature of the history of God's salvific engagement with human beings, and therefore truly "reads with" the biblical narrative of salvation that is (consciously or even unconsciously) embodied by the holy men and women who have manifested God's salvation in every time and place.[23] As Augustine Di Noia states, "it is only in the light of faith that the events of Christ's life can be understood in their historical reality as such."[24] If the "horizontal" and the "vertical" have been integrated historically, as Christians believe and as Scripture testifies, then this integration will manifest itself in the Church, which interprets Scripture ever anew in Christ and the Spirit.

Treating Aquinas as a model of exegetical practice, the biblical scholar Markus Bockmuehl remarks on a scene from William Tocco's and Bernard Gui's early fourteenth-century hagiographical lives of Aquinas:

This picture shows a master of systematicians employing the best of human reason in the demanding and persistent labour of engaging the text of the Old Testament as Christian Scripture. He is prompted and accompanied in this evidently communal, ecclesial task by the twin apostolic witness to the Jews and to the

Gentiles—Peter and Paul, who jointly laid the foundation of the Church. Thomas works, in other words, not in splendid critical isolation but as a disciple in the company of the saints. In that work, finally, he is further encouraged and prompted by the testimony of a third fellow disciple—the Mother of God, whose faithful ministry of pointing the world to her Son both illuminates and embodies the Christian interpreter's task.[25]

Bockmuehl's insight sums up the work of this book. I have proposed an approach to biblical interpretation founded on three steps: reclaiming history as a participatory rather than merely linear reality; understanding biblical exegesis as an ecclesial participation in God the Teacher; and renewing our sense of how the Church's wisdom-practices, and thus ultimately ecclesial authority, distinguish multilayered and embodied exegesis from the idolatrous distortions of eisegesis. By drawing on the work of many contemporary biblical scholars and theologians whose work can be seen as convergent, I hope to have shown that reclaiming patristic-medieval exegetical practice, rooted in a participatory theology of history and its attendant metaphysics, may fruitfully inform a contemporary renewal of the Church's biblical exegesis.

NOTES

Introduction

1. Throughout the book, indebted to John Paul II's encyclical *Fides et Ratio* (e.g., §§7–12, 16–17), I distinguish, without separating, "metaphysical" and "Christological-pneumatological" modes of participating in God. Influenced by the Reformers' rejection of philosophy, as well as by Kantian apophaticism and Hegelian dialectics, many modern theologians do not distinguish sufficiently the two modes of creaturely relationship to the Trinity (creation and redemption). What is lost is the Fathers' and the high scholastics' ability to account for natural teleology, for the divine names (most notably divine simplicity), and for the gratuitous character of grace. This insistence on a strictly Christological-pneumatological ontology mars Jens Zimmermann's *Recovering Theological Hermeneutics: An Incarnational-Trinitarian Theory of Interpretation* (Grand Rapids, Mich.: Baker, 2004), which is otherwise very much on the right track.

2. In correspondence with me, Philip McCosker has described this perspective as a "sacramental" view of reality (as opposed to a "scientific" view). In this regard Matthew L. Lamb's insights into the relationship of time and eternity have deeply influenced my perspective. The similar perspective of Francis Martin also bears the imprint of Lamb's insights on time and eternity: see for this debt Martin, *Sacred Scripture: The Disclosure of the Word* (Naples, Fla.: Sapientia Press, 2006), 239 f.

3. *Fides et Ratio* states in this regard: "What is distinctive about the biblical text is the conviction that there is a profound and indissoluble unity between the knowledge of reason and the knowledge of faith. The world and all that happens within it, including history and the fate of peoples, are realities to be observed, analyzed and assessed with all the resources of reason, but without

faith ever being foreign to the process. Faith intervenes not to abolish reason's autonomy nor to reduce its scope for action, but solely to bring the human being to understand that in these events it is the God of Israel who acts. Thus the world and the events of history cannot be understood in depth without professing faith in the God who is at work in them. Faith sharpens the inner eye, opening the mind to discover in the flux of events the workings of Providence" (§16).

4. R.W. L. Moberly, *The Bible, Theology, and Faith: A Study of Abraham and Jesus* (Cambridge: Cambridge University Press, 2000), 4–5. Cf. the similar concerns of the biblical scholar John Topel, "Faith, Exegesis, and Theology," *Irish Theological Quarterly* 69 (2004): 337–48, which attempts to move toward what I call "participatory" exegesis. After praising the advances accomplished by means of historical-critical research, the eminent Methodist theologian Geoffrey Wainwright notes, "But modern historical criticism has also been accompanied, and in some cases driven, by a thrust against traditional Christian dogmas and by philosophical presuppositions that exclude interaction between God and the world" (Wainwright, "Towards an Ecumenical Hermeneutic: How Can All Christians Read the Scriptures Together?" *Gregorianum* 76 [1995]: 639–62, at 648–49). Tracing the impact of these "philosophical presuppositions"—Wainwright has in mind Humean naturalism, which as Norris Clarke has shown emerges from Ockhamite presuppositions—constitutes a central theme of this book.

5. Cf. Richard Hays's discussion of Adolf Schlatter's 1909 essay "The Theology of the New Testament and Dogmatics" in Hays's "Reading Scripture in Light of the Resurrection," in *The Art of Reading Scripture*, ed. Ellen F. Davis and Richard B. Hays (Grand Rapids, Mich.: Eerdmans, 2003), 237–38. Hays asks, "What would critical study of the Bible look like if we heeded Schlatter's argument that dogmatics necessarily 'permeates the whole course of historical work' and that our location within the community of faith enhances rather than hinders our capacity to understand the past and the historical development of the tradition? What would biblical criticism look like if we sought to develop a consistent critical approach from within the community that knows itself to be given life by the resurrection of Jesus of Nazareth?" (238). Schlatter's essay can be found in English translation in *The Nature of New Testament Theology: The Contribution of William Wrede and Adolf Schlatter*, ed. and trans. Robert Morgan (London: SCM Press, 1973).

6. Walker, "Editorial: Fundamentalism and the Catholicity of Truth," *Communio* 29 (2002): 5–27, at 21. Just before this quotation Walker writes: "If, in fact, the inspiration of Scripture passes through the Church's participation in Jesus' 'traditioning,' though without ever being simply reducible to it, then the historical genesis of the Biblical text is *never* neutral with respect to Tradition—and, therefore, cannot be properly understood without participa-

tion in the Church's sharing in Jesus' traditioning. To be sure, the introduction of the traditional reading of Scripture into 'scientific' exegesis need not, indeed, *should not*, mean a proof-texting that ignores the *specificity* of Biblical discourse in order to dragoon the Scriptural text into the service of some a priori agenda. There can and should be a relatively autonomous scientific exegesis in the Church" (ibid.). I share Walker's sense that "participation" is the key to understanding what a "relatively autonomous scientific" exegesis of Scripture might look like.

7. John Duns Scotus was not a nominalist in the earlier sense regarding universals. Anthony Levi, Louis Dupré, and many others have identified the intellectual roots of the Renaissance in late-medieval nominalist metaphysical schemas; see Levi, *Renaissance and Reformation: The Intellectual Genesis* (New Haven: Yale University Press, 2002), 57; Dupré, *Passage to Modernity: An Essay in the Hermeneutics of Nature and Culture* (New Haven: Yale University Press, 1993). This point provides a corrective to positions such as that of Jean-Loup Seban, who argues that "it was the Renaissance, essentially humanist and naturalist, that sowed the seeds from which the historical-critical method germinated in the seventeenth century and flourished in the late eighteenth century" (Seban, "From Joseph-Juste Scaliger to Johann Gottfied Eichhorn: The Beginnings of Biblical Criticism," in *Biblical Theology: Problems and Perspectives*, ed. Steven J. Kraftchick, Charles D. Myers Jr., and Ben C. Ollenburger [Nashville: Abingdon Press, 1995]: 28–53, at 28). Seban credits especially Lorenzo Valla's philological work. Cf. Joseph M. Levine, *The Autonomy of History: Truth and Method from Erasmus to Gibbon* (Chicago: University of Chicago Press, 1999).

8. W. Norris Clarke, S.J., *The One and the Many: A Contemporary Thomistic Metaphysics* (Notre Dame: University of Notre Dame Press, 2001), 87–88. See also Michel Bastit's excellent analysis of the Aristotelian aspects of Aquinas's doctrine of participation: Bastit, "Le thomisme est-il un aristotélisme?" *Revue Thomiste* 102 (2001): 101–16; as well as Richard Schenk, O.P., "From Providence to Grace: Thomas Aquinas and the Platonisms of the Mid-Thirteenth Century," *Nova et Vetera* 3 (2005): 307–20. For the doctrine of participation in patristic theology and exegesis, see, e.g., Carolyn Schneider, "The Intimate Connection between Christ and Christians in Athanasius," *Scottish Journal of Theology* 58 (2005): 1–12. Murray A. Rae blames Greek (Platonic) metaphysics for denigrating the contingent realm of history and thereby disjoining history from theology, but it seems to me that in Plato's dialogues one finds the very opposite: Socrates' dialogic quest for transcendent truth is anything but "anti-historical." See Rae, *History and Hermeneutics* (Edinburgh: T. & T. Clark, 2005), 5–6.

9. Louis Dupré, *The Enlightenment and the Intellectual Foundations of Modern Culture* (New Haven: Yale University Press, 2004), 18–19. Dupré goes on to describe the rise, from the foundation of late-medieval nominalism, of mechanistic views of reality and the rejection of formal and final causality. Drawing

on Maimonides' overview of Muslim philosophical positions in *The Guide for the Perplexed*, trans. Shlomo Pines (Chicago: University of Chicago Press, 1974), as well as on primary texts, Richard Sorabji points out that behind late-medieval "occasionalism" one finds the influence of the Muslim Ash'arite theologians (followers of Ash'ari, who died in 935), and in particular of al-Ghazali (c. 1058–1111). Sorabji explains that "the Ash'arites held that every time-atom God creates an entirely new set of accidental properties, although they may be accidents of the same kind as before. If he omits to create new accidents, the substance which bore them will cease to exist. This shows why the blackness which we think is introduced into the cloth by the dye must in fact be created and re-created every time-atom by God" (Sorabji, *Time, Creation, and the Continuum: Theories in Antiquity and the Early Middle Ages* [Ithaca: Cornell University Press, 1983], 297). Al-Ghazali, in his *Destruction of the Philosophers*, "argues that there is no necessary connection and no logical implication between the contact of a piece of cotton with fire and its burning. God, either with or without the intermediacy of angels, does everything" (299). Aquinas responds to al-Ghazali in *Summa theologiae* I, q. 105, a. 5 and elsewhere. English translation, *Summa Theologica*, trans. the Fathers of the English Dominican Province (Westminster, Md.: Christian Classics, 1981).

10. Cf. James M. Starr, *Sharers in Divine Nature: 2 Pet 1.4 in Its Hellenistic Context* (Stockholm: Almqvist & Wiksell, 2000).

11. Gunton, "Martin Kähler Revisited: Variations on Hebrews 4:15," *Ex Auditu* 14 (1998): 21–30, at 28. Gunton appeals to "creation" (Creator–creature) in order to augment Barth's point, in Gunton's words, that "revelation is not a predicate of history, but history is a predicate of revelation" (27). On human rationality as participatory (although not in the full sense made possible by the affirmation of divine transcendence), see Hans-Georg Gadamer, *Reason in the Age of Science* (Cambridge: MIT Press, 1996), 18, as well as the excellent discussion of Gadamer in Jens Zimmermann, *Recovering Theological Hermeneutics*, 160–86. Cf. Martin Hengel's account of history as not strictly linear, but even in the Old Testament as containing "a number of lines run[ning] side by side" (242) and as united teleologically in Jesus Christ: Hengel, "'Salvation History': The Truth of Scripture and Modern Theology," in *Reading Texts, Seeking Wisdom: Scripture and Theology*, ed. David F. Ford and Graham Stanton (Grand Rapids, Mich.: Eerdmans, 2003), 228–44; also Christopher Seitz's point that the canonical organization of the prophetic books instantiates this providential (participatory) understanding of history, in Seitz, "What Lesson Will History Teach? The Book of the Twelve as History," in *"Behind" the Text: History and Biblical Interpretation*, ed. Craig Bartholomew et al. (Grand Rapids, Mich.: Zondervan, 2003), 443–67; also Joel Green's remark, "Thinking with history means that we locate ourselves in that biblical narrative whose fountainhead is creation and whose destination is new creation" (Green, "Rethinking History

(and Theology)," in *Between Two Horizons: Spanning New Testament Studies and Systematic Theology*, ed. Joel B. Green and Max Turner [Grand Rapids, Mich.: Eerdmans, 2000], 237–42, at 239). See also for a pneumatological participatory account of history, drawing on Barth, Mühlen, Pannenberg, Moltmann, Rahner, and von Balthasar as well as on the key shift from Newtonian to Einsteinian understandings of time, Wolfgang Vondey, "The Holy Spirit and Time in Contemporary Catholic and Protestant Theology," *Scottish Journal of Theology* 58 (2005): 393–409. Vondey concludes, "In the self-giving of the Holy Spirit into time, the 'wheel of history' is identical with the eschatological arrow of history" (409).

12. This is why it is not illegitimate to find the roots of historical methodologies in patristic-medieval exegesis, even though history is not understood there as *solely* linear. For an effort to identify such roots, see the Pontifical Biblical Commission's *The Interpretation of the Bible in the Church*, trans. John Kilgallen and Brendan Byrne (Boston: St. Paul's Books & Media, 1993); as well as, e.g., chapter 2 of Joseph Prior's *The Historical Critical Method in Catholic Exegesis* (Rome: Editrice Pontificia Univerità Gregoriana, 1999), 43–87.

13. Cf. Frances Young's *Virtuoso Theology: The Bible and Interpretation* (1993; Eugene, Ore.: Wipf & Stock, 2002). Young, seeking to explain and retrieve the allegorical reading of the Fathers, understands biblical interpretation as a "performance" of a "classic repertoire" rooted in the unity of Christ's two natures, human and divine. She observes, "The ancients recognized that like music or drama, the Logos moves the hearer to response, playing upon feelings of pity or fear, soothing out harried spirits, taming frenzied and disordered souls, and they knew that like music, the Logos brings rationality and order to the understanding. It is because the whole is meshed together as God's whole creation that two apparently distinct mimetic worlds never really worked, even for the Fathers. Music 'represented' the deep reality of the cosmic order, not a different world. Likewise whatever scripture 'represents,' it is not a different world, but our world understood as God's. In that sense the 'Two Natures' coinhere, and the 'spiritual meaning' is inseparable from the letter" (158–59; cf. 155). She argues that in this way historical-critical readings go together with spiritual/allegorical ones. As she states, "Rather more than the Fathers, we live conceptually in one world, but dare we let it become merely one-dimensional? If music be wholly itself yet both physical and spiritual, why should not scripture too speak with a human voice yet 'allegorically'? Why should the Word of God not be incarnate in real human sentences on real fragile papyrus, vulnerable as Christ was vulnerable to whatever the human race might choose to do with it?" (159). Earlier, following Irenaeus, she notes that the unity of the Bible "is given because the Bible is the Word of God," a unity that exists within the diversity of the "human historical process" by which the parts of the Bible were formed (44); and she similarly finds that "Cyril's sacramental view of the

scriptural text," uniting human and divine natures, means that the Church's performance of the scriptural texts makes Scripture's realities present (148). For Cyril, "The life and liturgy of the church was the contemporary embodiment of the Word embodied in scripture. The present was meshed in with the past by *mimesis* and by empathy" (148). The key is that, as Young says, there are not "two apparently distinct mimetic worlds." Otherwise the "human historical process" risks becoming a parallel track rather than the unfolding of spiritual realities in the very messiness of human history. Young's Christologically-pneumatologically participatory account of biblical interpretation accords with my approach, although a participatory metaphysics of creation would offer a richer (and more fully patristic) starting point than the hermeneutics of performance alone.

14. For the recovery of participatory metaphysics in biblical interpretation, see in particular Francis Martin's "The Spiritual Sense *(Sensus Spiritualis)* of Sacred Scripture: Its Essential Insight," in his *Sacred Scripture: The Disclosure of the Word* (Naples, Fla.: Sapientia Press, 2006), 249–75; as well as his "Revelation as Disclosure: Creation," in *Wisdom and Holiness, Science and Scholarship: Essays in Honor of Matthew L. Lamb*, ed. Michael Dauphinais and Matthew Levering (Naples, Fla.: Sapentia Press, 2007), 205–47. In "The Spiritual Sense" Martin states that the "dimension of economic participation—the fact that the events and persons, 'the wars and actions,' as well as the persons of Israel share proleptically but metaphysically in the reality of Christ—is the basis for the ancient understanding of the spiritual sense of the Old Testament" (274). See also Martin's earlier call for "a renewed investigation of what the ancients really meant by *analogia entis* and a modern application of this to the question of revelation in history" (Martin, "Literary Theory, Philosophy of History and Exegesis," *Thomist* 52 [1988]: 575–604, at 603). Cf. Martin, "*Sacra Doctrina* and the Authority of Its *Sacra Scriptura* according to St. Thomas Aquinas," *Pro Ecclesia* 10 (2001): 84–102; and "Historical Criticism and New Testament Teaching on the Imitation of Christ," *Anthropotes* 6 (1990): 261–87. The recovery of participatory metaphysics assists in emerging from the anthropocentric, transcendental-idealist modes of classical liberal theology that Hans Frei rightly cautions against in "The 'Literal Reading' of Biblical Narrative in the Christian Tradition: Does It Stretch or Will It Break?" in *Theology and Narrative*, ed. George Hunsinger and William C. Placher (Oxford: Oxford University Press, 1993), 117–52.

15. Hays, "Reading Scripture in Light of the Resurrection," in Davis and Hays, *The Art of Reading Scripture*, 237. Hays has laid out his approach to scriptural exegesis, to which I am significantly indebted, in his *Echoes of Scripture in the Letters of Paul* (New Haven: Yale University Press, 1989), 183–92. Among other points, Hays affirms that (1) "*If we learned from Paul how to read Scripture, we would learn to read it primarily as a narrative of election and promise,*

as a witness to the righteousness of God. God's faithfulness ensures that the story of his dealings with Israel extends into the present time and encompasses it" (183); (2) "*If we learned from Paul how to read Scripture, we would read it ecclesiocentrically,* as a word for and about the community of faith. . . . [T]he meaning of Scripture will never be understood at all until it is read in communities that embody the obedience of faith. Thus, true interpretation is a retrospective activity of communities whose reading is shaped by the grace of God in their midst" (184); (3) "*If we learned from Paul how to read Scripture, we would read it in the service of proclamation*" (184); (4) "*If we learned from Paul how to read Scripture, we would read as participants in the eschatological drama of redemption*" (185). In a similar vein, Willie James Jennings has attempted "to read the gospels as though the sinlessness of Jesus mattered" (Jennings, "Undoing Our Abandonment: Reading Scripture through the Sinlessness of Jesus. A Meditation on Cyril of Alexandria's *On the Unity of Christ*," *Ex Auditu* 14 [1998]: 85–96). See also, regarding the Trinity, Robert W. Jenson, "The Bible and the Trinity," *Pro Ecclesia* 11 (2002): 329–39; David Yeago, "The New Testament and Nicene Dogma," *Pro Ecclesia* 3 (1994): 152–64; C. Kavin Rowe, "Biblical Pressure and Trinitarian Hermeneutics," *Pro Ecclesia* 11 (2002): 295–312; idem, "The God of Israel and Jesus Christ: Luke, Marcion, and the Unity of the Canon," *Nova et Vetera* 1 (2003): 359–80; William S. Kurz, S.J., "Beyond Historical Criticism: Reading John's Prologue as Catholics," in Luke Timothy Johnson and William S. Kurz, S.J., *The Future of Catholic Biblical Scholarship: A Constructive Conversation* (Grand Rapids, Mich.: Eerdmans, 2002), 159–81; Gordon Fee, *God's Empowering Presence: The Holy Spirit in the Letters of Paul* (Peabody, Mass.: Hendrickson, 1994).

16. Ratzinger, "Biblical Interpretation in Crisis: On the Question of the Foundations and Approaches of Exegesis Today," in *Biblical Interpretation in Crisis: The Ratzinger Conference on Bible and Church*, ed. Richard John Neuhaus (Grand Rapids, Mich.: Eerdmans, 1989), 20; cf. Ratzinger's foreword to his *On the Way to Jesus Christ*, trans. Michael J. Miller (German, 2004; San Francisco: Ignatius Press, 2005), where he states, "The crisis of faith in Christ in recent times began with a modified way of reading Sacred Scripture—seemingly the sole scientific way. The question of how we should read the Bible is inseparably bound up with the question about Christ" (9). Ratzinger takes up this point particularly directly in two of the essays included in his volume: "Christ, the Redeemer of Mankind," 55–78, esp. 61–63, and "Is the *Catechism of the Catholic Church* Up-to-Date?" 142–65, where he explains, "The uniqueness of the Christian faith consists, first, of the fact that it is related to historical events, or, better yet, to a coherent story that has actually taken place in history. In this respect, the question about the fact, about the real event, is essential to it, and therefore it must allow room for the historical method. But these historical events are significant for the faith only because faith is certain that

God himself has acted in them in a specific way and that the events carry within themselves a surplus meaning that is beyond mere historical facticity and comes from somewhere else, giving them significance for all time and for all men. The surplus cannot be separated from the facts; it is not a meaning subsequently imposed upon them from without; rather, it is itself present in the event, even though it transcends mere facticity" (147–48). On these grounds, Ratzinger goes on to observe, the *Catechism of the Catholic Church* affirms "the twofold character of biblical exegesis" (149) in which historical-critical exegesis is combined with participatory modes. For the connections between the *Catechism's* approach and my own, see my forthcoming article in *Pro Ecclesia*, "Principles of Exegesis: Toward a Participatory Biblical Exegesis." For a position similar to Ratzinger's, see also Jean-Luc Marion, *God without Being: Hors-Texte*, trans. Thomas A. Carlson (1982; Chicago: University of Chicago Press, 1991), 144–45.

17. Understanding history as a strictly linear continuum has come under postmodern attack from critics who suggest that even the notion of a "linear continuum" is an imposition of a participatory/teleological pattern on past data. This postmodern critique is simply an extension of the modern critique of participatory/teleological accounts, although this point is not recognized by defenders of the strictly linear continuum. This point was recognized by Karl Löwith, *Meaning in History* (Chicago: University of Chicago Press, 1949). For the contemporary historiographical discussion, see Edward Hallett Carr, *What Is History?* (New York: Vintage Books, 1961); R. G. Collingwood, *The Idea of History* (Oxford: Oxford University Press, 1961); Herbert Butterfield, *The Whig Interpretation of History* (New York: W. W. Norton, 1965); G. R. Elton, *Return to Essentials: Some Reflections on the Present State of Historical Study* (Cambridge: Cambridge University Press, 1991); John Lewis Gaddis, *The Landscape of History: How Historians Map the Past* (Oxford: Oxford University Press, 2002); Joseph M. Levine, *The Autonomy of History*; Keith Jenkins, *On "What Is History?": From Carr and Elton to Rorty and White* (London: Routledge, 1995). Jenkins provides an overview of the postmodern perspective.

18. David M. Williams, *Receiving the Bible in Faith: Historical and Theological Exegesis* (Washington, D.C.: Catholic University of America Press, 2004), 203.

19. Ibid., 202.

20. Ibid., 210–11.

21. However, for historiographical reflections that move in a direction similar to mine, see Glenn W. Olsen, "Problems with the Contrast between Circular and Linear Concepts of Time in the Interpretation of Ancient and Early Medieval History," *Fides Quarens Intellectum* 1 (2001): 41–65. Drawing on and critiquing Mircea Eliade's *The Myth of the Eternal Return* (New York: Pantheon Books, 1954), which proposed that Judaism and Christianity replaced pagan "circular" understandings of history with a "linear" understanding, Olsen

observes that Augustine mixes "circular and linear patterns of thought. . . . Thus his idea that all the world and its history existed in God's eternity, to be brought forth in time by the Word and then returned to God, both allowed great weight to the linear unfolding of events, while seeing them as finally aiming upward toward God" (64–65). Olsen cites the critique of Eliade's proposal (as overgeneralized) in Arnaldo Momigliano's *History and the Concepts of Time* (Middletown, Conn.: Wesleyan University Press, 1966); idem, *On Pagans, Jews, and Christians* (Middletown, Conn.: Wesleyan University Press, 1987). See also such recent studies as Rae, *History and Hermeneutics*; Stratford Caldecott, ed., *Eternity in Time: Christopher Dawson and the Catholic Idea of History* (New York: T. & T. Clark, 1997); Nico T. Bakker, *History As a Theological Issue* (Leiden: Deo, 2000); Ben F. Meyer, *Reality and Illusion in New Testament Scholarship: A Primer in Critical Realist Hermeneutics* (Collegeville, Minn.: Liturgical Press, 1994), esp. 87–113. Meyer observes that "the critical a priori of history is the historian himself" (109), whose view "of knowledge and reality" shapes what counts as historical. On the theological writing of history that characterizes Scripture, see, e.g., Baruch Halpern, *The First Historians: The Hebrew Bible and History* (1988; University Park, Pa.: Pennsylvania State University Press, 1996); Marc Zvi Brettler, *The Creation of History in Ancient Israel* (London: Routledge, 1995). Brettler ultimately finds, on the basis of the historical-critical method, that "we can no longer recover the single truth of what the Torah describes as Revelation, nor of other religious issues that the ancient Hebrew texts address. The most we can do is to recognize the 'faces on every side'—the multiple ancient perceptions of God, preserved in our composite Bible" (Brettler, *How to Read the Bible* [Philadelphia: Jewish Publication Society, 2005], 283). He considers this postmodern perspective to be in accord with rabbinic understandings of Scripture, but what is largely missing is the "participatory" stance that affirms contact with the realities being described. See also, on the problems that plague historians of Christianity, Jonathan Z. Smith, *Drudgery Divine: On the Comparison of Early Christianities and the Religions of Late Antiquity* (Chicago: University of Chicago Press, 1990).

22. On Childs, see my "Ecclesial Exegesis and Ecclesial Authority: Childs, Fowl, and Aquinas," *Thomist* 69 (2005): 407–67 (parts of which appear here in chapter 5).

23. One might begin with Childs's important essay, "On Reclaiming the Bible for Christian Theology," in *Reclaiming the Bible for the Church*, ed. Carl E. Braaten and Robert Jenson (Grand Rapids, Mich.: Eerdmans, 1995), where he reflects on the failure of "the many serious attempts at a theological compromise that would build a confessional biblical theology directly on the foundation of the historical-critical method (Eichrodt, von Rad, Zimmerli, Bultmann, Jeremias, Stuhlmacher, Küng)" (5), and in this light describes the intended contribution of his canonical approach. As Roy A. Harrisville observes: "As far

as I can see, what has irritated Childs all his life is the separation between the descriptive and constructive elements of biblical interpretation, that is, the distance between 'Biblical Theology' as a primarily historical task *and* subsequent theological reflection, a distance celebrated, for example, by Krister Stendahl in his article on 'Biblical Theology,' in *The Interpreter's Dictionary of the Bible* [vol. 1, ed. Keith R. Crim and George A. Buttrick (Nashville: Abingdon Press, 1976)]" (Harrisville, "What I Believe My Old Schoolmate Is Up To," in *Theological Exegesis: Essays in Honor of Brevard S. Childs*, ed. Christopher Seitz and Kathryn Greene-McCreight [Grand Rapids, Mich.: Eerdmans, 1999], 7–25, at 7). For a survey of the fate of Childs's guiding theme of "canon" in biblical studies over the past half-century, with attention to Jewish–Christian dialogue, see Childs, "Critique of Recent Intertextual Canonical Interpretations," *Zeitschrift für die alttestamentliche Wissenschaft* 115 (2003): 173–84; and "The Canon in Recent Biblical Studies: Reflections on an Era," *Pro Ecclesia* 14 (2005): 26–45. For James Barr's extended critique of Childs's canonical approach (and more briefly of J. A. Sanders's quite distinct "canonical criticism" as well), see Barr, *Holy Scripture: Canon, Authority, Criticism* (Philadelphia: Westminster Press, 1983), esp. 130–71. In response to Barr's thoroughgoing attack (found throughout his work) against any form of "biblical theology," see the pointed comments of Francis Watson in his *Text and Truth: Redefining Biblical Theology* (Grand Rapids, Mich.: Eerdmans, 1997), 18–26. For Bultmann's project, see Michael D. Gibson, "Does Jesus Have a Say in the Kerygma? A Critical Remembrance of Bultmann," *Scottish Journal of Theology* 58 (2005): 83–103.

24. Childs, "The Sensus Literalis of Scripture: An Ancient and Modern Problem," in *Beiträge zur Alttestamentlichen Theologie*, ed. Herbert Donner, Robert Hanhart, and Rudolf Smend (Göttingen: Vandenhoeck & Ruprecht, 1977), 80–93, at 87.

25. Childs, *The Struggle to Understand Isaiah as Christian Scripture* (Grand Rapids, Mich.: Eerdmans, 2004): 162.

26. Cf. Harrisville, "What I Believe My Old Schoolmate Is Up To," 15.

27. Childs, *The Struggle to Understand Isaiah as Christian Scripture*, 163.

28. Ibid., 321.

29. Ibid., 320.

30. Ibid., 321. Here Childs's position is closer to Stephen Fowl's in *Engaging Scripture: A Model for Theological Interpretation* (Oxford: Blackwell, 1998); both hold that meaning cannot depend merely on reconstruction of the intentions of the authors, editors, and redactors, although Fowl unlike Childs is willing, depending on the interpretive circumstance, to do without such reconstruction altogether. In contrast to Childs, Fowl argues that texts do not *have* meanings: Fowl, "Texts Don't Have Ideologies," *Biblical Interpretation* 3 (1995): 15–34, which I think goes somewhat too far in separating "meaning" from "text" even while rightly noting that meaning requires not merely a text but

also an interpretive act. See also Fowl, "The Ethics of Interpretation, or What's Left Over After the Elimination of Meaning," in *The Bible in Three Dimensions*, ed. David J. A. Clines, Stephen E. Fowl, and Stanley E. Porter (Sheffield: Sheffield Academic Press, 1990), 379–98.

31. For his account of history as "dialectical," see Childs, *The Struggle to Understand Isaiah as Christian Scripture*, 317–21. On the New Testament canon, see Denis Farkasfalvy and William Farmer, *The Formation of the New Testament Canon: An Ecumenical Approach* (New York: Paulist, 1983); Denis Farkasfalvy, "'Prophets and Apostles': The Conjunction of the Two Terms before Irenaeus," in *Texts and Testaments*, ed. W. Eugene March (San Antonio: Trinity University Press, 1980), 109–34. For a Protestant perspective on the formation of the canon, with a valuable critique of Rahner's understanding of the Old Testament, see Stephen B. Chapman, "The Old Testament Canon and Its Authority for the Christian Church," *Ex Auditu* 19 (2003): 125–48; see also William M. Schniedewind's historical-critical study *How the Bible Became a Book: The Textualization of Ancient Israel* (Cambridge: Cambridge University Press, 2004); as well as James D. G. Dunn's reflections on the communal oral culture of the Second Temple period in his *A New Perspective on Jesus: What the Quest for the Historical Jesus Missed* (Grand Rapids, Mich.: Baker Academic, 2005). For an anthropological analysis, see the study of Walter Ong, *Orality and Literacy: The Technologizing of the Word* (1982; London: Routledge, 1988).

32. Similarly see Frank J. Matera's formulation in his "The Future of Catholic Biblical Scholarship: Balance and Proportion," *Nova et Vetera* 4 (2006): 120–32, at 125: "If Catholic biblical scholarship is to nourish the Church, it must be concerned with theology as well as with history, and with history as well as with theology—history in order to clarify the meaning of the text in its historical setting; theology to understand the text in light of the Church's faith. . . . To be sure, there will be moments when scholars will emphasize one more than the other, but at some point both must come into play. Theology must listen and learn from history, and history must leave room for theology to interpret." Matera, like Childs, seeks a unifying principle: "whereas the historian need not and should not begin by positing unity, the believer can and must" (126).

33. Childs, *The Struggle to Understand Isaiah as Christian Scripture*, 321. The opposition between "historical" and "theological" exegesis appears, as one would expect, throughout the literature; see, e.g., Ted M. Dorman's criticism of Francis Watson's *Text and Truth* for displaying "affinities to Barth's insistence that historical exegesis is only 'preliminary' to theological exegesis, since Jesus Christ is the sovereign subject matter of the entire Christian canon" (Dorman, "The Future of Biblical Theology," in *Biblical Theology: Retrospect and Prospect*, ed. Scott J. Hafemann [Downers Grove, Ill.: InterVarsity Press, 2002], 250–63, at 258). I argue in this book that what is required first is a deeper

understanding of the historical reality, although I am well aware that challenging the ingrained conception of the "historical" makes for a difficult job.

34. Childs, *The Struggle to Understand Isaiah as Christian Scripture*, 321.

35. Ibid.

36. On intertextuality, cf. Thomas R. Hatina, "Intertextuality and Historical Criticism in New Testament Studies: Is There a Relationship?" *Biblical Interpretation* 7 (1999): 28–43, which argues that the term's poststructuralist origin, as coined by Julia Kristeva, disqualifies it for use in historical-critical exegesis. While I would disagree with this, Hatina rightly sees that the term pushes past some of the barriers set up by traditional historical-critical exegesis. For intertextuality in its poststructural context, in which its goal is "a deconstructive search for the inherent conflicts, tensions, and aporias in the transposition of systems and subjectivities" (11), see George Aichele and Gary A. Phillips, "Introduction: Exegesis, Eisegesis, Intergesis," in their edited volume *Intertextuality and the Bible* (Atlanta: Scholars Press, 1995), 7–18.

37. Childs, *The Struggle to Understand Isaiah as Christian Scripture*, 160. For extended discussion of Childs's treatment of Aquinas in *Biblical Theology of the Old and New Testaments: Theological Reflection on the Christian Bible* (Minneapolis: Fortress Press, 1993), see my "Ecclesial Exegesis and Ecclesial Authority: Childs, Fowl, and Aquinas."

38. In his earlier *Biblical Theology of the Old and New Testaments*, in contrast, Childs states, within a broader response to David Kelsey's functionalist understanding of biblical authority: "Yet to speak of a reality in some form not identical with the biblical text as the grounds for theological reflection raises for many the spectre of a return to static dogmatic categories of the past. Thomas Aquinas assumed an analogy of being between divine and human reality which could be discerned to some degree by means of reason. Both the Reformers and the philosophers of the Enlightenment resisted strongly any direct move from general being to a sure knowledge of God, and such a move finds few modern defenders. A repristination of any form of traditional ontology seems out of the question for multiple reasons. . . . I would rather argue that the reality of God cannot be defined within any kind of foundationalist categories and then transferred to God. Rather it is crucial that the reality of God be understood as primary. Moreover, according to the Bible the reality of God has no true being apart from communion, first within God's self, and secondly with his creation" (82). Childs thus follows his rejection of "traditional ontology" with a metaphysical claim, drawn from the Bible, about God—a metaphysical claim that in fact needs the nuancing that traditional ontology could provide. Despite the effort to move from metaphysics to hermeneutics or to antifoundationalism, one finds oneself back at metaphysics!

39. Childs, *The Struggle to Understand Isaiah as Christian Scripture*, 164. Childs is responding to, among others, Eugene Rogers Jr., "How the Virtues

of the Interpreter Presuppose and Perfect Hermeneutics: The Case of Thomas Aquinas," *Journal of Religion* 76 (1996): 64–81. Against those—including the Pontifical Biblical Commission—who have seen Aquinas as the great precursor to historical-critical methodology, Rogers tends to imply that Aquinas is the precursor of postmodern readings. Aquinas is willing to allow for a certain indeterminacy in the literal sense. On this point, see John F. Boyle, "Authorial Intention and the *Divisio textus*," in *Reading John with St. Thomas Aquinas: Theological Exegesis and Speculative Theology*, ed. Michael Dauphinais and Matthew Levering (Washington, D.C.: Catholic University of America Press, 2005), 3–8; cf. Mark F. Johnson, "Another Look at the Plurality of the Literal Sense," *Medieval Philosophy and Theology* 2 (1992): 117–41. I thus disagree with Childs's early view that "Thomas's great contribution to the hermeneutical debate regarding the *sensus literalis* lay in his insistence that the words of the Bible can have only one meaning" (Childs, "The Sensus Literalis of Scripture: An Ancient and Modern Problem," 84). But in *The Struggle to Understand Isaiah as Christian Scripture* Childs rightly affirms that the *res* taught in God's *sacra doctrina* governs Aquinas's understanding of the "literal sense" and preserves it from postmodern fluidity. See also Francis Watson, *Text and Truth: Redefining Biblical Theology* (Grand Rapids, Mich.: Eerdmans, 1997): "Literal Sense, Authorial Intention, Objective Interpretation: In Defence of Some Unfashionable Concepts," 95–126.

40. Childs, *The Struggle to Understand Isaiah as Christian Scripture*, 161.

41. Interestingly, Rowan Williams praises Aquinas's attention to the literal sense while criticizing Childs's canonical interpretation as risking an "elision of *conflict* that has characterized other styles of non-literal exegesis" (Williams, "The Discipline of Scripture," in his *On Christian Theology* [Oxford: Blackwell, 2000], 44–59, at 48). For Williams, "'literal exegesis' has a particularly strong stake in the realities of *conflict*. The movement of our canonical texts is frequently a quite explicit response to or rebuttal of some other position *within* the same canonical framework; the world it opens to us is one of uneasy relationships and discontinuities. The meaning of one portion of scriptural text is constructed in opposition to another" (53). As an example he gives the relationship of the New to the Old Testament. Here Williams's distance from Aquinas's understanding of *sacra doctrina* could not be greater. For a critique of Williams's account from the perspective of a biblical scholar, see Markus Bockmuehl, "Reason, Wisdom and the Implied Disciple of Scripture," in *Reading Texts, Seeking Wisdom*, 53–68, at 59: "most of the biblical evidence adduced in support of his conflictual account lends itself more easily to a teleological dialectic of biblical theology, read in the light of a recognizably catholic rule of faith— a process that is no less eschatological in spirit and intent." Cf. Williams's moderated claims in "Historical Criticism and Sacred Text," in *Reading Texts, Seeking Wisdom*, 217–28; yet even here Williams proposes that "God names God

in Scripture as the unconditioned and uncaptured, apprehended as such only in the upheavals and new beginnings of the history of those God encounters in grace and freedom" (227). The influence of "nominalist" metaphysics, with its polarities and occasionalism, remains predominant in Williams's account, otherwise useful, of the contribution of historical-critical exegesis.

42. Childs, *The Struggle to Understand Isaiah as Christian Scripture*, 306–7. Childs is here responding to the positions of Rolf Rendtorff and Walter Brueggemann.

43. N. T. Wright, *The New Testament and the People of God* (Minneapolis: Fortress Press, 1992), 98 f. Wright's book contains a lengthy discussion of history and historiography, drawing on Carr, Collingwood, and Ben Meyer. See also for reflections on historical method and the New Testament Luke Timothy Johnson, *The Real Jesus: The Misguided Quest for the Historical Jesus and the Truth of the Traditional Gospels* (New York: HarperSanFrancisco, 1996), esp. 81–166; for a critique see Richard B. Hays, "Faith and History," *First Things* 64 (June/July 1996): 44–46. Hays fears that Johnson's approach "seems to reinforce the disastrous post-Kantian split between faith and history" (46). Hays is right to insist on Jesus' historicity and the value of historical research. Johnson is right to point out that at stake is the value not of history, but of historiography—and thus the risk of a normative exegetically reconstructed history understood in a strictly linear fashion. C. Stephen Evans has helpfully shown, in opposition to Ernst Troeltsch and others, that reading the gospel narrative with the eyes of faith cannot be philosophically ruled out as a fully historical reading, since philosophy cannot rule out the possibility of the occurrence of faith-inspiring supernatural events that are experienced and known historically. Evans, *The Historical Christ and the Jesus of Faith: The Incarnational Narrative as History* (Oxford: Clarendon Press, 1996). Evans presumes a reader whose knowledge of God justifies what I call a "participatory" account of history. See also Rae, *History and Hermeneutics*, chaps. 4–6, for a defense of the credibility of eyewitness testimony as mediated by oral tradition.

44. On simplicity in historical hypotheses, see Wright, *The New Testament and the People of God*, 107–8.

45. Ibid., 113.

46. This is the point nicely made by Robert Wilken in "Wilken's Response to Hays," *Communio* 25 (1998): 529–31. On this issue—the impossibility of avoiding a non-neutral "frame"—see also Jon D. Levenson's *The Hebrew Bible, the Old Testament, and Historical Criticism: Jews and Christians in Biblical Studies* (Louisville, Ky.: Westminster/John Knox Press, 1993).

47. Hans Urs von Balthasar, *The Glory of the Lord: A Theological Aesthetics*, vol. 1, *Seeing the Form*, trans. Erasmo Leiva-Merikakis (San Francisco: Ignatius Press, 1987), 543. Similarly Robert Jenson affirms the importance of historical-critical research in order to trace the development within the Bible, without holding that historical-critical research can demonstrate what is developing

(namely a unified story attested in a unified community). He writes, "This does not mean that historical-critical labors are futile or unnecessary. The story told by Scripture has been in progress for millennia, and *within* it there are historical distances in plenty, and so, in the narrative of this history, hermeneutical gaps in plenty" (Jenson, "Scripture's Authority in the Church," in Davis and Hays, *The Art of Reading Scripture*, 31; cf. Richard Bauckham's account in the same volume of the diversity and the unity of biblical writings, "Reading Scripture as a Coherent Story," 38–53). Jenson's account of our involvement in the drama of Scripture is close to von Balthasar's *Theo-Drama*, although for von Balthasar, somewhat more than for Jenson, the "drama" or "story" is the Church rather than (but not opposed to) Scripture. Jenson inscribes his own approach within that of Karl Barth; cf. the elaboration of Karl Barth's hermeneutical principles in Richard E. Burnett, *Karl Barth's Theological Exegesis: The Hermeneutical Principles of the* Römerbrief *Period* (Grand Rapids, Minn.: Eerdmans, 2004). As Burnett says of Barth, "He discovered the God who speaks for Himself" (35). Thus for Barth, "'Whoever does not continually 'read in' because he participates in the subject matter, cannot 'read out' either'" (112). Burnett emphasizes that such "reading in" does not unleash radical eisegesis or enclose the Bible self-referentially within itself because for Barth, "despite all our efforts to tell ourselves what we are to hear, there are occasions when, beyond all our attempts to grip, to subdue, and to master, we find *ourselves* really gripped, subdued, and mastered by a text's subject matter" (113).

48. Hans Urs von Balthasar, *Seeing the Form*, 542. In addition to Barth, one might note von Balthasar's debt to Johann Georg Hamann; on Hamann see John R. Betz, "Hamann's London Writings: The Hermeneutics of Trinitarian Condescension," *Pro Ecclesia* 14 (2005): 191–234. In his book on Barth, von Balthasar evaluates as both positive and negative Barth's debt to nominalism: "the real issue centers around what Barth tried to accomplish with his actualism: to pursue theology in the incomparable uniqueness of a theological *scientia de singularibus* or, as Barth says, of the *concretissimum*, where we get beyond the contrast of the mere historical fact and purely transhistorical doctrine; *where*, in other words, *the essence of event as well as doctrine is embedded in the person and activity of Jesus Christ.* Perhaps this was the theological point that historical nominalism meant to drive home" (von Balthasar, *The Theology of Karl Barth: Exposition and Interpretation*, trans. Edward T. Oakes, S.J. [German, 1951; San Francisco: Ignatius Press, 1992], 266).

49. This is the point of Bernd Sixtus in his helpful "Bridging the Gap? On Some Suggestions towards Solving the Normative Problem in Ecclesial Exegesis," *Scottish Journal of Theology* 58 (2005): 13–38. Sixtus reviews the approaches of N. T. Wright, Klaus Berger, Peter Stuhlmacher, and Luke Timothy Johnson. Sixtus summarizes the ongoing critique of Ernst Troeltsch: "Troeltsch's understanding of the nature of criticism and its criteria of analogy and correlation — still the (often only implicit) basis of modern liberal hermeneutics — rules out

that a text (any text) could credibly witness to events that are singular and not part of a chain of natural causation as understood in a quasi-deterministic sense" (17). The strictly linear chain of natural causation, by which Troeltsch ruled out miracles as "historical," has profound consequences not merely for miracles but for all aspects of the biblical witness. See also Murray Rae's response to Troeltsch's three hermeneutical principles in Rae, *History and Hermeneutics*, 154–55.

50. In contrast, Kevin Duffy has explained approvingly "how faith is and is not bracketed when the historical-critical method is used in the first stage of biblical interpretation in an ecclesial hermeneutic. In terms of the traditional distinction, the *fides quae*, the cognitive content of faith, is bracketed, the *fides qua*, the committed believing activity of the exegete, is not. . . . [T]he concrete, historical words of the Bible must be allowed to speak for themselves. To allow this to happen, an ascetical bracketing of doctrinal presuppositions emerges, paradoxically, as a religious imperative" (Duffy, "Exegetes and Theologians," *Irish Theological Quarterly* 63 [1998]: 219–31, at 230). This would be a paradox indeed: in order to understand the Bible in its historicity, we must bracket the realities that we know, in faith, to have been at the heart of that historicity. There must be a better way. However, I agree with Duffy (227), and with Henri de Lubac, that this way is not the "sensus plenior" (cf. Raymond Brown, S.S., *The Sensus Plenior of Sacred Scripture* [Baltimore: St. Mary's University, 1955]; and Henri de Lubac, S.J., *The Sources of Revelation*, trans. Luke O'Neill [New York: Herder, 1968]), if by this is meant a conflation of the literal and spiritual senses.

51. Cf. the essays in David B. Burrell, C.S.C., *Faith and Freedom: An Interfaith Perspective* (Oxford: Blackwell, 2004); as well as Kathryn Tanner, *God and Creation in Christian Theology* (Oxford: Blackwell, 1988). Thus the emphases of my third and fourth chapters are not opposed to each other—in contrast to metaphysical nominalism, which places God's freedom over against human freedom (making it difficult to understand, for example, how the divine Word could also be a human word). Following Barth, John Webster rightly emphasizes God's centrality, but for him this requires placing Scripture over against the Church: "the authority of Scripture is the authority of the church's Lord and his gospel, and so cannot be made an immanent feature of ecclesial existence. Scripture's authority *within* the church is a function of Scripture's authority *over* the church" (Webster, *Holy Scripture: A Dogmatic Sketch* [Cambridge: Cambridge University Press, 2003], 56; cf. 93 on the Magisterium and 123 ff. on theology, Church, and Scripture). Such polarities and tensions, even when defended on the grounds that the Church is an eschatological reality, manifest the lack of a fully sacramental (Christological and pneumatological) account of the Church. Telford Work shows how Ernst Käsemann—quite logically, I think—extends the alleged threat to God's free-

dom from the Church to Scripture itself. In Käsemann's rigorously nominalist defense of God's freedom, "Protestant Christianity has taken the same
wrong turn as New Testament-era early Catholicism. By identifying Scripture *itself* as the Church's ultimate authority, rather than God's Word spoken
out of Scripture, the Protestant movement has yielded to another human institution and has fallen prey to another form of Catholic idolatry." Work, *Living
and Active: Scripture in the Economy of Salvation* (Grand Rapids, Mich.: Eerdmans, 2002), 276.

    52. As Robert W. Jenson points out, "outside the church, no such entity as
the Christian Bible has any reason to exist" (Jenson, "Scripture's Authority in
the Church," in Davis and Hays, *The Art of Reading Scripture*, 27–37, at 27);
academic study of ancient Near Eastern languages and literature, Jenson argues, has proven this point. He adds, "What justifies churchly reading of Scripture is that there is no other way to read it, since 'it' dissolves under other
regimes. . . . The church reads her Scripture as a single plotted succession of
events, stretching from creation to consummation, plotted around exodus and
resurrection" (28–29). He therefore encourages Christians to "guide your reading by church doctrine" (28–29); cf. Jenson, *Systematic Theology*, vol. 1, *The Triune God* (Oxford: Oxford University Press, 1997), 25–33, 57–59; idem, "Hermeneutics and the Life of the Church," in Braaten and Jenson, *Reclaiming the
Bible for the Church*, 89–105.

    53. Thus John Webster, following Karl Barth, views theology as the task
of critically allowing Scripture, the Word of God, to judge and correct the
Church (Webster, *Holy Scripture*, 126 f.). Webster cites Rowan Williams in this
regard: "'[T]he Church's dogmatic activity, its attempts to structure its public and common language in such a way that the possibilities of judgement and
renewal are not buried, must constantly be chastened by the awareness that it
so acts in order to give place to the freedom of God—the freedom of God from
the Church's sense of itself and its power, and thus the freedom of God to renew
and absolve'" (131, citing Williams's "The Incarnation as the Basis of Dogma,"
in *The Religion of the Incarnation*, ed. Robert Morgan [Bristol: Bristol Classical
Press, 1989]). Similarly Childs, in "Toward Recovering Theological Exegesis," *Pro Ecclesia* 6 (1997): 16–26, argues, "There is, in addition, another aspect
of the Scripture's pressure which needs further exploration beyond Yeago's
description. The coercion of Scripture also functions critically in relation to
Christian dogmatics to fragment and shatter traditional dogmatic structures.
Especially in the Reformers' attack on the scholastics one sees how Scripture
exerted not only a centripetal, but also a centrifugal force in subjecting all
human traditions to radical criticism in light of the gospel. Right at this juncture one senses a decisive difference between Aquinas and Luther in the use
of the Bible" (17). Childs envisions Scripture as a self-standing entity that
radically calls to account non-scriptural entities. But what if the Church, as

sacramentally and dogmatically constituted, cannot be separated in this way from Scripture? For a sacramental perspective on Scripture, see Melkite Archbishop Neophytos Edelby's intervention during the Second Vatican Council's drafting of *Dei Verbum*, in Gerald O'Collins, S.J., *Retrieving Fundamental Theology: The Three Styles of Contemporary Theology* (New York: Paulist Press, 1993), app. 1, 174–77, at 175. See also the *Catechism of the Catholic Church*'s statement that "the Church has always venerated the Scriptures as she venerates the Lord's Body. She never ceases to present to the faithful the bread of life, taken from the one table of God's Word and Christ's Body" (§103), quoted appreciatively by the Protestant biblical scholar Markus Bockmuehl in his "Reason, Wisdom and the Implied Disciple of Scripture," 62. See also the insights of R. W. L. Moberly in *The Bible, Theology, and Faith: A Study in Abraham and Jesus* (Cambridge: Cambridge University Press, 2000).

54. As Corrine Patton has shown, biblical interpretation—beginning with the question, which remains in dispute as regards the Old Testament, of what books constitute the canon—ultimately requires some account of interpretive authority. For Thomas Aquinas, and I agree with him, this account relies (Christologically and pneumatologically) on apostolic succession and its ongoing conciliar and Petrine manifestations. See Patton, "Canon and Tradition: The Limits of the Old Testament in Scholastic Discussion," in *Theological Exegesis: Essays in Honor of Brevard S. Childs*, 75–95. See also the textual issues raised by Stephen D. Ryan, O.P., "The Text of the Bible and Catholic Biblical Scholarship," *Nova et Vetera* 4 (2006): 132–41.

55. See John Henry Newman, *An Essay on the Development of Christian Doctrine* (Notre Dame: University of Notre Dame Press, 1989).

56. Frank J. Matera observes that "Catholic biblical scholarship can and should embrace a variety of methods without claiming any particular one as distinctively its own. There is room for patristic and medieval exegesis, and a variety of modern approaches to the text—provided we maintain a sense of balance and proportion" (Matera, "The Future of Catholic Biblical Scholarship," 122). I strongly agree that a variety of approaches (although some have proven less fruitful than others) well serves the goal of biblical interpretation, even while I am proposing that fully "historical" and "critical" exegesis requires a participatory understanding of historical reality.

ONE
Late-Medieval Nominalism and Participatory Biblical Exegesis

1. Most medievalists, recognizing the subtlety of the differences between the various medieval theologians, would agree with A. J. Minnis's warning against "sweeping generalizations" based on Ockham's alleged "subversive

nominalism" (Minnis, "Material Swords and Literal Lights: The Status of Allegory in William of Ockham's *Breviloquium* on Papal Power," in *With Reverence for the Word: Medieval Scriptural Exegesis in Judaism, Christianity, and Islam*, ed. Jane Dammen McAuliffe, Barry D. Walfish, and Joseph W. Goering [Oxford: Oxford University Press, 2003], 305). When seen as a whole, however, the radical shift outlined by Olivier Boulnois, Servais Pinckaers, O.P., Louis Dupré, and others is undeniable.

2. Given my interest in Aquinas's *Commentary on John*, I have chosen it as a source for exegetical examples. For more on Aquinas's *Commentary on John*, see, e.g., Joseph W. Koterski, S.J., "The Doctrine of Participation in Aquinas's *Commentary on St. John*," in *Being and Thought in Aquinas*, ed. Jeremiah Hackett, William Murnion, and Carl Still (Binghamton, N.Y.: Global Academic Publishing, 2004), 109–21; *Reading John with St. Thomas Aquinas: Theological Exegesis and Speculative Theology*, ed. Michael Dauphinais and Matthew Levering (Washington, D.C.: Catholic University of America Press, 2005), with the extensive bibliography by Christopher Baglow; Matthew Levering, "Reading John with St. Thomas Aquinas," in *Aquinas on Scripture: An Introduction to His Biblical Commentaries*, ed. Thomas Weinandy, O.F.M. Cap., Daniel Keating, and John Yocum (New York: T. & T. Clark, 2005), 99–126. Regarding the *Commentary on John*, Koterski states that "a mindfulness of Platonism permeates this work. . . . Throughout the commentary on John, Thomas makes extensive use of participation adopted from the Neoplatonic tradition, but carefully adapted in light of the criticisms raised against the very idea by Aristotle" (109, 115), so as to "deny any necessity to the Divine activity (such as a standard Neoplatonic discussion of emanation might suggest) and to affirm the efficacy of participation as causing being" (116). An earlier version of this chapter appears as "Participation and Exegesis: Response to Catherine Pickstock," *Modern Theology* 21 (2005): 587–601.

3. Charles Taylor, "A Digression on Historical Explanation," chapter 12 of Taylor, *Sources of the Self: The Making of Modern Identity* (Cambridge: Harvard University Press, 1989), 199–207, at 203.

4. See Francis Martin's "Revelation as Disclosure: Creation," in *Wisdom and Holiness, Science and Scholarship: Essays in Honor of Matthew L. Lamb*, ed. Michael Dauphinais and Matthew Levering (Naples, Fla.: Sapientia Press, 2007), 205–47, which Fr. Martin generously made available to me as I was completing the chapters of this study. Martin sets forth the change in our understanding of history that results from participatory metaphysics open to Trinitarian action, and he shows how participatory metaphysics belongs at the heart of the Old and New Testaments. See also his "The Spiritual Sense *(Sensus Spiritualis)* of Sacred Scripture: Its Essential Insight" in Martin, *Sacred Scripture: The Disclosure of the Word* (Naples, Fla.: Sapientia Press, 2006), 249–75; as well as his earlier "Historical Criticism and New Testament Teaching on the

Imitation of Christ," *Anthropotes* 6 (1990): 261–87; idem, "Israel as the Spouse of YHWH: A Story of Sin and Renewed Love," *Anthropotes* 16 (2000): 129–54, at 151–54; also D. Stephen Long, "Response to Abraham," *Ex Auditu* 19 (2003): 76–80, at 79; Ignace de la Potterie, "The Spiritual Sense of Scripture," *Communio* 23 (1996): 738–56. In "Historical Criticism and New Testament Teaching on the Imitation of Christ," Martin emphasizes the biblical, and patristic-medieval, apprehension of "the intrinsic relation of all created reality to God," and argues that "as the vertical dimension of the biblical view of events faded from consciousness, the very nature of the biblical narratives themselves was misunderstood" (274). He concludes that "it is possible to move beyond the impasse so eloquently described by Schweitzer by complementing the historical-critical approach to the NT with an 'analogical' approach that seeks to recover what was sound in the basic insight of generations of believers I have already described. This insight may be called an analogy of *historical* being based on the action of God, the creator, in the world as this is supremely realized in Jesus Christ" (279).

5. Referencing R. R. Reno and John J. O'Keefe's *Sanctified Vision: An Introduction to Early Christian Interpretation of the Bible* (Baltimore: Johns Hopkins, 2005), David S. Yeago observes that "faith in divine providence is at the heart of the classical Christian engagement with Scripture, that one providence that has enfolded the whole world in an '*oikonomia* for the fullness of the times, to recapitulate all things in Christ, things in heaven and things on earth' (Eph 1:10), and has likewise designed in the literary 'economy' of the scriptural canon an unsurpassably rich representation of the Christologically centered order of reality" (Yeago, "Re-Entering the Scriptural World," *Nova et Vetera* 4 [2006]: 159–71, at 169).

6. This is not to say that getting the metaphysics right will, by itself, solve the problem. Rather, it is to suggest that renewing biblical interpretation, as part of the new evangelization and the quest for Christian unity, requires challenging the metaphysics assumed by much contemporary biblical interpretation. See Yeago, "Re-Entering the Scriptural World," 170, esp. n. 20.

7. Catherine Pickstock, "Duns Scotus: His Historical and Contemporary Significance," *Modern Theology* 21 (2005): 543–74, at 548; one can appreciate this passage without accepting Pickstock's account of human knowing as presented in John Milbank and Catherine Pickstock, *Truth in Aquinas* (London: Routledge, 2000). On human knowing, see, e.g., Josef Pieper, *The Truth of All Things*, in *Living the Truth* (San Francisco: Ignatius Press, 1989), 11–105; Wayne J. Hankey, "*Participatio divini luminis*, Aquinas' Doctrine of the Agent Intellect: Our Capacity for Contemplation," *Dionysius* 22 (2004): 149–78. On the unity of the conceptual and the mystical, see Gilles Emery, O.P., "Le propos de la théologie trinitaire spéculative chez saint Thomas d'Aquin," *Nova et Vetera* (French) 79 (2004): 13–43 (English trans. in Emery, *Trinity, Church, and*

the Human Person, 1–32); Jean-Pierre Torrell, O.P., *Saint Thomas Aquinas*, vol. 2, *Spiritual Master*, trans. Robert Royal (Washington, D.C.: Catholic University of America Press, 2003); A. N. Williams, "Contemplation: Knowledge of God in Augustine's *De Trinitate*," in *Knowing the Triune God: The Work of the Spirit in the Practices of the Church*, ed. James J. Buckley and David S. Yeago (Grand Rapids, Mich.: Eerdmans, 2001), 121–46; and my *Scripture and Metaphysics: Aquinas and the Renewal of Trinitarian Theology* (Oxford: Blackwell, 2004).

8. See, e.g., Wayne J. Hankey, "Radical Orthodoxy's *Poiesis*: Ideological Historiography and Anti-Modern Polemic," *American Catholic Philosophical Quarterly* 80 (2006): 1–21; idem, "Why Philosophy Abides for Aquinas," *Heythrop Journal* 42 (2001): 329–48; Paul D. Janz, "Radical Orthodoxy and the New Culture of Obscurantism," *Modern Theology* 20 (2004): 362–405. Hankey has also recently co-edited with Douglas Hedley *Deconstructing Radical Orthodoxy: Postmodern Theology, Rhetoric and Truth* (Aldershot: Ashgate, 2005).

9. Drawing on an earlier essay of Pickstock's, Denys Turner has noted that for Pickstock "this intellectual shift is not said to have been uniquely causal of subsequent developments in Western intellectual history, but only in the long run to have removed a conceptual barrier, set firmly in place by Thomas's doctrine of 'analogy,' standing in the way of the development of a rationalist and secularist ideology, of which Kant is the classical 'modern' inheritor" (Turner, *Faith, Reason and the Existence of God* [Cambridge: Cambridge University Press, 2004], 126). For further analysis of this shift, see, e.g., Olivier Boulnois's brilliant *Être et représentation. Une généalogie de la métaphysique moderne à l'époque de Duns Scot (XIIIe–XIVe siècle)* (Paris: Presses Universitaires de France, 1999); Emmanuel Perrier, O.P., "Duns Scotus Facing Reality: Between Absolute Contingency and Unquestionable Consistency," *Modern Theology* 21 (2005): 619–43, esp. 634–36; Louis Dupré, *Passage to Modernity: An Essay in the Hermeneutics of Nature and Culture* (New Haven: Yale University Press, 1993); Amos Funkenstein, *Theology and the Scientific Imagination from the Middle Ages to the Seventeenth Century* (Princeton: Princeton University Press, 1986); Charles Morerod, O.P., *Ecumenism and Philosophy*, trans. Therese Scarpelli (Naples, Fla.: Sapientia Press, 2005); Jerome B. Schneewind, *The Invention of Autonomy: A History of Modern Moral Philosophy* (Cambridge: Cambridge University Press, 1998); Richard Popkin, *The History of Scepticism: From Savonarola to Bayle*, rev. and expanded ed. (Oxford: Oxford University Press, 2003). See also, for later time periods, works such as Jonathan I. Israel, *Radical Enlightenment: Philosophy and the Making of Modernity 1650–1750* (Oxford: Oxford University Press, 2001); Tad M. Schmaltz, *Radical Cartesianism: The French Reception of Descartes* (Cambridge: Cambridge University Press, 2002); Antonio Levi, "The Philosophical Category of 'Faith' at the Origins of Modern Scepticism," *Nova et Vetera* 1 (2003): 321–40; Gordon Michalson, *Lessing's "Ugly Ditch": A Study of Theology and History* (Philadelphia: Pennsylvania State University Press, 1985).

10. Olivier Boulnois, "Reading Duns Scotus: From History to Philosophy," *Modern Theology* 21 (2005): 603–7, at 604–5.

11. Mary Beth Ingham and Mechthild Dreyer, *The Philosophical Vision of John Duns Scotus* (Washington, D.C.: Catholic University of America Press, 2004), 147. Earlier they explain, "The human will can will or attend to all possible actions. It is in itself not a power having pre-determined acts, as is the intellect which always stands in relation to the cognitive act and cannot restrain itself from cognizing in the case of sufficient conditions. The human will is indifferent to contrary acts and not determined with respect to them. It is also indifferent and undetermined with regard to possible objects and the effects of actions" (97). The will's indifference toward possible objects is, for Scotus, a perfection. As Ingham and Dreyer observe, "In this deeper capacity to choose or not, the will reveals itself as a self-mover in the purest sense" (149). For Scotus, "when the will is shown happiness, it still chooses freely because no object can necessitate it. Hence, when it is shown happiness, it can refrain from acting at all. In regard to any object, then, the will is able not to will or (nec) nill it, and can suspend itself from eliciting any act in particular with regard to this or that.' This act of self-suspension defines the nature of rational human freedom as understood by Scotus. Such freedom remains in heaven" (150; the citation is from *Ordinatio* IV, d. 49, qq. 9–10 [codex A, f. 282va]). On this freedom in heaven, see Thomas Williams, "From Metaethics to Action Theory," in *The Cambridge Companion to Duns Scotus*, ed. Thomas Williams (Cambridge: Cambridge University Press, 2003), 332–51, at 348. For Aquinas's contrasting view on freedom in heaven (understanding "freedom" as "freedom for excellence"), see Simon Francis Gaine, O.P.'s superb *Will There Be Freedom in Heaven? Freedom, Impeccability and Beatitude* (New York: T. & T. Clark, 2003). On Scotus's account of freedom in comparison with Aquinas's, see also Christopher Toner, "Angelic Sin in Aquinas and Scotus and the Genesis of Some Central Objections to Contemporary Virtue Ethics," *Thomist* 69 (2005): 79–125; David B. Burrell, C.S.C., "Aquinas and Scotus: Contrary Patterns for Philosophical Theology," in idem, *Faith and Freedom* (Oxford: Blackwell, 2004), 105–11; cf. in the same volume Burrell's preface describing human freedom as "a response to the gift of being, whereby persons are drawn to return what they have received; ideally, even returning everything to the One from whom they have received everything" (vii), as well as his essay "Creation, Will, and Knowledge in Aquinas and Duns Scotus," 176–89: "The contrast between these two medieval and Christian thinkers on this crucial point also nicely delineates a divide among theologians regarding man's relation to God, as well as characterizing two tempers often contrasted as 'classical' and 'modern.' It is characteristic of the modern temper to regard freedom as auto-determination, while the classical prefers to think of it as the capacity to attune oneself with the 'true joints' of reality" (188). The consequences of Scotus's position as de-

veloped by Ockham are explored by Servais Pinckaers, O.P., *The Sources of Christian Ethics*, trans. from the 3d ed. by Mary Thomas Noble, O.P. (Washington, D.C.: Catholic University of America Press, 1995). Thomas M. Osborne Jr. has demonstrated, through a textual study of Ockham and in response to Marilyn McCord Adams and Peter King, the accuracy of Pinckaers's depiction of Ockham's divine-command ethics as constituting a profound shift in Christian ethics: see Osborne, "Ockham as a Divine-Command Theorist," *Religious Studies* 41 (2005): 1–22.

12. See Hannes Möhle, "Scotus's Theory of Natural Law," in *The Cambridge Companion to Duns Scotus*, 312–31, at 325, quoting Scotus's *In Metaph.* 9, q. 14, n. 47; cf. 327. He adds, "In Aquinas's system moral goodness is understood ontologically, as being that contributes to perfection and is operative as final cause: as *ens perfectivum per modum finis*. Scotus, by contrast, understands moral goodness as a relational concept. The morally good is constituted by a *convenientia* that is to be ascertained in a judgment" (327). As Möhle points out at the beginning of his essay, "What takes center stage in Scotus's ethics is the obligation on the part of reason to what is apprehended in the natural law as a practical truth, rather than what befits the agent's end-directed nature as it is manifested in the virtues" (312). Möhle shows how this position shapes Scotus's non-participatory account of natural law. The key text for Scotus's natural law theory is *Ordinatio* III, suppl., dist. 37; for an English translation, see Allan B. Wolter, O.F.M., ed. and trans., and William A. Frank, ed., *Duns Scotus on the Will and Morality* (Washington, D.C.: Catholic University of America Press, 1997), 198–207.

13. Williams, "From Metaethics to Action Theory," 334–35.

14. See Emmanuel Perrier, O.P., "Duns Scotus Facing Reality: Between Absolute Contingency and Unquestionable Consistency," 635–36. On God's knowledge of creatures according to Scotus and Ockham, see also the essays in *Le contemplateur et les idées: Modèles de la science divine du néoplatonisme au XVIIIe siècle*, ed. Olivier Boulnois, Jacob Schmutz, and Jean-Luc Solère (Paris: Vrin, 2002), esp. Boulnois's "Ce dont Dieu n'a pas idée. Problèmes de l'idéalisme médiéval (XIIIe–XIVe siècles)," 45–78, at 70–78. For further development in the sixteenth and seventeenth centuries away from participatory accounts of God's knowledge, see Jacob Schmutz's essay in the same volume, "Un Dieu indifférent: La crise de la science divine durant la scolastique moderne," 185–221. For an excellent discussion of Scotus's rejection of analogy in favor of univocity, see Olivier Boulnois, *Être et représentation*, 223–91; for a defense of Scotus's position, see Thomas Williams, "The Doctrine of Univocity Is True and Salutary," *Modern Theology* 21 (2005): 575–85. Amos Funkenstein has observed in his *Theology and the Scientific Imagination from the Middle Ages to the Seventeeth Century*, "The Nominalists had to reject the doctrine of analogy because they had already desymbolized the universe (as well as history) almost

completely" (58). See also Pierre Manent's account of modern historicism in his *The City of Man* (Princeton: Princeton University Press, 1998). For discussion of Hans Urs von Balthasar's attempt to recover "analogy" for biblical interpretation, see W. T. Dickens, *Hans Urs von Balthasar's Theological Aesthetics: A Model for Post-Critical Biblical Interpretation* (Notre Dame: University of Notre Dame Press, 2003), 48–50; cf., for problems in von Balthasar's deployment of analogy, Bernhard Blankenhorn, O.P.'s "Balthasar's Method of Divine Naming," *Nova et Vetera* 1 (2003): 245–68.

15. See Servais Pinckaers, *The Sources of Christian Ethics*, 242; cf. 342. Pinckaers has William of Ockham in mind. In addition to chapter 10 of *The Sources of Christian Ethics*, from which this quotation is taken, the chapters in "Part III: Freedom and Natural Law" merit close attention. Thomas M. Osborne Jr. argues that Scotus's account of the will remains "teleological" insofar as Scotus "thinks that the will has a direction towards certain goods which are preestablished. In contrast, some later medievals argued that free choice implies an ability to will anything whatsoever" (Osborne, *Love of Self and Love of God in Thirteenth-Century Ethics* [Notre Dame: University of Notre Dame Press, 2005], 206). For background in Henry of Ghent, to whom Scotus largely responds, see Bonnie Kent, *Virtues of the Will: The Transformation of Ethics in the Late Thirteenth Century* (Washington, D.C.: Catholic University of America Press, 1995), summarized on 252: "When understood as habits, and thus as potential sources of determination, the virtues themselves may pose a threat to morality. Hence Henry of Ghent's refusal to posit virtues in the will as free. In Henry's opinion, the very notion of a habit of choosing freely is bizarre. To be free, the will must be both indeterminate and indeterminable. Though Scotus rejected Henry's position and himself attributed virtuous habits to the will as free, he argued that the habit is never more than a partial efficient cause of a virtuous act. The will itself must always be a partial cause, and the principal one" (252). More broadly, Kent argues that the thirteenth-century account of freedom and of habits of the will was, due to the contrast between Aristotle and Augustine, inherently unstable, but this seems to me to misunderstand Augustine.

16. Pickstock points out that for Jean-Luc Marion and Olivier Boulnois, the shift is bad as "onto-theology" but good in opening the way for recovery of a radical notion of charity; for Orlando Todisco and Isiduro Manzano, the shift is good because it weakens reason and (in Kantian fashion) inspires a new awareness of both divine and human autonomy that reveals the full freedom of love; and postmoderns rejoice in the gaps opened by univocity (Pickstock, "Duns Scotus: His Historical and Contemporary Significance," 544 and elsewhere). Cf. Boulnois's *Duns Scot. La rigueur de la charité* (Paris: Cerf, 1998). For a recent defense of Scotus, see Allan B. Wolter, O.F.M., "The Unshredded Scotus: A Response to Thomas Williams," *American Catholic Philosophical Quarterly* 77 (2003): 315–56; cf. Adrian Pabst, "De la chrétienté à la modernité? Lecture critique des theses de *Radical Orthodoxy* sur la rupture scotiste et ock-

hamienne et sur le renouveau de la théologie de saint Thomas d'Aquin," *Revue des sciences théologiques et philosophiques* 86 (2002): 561–99.

17. Anthony Levi, *Renaissance and Reformation: The Intellectual Genesis* (New Haven: Yale University Press, 2002), 368–69.

18. For philosophical and theological accounts of such teleology, see Thomas S. Hibbs, *Virtue's Splendor: Wisdom, Prudence, and the Human Good* (New York: Fordham University Press, 2001); Romanus Cessario, O.P., *Introduction to Moral Theology* (Washington, D.C.: Catholic University of America Press, 2001); David L. Schindler, "Biotechnology and the Givenness of the Good: Posing Properly the Moral Question Regarding Human Dignity," *Communio* 31 (2004): 612–44.

19. For a response to the latter, see John Rist's *On Inoculating Moral Philosophy against God* (Milwaukee: Marquette University Press, 1999); and *Real Ethics: Reconsidering the Foundations of Morality* (Cambridge: Cambridge University Press, 2002). For a response to the former, indicating the unity of truth and love, see Michael S. Sherwin, O.P., *By Knowledge and By Love: Charity and Knowledge in the Moral Theology of St. Thomas Aquinas* (Washington, D.C.: Catholic University of America Press, 2005).

20. See Matthew L. Lamb, "Eternity and Time," in *Gladly to Learn and Gladly to Teach: Essays on Religion and Political Philosophy in Honor of Ernest L. Fortin, A.A.*, ed. Michael P. Foley and Douglas Kries (Lanham, Md.: Lexington Books, 2002), 195–214, at 205–6; cf. Lamb, *Solidarity with Victims: Toward a Theology of Social Transformation* (New York: Crossroad, 1982). See also Burrell, "Aquinas and Scotus: Contrary Patterns for Philosophical Theology."

21. Cf. Louis Dupré's observation, "Earlier autobiographies had described the self in its relation to others. Augustine's had entirely consisted of a dialogue with God and Teresa of Avila's *Life* of her relations with superiors and fellow sisters. Yet during the Enlightenment the relation with others ceased to be a dialogue and instead displayed the controlling presence of the author. Modern autobiographies became increasingly self-centered and self-conscious" (Dupré, *The Enlightenment and the Intellectual Foundations of Modern Culture* [New Haven: Yale University Press, 2004], 62). Similarly Francis Martin remarks, "The difference between Ignatius of Antioch and Jean Jacques Rousseau lies precisely in the way they view the presence of Christ to history" (Martin, "Historical Criticism and New Testament Teaching on the Imitation of Christ," *Anthropotes* 6 [1990]: 261–87, at 286).

22. Matthew L. Lamb, "Nature, History, and Redemption," in *Jesus Crucified and Risen*, ed. William P. Loewe and Vernon J. Gregson (Collegeville, Minn.: Liturgical Press, 1998), 117–32, at 126–27; cf. Francis Martin's excellent handling of this theme, indebted to Lamb, in Martin's "Revelation as Disclosure: Creation." Lamb is influenced by Bernard Lonergan, S.J.'s account of theology and history: see Lonergan, *The Way to Nicea: The Dialectical Development of Trinitarian Theology* (Philadelphia: Westminster Press, 1976).

23. In this regard see Louis Dupré, "The New Science of History," in his *The Enlightenment and the Intellectual Foundations of Modern Culture*, 187–228, esp. 188–89.

24. Hans W. Frei, *The Eclipse of Biblical Narrative: A Study in Eighteenth and Nineteenth Century Hermeneutics* (New Haven: Yale University Press, 1973), 89; see also Frei's "'Narrative' in Christian and Modern Reading," in *Theology and Dialogue*, ed. Bruce Marshall (Notre Dame: University of Notre Dame Press, 1990), 149–63. Frei identifies a key dynamic of modern exegesis, even if, in seeking a way out of the nominalist options, he finds himself denying the importance of extratextual reference. In an early essay, "Remarks in Connection with a Theological Proposal," Frei makes an intriguing distinction between "ontology" and "metaphysics"—the former adopting an anthropocentric approach to "being"—but he does not pursue this point and it does not appear in his important "Theological Reflections on the Accounts of Jesus' Death and Resurrection": for these two essays see his *Theology and Narrative*, ed. George Hunsinger and William C. Placher (Oxford: Oxford University Press, 1993), 26–93. For appreciative discussion of Frei's work, see Cyril O'Regan, "*De Doctrina christiana* and Modern Hermeneutics," in *De Doctrina Christiana: A Classic of Western Culture*, ed. Duane W. H. Arnold and Pamela Bright (Notre Dame: University of Notre Dame Press, 1995), 217–43; David Dawson, "Figural Reading and the Fashioning of Christian Identity in Boyarin, Auerbach and Frei," *Modern Theology* 14 (1998): 181–96. Nicholas Wolterstorff, in addition to showing the importance of Frei's *The Identity of Jesus Christ* (Eugene, Ore.: Wipf & Stock Publishers, 1997) for understanding (in both critical and appreciative ways) *The Eclipse of Biblical Narrative*, provides a crystal-clear summary of Frei's argument in the latter book: see Wolterstorff, *Divine Discourse: Philosophical Reflections on the Claim That God Speaks* (Cambridge: Cambridge University Press, 1995), 230–36. For a critical response to Frei's *The Eclipse of Biblical Narrative*, from a literary perspective, see Nicholas Boyle, "Revelation and Realism: Frei and Ricoeur," in *Sacred and Secular Scriptures: A Catholic Approach to Literature* (Notre Dame: University of Notre Dame Press, 2005), 58–75.

25. For a critical theological reading of Frei's position as depending too heavily on an intratextual understanding of literary realism, see Francis Watson, *Text, Church and World: Biblical Interpretation in Theological Perspective* (Grand Rapids, Mich.: Eerdmans, 1994), 20–29. Watson is responding to Frei's *The Eclipse of Biblical Narrative* as well as later work such as "The Encounter of Jesus with the German Academy," in Frei, *Types of Christian Theology*, ed. George Hunsinger and William C. Placher (New Haven: Yale University Press, 1992), 133–46. I cannot disagree with Watson's concern—expressed more polemically than I would put it—that "Frei's self-contained text is a privileged space in which one unsubstitutable individual (the reader) encounters another (Jesus). In its largely justified emphasis on the important tautology that narra-

tive is narrative, this hermeneutic of self-containment proves unable to achieve an adequate correlation of the text with the church and the world" (29). Watson criticizes George Lindbeck's work on the same grounds (135). For Lindbeck's work, see in particular *The Nature of Doctrine: Religion and Theology in a Postliberal Age* (Philadelphia: Westminster, 1984); "Scripture, Consensus, and Community," in *Biblical Interpretation in Crisis: The Ratzinger Conference on Bible and Church*, ed. Richard John Neuhaus (Grand Rapids, Mich.: Eerdmans, 1989), 74–101; as well as his description of his position during the roundtable discussion of his work, summarized by Paul Stallsworth in "The Story of an Encounter," in *Biblical Interpretation in Crisis*, 167–89; "Two Kinds of Ecumenism: Unitive and Interdenominational," *Gregorianum* 70 (1989): 647–60. Without escaping its element of truth, Lindbeck's writings demonstrate the severe limitations of Watson's critique. Lindbeck seeks continually to engage with real-world problems and concerns, far from seeking refuge in textual self-containment, and he affirms that "the stories of Jesus" narrate what "actually happened to an actual Palestinian Jew who died for our sins and was resurrected" (from the roundtable discussion as summarized by Paul Stallsworth in "The Story of an Encounter," in *Biblical Interpretation in Crisis*, 153). Yet Lindbeck's thesis in "Scripture, Consensus, and Community," reflecting *The Nature of Doctrine*, undeniably evinces the problem—however moderated elsewhere— that Watson observes. Lindbeck writes, "Stated compactly and technically, the issue which concerns us is the extent to which the Bible can be profitably read in our day as a canonically and narrationally unified and internally glossed (that is, self-referential and self-interpreting) whole centered on Jesus Christ, and telling the story of the dealings of the Triune God with his people and his world in ways which are typologically (though not, so at least the Reformers would say, allegorically) applicable to the present" (75). Cf. Rowan Williams's critique of Lindbeck in "The Judgement of the World," in Williams, *On Christian Theology* (Oxford: Blackwell, 2000), 29–43, which misreads Lindbeck's project as an attempt to set boundaries; Stephen Fowl's criticism of Watson's account of Frei and Lindbeck in *Engaging Scripture: A Model for Theological Interpretation* (Oxford: Blackwell, 1998), 23–24. For European response to Lindbeck's thought, see Marc Boss, Gilles Emery, O.P., and Pierre Gisel, eds., *Postlibéralisme? La théologie de George Lindbeck et sa réception* (Geneva: Labor et Fides, 2004), especially the two essays by Gilles Emery, O.P., "L'intérêt de théologiens catholiques pour la proposition postlibérale de George Lindbeck," 39–57; and "Thomas d'Aquin postliberal? La lecture de saint Thomas par George Lindbeck," 85–111 (English trans. in Emery, *Trinity, Church, and the Human Person*, 263–90).

26. For an attempt to pursue such a reading of the Bible for catechetical purposes, see Michael Dauphinais and Matthew Levering, *Holy People, Holy Land: A Theological Introduction to the Bible* (Grand Rapids, Mich.: Brazos Press,

2005). Reading the Bible as a whole, rather than merely each book separately, is ably defended by Trevor Hart, "Tradition, Authority, and a Christian Approach to the Bible as Scripture," in *Between Two Horizons: Spanning New Testament Studies and Systematic Theology*, ed. Joel B. Green and Max Turner (Grand Rapids, Mich.: Eerdmans, 2000), 183–204.

27. Joseph M. Levine, *The Autonomy of History: Truth and Method from Erasmus to Gibbon* (Chicago: University of Chicago Press, 1999): 25–26.

28. Ibid., 26. Levine observes, "The whole Erasmian hermeneutic depended (as he explained in his enlarged *Methodus*) on reading the biblical passages in their context, on gauging their moment and their milieu—the occasion, tone, intention, and order of each discourse for each speaker" (39). Of course, Erasmus's contributions are too extensive to be evaluated simply with respect to his understanding of history.

29. Ibid., 27. See also Anthony Grafton, "The Identities of History in Early Modern Europe: Prelude to a Study of the *Artes Historicae*," in *Historia: Empiricism and Erudition in Early Modern Europe*, ed. Gianna Pomata and Nancy G. Siraisi (Cambridge: MIT Press, 2005), 41–72. Grafton points out that "Jean Bodin [1536–90] argued, influentially, that one should distinguish *historia humana* from *historia naturalis* and *historia divina*" (51). Spatiotemporal data governed the writing of *historia humana* and *historia naturalis*. Grafton states that early modern "[w]riters on the *ars historica* emphasized the resemblance between civil history and other forms of empirical knowledge—for example, by stressing that history had a strong visual component, best mastered by studying chronological tables, which revealed the course of history at a glimpse, and maps, which made it possible to know 'the sites and distances of the kingdoms and places in which events are said to have taken place'" (51–52). Grafton remarks that in contrast to Jean Bodin, Tommaso Campanella (1568–1639), a Dominican who spent a total of twenty-seven years in prison on charges of teaching naturalistic doctrine, "strongly emphasized the identity of all forms of *historia*, divine, natural, or human, as narratives that provided just the facts without offering causal explanations" (52). For further background, see John M. Headley, *Tommaso Campanella and the Transformation of the World* (Princeton: Princeton University Press, 1997); cf. Ernst Cassirer's classic *The Individual and the Cosmos in Renaissance Philosophy*, trans. Mario Domandi (1927; New York: Harper & Row, 1964). In his introduction, Domandi summarizes what for us is Cassirer's key insight: "Cassirer demonstrates carefully how Renaissance thinkers arrived at their vision of the orderliness of nature—an orderliness reducible to and definable through mathematical principles. He shows how the hierarchical, Neo-Platonic view of the cosmos, with its qualitative differences between the various strata that constitute the spiritual and physical universe, gave way to the ideas of the homogeneity of nature and the essential similarity of historical phenomena" (viii).

30. Cf. Claus Westermann, "The Old Testament's Understanding of History in Relation to That of the Enlightenment," in *Understanding the Word: Essays in Honor of Bernhard W. Anderson*, ed. James T. Butler, Edgar W. Conrad, and Ben C. Ollenburger (Sheffield: JSOT Press, 1985), 207–19. Westermann emphasizes that "the Bible is not in agreement with [the Enlightenment conception of] *history*, because the latter does not recognize the beginning or the end of humankind" (216). Biblical "history," in other words, is teleological (cf. 217).

31. John Webster, *Holy Scripture: A Dogmatic Sketch* (Cambridge: Cambridge University Press, 2003), 19–20; see also his forthcoming essay calling for a metaphysics adequate to biblical exegesis. Among early modern philosophers, Giambattista Vico is well known for his effort to renew the understanding of history by reclaiming a form of "providence." His thought has therefore generated considerable contemporary interest as postmodern thinkers have come to recognize that there is nothing to unite the modern linear-historical continuum. Karl Löwith remarks, "His leading idea is neither the progression toward fulfilment nor the cosmic cycle of a merely natural growth and decay, but a historicocyclic progression from *corso* to *ricorso* in which the cycle itself has providential significance by being an ultimate remedy for man's corrupted nature. Vico's perspective is still a theological one, but the means of providence and salvation are in themselves historiconatural ones. History as seen by Vico has a prehistoric beginning but no end and fulfilment, and yet it is ruled by providence for the sake of mankind" (Löwith, *Meaning in History* [Chicago: University of Chicago Press, 1949], 135). For Löwith Vico's approach "is precisely on the border line of the critical transition from theology to the philosophy of history and, therefore, deeply ambiguous" (ibid.). On Vico and history, see also Robert Miner, *Vico, Genealogist of Modernity* (Notre Dame: University of Notre Dame Press, 2002); John Milbank, *The Religious Dimension of the Thought of Giambattista Vico*, pt. 2, *Language, Law, and History* (Lewiston, N.Y.: Edwin Mellen Press, 1992); Levine, *The Autonomy of History*, chap. 6: "Giambattista Vico and the Quarrel between the Ancients and the Moderns." Löwith's book, which compares a variety of historical paradigms from the Bible through Jacob Burckhardt, retains its value. As Löwith observes in his introduction, "We are neither ancient ancients nor ancient Christians, but moderns—that is, a more or less inconsistent compound of both traditions. The Greek historians wrote pragmatic history centered around a great political event; the Church Fathers developed from Hebrew prophecy and Christian eschatology a theology of history focused on the supra-historical events of creation, incarnation, and consummation; the moderns elaborate a philosophy of history by secularizing theological principles and applying them to an ever increasing number of empirical facts" (19). This secularization cannot be understood apart from the fourteenth-century shift.

32. Lamb, "Nature, History, and Redemption," 129–30. For a similar view on biblical exegesis, see Jean-Luc Marion, *God without Being: Hors-Texte*, trans. Thomas A. Carlson (1982; Chicago: University of Chicago Press, 1991), 155. Cf. Ben Meyer's observation, following Gadamer, that "C. S. Lewis has Screwtape instruct Wormwood, 'The Historical Point of View, put briefly, means that when a learned man is presented with any statement in an ancient author, the one question he never asks is whether it is true'" (Meyer, *Reality and Illusion in New Testament Scholarship: A Primer in Critical Realist Hermeneutics* [Collegeville, Minn.: Liturgical Press, 1994], 95).

33. Joseph Cardinal Ratzinger, preface to the Pontifical Biblical Commission's *The Interpretation of the Bible in the Church*, trans. John Kilgallen and Brendan Byrne (Boston: St. Paul's Books & Media, 1993), 27–29, at 29. Ratzinger similarly observes in the roundtable discussion summarized by Paul Stallsworth in *Biblical Interpretation in Crisis*: "'For the medieval and for the patristic theory of exegesis there is an interpenetration of the dimension of factum and the dimension of Christology, moral life, and eschatology. Substantially, the first dimension is the indispensable dimension of the facticity of the Christian event. The three others correspond to faith, charity, and hope. Thus the facticity of the text is open to the other three dimensions—to the Christological fact and presence, to the application and realization of the grace of Christ in our charity life, and to the eschatological tension in the hope of the complete reign of God'" (155).

34. Cf. for its influence on Ratzinger, as well as for its value in itself, Hans Urs von Balthasar, *A Theology of History* (New York: Sheed & Ward, 1963).

35. Thus the issue cannot be reduced, as the Pontifical Biblical Commission does in *The Interpretation of the Bible in the Church*, to "synchronic" versus "diachronic" readings: see *The Interpretation of the Bible in the Church*, 41–42, 133–34. Granted that historical-critical research has greatly contributed to our diachronic understanding of Scripture, one should point out that the opposition "synchronic/diachronic" does not adequately express the participatory aspect of history: the terms denote either a uniformity or a diversity, but not the participatory aspect (analogy) that moves beyond univocity on the one hand and equivocity on the other. This nominalist inheritance goes unrecognized in *The Interpretation of the Bible in the Church*, which not unimportantly begins its narrative of the development of the historical-critical method, after a brief glance at the Fathers, with the Renaissance (35). The medieval period is entirely passed over, and the document confidently affirms, "For a long time now scholars have ceased combining the method with a philosophical system" (41; cf. 76–80 for discussion of contemporary philosophical hermeneutics). For an exposition of *The Interpretation of the Bible in the Church*, see Peter S. Williamson, *Catholic Principles for Interpreting Scripture: A Study of the Pontifical Biblical Commission's* The Interpretation of the Bible in the Church (Rome: Edi-

trice Pontificio Istituto Biblico, 2001), which includes a preface by the secretary of the Commission, Albert Vanhoye, S.J.; idem, "Catholic Principles for Interpreting Scripture," *Catholic Biblical Quarterly* 65 (2003): 327–49, which summarizes his book; idem, "Catholicism and the Bible: An Interview with Albert Vanhoye," *First Things* 74 (June/July 1997): 35–40. For discussion of *The Interpretation of the Bible in the Church* in light of a 1999 Vatican symposium on the same theme, see Donath Hercsik, S.J., "Das Wort Gottes in der nachkonziliaren Kirche und Theologie," *Gregorianum* 86 (2005): 135–62. See also Paul Blowers, Jon D. Levenson, and Robert Wilken, "Interpreting the Bible: Three Views," *First Things* 45 (August/September 1994): 40–46; Avery Dulles, S.J., "The Interpretation of the Bible in the Church: A Theological Appraisal," in *Kirche sein: nachkonziliare Theologie im Dienst der Kirchenreform*, ed. W. Geerlings and M. Seckler (Freiburg: Herder, 1994); Eduardo Pérez-Cotapos Larraín, "El valor hermenéutico de la eclesialidad para la interpretación de la Sagrada Escritura," *Teología y Vida* 37 (1996): 169–85; as well as Christopher Rowland's critique, in passing, of the Pontifical Biblical Commission's reliance on historical-critical methods in "An Open Letter to Francis Watson on *Text, Church and World*," *Scottish Journal of Theology* 48 (1995): 508, and the similar, but more extensive, critique found in Lewis Ayres and Stephen E. Fowl, "(Mis)reading the Face of God: *The Interpretation of the Bible in the Church*," *Theological Studies* 60 (1999): 513–28. Blowers hails *The Interpretation of the Bible in the Church* for making clear that "the Church is still the foundational context for expounding Scripture and the only promising medium for actualizing the Word of God through new 'retellings' *(relectures)* of the biblical story" (40) and for balancing "diachronic" and "synchronic" interpretation (41), and Wilken largely agrees, while adding his own (welcome) gloss that "[t]he spiritual understanding of the Bible is not a relic from the Middle Ages, a precritical expedient to make do until the advent of historical science. It is the distinctively Christian way of interpreting the Bible" (46). For his part, Levenson rightly warns that the document does not adequately address Joseph Ratzinger's concern in his preface that the academy's practice of the allegedly neutral historical-critical method, when given primacy, limits the meaning of biblical texts to the human past and makes impossible privileging theologically normative texts (42–43). Levenson also notes that the document applies historical-critical methodology more rigorously to the Old Testament than the New. One might also see a similar document of the Pontifical Biblical Commission, "Bible et christologie" (1984), in Joseph Fitzmyer, S.J., *Scripture and Christology: A Statement of the Biblical Commission with a Commentary* (New York: Paulist Press, 1986).

36. Webster, *Holy Scripture: A Dogmatic Sketch*, 21; cf. Gilles Emery, O.P., *La Trinité créatrice* (Paris: Vrin, 1995); idem, "The Personal Mode of Trinitarian Action in Saint Thomas Aquinas," trans. Matthew Levering, *Thomist* 69 (2005): 31–77. For Webster, admittedly, the answer seems to be avoiding metaphysical

discourse as much as possible, and instead substituting explicitly theological language. He writes, "This frankly dualistic framework can only be broken by replacing the monistic and monergistic idea of divine causality with an understanding of God's continuing free presence and relation to the creation through the risen Son in the Spirit's power" (21). No doubt this is the case, but the point is that if this Trinitarian "free presence and relation to the creation" is understood in nominalist categories, then distortion inevitably results, no matter how much theological language is imported.

37. David Bentley Hart, *The Doors of the Sea: Where Was God in the Tsunami?* (Grand Rapids, Mich.: Eerdmans, 2005), 72–73.

38. Hart, *The Beauty of the Infinite: The Aesthetics of Christian Truth* (Grand Rapids, Mich.: Eerdmans, 2003), 224; cf. his "The Offering of Names: Metaphysics, Nihilism, and Analogy," in *Reason and the Reasons of Faith*, ed. Paul J. Griffiths and Reinhard Hütter (New York: T. & T. Clark, 2005), 255–91. Commenting on a Heideggerian study, Hart notes, "To think of God as a supreme being among lesser beings in the fashion Scharlemann has in mind requires a profoundly modern concept of what beings are: objective, unitary instantiations, not 'participating' in being but standing forth as punctiliar substances, devoid of analogical tension within themselves, and as discrete 'entities' embraced within the empty and abstract category of being or—more properly—existence" (*The Beauty of the Infinite*, 230).

39. Pickstock, "Duns Scotus: His Historical and Contemporary Significance," 548. Thus whereas Frei locates the problem in the displacement of the "narrative meaning" by a foundationalist/correlationist search for facts outside the narrative (see also George Lindbeck, "Scripture, Consensus, and Community," in *Biblical Interpretation in Crisis: The Ratzinger Conference on Bible and Church*, 82–86), I suggest—indebted to numerous other scholars—that the problem has its roots in the nominalist rejection of participation, which produced an understanding of time and history that could not sustain a narrative encompassing the past, present, and future modes of one reality. In "Scripture, Consensus, and Community," Lindbeck begins his account of the rise of historical-critical biblical scholarship, as most do, with the sixteenth century (84). Lindbeck does not view historical-critical scholarship as lacking in good fruits (see 86): he advocates, as do I, a mode of exegesis that recovers a deeper meaning of "history" without thereby throwing out historical-critical exegesis. As Lindbeck puts it, the key difficulty in exegesis as presently constituted (by the nominalist inheritance, I would add) is that "[t]here seems to be no exegetical bridge between past and present. This gap, much more than questions about inerrancy or inspiration, is the heart of the current crisis of scriptural authority and the source of the conflict of interpretations" (86). Similarly, Lindbeck is fully aware that all interpretation requires philosophical resources (86–87).

40. In suggesting that the gospels are "narrated history," Francis Watson proposes, following Paul Ricoeur, that in order to describe a "historically particular 'limit-experience'" an author would be justified in going outside the bounds of historiography and employing metaphorical/fictive description, without thereby destroying the historical caliber and extratextual reference of the account (Francis Watson, *Text and Truth: Redefining Biblical Theology* [Grand Rapids, Mich.: Eerdmans, 1997], 63). Watson draws specifically on Ricoeur's *Time and Narrative*, 3 vols. (Chicago: University of Chicago Press, 1984–1988); cf. the reflections in Kevin J. Vanhoozer, *Biblical Narrative in the Philosophy of Paul Ricoeur: A Study in Hermeneutics and Theology* (Cambridge: Cambridge University Press, 1990). Like Ricoeur (and Troeltsch whose attempt is superbly critiqued by Ricoeur), Watson is attempting to get away from history as conceived in terms of the natural sciences, with general laws that make possible "a comprehensive and totalizing understanding of all phenomena in the human sphere" (58). Yet as Matthew Lamb has noted, Ricoeur fails in *Time and Narrative* to grasp the participatory metaphysics of Augustine's understanding of time and eternity (see Lamb, "The Resurrection and Christian Identity as *Conversatio Dei*," *Concilium* 249 [1993]: 112–23, at 119). Watson's account, while valuable in many ways, therefore remains unsatisfying. If one rejects the model of the natural sciences without adverting to a participatory metaphysics, one is ultimately left with metaphorical rather than analogical *doctrina* (see Lamb, "Eternity and Time," 207). One can see the difficulties in Ricoeur's understanding of time in the appropriation of Franz Rosenzweig found in Ricoeur's wonderfully suggestive essay "Thinking Creation," in André LaCocque and Paul Ricoeur, *Thinking Biblically: Exegetical and Hermeneutical Studies*, trans. David Pellauer (Chicago: University of Chicago Press, 1998), 31–67, where Ricoeur argues that Creation, Revelation, and Redemption possess a "profound temporality" that is "irreducible to any chronology or to any linear representation. If it were to be a question of a time of succession, we would have to say that Creation, Revelation, and Redemption do not succeed one another along the same line. Rather it is a matter of a sequence of strata. Redemption—utopia, if one prefers—constitutes the highest level; Revelation, the middle level; and Creation the lowest level" (66–67). Although Ricoeur is close to succeeding in moving beyond the strictly linear continuum, his thought is finally not participatory enough. In part this is due to the influence of Heidegger, whose complex influence on Ricoeur's thought—Ricoeur both rejects Heidegger's criticism of Aquinas's metaphysics of being, and grants the necessity after Heidegger of rejecting that metaphysics in favor of a phenomenology of love (Marion)—appears in Ricoeur's "From Interpretation to Translation," in *Thinking Biblically*, 331–61; this essay, which explores the history of interpretation of Exodus 3:14, is less Heideggerian than Ricoeur's earlier work. For an example of the latter, see Alasdair MacIntyre and

Paul Ricoeur, *The Religious Significance of Atheism* (New York: Columbia University Press, 1969).

41. The Revised Standard Version, which I have quoted here, ends the discourse of John the Baptist at verse 30, but acknowledges that this decision is controverted. Aquinas considers the whole passage to belong to the discourse of John the Baptist.

42. Cf. Frei, *The Eclipse of Biblical Narrative*, 127–30, 152–54, and elsewhere. What Paul M. Blowers says of Irenaeus's theology would apply to Aquinas as well: "the presupposition of Irenaeus's whole theology of revelation is that the church here and now, in its current witness, dwells in one and the same narrative world with the scriptural witnesses themselves, 'prophets and apostles.' There is a coherent trinitarian and christocentric perspective in 'Scripture' (broadly speaking), discerned and traditioned by the church, that sets the stage in advance for what a 'faithful' hearing and interpretative performance of it will be" (Blowers, "The *Regula Fidei* and the Narrative Character of Early Christian Faith," *Pro Ecclesia* 6 [1997]: 199–228, at 210). Blowers is drawing on two articles by Denis Farkasfalvy, O. Cist., "'Prophets and Apostles': The Conjunction of the Two Terms before Irenaeus," in *Texts and Testaments: Critical Essays on the Bible and Early Church*, ed. W. Eugene March (San Antonio: Trinity University Press, 1980), 109–34; and "Theology of Scripture in St. Irenaeus," *Revue Bénédictine* 78 (1968): 319–33. Blowers gives a useful survey of scholarly interpretation of the "Rule of Faith" since the late nineteenth century.

43. The neo-Platonic aspects of Aquinas's participatory metaphysics, as intrinsic to his reading of Scripture, have been emphasized in Wayne Hankey, "Aquinas, Pseudo-Denys, Proclus and Isaiah VI.6," *Archives d'histoire doctrinale et littéraire du Moyen Âge* 64 (1997): 59–93. On Aquinas's metaphysical appropriation of Scripture, see Waclaw Swierzawski, "God and the Mystery of His Wisdom in the Pauline Commentaries of Saint Thomas Aquinas," *Divus Thomas* 74 (1971): 466–500.

44. Rather than identify in the endnotes the citations from Aquinas's *Commentary on John*, I place the paragraph number from the Marietti edition in parentheses after each quotation. For the English translation of Aquinas's commentary on John 3:27–36, see Aquinas, *Commentary on the Gospel of St. John*, trans. James A. Weisheipl, O.P., and Fabian R. Larcher, O.P., pt. I (Albany, N.Y.: Magi Books, 1980): chap. 3, lectures 5–6, pp. 211–25.

45. As the Fathers recognized as well; cf. J. P. Williams, "The Incarnational Apophasis of Maximus the Confessor," *Studia Patristica* 37 (2001): 631–35.

46. On the theological role in Aquinas's biblical commentaries of the "divisio textus," see John F. Boyle, "The Theological Character of the Scholastic 'Division of the Text' with Particular Reference to the Commentaries of Saint Thomas Aquinas," in *With Reverence for the Word: Medieval Scriptural Exegesis in*

Judaism, Christianity, and Islam, ed. Jane Dammen McAuliffe, Barry D. Walfish, and Joseph W. Goering (Oxford: Oxford University Press, 2003), 276–83; idem, "Authorial Intention and the *Divisio textus*," in Dauphinais and Levering, *Reading John with St. Thomas Aquinas*, 3–8.

47. Pickstock, "Duns Scotus: His Historical and Contemporary Significance," 548.

48. For a response to criticism of John's Gospel as "dualistic" or locked in the conflict between wrath and love, see Miroslav Volf, "Johannine Dualism and Contemporary Pluralism," *Modern Theology* 21 (2005): 189–217.

49. This is the concept of history that Alan Richardson has in mind in "The Rise of Modern Biblical Scholarship and the Authority of the Bible," in *The Cambridge History of the Bible: The West from the Reformation to the Present Day*, vol. 3, ed. S. L. Greenslade (Cambridge: Cambridge University Press, 1963). He writes, "It is not difficult to see that the rise of modern biblical scholarship must also have necessitated the abandonment of traditional methods of scriptural exegesis and the development of new ones. . . . In other words, the significance of the fact that the Christian revelation was a *historical* revelation was not yet properly understood. If the biblical revelation be historical, as the nineteenth century came to understand history, then a new type of exegesis will be required to elucidate the Scriptures, namely one which is based upon sound historical scholarship" (300).

50. Cf. Mary Healy, "Behind, in Front of . . . or Through the Text? The Christological Analogy and the Lost World of Biblical Truth," in *"Behind" the Text: History and Biblical Interpretation*, ed. Craig Bartholomew et al. (Grand Rapids, Mich.: Zondervan, 2003), 187.

51. Klyne R. Snodgrass voices a common concern at this stage: what happens if the "ongoing Church" is corrupted? Commenting on the exegesis of Jesus' parables, Snodgrass observes that "allegorizing is no legitimate means of interpretation. It obfuscates the message of Jesus and replaces it with the teaching of the church. Such an interpretive procedure assumes that one knows the truth before reading a text, and then finds the truth paralleled by the text being read—even if the text is about another subject" (Snodgrass, "From Allegorizing to Allegorizing: A History of the Interpretation of the Parables of Jesus," in *The Challenge of Jesus' Parables*, ed. Richard N. Longenecker [Grand Rapids, Mich.: Eerdmans, 2000], 3–29, at 5). While observing that even Luther and Calvin sometimes fell into allegory, Snodgrass takes Augustine as his primary example: "The best-known example of such theological allegorization is Augustine's interpretation of the Parable of the Good Samaritan (Luke 10:30–37), where virtually every item is given a theological significance: (1) the man is Adam; (2) Jerusalem is the heavenly city; (3) Jericho is the moon, which stands for our mortality; (4) the robbers are the devil and his angels, who strip the man of his immortality and beat him by persuading him to sin; (5) the

priest and Levite are the priesthood and the ministry of the Old Testament; (6) the good Samaritan is Christ; (7) the binding of the wounds is the restraint of sin; (8) the oil and wine are the comfort of hope and the encouragement to work; (9) the donkey is the incarnation; (10) the inn is the church; (11) the next day is after the resurrection of Christ; (12) the innkeeper is the apostle Paul; and (13) the two denarii are the two commandments of love, or the promise of this life and that which is to come (summary from *Quaestiones Evangeliorum* 2.19)" (4). Snodgrass finds the same problem in Aquinas: "for example, Thomas Aquinas took God's statement of Gen 1:3, 'Let there be light,' to refer literally to creation, but also allegorically to mean 'Let Christ be born in the church,' ethically to mean 'May we be illumined in mind and inflamed in heart through Christ,' and with regard to heaven to mean 'May we be conducted to glory through Christ' (see his *Commentary on the Epistle to the Galatians* 4:7)" (4). The key issue is the assumption, in Snodgrass's words, "that one knows the truth before reading a text," and that this (ecclesial) truth then colors and distorts one's reading of the biblical text. At stake is whether the biblical text can legitimately be seen as having more than one accessible dimension (the linear-historical one), and whether the reduction of Scripture to the linear-historical dimension does not itself distort, even historically, the exegesis of biblical texts.

52. Robert Jenson, "Scripture's Authority in the Church," in *The Art of Reading Scripture*, ed. Ellen F. Davis and Richard B. Hays (Grand Rapids, Mich.: Eerdmans), 35.

53. Cf. Matthew L. Lamb, "The Resurrection and Christian Identity as *Conversatio Dei*," *Concilium* 249 (1993): 112–23.

TWO
From Aquinas to Raymond Brown

1. See Henri de Lubac, S.J., *Exégèse médiévale: Les quatre sens de l'Écriture*, Seconde Partie, II (Paris: Aubier, 1962). De Lubac sees the fourteenth and fifteenth centuries, in general, as a period of profound exegetical "decadence" (369 f.). By the sixteenth century, de Lubac shows, university theologians viewed Scripture largely through lists of authorities (385). The fact that the shift predates the crisis of the Reformation is highly important, although I do not mean to deny the impact of the post-Reformation "wars of religion" on hastening the demise of the patristic-medieval understanding of historical reality. David Yeago argues in this vein that "historical-critical biblical scholarship, as it exists today, is not simply a Protestant phenomenon, but a synthesis of Protestant motifs with something else, with the *secularism* that arose in the seventeenth and eighteenth centuries as a reaction to a lamentable *joint* 'achievement'

of Catholics and Protestants, the physical and moral devastation of Europe by the wars of religion. Secularism, as John Milbank and others have described it, was the cultural and political construction of a world in which Christianity was defined as 'religion,' inward and private, and thus banished from the public realm, where it was deemed to have proven itself incurably destructive. Such a project could not succeed without breaking down the precritical tradition of scriptural exegesis in which Scripture was read, in Ephraim Radner's terms, as 'the providential exponent of the world's divine order.'" See Yeago, "Re-Entering the Scriptural World," *Nova et Vetera* 4 (2006): 159–71, at 167, citing Ephraim Radner, *Hope among the Fragments: The Broken Church and its Engagement with Scripture* (Grand Rapids, Mich.: Brazos, 2004), 103.

2. The generally "conservative" character of exegetical traditions, including the tradition of historical-critical interpretation (as well as the interpretive traditions inaugurated by the Reformers, which I do not have space to treat in this chapter), lies behind Luke Timothy Johnson's perceptive remark, "The most imaginative and original and important biblical interpretations of Scripture in Christianity's first 1,500 years . . . did not take place in biblical commentaries, but in other literary and liturgical expressions. Biblical commentaries tended to have an explanatory function. In them, the literal sense of Scripture was explicated. Commentaries then, as now, quickly became encyclopedic, as one generation borrowed lexical and grammatical and historical information from another. Commentaries rarely had anything original to say. This is one reason why modern scholars find so little of interest in ancient interpretation. They assume that the commentary is where interpretation is to be found. But it is not. The most vibrant forms of interpretation in antiquity occur when the Scripture is *used* to explicate the Christian life. The way such uses bear within them an implicit understanding also of the biblical text requires careful analysis" (Johnson, "Rejoining a Long Conversation," in Luke Timothy Johnson and William S. Kurz, S.J., *The Future of Catholic Biblical Scholarship: A Constructive Conversation* [Grand Rapids, Mich.: Eerdmans, 2002], 45).

3. Cf. Michael Cahill's proposal that the history of biblical exegesis should play a significant role in biblical exegesis: Cahill, "The History of Exegesis and Our Theological Future," *Theological Studies* 61 (2000): 332–47. On different, more theological grounds Lewis Ayres also argues for the exegetical importance of the history of exegesis: see Ayres, "On the Practice and Teaching of Christian Doctrine," *Gregorianum* 80 (1999): 65f. Ayres states, "Becoming a good reader of Scripture will in part involve developing attention to these persistent patterns as they have arisen in the body of Christ. Appropriate attention to Scripture as that which identifies Christ thus necessarily involves attention to the providentially ordered patterns of figuration of Scripture which have arisen through the course of Christian history as part of revealing and achieving the identity of Christ indicated by Scripture" (72). See

also the Blackwell Bible Commentaries series, which pays significant attention to the entire history of exegesis.

4. Although the Reformers commented on the Bible, within later Protestant ecclesial traditions the split between biblical scholarship and theology reemerged. I should note that this chapter does not treat the history of Protestant or Eastern Orthodox exegesis, since to do so would require another book. Yet, I hope that my effort briefly to present Catholic biblical exegesis from the fourteenth to the twentieth centuries assists ecumenical dialogue, since Protestants and Catholics (and to a lesser degree Eastern Orthodox) are currently struggling with the dilemma of how to reincarnate a theological exegesis. For exploration of the Protestant tradition of exegesis during this time period, see Brevard S. Childs, *The Struggle to Understand Isaiah as Christian Scripture* (Grand Rapids, Mich.: Eerdmans, 2004), 148–298; cf. such studies as Hans Frei, *The Eclipse of Biblical Narrative: A Study in Eighteenth and Nineteenth Century Hermeneutics* (New Haven: Yale University Press, 1973); Richard Burnett, "John Calvin and the *Sensus Literalis*," *Scottish Journal of Theology* 57 (2004): 1–13. After his chapters on Aquinas and Nicholas of Lyra, Childs focuses entirely on Protestant exegetes from the sixteenth to the twentieth centuries. For an Eastern Orthodox approach to exegesis similar to the approach advocated in this book, see Stanley Samuel Harakas, "Doing Theology Today: An Orthodox and Evangelical Dialogue on Theological Method," *Pro Ecclesia* 11 (2002): 435–62. See also Georges Florovsky, *Bible, Church, Tradition: An Eastern Orthodox View* (Belmont, Mass.: Nordland Publishing Co., 1972); Thomas Hopko, "The Church, the Bible, and Dogmatic Theology," in *Reclaiming the Bible for the Church*, ed. Carl Braaten and Robert Jenson (Grand Rapids, Mich.: Eerdmans, 1995), 107–18. After noting the creed's scriptural language, Florovsky writes, "The deposits are alive—*depositum juvenescens*, to use the phrase of St. Irenaeus. The creed is not a relic of the past, but rather the 'sword of the Spirit'" (12). It is this sense of how the realities depicted in Scripture are present and active that informs participatory history, a history that is never strictly linear but is instead always joined—preeminently in the Church as the Body of Christ, the center of history—to all other times and places by participation in the triune God's creative and redemptive action.

5. Hans Urs von Balthasar, *Theo-Drama: Theological Dramatic Theory*, vol. 4, *The Action*, trans. Graham Harrison (German, 1980; San Francisco: Ignatius Press, 1994), 458. Von Balthasar, following Gustav Siewerth, adds that "the *ratio*, abandoning all restraint, thinks itself empowered and authorized to plumb the ultimate mysteries of God. In the end, this leads to Hegel's God, who is without all mystery: behold the door to atheism" (ibid.). Von Balthasar does not entirely leave Aquinas without blame. He agrees with Louis Bouyer that "High Scholasticism had made the mistake of thinking that it had to give an appropriate answer to every inquisitive question, however untheological" (ibid.).

6. In his valuable "The Bible in the Fourteenth Century: Some Observations," *Church History* 54 (1985): 176–87, William J. Courtenay points out that "[u]niversity scholars again began to publish biblical commentaries in the third quarter of the fourteenth century," with John Wyclif's work being a turning point. Other than Jean Gerson, however, the scholars he names are of lesser note. For further discussion see, e.g., Jacques Verger, "L'exégèse de l'Université," in *Le moyen âge et la Bible*, ed. Pierre Riché and Guy Lobrichon (Paris: Beauchesne, 1984), 199–232, at 226. A. J. Minnis has shown that Ockham's view of biblical interpretation can to some degree be examined through Ockham's *Breviloquium de principatu tyrannico super divina et humana* (English trans. John Kilcullen), which Ockham wrote after his excommunication in 1328 in order to criticize Pope Boniface VIII's claim in the papal bull *Unam sanctam* (1302) to authority over the secular realm. Much of the debate over this bull centered on the interpretation of two biblical passages: "See, here are two swords" (Lk 22:38) and "God made two great lights, a larger one to rule the day and a lesser one the night" (Gen 1:16). While others, including Dante Alighieri, Marsilius of Padua, and John of Paris, criticized the popes' claim, Ockham's *Breviloquium* devalues allegorical reading in a way that goes beyond what these others were prepared to do. See Minnis, "Material Swords and Literal Lights: The Status of Allegory in William of Ockham's *Breviloquium* on Papal Power," in *With Reverence for the Word: Medieval Scriptural Exegesis in Judaism, Christianity, and Islam*, ed. Jane Dammen McAuliffe, Barry D. Walfish, and Joseph W. Goering (Oxford: Oxford University Press, 2003), 292–308. For similar "occasional" writings by Ockham, in which biblical quotations are relatively frequent, see the material translated by John Kilcullen in William of Ockham, *A Letter to the Friars Minor and Other Writings*, ed. Arthur Stephen McGrade and John Kilcullen (Cambridge: Cambridge University Press, 1995).

7. Meister Eckhart, *Die Deutschen und Lateinischen Werke*, ed. Josef Quint, Dritter Band: *Expositio Sancti Evangelii secundum Iohannem*, ed. Karl Christ, Bruno Deder, Joseph Rodj, Heribert Fischer, and Albert Zimmermann (Stuttgart: W. Kohlhammer Verlag, 1953), 302–14. For a fuller treatment of Eckhart's theology and exegesis, see Bernard McGinn, *The Mystical Thought of Meister Eckhart: The Man from Whom God Hid Nothing* (New York: Herder & Herder, 2003).

8. On the *Glossa Ordinaria*, cf. M. T. Gibson, "The Place of the *Glossa ordinaria* in Medieval Exegesis," in *Ad Litteram: Authoritative Texts and Their Medieval Readers*, ed. Mark Jordan and Kent Emery Jr. (Notre Dame: University of Notre Dame Press, 1992), 5–27. Gibson argues that the *Glossa Ordinaria*, completed in the twelfth century, "is the junction between traditional patristic exegesis and modern scholastic method. It is the side of the hinge that is fixed to the doorpost, while scholastic exegesis swings with the door. In that capacity, the *Glossa ordinaria* remained available and consulted, but

essentially unchanged, until well into the fifteenth century. Only the ambitions of the early printers and the new demands of Reformation controversy radically altered first the format and then the content of the *Glossa ordinaria*" (21).

9. For the argument that Nicholas of Lyra's commentaries owe a debt to his nominalist contemporaries, see James Samuel Preus, *From Shadow to Promise: Old Testament Interpretation from Augustine to the Young Luther* (Cambridge: Harvard University Press, 1969), 62 ff. For Joachim of Fiore's influence on some aspects of Nicholas of Lyra's biblical interpretation, see Henri de Lubac, S.J., *Exégèse médiévale: Les quatre sens de l'Écriture*, Seconde Partie, II (Paris: Aubier, 1962), 344 ff., which focuses on Nicholas's interpretation of the Book of Revelation. For Nicholas's relationship to Scotus, see also the brief remarks in Edward Synan, "The Four 'Senses' and Four Exegetes," in *With Reverence for the Word: Medieval Scriptural Exegesis in Judaism, Christianity, and Islam*, ed. Jane Dammen McAuliffe, Barry D. Walfish, and Joseph W. Goering (Oxford: Oxford University Press, 2003), 225–36, at 230. Corrine Patton in contrast observes regarding Nicholas's biblical commentaries that his "philosophical interpretations often align with those of Aquinas, while his exegetical principles closely follow the Victorine school" (Patton, introduction to "Selections from Nicholas of Lyra's *Commentary on Exodus*, in *The Theological Interpretation of Scripture: Classic and Contemporary Readings*, ed. Stephen E. Fowl [Oxford: Blackwell, 1997], 115). Patton explores Nicholas's view of what books belong in the Old Testament canon in her "Canon and Tradition: The Limits of the Old Testament in Scholastic Discussion," in *Theological Exegesis*, ed. Christopher Seitz and Kathryn Greene-McCreight (Grand Rapids, Mich.: Eerdmans, 1999), 75–95. See also Denys Turner's discussion of Nicholas's "pedantic historicism"—although Turner holds that Nicholas is following Aquinas—as regards the Song of Songs: Turner, "Metaphor, Poetry and Allegory: Erotic Love in the *Sermons on the Song of Songs* of Bernard of Clairvaux," in *Reading Texts, Seeking Wisdom*, ed. David F. Ford and Graham Stanton (Grand Rapids, Mich.: Eerdmans, 2003), 202–16.

10. *Bibliorum Sacrorum Tomus Quintus cum Glossa Ordinaria, & Nicolai Lyrani expositionibus, literali & morali: Additionibus insuper & Replicis* (Lugduni: 1545), 196–97.

11. Terence O'Reilly, introduction to *Spiritual Writings* by Denis the Carthusian, trans. Íde M. Ní Riain (Dublin: Four Courts Press, 2004), ix.

12. Ibid., x.

13. Denys Turner, *The Darkness of God: Negativity in Christian Mysticism* (Cambridge: Cambridge University Press, 1995), 224–25, quoted in O'Reilly, "Introduction," xi. Romanus Cessario, O.P. states that Denys the Carthusian "combined a comprehensive treatment of Aquinas's theology with a retrieval of biblical science and patristic learning, modeling the kind of return-to-the-sources theology that would revitalize Thomism at other moments in its his-

tory" (Cessario, *A Short History of Thomism* [Washington, D.C.: Catholic University of America Press, 2005], 63).

14. Dionysius the Carthusian, *Opera Omnia*, ed. by the Carthusian Order with the support of Pope Leo XIII, *In Lucam (X–XXI), et Joannem* (Monstolii: Typis Cartusiae S. M. de Pratis, 1901), 339–44.

15. As the biblical scholar James D. G. Dunn observes, "The Renaissance gave us two lasting criteria for appropriate handling of historical texts: historical philology and textual criticism" (Dunn, "Criteria for a Wise Reading of a Biblical Text," in *Reading Texts, Seeking Wisdom: Scripture and Theology*, ed. David F. Ford and Graham Stanton [Grand Rapids, Mich.: Eerdmans, 2003], 38–52, at 38). Dunn explains, quoting a Petrarch scholar, "'This meant that the languages of antiquity had to be studied as the ancients had used them and not as vehicles for carrying modern thoughts.' It would be a mistake to treat this development lightly, or to assume that it is so obvious that it requires no emphasis. On the contrary, its absolutely fundamental character for any and all reading of biblical texts should always provide one of the beginning points for the hermeneutical task" (39). Noting that without the Renaissance scholars and their successors the texts would not have been read in this way, Dunn argues that only thereby was the real meaning of the Scriptures uncovered: "in order to convey meaning they must be read within the context of the language usage of their time. For Schleiermacher, the founder of modern hermeneutics, this was the 'first canon' of interpretation: 'A more precise determination of any point in a given text must be decided on the basis of the use of language common to the author and his original public'" (ibid.). Dunn goes on to describe the impact of Renaissance textual criticism, which made it possible "to recognize *the character of historical texts as historical texts*" (41). The Reformation, Dunn states, took up these insights and insisted on the literal sense of the biblical text in its original historical context (42–43). Dunn ably defends, against postmodern hermeneutics, the strictly linear understanding of history developed during this time period. However, in not apprehending—or perhaps in rejecting as granting too much to tradition and Church over against Scripture (48–49)—the participatory aspect of history, he manifests precisely the difficulties that theological exegesis must overcome. Dunn does affirm that "faith is an integral part of the critical theological dialogue which is the interpretation of the NT" (48). See also James Barr's description of the influence of the Renaissance's linear-historical model on the Reformers: "In the Middle Ages text, interpretation, theology, and metaphysics formed, for many, one unitary body of knowledge, with an infinite network of interrelations between these different strata. Allegorical interpretation bound the details of the text and the convictions of theology and metaphysics together. The Reformers questioned the harmony in which all this knowledge was supposed to stand. As against the synthesis of the later Middle Ages, a global picture of reality which looked

as if it had always been so, the Reformers were easily able to show that this or that doctrinal element, far from having been there from eternity, had not been there in the Fathers, still less in the New Testament. The effect of this was to split up the global picture of reality into one involving temporally successive strata: in other words, it was a historical-critical operation, and one without which the Reformational position could not have sustained itself. . . . There was, from the Renaissance on, a certain distance between questions of different orders, and in particular between questions of the proximate meaning of texts on the one hand, and questions of the ultimate meaning of the universe on the other. The full recognition of this belongs, we may say, to the Enlightenment. Literary genres and the historical role of a writing can be discussed without *immediate* involvement in the ultimate questions of reality" (Barr, *Holy Scripture: Canon, Authority, Criticism* [Philadelphia: Westminster Press, 1983], 35–36). See also the similar account, from a different theological perspective, in Peter Stuhlmacher, *Historical Criticism and Theological Interpretation of Scripture: Toward a Hermeneutics of Consent*, trans. Roy A. Harrisville (Philadelphia: Fortress Press, 1977), 33–35. Stuhlmacher argues for both the return to origins and an adherence to the tradition of the Reformers. As he later puts it, "Protestant exegesis had thus first to free itself from the Procrustean bed [first Catholic and then seventeenth-century Protestant] of an orthodox, ahistorical, theological treatment of the Bible. It had to achieve an unrestricted view of the original shape of the Old and New Testaments and establish possibilities for a historical-critical exegesis of the Bible. But once Protestant exegesis has established these possibilities and with that perceived what historical method can and cannot do, it can and must recall that exegesis which serves the church must be hermeneutically equipped to deal with the self-sufficiency of the scriptural word, the horizon of the Christian community's faith and experience, and the truth of God encountering us from out of transcendence" (88).

16. Richard Muller affirms that "Calvin's interests do not presage the nineteenth and twentieth century; they rather emerge from the legacy of his forebears" (Muller, "Biblical Interpretation in the Era of the Reformation: The View from the Middle Ages," in *Biblical Interpretation in the Era of the Reformation: Essays Presented to David C. Steinmetz*, ed. Richard A. Muller and John L. Thompson [Grand Rapids, Mich.: Eerdmans, 1996], 3–22, at 8). Muller goes on to make clear that by "forebears" he primarily means the late-medieval theologians (along with Nicholas of Lyra and Lefèvre d'Etaples, Muller includes Aquinas) who emphasized the "literal sense." This "literal sense" is more participatory than that allowed by what Muller calls "the modern, higher-critical paradigm for biblical interpretation" (11). As Muller points out as regards Calvin: "The exegetical practice is far more textual, the hermeneutics is far more grammatical and philological, and (in justice to Calvin's intentions and

actual procedure) the sense of the text is focused in its literal meaning, but the underlying assumption that the meaning of the text is ultimately oriented to the belief, life, and future of the church retains significant affinities with the *quadriga*, the basic pattern of the so-called 'allegorical exegesis' of the Middle Ages. A step back in time from Calvin to Luther makes the same point still more clearly" (11–12). I agree with Muller that the participatory-historical dimension, which enables interpreters to read the biblical text in light of the active presence of such realities as the Trinity and the risen Christ, does not disappear during this period either for the Reformers or for Catholic exegetes. As Brevard Childs (following Gerhard Ebeling and J. S. Preus) is at pains to show by emphasizing Luther's identification of the Old Testament's literal sense as "promise," Luther "found Erasmus's *sensus grammaticus* to be flat, sterile, and a fully inadequate wrestling with the subject matter of the Bible" (Childs, "The Sensus Literalis of Scripture: An Ancient and Modern Problem," in *Beiträge zur Alttestamentlichen Theologie*, ed. Herbert Donner, Robert Hanhart, and Rudolf Smend [Göttingen: Vandenhoeck & Ruprecht, 1977], 86). Yet James Barr's observations regarding the developing understanding of history seem accurate to me: "Did Jesus cleanse the temple of the money-changers at the beginning of his ministry, as in John, or almost at the end, after his final entry into Jerusalem, as in the other Gospels? In the Middle Ages the question might not have seemed very important; but after the Reformation it was a serious matter. . . . Consider all these various influences together, and one cannot avoid the conclusion: it was the dynamics of Reformation theology that created the needs which biblical criticism was developed to answer" (*Holy Scripture*, 37). Muller, too, grants a discontinuity within continuity: "we can identify the major impact of Renaissance humanism on the history of exegesis: philological and rhetorical expertise, not absent from the field of medieval exegesis, became the norm with the rise of humanism. The task of establishing the text and of closely examining its grammar and syntax in the original languages became, by way of their humanistic training, one of the basic tasks of the Reformers' exegesis" (14).

17. Mystical theology retains its vigor during this period, influenced by neo-Platonic Renaissance philosophy. See, e.g., Henri de Lubac, S.J., *Exégèse médiévale*, Seconde Partie, II, "Humanistes mystiques," 391–427. Cf. Michel de Certeau, *The Mystic Fable*, vol. 1, *The Sixteenth and Seventeenth Centuries*, trans. Michael B. Smith (French, 1982; Chicago: University of Chicago Press, 1992), 103. Among the direct contemporaries of Erasmus, Jacques Lefèvre d'Etaples (1455–1536) combined humanist biblical scholarship and studies of medieval mystics. For discussion of his exegesis, see Guy Bedouelle, O.P., *Lefèvre d'Étaples et l'Intelligence des Écritures* (Geneva: Librairie Droz, 1976); de Lubac, *Exégèse médiévale*, Seconde Partie, II, 411–22; as well as a brief summary in Jean-Michel Poffet, O.P., *Les chrétiens et la Bible. Les Anciens et les Modernes*

(Paris: Cerf, 1998), 95–98. As de Lubac observes, "We find again, in part, the traditional exegesis and its fourfold sense in Jacques Lefèvre d'Etaples" (411)— "in part" being, for de Lubac, the key phrase. For an English translation of his preface to his *Commentaries on the Four Gospels* (1521) as well as a brief historical sketch of his life, see chapter 8 of *The Catholic Reformation: Savonarola to Ignatius Loyola*, ed. John C. Olin (New York: Fordham University Press, 1992): 107–17.

    18. Barr, *Holy Scripture*, 36.

    19. Ibid.

    20. Robert M. Grant notes that in comparison with other humanist Catholics of the time such as John Colet, Erasmus was a moderate in his attitude to the spiritual senses and patristic-medieval exegesis. See Grant (with David Tracy), *A Short History of the Interpretation of the Bible*, 2d ed. (Philadelphia: Fortress, 1984), 102–3.

    21. Erasmus at times does not seem to grant to Old Testament history a significant participatory dimension. He says of the Old Testament, "I would prefer the New Testament to be left untouched and that the whole of the Old Testament should be destroyed rather than that peace should be shattered among Christians because of the Jewish books [Iudaeorum libros]." Letter to J. Caesarius (November 3, 1517), *Ep.* 701, in the *Opus epistolarum*, vol. III, ed. P. S. Allen et al. (1906–57), 127; quoted in Reventlow, *The Authority of the Bible and the Rise of the Modern World*, 47. Cf. de Lubac, *Exégèse médiévale*, Seconde Partie, II, 444–45. Henning Graf Reventlow points out, "Erasmus is methodically following the course of customary allegorical interpretation, but he has his own ends in view: positively, he seeks to interpret the Old Testament in moralistic and didactic terms . . . while negatively he seeks to devalue its literal statements which as historical narratives cannot mean more to him than Livy" (Reventlow, *The Authority of the Bible and the Rise of the Modern World*, trans. John Bowden [German, 1980; London: SCM Press, 1984 (English edition contains additional material supplied by the author)], 43–44. It is worth noting that the humanist Lefèvre d'Etaples (also known as Faber Stapulensis) earlier makes a similar move: see Muller, "Biblical Interpretation in the Era of the Reformation," 11. See also Reventlow, *The Authority of the Bible and the Rise of the Modern World*, 39–48; Istvan Bejczy, *Erasmus and the Middle Ages: The Historical Consciousness of a Christian Humanist* (Leiden: Brill, 2001). Catholic evaluation of Erasmus is still in its infancy.

    22. Louis Bouyer, "Erasmus in Relation to the Medieval Biblical Tradition," in *The Cambridge History of the Bible*, vol. 2, ed. G. W. H. Lampe (Cambridge: Cambridge University Press, 1969), 492–505, at 502.

    23. Ibid. See also Bouyer's account on p. 504, where he appreciatively notes Erasmus's efforts to distinguish eisegesis from exegesis, to be attuned to the meanings of the original Hebrew and Greek, to urge the development of

a critical concordance, and "to quote Scripture always at first hand, paying attention at the same time to context. This gives him a good opportunity to set out a list of scriptural expressions misconstrued even by such writers as Ambrose, Bede or Augustine."

24. Ibid., 505. On Erasmus's philological work (as well as his exegesis and theology), see Joseph M. Levine, *The Autonomy of History: Truth and Method from Erasmus to Gibbon* (Chicago: University of Chicago Press, 1999), chap. 2, "Erasmus and the Problem of the Johannine Comma."

25. Desiderius Erasmus, *Paraphrase on John (Paraphrasis in Ioannem)*, trans. Jane E. Phillips, in *Collected Works of Erasmus: New Testament Scholarship*, ed. Robert D. Sider (Toronto: University of Toronto Press, 1991), 51.

26. Tommaso de Vio Cardinal Cajetan, *Opera Omnia, In S. Scripturam Commentarii*, vol. 4, pp. 304–10.

27. Richard Popkin has briefly chronicled the work of Cardinal Ximinez of Spain, beginning in 1506, on the Polyglot Bible project, which endeavored "to publish the Hebrew and Greek texts of the New and Old Testament and the Latin Vulgate of St. Jerome, as well as Aramaic paraphrases" (Popkin, *The History of Scepticism: From Savonarola to Bayle*, rev. and expanded ed. [Oxford: Oxford University Press, 2003], 220). Cajetan, Maldonado, and Toledo show the influence of this work. For discussion of Cardinal Ximinez's project, see also Levine, *The Autonomy of History*, 45 f.

28. F. J. Crehan, S.J., "The Bible in the Roman Catholic Church from Trent to the Present Day," in *The Cambridge History of the Bible*, vol. 3, *The West from the Reformation to the Present Day*, ed. S. L. Greenslade (Cambridge: Cambridge University Press, 1963), 199–237, at 213. In addition to Maldonado and Toledo, Crehan mentions Alfonso Salmeron, who was one of the original companions of St. Ignatius Loyola and to whom goes much of the credit for the flourishing of Spanish exegetes.

29. For discussion of this Thomistic commentary, indicating some of its weaknesses, see G. J. McAleer, *Ecstatic Morality and Sexual Politics: A Catholic and Antitotalitarian Theory of the Body* (New York: Fordham University Press, 2005), 94–99. Cessario does not mention Toledo's work in his *A Short History of Thomism*.

30. Cf. Crehan, "The Bible in the Roman Catholic Church from Trent to the Present Day," 213.

31. Joannes Maldonatus, S.J., *Commentarii in Quatuor Evangelistas*, ed. Conrad Martin, vol. 2 (Moguntiae: Francisci Kirchhemii, 1863), 501–11.

32. Crehan, "The Bible in the Roman Catholic Church from Trent to the Present Day," 214.

33. Crehan points out that Toledo "was a pioneer in having his commentary printed separately from the notes on the texts of John, in a fashion that is now common" (ibid., 214).

34. Francisco de Toledo, S.J., *In Sacrosanctum Ioannis Evangelium Commentarii* (Rome: Iacobum Tornerium, 1588), 317–34.

35. For Erasmus's criticism of the scholastic theology of his day, see his remarks in *The Praise of Folly*, where he observes that "these most subtle subtleties are rendered even more subtle by the various 'ways' or types of scholastic theology, so that you could work your way out of a labyrinth sooner than out of the intricacies of the Realists, Nominalists, Thomists, Albertists, Occamists, Scotists—and I still haven't mentioned all the sects, but only the main ones. In all of these there is so much erudition, so much difficulty, that I think the apostles themselves would need to be inspired by a different spirit if they were forced to match wits on such points with this new breed of theologians" (*The Praise of Folly*, trans. Clarence H. Miller [New Haven: Yale University Press, 1979], 90). He grants that "among the theologians themselves there are some better educated men who are disgusted by these theological quibbles, which they consider utterly pointless. There are those who denounce it as a form of sacrilege and consider it the worst sort of impiety to talk in such a tawdry fashion, to dispute with the worldly subtleties of the pagans, to lay down such arrogant definitions, about sacred mysteries which should be reverently contemplated rather than explicated, and to besmirch the majesty of divine theology with words and ideas so bloodless and even squalid. But meanwhile they themselves are so completely contented and self-satisfied, they even applaud themselves so enthusiastically, that they spend their days and nights in these most delightful trifles and have not a moment to spare to read through the gospel or Paul's epistles even once" (95). In contrast, Erasmus admires the works of the Fathers, which are not contaminated with the rationalism of Aristotle ("Letter to Martin Dorp" [1514], appendix to *The Praise of Folly*, 155, cf. 164f.) but which instead seek critical knowledge of Scripture as does Erasmus through the critical apparatus of his day. As Joseph Levine points out, "Erasmus was not so kind to Aquinas, whose Biblical authority he challenges frequently in his annotations. . . . In the note to 1 Cor. 13:4 (LB 6: 725–26), Erasmus says frankly that St. Thomas should not have used the rubbish of unscholarly sources for his commentary; it was *indignus*. Elsewhere he writes that the saint would have done better had he lived in a happier intellectual time; see Erasmus to Hermannus Buschius, July 31, 1520, *CWE*, no. 1126, 8: 15" (Levine, *The Autonomy of History*, 46 n. 83). See Henri de Lubac, S.J., *Exégèse médiévale*, Seconde Partie, II, 448, for discussion of Erasmus's position on the fourfold sense. Erasmus warns against mechanical application of the senses, and holds up Origen, known for his allegorizing of the Old Testament, as a model of one who avoids mechanical application.

36. For discussion of Richard Simon, who remains well known for his groundbreaking textual criticism of the Old Testament and who was a direct

contemporary of Natalis (so far as I know Simon did not comment on the Gospel of John), see Crehan, "The Bible in the Roman Catholic Church from Trent to the Present Day," 218–21. Simon embodies, not least in his 1712 biblical encyclopedia, the linear understanding of history in both its strengths and its weaknesses. Lamenting that "precritical Protestant exegesis" has fallen "so completely down the memory hole," David S. Yeago has pointed to the significance of Natalis's strikingly similar Protestant contemporary, the German Pietist exegete August Herman Francke (1662–1727), "who combined philological expertise with the lifelong hermeneutical project of a unified Christocentric reading of the whole Bible, not only in the dogmatic mode promoted by confessional controversy, but also as a spiritually transformative enterprise" (Yeago, "Re-Entering the Scriptural World," 167).

37. Alexander Natalis, *Scripturae Sacrae. Cursus Completus*, vol. 23, ed. Jacque-Paul Migne (Paris: 1840), 123–43.

38. We might also note a famous exegete from the same time period, Cornelius a Lapide, S.J. (Holland, 1567–1637). In his commentary on John 3:27–36, he includes extensive lists of patristic authorities where Chrysostom, Theophylactus, and Euthymius join forces. He quotes pagan authorities, in his case Claudianus and Plutarch in support of his reading of verse 29. He shows awareness of the Greek text. When he pauses to ask and answer technical theological questions, both the questions and the answers show his indebtedness to his forebears. Yet the commentary displays something of an encyclopedic character. See Cornelius a Lapide, S.J., *Commentaria in Quatuor Evangelia*, vol. 4, 3d rev. ed. (Paris: Marietti, 1922), 86–90. Michael Cahill, in "The History of Exegesis and Our Theological Future," values Lapide precisely for this encyclopedic character. He notes that Lapide's commentaries "are characterized by a systematic tabling of the opinions of earlier commentators, especially the Fathers, on a verse-by-verse basis. In this regard Lapide's commentaries remain a useful resource today," although Cahill adds that caution has to be taken with regards to Lapide's occasional misidentification of patristic texts now known to be pseudonymous (334). In "The Bible in the Roman Catholic Church from Trent to the Present Day," Crehan remarks that Lapide "is copious, giving as many interpretations as he thinks can reasonably be defended and catering for all types of readers, much as the Baroque church was calculated to appeal to every type of worshipper" (217).

39. In "The Bible in the Roman Catholic Church from Trent to the Present Day," Crehan praises Lagrange's contributions: "The school of S. Étienne at Jerusalem had been founded by Père Lagrange in 1890 and in 1892 the *Revue biblique* began to issue from it; ten years later, at Toulouse in 1902, Lagrange gave his famous course on 'Historical method in the Old Testament' which presented a detailed working out of the analogy between the statements in the Old Testament about physical science and those which purported to be historical.

Here the consideration of the literary genera was for the first time suggested, though not as the main principle for overcoming discrepancies between the Bible and the findings of historians" (231). Crehan, writing just before the Second Vatican Council, also summarizes the content and impact of the encyclicals *Providentissimus Deus* (1893) and *Divino Afflante Spiritu* (1943). For a survey of these encyclicals (along with Pontifical Biblical Commission decisions from the same period) with a focus on their contribution to contemporary Catholic practice of historical-critical exegesis, see Joseph G. Prior, *The Historical Critical Method in Catholic Exegesis* (Rome: Editrice Pontificia Università Gregoriana, 1999), 89–127.

40. Lagrange's commitment to ecclesial biblical interpretation is clear throughout his corpus; see, e.g., his "L'interprétation de la Sainte Écriture par l'Église," *Revue Biblique* 9 (1900): 135–42.

41. Marie-Joseph Lagrange, O.P., *Évangile selon saint Jean,* 4th ed. (Paris: Librairie Victor Lecoffre, 1927), 94–99.

42. In *The Critical Meaning of the Bible: How a Modern Reading of the Bible Challenges Christians, the Church, and the Churches* (New York: Paulist Press, 1981), Brown focuses on refuting his Catholic critics: see the dedication page, 17, 26–28, 35, etc. Noting that "critical biblical thought" has not influenced significantly the thought of many theologians trained in the preconciliar period and has been relatively ignored by "Roman statements," he states, "To Catholics who express fears about biblical criticism, one may well reply in the crude argot of the street: 'Don't knock it till you've tried it.' And I would add to that maxim '—tried it and been judged by your fellow-scholars as knowing what you are doing'" (28). He goes on to affirm the necessity of historical-critical interpretation for ensuring that the time-conditioned aspects of the word of God are recognized. Thinking that the issue is the orthodoxy of historical-critical reconstruction—whose validity he finds affirmed in the Pontifical Biblical Commission's short 1964 document "The History of the Gospels"—Brown does not see that his understanding of history might be lacking. For further discussion of "The Historicity of the Gospels" in its context, see Joseph Fitzmyer, S.J., "The Biblical Commission's Instruction on the Historical Truth of the Gospels," *Theological Studies* 25 (1964): 386–408. In *The Critical Meaning of the Bible,* Brown demonstrates some sympathy for Childs's emphasis on canon as a way of avoiding the radical fragmentation brought about by the various reconstructions of the biblical texts, but Brown affirms that the "literal sense" remains that of the original author and thus the historical-critical method retains its priority for understanding the Bible, if not for understanding the evolving meaning of the Bible today as received through the Church's added insights (cf. 31–35). Here Brown agrees with the criticisms of Childs by James A. Sanders, "Canonical Context and Canonical Criticism," *Horizons in Biblical Theology* 2 (1980): 173–97, reprinted in Sanders's *From Sacred Story to Sacred Text: Canon as Paradigm* (Philadelphia: Fortress Press, 1987), 153–74.

Sanders sees his project as an extension and development of historical-critical scholarship—now more aware of the ongoing role of believing communities— rather than an appeal to a normative text that stands above the ever-changing historical contexts identified by historical criticism (*From Sacred Story to Sacred Text*, 170–72).

43. See Raymond E. Brown, S.S., *The* Sensus Plenior *of Sacred Scripture* (Baltimore: St. Mary's University, 1955), esp. 91–93. As understood by Brown (entering into a discussion that was widely current at the time but that largely disappeared within a decade), the concept of the *sensus plenior* grants that a divinely intended "fuller sense exists *in the words of the text*" (92). Yet, the *sensus plenior* remains strictly on the textual level. It does not augment metaphysically the understanding of history. This is the crucial problem, since history and theological realities remain unbridged. For Brown the *sensus plenior* is first "the homogeneous enrichment in meaning that a text assumes when placed in its setting in the whole Bible" (97). Aware that "in secular history . . . our outlook on an event is colored by our philosophy of history," Brown hopes that granting a text's "enrichment in meaning" will serve to account adequately for the depths of Israel's history (98). But if the *sensus plenior* pertains to words but not in a real way to things, then it cannot reach the metaphysical level of history. Brown's account of prophecy similarly avoids attributing much participatory depth to the prophet or inspired author. Summarizing a view with which he agrees, Brown states, "*Theoria* then involves a fuller meaning of the text itself, evident to later generations through a development in revelation, and foreseen somewhat vaguely and imprecisely by the prophet" (110; cf. 133). Again the *sensus plenior* is relegated to the text and its later interpretation, although a certain vague knowledge can be granted to the prophet. Likewise Brown states as regards the typology found in the Bible: "the *sensus plenior* and the typical sense are two different things: one deals primarily with words; the other, with 'things.' Yet since they both outstrip the *clear* consciousness of the author, they have a very basic attribute in common" (118)—namely that they are not the literal sense.

44. Ibid., 105: since the "literal sense" includes solely "that which the human author clearly intended when he wrote the text," it follows that "the *sensus plenior* is not strictly speaking a literal sense"; cf. 113 and 122 for the same point. He explains that the *sensus plenior* properly relates to the literal sense in the following fashion: "(1) that the doctrines concerned be related, and there be some authoritative testimony of this relation; (2) that the fuller meaning be close to the literal meaning, so that the words are not used in an entirely different sense, but in one closely connected to the original" (129).

45. Brown, *The Gospel according to John (I–XII)*, vol. 29 of *The Anchor Bible* (New York: Doubleday, 1966), vi. See also Brown's "The Contribution of Historical Biblical Criticism to Ecumenical Church Discussion," in *Biblical Interpretation in Crisis: The Ratzinger Conference on Bible and Church*, ed. Richard John Neuhaus (Grand Rapids, Mich.: Eerdmans, 1989), 24–49. For criticism of

Brown's assumption about the accessibility of the literal meaning of Scripture, see Jon D. Levenson, *The Hebrew Bible, the Old Testament, and Historical Criticism: Jews and Christians in Biblical Studies* (Louisville: Westminster/John Knox Press, 1993); idem, "Is Brueggemann Really a Pluralist?" *Harvard Theological Review* 93 (2000): 265–94. For an extension of Brown's position, see Pheme Perkins, "The Theological Implications of New Testament Pluralism," *Catholic Biblical Quarterly* 50 (1988): 5–23.

46. Brown returns to this theme in a 1980 address, published in his *The Critical Meaning of the Bible* as "What the Biblical Word Meant and What It Means." His preface to that book explains that "the meaning of the Bible as the Church's collection of sacred and normative books goes beyond what the authors *meant* in a particular book. Not only scholarship but also church tradition and teaching enters into the complex issue of what the Bible *means* to Christians" (x); cf. Brown's insistence on the Church's magisterial role, given the general paucity of New Testament evidence for Catholic doctrine, in his "Critical Biblical Exegesis and the Development of Doctrine," in *Biblical Exegesis and Church Doctrine* (New York: Paulist Press, 1985), 26–53. On "what it meant" versus "what it means"—a formulation developed by Krister Stendahl—see, however, Ben C. Ollenburger, "What Krister Stendahl 'Meant'—A Normative Critique of 'Descriptive Biblical Theology,'" *Horizons of Biblical Theology* 8 (1996): 61–98. See also, for a critique of Stendahl's position, Francis Watson, *Text, Church and World: Biblical Interpretation in Theological Perspective* (Grand Rapids, Mich.: Eerdmans, 1994), 30–33; A. K. M. Adam, *Making Sense of New Testament Theology: "Modern" Problems and Prospects* (Macon, Ga.: Mercer University Press, 1995), 76–86 and 129–32; Brevard Childs, "Interpretation in Faith," *Interpretation* 18 (1964): 259–71, to which Stendahl briefly responds in "Method in the Study of Biblical Theology," in *The Bible in Modern Scholarship*, ed. J. Philip Hyatt (Nashville: Abingdon Press, 1965), 203. The problem with this view is that "what it meant" is inscribed within the triune God's creative and redemptive presence so profoundly as to defeat any strict version of the past tense: the past, as *history* and not solely when viewed from the perspective of the divine Author, is participatory. Were Brown alive today, he might well agree with this point and revise, on the basis of an expanded understanding of the historical, his conception of the *historical*-critical method as providing the strictly linear past meaning to which theologians then add (extrinsically) other evolving meanings. As Nicholas Lash says, "there is . . . a sense in which the articulation of what the text might 'mean' today, is a necessary condition of hearing what the text 'originally meant'" (Lash, *Theology on the Way to Emmaus* [London: SCM Press, 1986], 81, quoted in R. W. L. Moberly, *The Bible, Theology, and Faith* [Cambridge: Cambridge University Press, 2000], 40). Stephen E. Fowl and L. Gregory Jones make good use of Lash's point in their *Reading in Communion: Scripture and Ethics in Christian Life* (Grand Rapids, Mich.: Eerdmans, 1991), 57–58.

47. Brown, *The Gospel according to John (I–XII)*, 156.
48. Ibid., 155.
49. Ibid., 156.
50. Ibid., 160.
51. Ibid., 161. This kind of interpretive move, relying on the hypothetical reconstruction to interpret the text, is criticized by Brevard Childs with regard to Brown's exegesis of 1 John. See Childs, *The New Testament as Canon: An Introduction* (London: SCM Press, 1984), 482 f. Childs elsewhere cautions that Catholic exegetes, uncritical prior to the twentieth century, are now in danger of shifting too far in the other direction: "In modern Catholicism since the encyclical of 1943, the historical critical approach to biblical studies has been fully embraced. I judge this move to have been correct, especially when viewed in the historical context of the Catholic Church's earlier dogmatic position. However, I think that this hermeneutical relationship [between historical-critical and canonical biblical interpretation] must be viewed in a far more subtle, indeed dialectical manner, because of the unique character of the biblical subject matter" (Childs, "The Canon in Recent Biblical Studies: Reflections on an Era," *Pro Ecclesia* 14 (2005), 26–45, at 44).

52. Compare, in contrast, Markus Bockmuehl's concern: "The Nicene Creed, as a reviewer recently admonished us yet again, is hardly the faith of the 'undivided Church', but must instead be understood as the symbol of the victors in a political battle fought 'with considerable strong-arm tactics.' New Testament scholars, too, have been brought up to insist that the socio-political controversies and the literary dependencies behind the historical genesis of each biblical document are vital for an accurate understanding. . . . Nagging doubts did, alas, intrude upon my reading of that review. Is it *really* of the slightest consequence to the congregation of Little Snoring that 1,800 years ago the formulations of Nicaea happen to have flattered the convictions of the party that triumphed in a long-forgotten feud? Might it not rather be the case that for all its historically contingent, socially fraught and politically dubious origins, the Creed came to be universally adopted in the Church precisely because successive generations found it to be a widely serviceable expression of 'essential' Christian doctrines—that is to say, truths accepted as being of transcendent and abiding significance rather than specific to a particular culture, clique or context? And if this is even vaguely true for the Creed, must not an equivalent judgement apply a fortiori to the case of Holy Scripture? And what might be the implications of such ecclesial realism for the exercise known as New Testament theology?" (Bockmuehl, "Humpty Dumpty and New Testament Theology," *Theology* 101 [1998]: 330–38, at 330). "Humpty Dumpty" here refers to the unity of the New Testament that lies in shards, so to speak, after biblical scholarship has done theorizing about the conflicts behind the texts. See also Bockmuehl, "'To Be or Not to Be': The Possible Futures of New Testament Scholarship," *Scottish Journal of Theology* 51 (1998): 271–306.

53. For further discussion of these figures, see Richard Popkin's chapter "Biblical Criticism and the Beginning of Religious Scepticism" in his *The History of Scepticism*, 219–38; idem, *Isaac La Peyrère, 1596–1676* (Leiden: Brill, 1987); Anthony Grafton, "Isaac La Peyrère and the Old Testament," in idem, *Defenders of the Text: The Traditions of Scholarship in an Age of Science, 1450–1800* (Cambridge: Harvard University Press, 1991), 204–13; Louis Dupré, *The Enlightenment and the Intellectual Foundations of Modern Culture* (New Haven: Yale University Press, 2004), 231–37. For discussion of key Protestant figures in the development of historical criticism from Spinoza to the twentieth-century exegete Ernst Käsemann, see Roy A. Harrisville and Walter Sundberg, *The Bible in Modern Culture: Theology and Historical-Critical Method from Spinoza to Käsemann* (Grand Rapids, Mich.: Eerdmans, 1995).

54. Robert Sweetman points out that Beryl Smalley's research on medieval exegesis overlooks medieval "performative" (e.g., liturgical, pastoral) readings of Scripture, whether such readings focus on the literal sense or on the spiritual senses. Sweetman speaks for Aquinas and the patristic-medieval tradition in noting: "For the university master, too, the scriptures maintained an authority that invited the reader's submission, a submission whereby the text was to inscribe itself upon the reader's subsequent understanding and practice of life" (Sweetman, "Beryl Smalley, Thomas of Cantimpré, and the Performative Reading of Scripture: A Study in Two *Exempla*," in *With Reverence for the Word: Medieval Scriptural Exegesis in Judaism, Christianity, and Islam*, ed. Jane Dammen McAuliffe, Barry D. Walfish, and Joseph W. Goering [Oxford: Oxford University Press, 2003], 256–75, at 269). See also William T. Flynn, *Medieval Music as Medieval Exegesis* (Lanham, Md.: Scarecrow Press, 1999), esp. chaps. 3 and 4 on "Liturgy and Scripture Study: Interpreting Scripture within the Liturgy" and "Liturgical *Sacra Pagina*: Christmas and Easter Services at Autun in the Early Eleventh Century" respectively. This is participatory exegesis in perhaps its highest form, that of worship. Cf. Aidan J. Kavanaugh, O.S.B., "Scriptural Word and Liturgical Worship," in Braaten and Jenson, *Reclaiming the Bible for the Church*, 131–37.

55. Cf. Bockmuehl, "Humpty Dumpty and New Testament Theology," 336: "Any properly *Christian* interpretation of Scripture is a fundamentally corporate and indeed ecclesial task, to be carried out in common loyalty to fellow Christian authors and in dialogue with the living tradition to which they gave rise." Bockmuehl makes the same point in his excellent "Reason, Wisdom and the Implied Disciple of Scripture," in *Reading Texts, Seeking Wisdom: Scripture and Theology*, ed. David F. Ford and Graham Stanton (Grand Rapids, Mich.: Eerdmans, 2003), 53–68. He draws helpfully on Aidan Nichols, O.P., "François Dreyfus on Scripture Read in Tradition," in Aidan Nichols, *Scribe of the Kingdom: Essays on Theology and Culture* (London: Sheed & Ward, 1994), 32–77.

56. Joseph Ratzinger has pointed out, "Exegesis can no longer be studied in a unilinear, synchronic fashion, as is the case with scientific findings which do not depend upon their history but only upon the precision of their data. Exegesis must recognize itself as a historical discipline. . . . Philological and scientific literary methods are and will remain critically important for a proper exegesis. But for their actual application to the work of criticism—just as for an examination of their claims—an understanding of the philosophic implications of the interpretative process is required. The self-critical study of its own history must also imply an examination of the essential philosophic alternatives for human thought. Thus, it is not sufficient to scan simply the last one hundred and fifty years. The great outlines of patristic and medieval thought must also be brought into the discussion. It is equally indispensable to reflect on the fundamental judgments made by the Reformers and the critical importance they have had in the history of exegesis" (Ratzinger, "Biblical Interpretation in Crisis: On the Question of the Foundations and Approaches of Exegesis Today," in *Biblical Interpretation in Crisis: The Ratzinger Conference on Bible and Church*, ed. Richard John Neuhaus [Grand Rapids, Mich.: Eerdmans, 1989], 22).

57. Wilken, "Wilken's Response to Hays," *Communio* 25 (1998): 529–31, at 529–30.

THREE
Participatory Biblical Exegesis and God the Teacher

1. Responding to the loss incurred by non-participatory historical readings, literary-aesthetic readings have emerged that seek to retain a transformative power of the text without grounding the text's power in judgments (beyond metaphor) about extratextual reality. See, e.g., Robert Alter, *The Art of Biblical Narrative* (New York: Basic Books, 1981); Gabriel Josipovici, *The Book of God: A Response to the Bible* (New Haven: Yale University Press, 1988); Stephen Prickett, *Words and* The Word: *Language, Poetics and Biblical Interpretation* (Cambridge: Cambridge University Press, 1986); as well as the classic works of Robert Lowth, Coleridge, Hamann, Herder, and others; cf. Nicholas Boyle, "History and Hermeneutics (1): Herder," in Boyle's *Sacred and Secular Scriptures: A Catholic Approach to Literature* (Notre Dame: University of Notre Dame Press, 2005), 17–29. For an excellent critique of such approaches, see George Steiner, "The Good Books," *Religion and Intellectual Life* 6 (1989): 15–16, a review of *The Literary Guide to the Bible*, ed. Robert Alter and Frank Kermode (Cambridge: Harvard University Press, 1987).

2. R. R. Reno, *The Ruins of the Church* (Grand Rapids, Mich.: Brazos Press, 2002), 180. Such "hermeneutical discipline" must remain metaphysically (Creator–creature) rather than epistemologically oriented in order to attain in

Christ its spiritually transformative potential. For discussion of Friedrich Schleiermacher's role in the anthropocentric shift in biblical interpretation, see Nicholas Boyle, "History and Hermeneutics (2): Schleiermacher," in *Sacred and Secular Scriptures*, 30–45, esp. 42: "In Schleiermacher's hands the concept of the Bible as literature [Herder] leads not to an aestheticization of our response but to an academicization. Understanding the Bible becomes a matter of following the rules for a school exercise in *explication de texte*. It becomes the affair not of the whole church but of an academic caste of hermeneuts for whom the biblical texts are, emphatically, texts like any other: literature with its own particular problems no doubt but simply literature—the distinction between sacred and secular is, for Schleiermacher's hermeneutics, simply irrelevant."

3. McGrath, "Reclaiming Our Roots and Vision: Scripture and the Stability of the Christian Church," in *Reclaiming the Bible for the Church*, ed. Carl Braaten and Robert Jenson (Grand Rapids, Mich.: Eerdmans, 1995), 63–88, at 67. McGrath points out, "It is not a question of *either* the Bible *or* Jesus Christ, as if they can or should be separated. There is an organic and essential connection between them. We honour Christ by receiving both the Scriptures that he received, and those that the church has handed down to us as a divinely inspired witness to Christ" (66–67). Or as Frank J. Matera puts it, "Searching for the unity of Scripture is another way of searching for God" (Matera, "The Future of Catholic Biblical Scholarship: Balance and Proportion," *Nova et Vetera* 4 [2006]: 120–32, at 126–27).

4. Raymond Brown expresses this concern in his *The Critical Meaning of the Bible: How a Modern Reading of the Bible Challenges Christians, the Church, and the Churches* (New York: Paulist Press, 1981), chap. 1, "The Human Word of the Almighty God." He fears that theologians of his generation "continue to use basic terms shaped in a precritical era without stopping to examine the meaning of those terms when rethought in a critical context" (2). Affirming as a matter of faith that the Bible is "the word of God," Brown seeks to probe into the reality that this word is also "a time-conditioned word, affect by limitations of human insight and problems" (4), on which basis he holds that "[t]he attribution of a word to God, to Jesus, or to the Church would not enable that word to escape limitation" (4). Theology, he suggests, has not yet fully come to grips with the human limitations inscribed into revelation: "To the jaundiced eye of a biblical scholar it often seems as if theologians phrase their theories of inspiration by reflecting on books like Genesis, the Gospels, and Romans; they might do better by trying their theories out on the first nine chapters of I Chronicles!" (7). Having limited biblical interpretation to reconstructing the historical past, Brown attempts to construct an understanding of revelation on the basis of the identification of problems in the biblical text. What is missing is a sufficiently rich understanding of *sacra doctrina* to avoid making the difficult texts normative for the theology of revelation. The question must first be what

are the realities that God is teaching—which is why theologians begin with, for example, Genesis, the Gospels, and Romans.

5. For a brief introduction to *Dei Verbum*, see Gerald O'Collins, S.J., *Retrieving Fundamental Theology: The Three Styles of Contemporary Theology* (New York: Paulist Press, 1993), chap. 4, 48–62; along with "*Dei Verbum*: A Bibliography," app. 2, 178–217. Among the most important commentaries on *Dei Verbum* are Augustinus Bea, *The Word of God and Mankind* (London: 1968); Henri de Lubac, S.J., *La révélation divine. Commentaire du préambule et du chapitre I de la constitution 'Dei verbum' du Concile Vatican II*, 3d ed. (Paris: 1983); and Joseph Ratzinger's "Origin and Background," "Preface," and commentary on chaps. 1 ("Revelation Itself"), 2 ("The Transmission of Divine Revelation"), and 6 ("Sacred Scripture in the Life of the Church") in *Commentary on the Documents of Vatican II*, vol. 3, ed. Herbert Vorgrimler, trans. William Glen-Doepel et al. (German, 1967; New York: Crossroad, 1989), 155–98, 262–72. The passage from *Dei Verbum* that I examine (following Kurz) is commented on by Alois Grillmeier, "The Divine Inspiration and the Interpretation of Sacred Scripture," in Vorgrimler, *Commentary on the Documents of Vatican II*, vol. 3, 199–246.

6. See Denis Farkasfalvy, O. Cist., "How to Renew the Theology of Biblical Inspiration?" *Nova et Vetera* 4 (2006): 231–54.

7. I have chosen St. Augustine in part for his influence on Aquinas, but I could just as well, or better, have chosen to exposit St. Athanasius's *On the Incarnation* (Crestwood, N.Y.: St. Vladimir's Seminary Press, 1975). Fortunately, this task has been masterfully performed by Telford Work in his *Living and Active: Scripture in the Economy of Salvation* (Grand Rapids, Mich.: Eerdmans, 2002), 36–50, 129, 132–33, 193, 213, 309. Work traces the theme of teaching, *doctrina*, in *On the Incarnation* particularly on 42–44. The Logos's external and interior teaching, and its reception and mediation in the Church, constitutes the pattern of salvation for Athanasius, as the human *imago Dei*, bowed low by the foolishness of idolatry, is raised once again to its non-idolatrous modeling of the divine Wisdom of the divine *Imago*. Work's account of Augustine's *On Christian Doctrine* also is valuable: see *Living and Active*, 50–59, 226–33, 304–8. Work's approach to Scripture is influenced by William J. Abraham's *Canon and Criterion in Christian Theology*, paperback ed. with a new preface (Oxford: Clarendon Press, 2002), which urges that the Church's "canonical heritage," including Scripture, be viewed in soteriological rather than epistemological terms. See Work, *Living and Active*, 256–59; for a similar debt to Abraham's thesis, see John Webster, "The Dogmatic Location of the Canon," in Webster, *Word and Church: Essays in Christian Dogmatics* (Edinburgh: T. &. T. Clark, 2001), 9–46; and N. T. Wright, *The Last Word: Beyond the Bible Wars to a New Understanding of the Authority of Scripture* (New York: HarperSanFrancisco, 2005), 64–65. Unfortunately, Abraham's historical account hinges in a misleading way on Aquinas: see my "William Abraham and St. Thomas Aquinas," *New Blackfriars* 88 (2007):

46–65; as well as D. Stephen Long, "Response to Abraham," *Ex Auditu* 19 (2003): 76–80.

8. Saint Augustine, *On Christian Doctrine*, trans. D. W. Robertson Jr. (New York: Macmillan, 1958), Prologue, §1 (p. 3). For a valuable discussion of Augustine's interpretation of Scripture, complementing the account offered here (and deepening it through erudite and wide-ranging reading of Augustine's texts), see Robert Dodaro, *Christ and the Just Society in the Thought of Augustine* (Cambridge: Cambridge University Press, 2004), chap. 4: "Divine Eloquence and Virtue in the Scriptures." See also, e.g., the essays (and Lewis Ayres's excellent bibliography) in *De Doctrina Christiana: A Classic of Western Culture*, ed. Duane W. H. Arnold and Pamela Bright (Notre Dame: University of Notre Dame Press, 1995); Bertrand de Margerie, S.J., *An Introduction to the History of Exegesis*, vol. 3, *Saint Augustine*, trans. Pierre de Fontnouvelle (Petersham, Mass.: Saint Bede's Publications, 1991); Gerald W. Schlabach, *For the Joy Set before Us: Augustine and Self-Denying Love* (Notre Dame: University of Notre Dame Press, 2001); Jaroslav Pelikan, "*Canonica regula*: The Trinitarian Hermeneutics of Augustine," in *Proceedings of the Patristic, Medieval and Renaissance Conference* 12–13 (1987–88): 17–29; and Lewis Ayres's *Nicaea and Its Legacy: An Approach to Fourth-Century Trinitarian Theology* (Oxford: Oxford University Press, 2004). In what follows I concentrate on Book I, composed in the 390s.

9. Augustine, *On Christian Doctrine*, Prologue, §6 (p. 5).

10. Confirming this emphasis on teaching, Brevard Childs remarks, "In his final section of his treatise *On Christian Doctrine* Augustine brought to bear a perspective on the Bible and its reader which remains quite unique for much of later Christianity. He set out to describe the necessary qualities of the teacher for interpreting the message of Scripture to others. However, before he set out in some detail the manner of Christian living necessary for the teacher, he sought to demonstrate that the biblical writers themselves had these same qualities." See Childs, *Biblical Theology of the Old and New Testaments: Theological Reflection on the Christian Bible* (Minneapolis: Fortress Press, 1993), 38.

11. Augustine, *On Christian Doctrine*, Book I, 3, §4 (p. 9).

12. Ibid., Book I, 7, §7 (p. 11).

13. Ibid., Book I, 10, §10 (p. 13).

14. Ibid., Book I, 11, §11 (p. 13); cf. 14, §13 (pp. 14–15), as well as 34, §38 (p. 29).

15. Ibid., Book I, 12, §§11–12 (pp. 13–14).

16. Ibid., Book I, 19–22 (pp. 17–18). As Telford Work points out, "Augustine's semiotics of Scripture presupposes a context in which biblical signs become intelligible; and that context is the Church, Scripture's reading community" (Work, *Living and Active*, 308).

17. Hence the many modern problems that stem from a lack of belief in a future life even, perhaps, when there is some kind of belief in God. Partici-

patory weakness is linked to eschatological weakness, since both are the consequence of a narrowing of vision and horizon.

18. Augustine, *On Christian Doctrine*, Book I, 24, §24 (p. 20).

19. Ibid., Book I, 26–32 (pp. 22–28).

20. Ibid., Book I, 35, §39 (p. 30).

21. Telford Work cites an article by Mark Jordan that makes clear how Augustine keeps the Teacher, rather than the texts, primarily in view. As Jordan recognizes, for Augustine "'any method of reading the Scriptures is fundamentally a reflection on words as analogous to Christ the Word.' Biblical practices actualize the incarnation in the context of the Church, disclosing its mystery to those chosen to receive it. The point of Augustine's argument 'is to construct fundamental analogies between signification and Incarnation'" (Work, *Living and Active*, 52, citing Jordan's "Words and Word: Incarnation and Signification in Augustine's *De Doctrina Christiana*," *Augustinian Studies* 11 [1980]: 177–96, at 177–78). See also two valuable studies on Christ's teaching and Christian teaching, according to Aquinas, in *Reading John with St. Thomas Aquinas: Theological Exegesis and Speculative Theology*, ed. Michael Dauphinais and Matthew Levering (Washington, D.C.: Catholic University of America Press, 2005): Michael Sherwin, O.P., "Christ the Teacher in St. Thomas's *Commentary on the Gospel of John*," 173–93; and Serge-Thomas Bonino, O.P., "The Role of the Apostles in the Communication of Revelation according to the *Lectura super Ioannem* of St. Thomas Aquinas," trans. Teresa Bede and Matthew Levering, 318–46.

22. Augustine, *On Christian Doctrine*, Book I, 36, §40 (p. 30).

23. Ibid., Book I, 37, §41 (p. 31); cf. Book II, 7, §9 (pp.38–39).

24. Ibid., Book I, 39, §43 (p. 32).

25. On the engagement of divine love as the meaning of Israel's history and that of the world, cf. Yves Congar, O.P.'s *The Mystery of the Temple or the Manner of God's Presence to His Creatures from Genesis to the Apocalypse*, trans. Reginald Trevett (London: Burns & Oates, 1962); for discussion, see James Hanvey, S.J., "In the Presence of Love: The Pneumatological Realization of the Economy: Yves Congar's *Le Mystère du Temple*," *International Journal of Systematic Theology* 7 (2005): 383–98. Without then knowing of Congar's book, Michael Dauphinais and I pursue much the same themes in *Holy People, Holy Land: A Theological Introduction to the Bible* (Grand Rapids, Mich.: Brazos, 2005).

26. For detailed discussion of an example of Augustine's exegesis, see my "Augustine and Aquinas on the Good Shepherd: The Value of an Exegetical Tradition," in *Aquinas the Augustinian*, ed. Michael Dauphinais, Barry David, and Matthew Levering (Washington, D.C.: Catholic University of America Press, 2007), 205–42.

27. Augustine, *On Christian Doctrine*, Book II, 6, §7 (p. 37).

28. Ibid., Book II, 7, §10 (p. 39).

29. Ibid., Book II, 7, §§10–11 (pp. 39–40). For further discussion of this pattern, see Work, *Living and Active*, 304–7.

30. My use of *doctrina*, following Augustine and Aquinas, has similarities with A. K. M. Adam's use of Julia Kristeva's concept of "signifying practice," insofar as we are both attempting to describe the source of the unity, despite differing methodologies, of speculative theology and biblical exegesis as theological disciplines. I find *doctrina* particularly useful because it analogously expresses both God's Word and human teaching, rather thereby ensures that the source is not our practice, but God's living Word—put differently, *doctrina* expresses a metaphysical/theological rather than hermeneutical/epistemological framework. Adam's work on "signifying practice," grounded in the Word's signifying, complements my approach. See Adam's forthcoming "'He Placed Himself in the Order of Signs': Exegesis Signifying Theology." The need to articulate the unity of the two disciplines is made clear in Adam's "Docetism, Käsemann, and Christology: Why Historical Criticism Can't Protect Christological Orthodoxy," *Scottish Journal of Theology* 49 (1996): 391–410.

31. Wolterstorff, *Divine Discourse: Philosophical Reflections on the Claim That God Speaks* (Cambridge: Cambridge University Press, 1995), 242. Cf., for philosophical arguments in favor of reading Scripture as a unified whole, Stephen T. Davis, "Philosophical Presuppositions and Biblical Exegesis," in *Truth, Religious Dialogue and Dynamic Orthodoxy: Essays on the Work of Brian Hebblethwaite*, ed. Julius J. Lipner (London: SCM Press, 2005), 71–84. In the process of making his case, Davis notes that the Bible affirms that "time is linear," in the sense that time moves progressively toward a goal, the kingdom of God (81). Insofar as all time is already in some respect caught up in relation to the kingdom of God, however, I would add that time is more than linear.

32. Cf. I. Howard Marshall's appeal to "a mind nourished on the gospel" (Marshall, *Beyond the Bible: Moving from Scripture to Theology* [Grand Rapids, Mich.: Baker, 2004], 70), or Kevin J. Vanhoozer's appeal, in response to Marshall in the same volume, to "the mind of the canon" (93). Vanhoozer states, "According to Luke 24, it was Jesus himself who taught his disciples to go beyond the Scriptures in order to see how they point to him. Here is a canonical practice—figural reading—that proceeds from Christ's very own prophetic office! As with all the other canonical practices, the point is to train us to see, think, and judge so that we will be fit participants in the ongoing drama of redemption. Canonical practices are rule-governed forms of covenantal behavior that direct the seeing, judging, and acting of the believing community. We acquire canonical competence—a mind nurtured on the Christ-centered canon—when we learn how to make the same kind of judgments about God, the world, and ourselves as those embedded in Scripture. To exposit the Scriptures is to participate in the canonical practices—practices that form, inform, and transform our speaking, thinking, and living" (94). See also Vanhoozer's

The Drama of Doctrine: A Canonical-Linguistic Approach to Theology (Louisville: Westminster/John Knox, 2004).

33. This understanding of *sacra doctrina* serves to bridge what R. R. Reno calls "the historical and metaphysical problems of distance. . . . Time separates us from what is said, and the finite form of all signs and texts makes the Bible a peculiar instrument for speaking about God" (Reno, *The Ruins of the Church* [Grand Rapids, Mich.: Brazos Press, 2002], 169). As Reno shows, the Fathers of the Church engage these problems of "distance" from the perspective of the human "conversation" with God, in which the fundamental distance consists in sin that breaks off communion between human beings and God.

34. See also my "Augustine and Aquinas on the Good Shepherd."

35. Thomas Aquinas, "Commendation of and Division of Sacred Scripture," in *Thomas Aquinas: Selected Writings*, ed. and trans. Ralph McInerny (New York: Penguin, 1998), 5. For historical study of the genre of the "sermon" in the Middle Ages (a genre mirrored in Aquinas's lecture), see, e.g., Louis-Jacques Bataillon, O.P., "Chronique de doctrines médiévales. Études récentes sur les sermons," *Revue des sciences philosophiques et théologiques* 88 (2004): 789–805. He treats the massive volume edited by Beverly Mayne Kienzle, *The Sermon* (Turnhout: Brepols, 2000) as well as David d'Avray, *Medieval Marriage Sermons: Mass Communication in a Culture without Print* (Oxford: Oxford University Press, 2001); idem, *Death and the Prince: Memorial Preaching before 1350* (Oxford: Oxford University Press, 1994); and Christoph Maier, *Preaching the Crusades: Mendicant Friars and the Cross in the Thirteenth Century* (Cambridge: Cambridge University Press, 1994), among others. See also Bataillon, "Early Scholastic and Mendicant Preaching as Exegesis of Scripture," in *Ad litteram: Authoritative Texts and Their Medieval Readers*, ed. Mark D. Jordan and Kent Emery Jr. (Notre Dame: University of Notre Dame Press, 1992).

36. For Aquinas's theology of revelation, see especially Leo J. Elders, S.V.D., "Aquinas on Holy Scripture as the Medium of Divine Revelation," in *La doctrine de la révélation divine de saint Thomas d'Aquin*, ed. Leo J. Elders (Vatican City: Libreria Editrice Vaticana, 1990), 132–52.

37. Cf. the observation by Denis Farkasfalvy, O. Cist., following Origen and other Fathers, that "[t]he encounter between God and man is consummated on a spiritual level: spirit becomes united to Spirit. Consequently, the exegete must operate on the supposition that the divine words and deeds, witnessed to in the Bible, are ultimately addressed to man's spiritual faculties in order to elicit from them the response of faith and love" (Farkasfalvy, "The Case for Spiritual Exegesis," *Communio* 10 [1983]: 348). See also for Aquinas's theocentric—thus intrinsically metaphysical—reading of Scripture Waclaw Swierzawski's marvelous "God and the Mystery of His Wisdom in the Pauline Commentaries of Saint Thomas Aquinas," *Divus Thomas* 74 (1971): 466–500.

38. Aquinas, "Commendation of and Division of Sacred Scripture," 6.

39. Ibid.

40. Ibid. The divine Teacher's work is manifested not only in the canonical form of the Bible, but also already in the communities in which the texts of the Bible were authored and canonized under the inspiration of the Holy Spirit. Michael Dauphinais and I try to draw out this unity in *Holy People, Holy Land*.

41. Aquinas, "Commendation of and Division of Sacred Scripture," 6.

42. Ibid., 7.

43. Ibid.

44. St. John of Damascus, *An Exact Exposition of the Orthodox Faith*, Book IV, ch. 17, in *St. John of Damascus: Writings*, trans. Frederic H. Chase Jr. (Washington, D.C.: Catholic University of America Press, 1958), 374; cf. Telford Work's attention to Athanasius in *Living and Active*.

45. *The Future of Catholic Biblical Scholarship* begins with Johnson's "What's Catholic about Catholic Biblical Scholarship? An Opening Statement": see Luke Timothy Johnson and William S. Kurz, S.J., *The Future of Catholic Biblical Scholarship: A Constructive Conversation* (Grand Rapids, Mich.: Eerdmans, 2002), 3–34. This marvelous essay, originally an address to the 1997 meeting of the Catholic Biblical Association, compares twentieth-century Catholic biblical scholarship with the acculturation process undergone by immigrants: the first generation still follows the traditional ways, the second generation seeks to "inculturate" in every respect, and the third generation, while embedded firmly in the new culture, seeks to recover some of the neglected traditional ways. Johnson presents his work as an example of "third-generation" Catholic biblical scholarship, in which he seeks to recover patristic-medieval modes of exegesis while incorporating the insights of historical-critical research. On this model, which I think is accurate, "second-generation" Catholic exegetes include Raymond Brown, Joseph Fitzmyer, S.J., and Roland E. Murphy, O. Carm. All three have published books and articles defending historical-critical biblical scholarship against the rising tide of alternative methods. For the situation in the late-nineteenth through the mid-twentieth centuries, in which nascent historical-critical biblical scholarship (what might be called the "first generation") was first suppressed among Catholic scholars in the United States and then gradually developed, see Gerald P. Fogarty, S.J., *American Catholic Biblical Scholarship: A History from the Early Republic to Vatican II*, with a foreword by Roland Murphy (San Francisco: Harper & Row, 1989). For a positive response to Johnson, see Bernd Sixtus, "Bridging the Gap? On Some Suggestions towards Solving the Normative Problem in Ecclesial Exegesis," *Scottish Journal of Theology* 58 (2005): 13–38. For a negative response, see Roland Murphy, O. Carm., "What Is Catholic about Catholic Biblical Scholarship?—Revisited," *Biblical Theology Bulletin* 28 (1998): 112–19. Since his speciality is the Old Testament Wisdom literature, Murphy gives as an example the interpretation of the Song of Songs. He argues for "the age-old interpretation that finds God

and humans in an intimate relationship. That still remains valid and valuable. It has fed, and will continue to feed, the mystical experiences of many ardent lovers of God. The relationship between God and the people of God, important as it is, can be illustrated by so many other data in the Bible. Besides, the allegorical features in this body of tradition are largely superficial according to modern taste. We do not need such a complicated allegorical portrayal to view the love of God and humans. But we do need, as sexual creatures, to hear what the inspired word communicates about the relationship between the sexes" (118; cf. Murphy, "The Song of Songs: Critical Biblical Scholarship vis-à-vis Exegetical Traditions," in *Understanding the Word: Essays in Honor of Bernhard W. Anderson*, ed. James T. Butler, Edgar W. Conrad, and Ben C. Ollenburger [Sheffield: JSOT Press, 1985], 63–69). This seriously misunderstands patristic-medieval approaches. See also Joseph A. Fitzmyer, S.J., "Historical Criticism: Its Role in Biblical Interpretation and Church Life," *Theological Studies* 50 (1989): 244–59; Raymond E. Brown, S.S., *Biblical Exegesis and Church Doctrine* (New York: Paulist Press, 1985); T. R. Curtin, *Historical Criticism and the Theological Interpretation of Scripture: The Catholic Discussion of a Biblical Hermeneutic: 1958–1983* (Rome: Gregorian University, 1987). For a comparison of Murphy's exegesis with that of St. Bonaventure that is appreciative of both, see Jeremy Holmes, "Biblical Scholarship New and Old: Learning from the Past," *Nova et Vetera* 1 (2003): 303–20.

46. Johnson and Kurz, *The Future of Catholic Biblical Scholarship*, 119. Out of concern to avoid an idealism that would crystallize Scripture's message into a disembodied "essence," Johnson distinguishes "imagination" and "images" from less embodied "ideas." Johnson is too hesitant here, because the biblical authors, as he himself makes clear, certainly advance ideas and not merely metaphors and images. See the criticisms posed to this aspect of Johnson's approach by David S. Yeago, "Re-Entering the Scriptural World," *Nova et Vetera* 4 (2006): 159–71, esp. 169–70. For an account of biblical interpretation as imagination-reliant, cf. Walter Brueggemann, "Imagination as a Mode of Fidelity," in Butler, Conrad, and Ollenburger, *Understanding the Word*, 13–36. In this regard Brevard Childs's critique of Brueggemann as ultimately falling into the liberal Protestant exegetical mode described by Hans Frei strikes me as correct. In response to Brueggemann's approach to canonical exegesis in "Canonization and Contextualization" (in Brueggemann, *Interpretation and Obedience* [Philadelphia: Fortress, 1991]), Childs observes that Brueggemann— drawing on David Tracy's terminology—relies on the voices of the oppressed, mediated by the interpreter, to actualize the "classic" text and thereby instantiate the Church's "canonical interpretation" today. This procedure, in which "[t]he inert text of the classic receives its meaning when it is correlated with some other external cultural force, ideology, or mode of existence," is as Childs says "exactly the hermeneutical typology which H. Frei so brilliantly described

in his book, *The Eclipse of Biblical Narrative*. It makes little difference whether the needed component for correctly interpreting the Bible is the Enlightenment's appeal to reason, consciousness, and pure spirit, or to Karl Marx's anti-Enlightenment ideology of a classless society and the voice of the proletariat. The hermeneutical move is identical. . . . The theological appeal to an authoritative canonical text which has been shaped by Israel's witness to a history of divine, redemptive intervention has been replaced by a radically different construal" (Childs, *Biblical Theology of the Old and New Testaments*, 73). As Childs makes clear, modern and postmodern biblical interpretation imagines the text as fundamentally "inert" rather than as bespeaking ecclesially identifiable realities of faith. See also the parallel critique offered by Jon D. Levenson, "Is Brueggemann Really a Pluralist?" *Harvard Theological Review* 93 (2000): 265–94.

47. Johnson and Kurz, *The Future of Catholic Biblical Scholarship*, 121.

48. On the need for repentance in order to purify the imagination, see Ellen F. Davis, "Teaching the Bible Confessionally in the Church," in *The Art of Reading Scripture*, ed. Ellen F. Davis and Richard B. Hays (Grand Rapids, Mich.: Eerdmans, 2003), 11–12. Davis's emphasis on the Bible's symbols could be augmented by attention to the analogical and metaphysical dimension of biblical language, which would also assist Davis in assessing truth claims.

49. Johnson and Kurz, *The Future of Catholic Biblical Scholarship*, 271.

50. On this difference, see ibid., 36–39, 266. Augustine's Christological reflection on *sapientia* and *scientia* may provide the inspiration here, with the former connected with the divine realities and the latter with the human realities (cf. Augustine, *The Trinity*, trans. Edmund Hill, O.P. [Brooklyn, N.Y.: New City Press, 1991], Book XII, ch. 4, 334–37). For another understanding of "wisdom" in biblical interpretation, where wisdom is connected with the practical dimension in contrast to mere rational information, see David F. Ford, "Jesus Christ, the Wisdom of God (1)," in *Reading Texts, Seeking Wisdom: Scripture and Theology*, ed. David F. Ford and Graham Stanton (Grand Rapids, Mich.: Eerdmans, 2003), 4–21.

51. See Johnson and Kurz, *The Future of Catholic Biblical Scholarship*, 39.

52. Ibid.

53. Cf. Johnson's *Living Jesus: Learning the Heart of the Gospel* (New York: HarperSanFrancisco, 1999). In his preface to *Living Jesus* Johnson indicates his keen awareness of the task faced by biblical interpreters: "Is there a place between a historicism that wants to keep Jesus locked in his past and a mysticism that threatens to vaporize the particularity of Jesus altogether? I try to locate that place in a process of intersubjective learning within the community of faith—a process in which the diverse portrayals of Jesus in the writings of the New Testament play a positive rather than a negative role."

54. Johnson and Kurz, *The Future of Catholic Biblical Scholarship*, 252.

55. A mystery is not "a puzzle which ceases to be a puzzle as soon as enough information becomes available" but instead "something whose intrinsic

depth cannot be exhausted—simply expressed, the more you know, the more you know you do not know" (R. W. L. Moberly, *The Bible, Theology, and Faith: A Study of Abraham and Jesus* [Cambridge: Cambridge University Press, 2000], 42). Thomas Weinandy, O.F.M. Cap., in his chapter "Theology—Problems and Mysteries," in *Does God Suffer?* (Notre Dame: University of Notre Dame Press, 2000), 27–39, traces this distinction between a "mystery" and a "problem" (or "puzzle") to Gabriel Marcel's *The Mystery of Being*, vol. 1, *Reflection and Mystery* (London: Harvill, 1950), 204–19.

56. Joseph Ratzinger comments that theological biblical interpretation "must recognize that the faith of the church is that form of 'sympathia' without which the Bible remains a *closed* book. It must come to acknowledge this faith as a hermeneutic, the space for understanding, which does not do dogmatic violence to the Bible, but precisely allows the solitary possibility for the Bible to be itself" (Ratzinger, "Biblical Interpretation in Crisis: On the Question of the Foundations and Approaches of Exegesis Today," in *Biblical Interpretation in Crisis: The Ratzinger Conference on Bible and Church*, ed. Richard John Neuhaus [Grand Rapids, Mich.: Eerdmans, 1989], 22–23).

57. Cf. Johnson's *The Real Jesus: The Misguided Quest for the Historical Jesus and the Truth of the Traditional Gospels* (New York: HarperSanFrancisco, 1996). Johnson's chapters on "The Limitations of History" and "What's Historical about Jesus?" in *The Real Jesus*, written in response to the Jesus Seminar, are particularly valuable in setting forth what historical-critical research can and cannot demonstrate. Johnson identifies Luther as the key figure in the transition from ecclesial exegesis to modern academic exegesis, although Luther hardly would have accepted the results of the latter: "Luther was from beginning to end not only an interpreter of the Bible but a passionate lover of the texts and of the One to whom they pointed. Nevertheless, his approach to the New Testament (which was to prove overwhelmingly influential in the development of critical scholarship) was deeply if unconsciously affected by the intellectual climate of the Renaissance. This can be seen not only in his preference for the recovered Greek text over the Latin Vulgate proclaimed in the church (note here the implicit authority of the Greek-reading scholar over the Latin-dependent clergy), but above all in his commitment to a certain kind of historical understanding. The recovery of the original text was key to the recovery of original Christianity. Just as Renaissance scholars, once classical texts were recovered, could measure the inadequacy of late-medieval society against the grandeur of Greece and Rome, so could the theologian measure the inadequacy of medieval Christianity against the norm of the primitive church, or even better, the figure of Jesus himself" (68). Johnson identifies two Renaissance assumptions in this move: the superiority of the period of origins, and the use of the recovery of the period of origins as an instrument of societal reform. This attempt to return to the purity of origins, in Johnson's view, separates biblical scholarship from its ecclesial and theological matrix ("church, canon, and creed"

[67]) and ties it to history. See also Christopher Seitz, "'In Accordance with the Scriptures': Creed, Scripture, and 'Historical Jesus,'" in his *Word without End: The Old Testament as Abiding Theological Witness* (Grand Rapids, Mich.: Eerdmans, 1998), 51–60, which nicely captures the irony of ahistorical historical reconstruction.

58. On the relationship between Scripture and Tradition in *Dei Verbum*, see most recently Carmen Aparicio Valls, "La tradición según la *Dei Verbum* y su importancia en la teología ecuménica actual," *Gregorianum* 86 (2005): 163–81; among the vast literature, cf. A. Franzini, *Tradizione e scrittura. Il contributo del Concilio Vaticano II* (Brescia: 1978); F. Castro Aguayo, *Relación entre Sagrada Escritura y tradición según la constitución Dei Verbum* (Pamplona: 1987); J. Feiner, "La contribution du secrétariat pour l'unité des chrétiens à la Constitution dogmatique sur la Révélation divine," in *La Révélation divine*, vol. 1, ed. B.-D. Dupuis (Paris: 1968). See also the essays in *Your Word Is Truth: A Project of Evangelicals and Catholics Together*, ed. Charles Colson and Richard John Neuhaus (Grand Rapids, Mich.: Eerdmans, 2002), esp. Avery Dulles, S.J.'s "Revelation, Scripture and Tradition." See also the work of George Tavard, *Holy Writ or Holy Church: The Crisis of the Protestant Reformation* (New York: Harper & Brothers, 1959); and Yves Congar, O.P., *The Meaning of Tradition*, trans. A. N. Woodrow (1964; reprint, with a new foreword by Avery Dulles, S.J., San Francisco: Ignatius Press, 2004).

59. Johnson and Kurz, *The Future of Catholic Biblical Scholarship*, 257; cf. 273. See also Richard B. Hays, "The Future of *Christian* Biblical Scholarship," *Nova et Vetera* 4 (2006): 95–120, a response to Johnson and Kurz's book. Hays critiques Kurz in particular: "Kurz is, from start to finish, committed to performing biblical interpretation within the framework of Catholic teaching, as mediated through the Church's *magisterium*. He champions the *Catechism of the Catholic Church* as an appropriate guide to reading Scripture, and his sample exegetical probes unfailingly support contemporary Catholic doctrine and practice, whether the issue is Christology, abortion, Eucharist, or the sacrament of reconciliation. At no point does he entertain the notion that Scripture might play a critical role in relation to tradition, or that received ecclesiastical interpretations might be in need of some correction. He comes across, in these chapters at least, as a good company man, who strongly believes that the institution of the Catholic Church provides comprehensive and satisfying guidelines for interpreting Scripture. This gives his chapters the virtue of clarity and consistency, but one never has the sense that Kurz is actually *learning* anything through his exegesis or that Scripture might have the capacity to *surprise* the Catholic reader. Rather, his exegesis consistently reinforces preestablished beliefs and practices—and vice-versa" (109). As a preliminary response to Hays, I would suggest that his notion of "the Catholic reader" is perhaps outdated. Many Catholic readers, as Kurz recognizes, would be surprised to find that biblical exegesis supports Magisterial interpretation of Scripture. Among other

things, the Catholic reader learns from Kurz's exegesis a surprising valuation of the Church's exegesis. See also Olivier-Thomas Venard, O.P.'s comments in "'La Bible en ses Traditions': The New Project of the *École biblique et archéologique française de Jérusalem* Presented as a 'Fourth-Generation' Enterprise," *Nova et Vetera* 4 (2006): 142–59, at 154–55.

60. For succinct analysis of human authorial intention that distinguishes "authorial motives" from "an author's communicative intention" (the latter being accessible in the text), see Stephen E. Fowl, "The Role of Authorial Intention in the Theological Interpretation of Scripture," in *Between Two Horizons: Spanning New Testament Studies and Systematic Theology,* ed. Joel B. Green and Max Turner (Grand Rapids, Mich.: Eerdmans, 2000), 71–87; cf., for further discussion of this distinction, Kevin Vanhoozer, *Is There a Meaning in This Text? The Bible, the Reader, and the Morality of Literary Knowledge* (Grand Rapids, Mich.: Zondervan, 1998). Fowl points out in his article, as he does elsewhere, that Aquinas's account of the literal sense does not restrict the number of possible meanings to one, because God's authorial intention is involved in the biblical text and God can intend many meanings even in the literal sense, because of the comprehensive scope of God's knowledge. Yet this point does not mean for Aquinas that the literal sense is radically undetermined, as at times some scholars seem to think.

61. The question of Jesus' human knowledge of divine *doctrina* is a complex one that tends to be caricatured by reduction of Jesus' knowing to a set of concepts whose value for our salvation is then difficult to see. I have tried to indicate a better course for Jesus' human knowledge as it pertains to our salvation in *Christ's Fulfillment of Torah and Temple: Salvation according to Thomas Aquinas* (Notre Dame: University of Notre Dame Press, 2002); and *Sacrifice and Community: Jewish Offering and Christian Eucharist* (Oxford: Blackwell, 2005). This question remains plagued by both theological rationalism and epistemological conceptualism.

62. Aquinas, *De potentia* q. 4, a. 1, ad 8. I am using the translation done by the English Dominican Fathers in Thomas Aquinas, *On the Power of God: Quaestiones disputatae de potentia dei* (1932; Eugene, Ore.: Wipf & Stock, 2004). With the Fathers' exegesis in mind, Aquinas adds that "every truth that can be adapted to the sacred text without prejudice to the literal sense, is the sense of Holy Scripture." For an example, see Rowan Greer's treatment of the Fathers' various interpretations of John 10 in his "The Good Shepherd: Canonical Interpretations in the Early Church?" in *Theological Exegesis: Essays in Honor of Brevard S. Childs,* ed. Christopher Seitz and Kathryn Greene-McCreight (Grand Rapids, Mich.: Eerdmans, 1999), 306–30, as well as my "Augustine and Aquinas on the Good Shepherd."

63. David C. Steinmetz, "Uncovering a Second Narrative: Detective Fiction and the Construction of Historical Method," in Davis and Hays, *The Art of Reading Scripture,* 54–65, at 65.

64. In the roundtable discussion summarized by Paul Stallsworth in *Biblical Interpretation in Crisis*, ed. Richard John Neuhaus (Grand Rapids, Mich.: Eerdmans, 1989), David Wells points out that "'of course the autonomy of the individual interpreter opens the door to great abuse. But I think you should hear the other side of the argument: The autonomy of the church also opens itself to great abuse. If it is true that the interpreter can be overcome by vested interests in his or her reading of the text, it is equally true that an interpreting church can be overcome by vested interests in its reading of the text" (161). Similarly, speaking on the basis of notes prepared by John Rodgers, Wells later cautions that "where you have this very neat conjunction between Scripture, tradition, and the church, what you are really looking at is a kind of translation theology. In principle, it does the same thing that radical feminists and liberationists do. Only here the Word of God is faded out into a kind of ecclesiastical vernacular. John Rodgers's concern is that the Word of God must be unfettered. If the church attempts to fetter or control the Scriptures, then Christ is no longer free to speak through it" (173). In his *Biblical Theology of the Old and New Testaments*, Childs struggles with the same problem: will not a robust account of the Church's participation in and mediation of the Word of God result in the Church's controlling and eventually muting Christ, in a profound distortion of what should be? In contrast Catholics, recognizing the sinfulness of human beings, nonetheless trust in faith that Christ, through the gift of the Holy Spirit, will sustain his Bride in faithfully witnessing, though not with eschatological fullness, to his cruciform image by mediating sacramentally and doctrinally his deifying wisdom and love to the world. This confidence in Christ, which fuels rather than mitigates the call for constant renewal of the Church in holiness, partakes in Christian "foolishness" (1 Cor 1:18–31). As John Paul II observes with respect to the Incarnation, "In a certain sense God has gone too far!" (*Crossing the Threshold of Hope*, ed. Vittorio Messori, trans. Jenny and Martha McPhee [New York: Knopf, 1995], 40).

65. John Webster makes this point in *Holy Scripture: A Dogmatic Sketch* (Cambridge: Cambridge University Press, 2003), 106. See also Robert Jenson's remark: "In the church any passage of Scripture is to be read for its contribution to the telling of Scripture's whole story" (Jenson, "Scripture's Authority in the Church," in Davis and Hays, *The Art of Reading Scripture*, 29).

66. *Summa theologiae* I, q. 68, a. 1.

67. *On Christian Doctrine*, Book I, 35–36, §§39–40 (p. 30).

68. Alois Grillmeier provides a detailed survey, favoring the interventions of Cardinal König, of the genesis and intent of §§11–13 of *Dei Verbum* in "The Divine Inspiration and the Interpretation of Sacred Scripture," in Vorgrimler, *Commentary on the Documents of Vatican II*, vol. 3, 199–246; for §12, see 215–26, 237–45. For additional insight, see Thomas J. McGovern, "The Interpretation of Scripture 'in the Spirit': The Edelby Intervention at Vatican II," *Irish Theo-*

logical Quarterly 64 (1999): 245–59. McGovern recounts the influence of the Melchite Archbishop Neophytos Edelby of Edessa's intervention on October 5, 1964, emphasizing the action of the Holy Spirit, during the drafting of §12 (for the text of the intervention, in English translation, see "Appendix One: A Neglected Conciliar Intervention," in Gerald O'Collins, S.J., *Retrieving Fundamental Theology*, 174–77, although in O'Collins's view Archbishop Edelby's intervention "came too late and hardly affected the final shape of *Dei Verbum*" [*Retrieving Fundamental Theology*, 56]). In understanding biblical interpretation as ecclesial, participatory *sacra doctrina* in which the aim is (deifying) learning of the triune God, I am in agreement with Archbishop Edelby's vision of the goal and context of biblical interpretation. See also the discussion of §12 in Kevin Duffy, "Exegetes and Theologians," *Irish Theological Quarterly* 63 (1998): 219–31; Norbert Lohfink, "Der weiße Fleck in *Dei Verbum*, Artikel 12," *Trierer Theologische Zeitschrift* 101 (1992): 20–35; Walter Kasper, "Prolegomena zur Erneuerung der geistlichen Schriftauslegung," in *Vom Urchristentum zu Jesus: Für Joachim Gnilka*, ed. H. Frankemölle and K. Kertelge (Freiburg: Herder, 1989).

69. For discussion of this text, see also Ignace de la Potterie, "Interpretation of Holy Scripture in the Spirit in Which It Was Written," in *Vatican II: Assessment and Perspectives*, vol. 1, ed. René Latourelle (New York: Paulist Press, 1988), 220–66; Francis Martin, "Some Aspects of Biblical Studies since Vatican II: The Contribution and Challenge of *Dei Verbum*," in Martin, *Sacred Scripture: The Disclosure of the Word* (Naples, Fla.: Sapientia Press, 2006), 227–47. I have slightly modified the translation in *Vatican Council II*, vol. 1, *The Conciliar and Post Conciliar Documents*, ed. Austin Flannery, O.P., rev. ed. (Northport, N.Y.: Costello, 1975). The Latin text reads (with the addition, made after Archbishop Edelby's intervention, in italics): "*Sed*, cum sacra scriptura eodem Spiritu quo scripta est etiam legenda et interpretanda sit, *ad recte sacrorum textuum sensum eruendum, non minus diligenter respiciendum est ad contentum et unitatem totius scripturae, ratione habita vivae totius ecclesiae traditionis et analogiae fidei.* Exegetarum autem est secundum has regulas adlaborare ad sacrae scripturae sensum penitius intelligendum et exponendum, ut quasi praeparato studio, iudicium ecclesiae maturetur. Cuncta enim haec, de ratione interpretandi scripturam, ecclesiae iudicio ultime subsunt, quae verbi Dei servandi et interpretandi divino fungitur mandato et ministerio" (*Decrees of the Ecumenical Councils*, vol. II, *Trent–Vatican II*, ed. Norman P. Tanner, S.J. [Washington, D.C.: Georgetown University Press, 1990], 976–77). The English translation of *Dei Verbum* included in Tanner's volume is poor.

70. For Johnson's five "premises of premodern interpretation," and his commentary on these premises, see Johnson and Kurz, *The Future of Catholic Biblical Scholarship*, 47–60. For Kurz's comparison of these premises with *Dei Verbum*, see ibid., 152–53.

71. Thomas McGovern points out with regard to this principle in *Dei Verbum* §12: "The content and unity of Scripture, as a manifestation of the Spirit, is not then a literary criterion. It does not refer to the *books* of Scripture themselves, but to the reality to which these books give testimony" (McGovern, "The Interpretation of Scripture 'in the Spirit': The Edelby Intervention at Vatican II," 253). This reality ultimately is the gospel of Jesus Christ (cf. Lk 24:27, 32). As McGovern says, "Consequently, reading and interpreting any biblical text from the perspective of the unity and content of Scripture is, in the first place, a *dynamic* operation. Not all the texts have the same significance although all are inspired; they illuminate one another when they are seen in their historical-salvific dynamic, not just by mere juxtaposition" (254).

72. For further discussion of the Tradition, in light of the mission of the Holy Spirit, see McGovern, "The Interpretation of Scripture 'in the Spirit': The Edelby Intervention at Vatican II," 254–57. McGovern probes with similar acuity the analogy of faith, pointing to its biblical source in Romans 12:6 (257–58).

73. Translation from Flannery, *Vatican Council II*, 756.

74. Ibid., 757. The nuances of the Latin text somewhat escape translation: "Cum ergo omne id, quod auctores inspirati seu hagiographi asserunt, retineri debeat assertum a Spiritu sancto, inde scripturae libri veritatem, quam Deus nostrae salutis causa litteris sacris consignari voluit, firmiter, fideliter et sine errore docere profitendi sunt" (Tanner, 976).

75. Without judging individual souls, one should consider the role of interior conversion in interpretation. As Hans Urs von Balthasar has remarked (to the discomfort of those who consider exegesis a strictly objective science), "behind the front lines of the 'scientific' arguments, with their endless skirmishing, we can discern the two fundamental attitudes of faith and unbelief, in whose service the arguments are used. These fundamental attitudes are irreducible: one sees the form *[Gestalt]*, the other is blind to it" (von Balthasar, *Theo-Drama*, vol. 4: *The Action*, trans. Graham Harrison [San Francisco: Ignatius Press, 1994 (German 1980)], 461). A similar point is made by Roy A. Harrisville, "The Loss of Biblical Authority and Its Recovery," in Braaten and Jenson, *Reclaiming the Bible for the Church*, 47–61, at 60–61.

76. For excellent discussion of this Christological analogy, which *Lumen Gentium* takes from Pius XII's encyclical *Divino Afflante Spiritu* (§37), and which is also found in such theologians as Karl Barth and Aidan Nichols, O.P., see Work, *Living and Active*, 19–32. Work discusses the objections of Markus Barth and James Barr. The Pontifical Biblical Commission, in its 1993 document *The Interpretation of the Bible in the Church*, trans. John Kilgallen and Brendan Byrne (Boston: St. Paul Books & Media, 1993), makes the Christological analogy the grounds for affirming the necessity and priority of historical-critical biblical interpretation. For a critique of the document in this regard,

see Lewis Ayres and Stephen E. Fowl, "(Mis)reading the Face of God: *The Interpretation of the Bible in the Church*," *Theological Studies* 60 (1999): 513–28; see also two articles that can be read partially as responses to Ayres and Fowl's critique, Michael Cahill, "The History of Exegesis and Our Theological Future," *Theological Studies* 61 (2000): 332–47, and Marie Anne Mayeski, "Quaestio Disputata: Catholic Theology and the History of Exegesis," *Theological Studies* 62 (2001): 140–53. Cahill argues for retaining the primacy of the historical-critical approach (346) by focusing on the history of exegesis as itself a further historical-exegetical tool. Mayeski surveys the discussion of typology involving de Lubac, Daniélou, Bouyer, Jean Leclerq, and others in the 1940s–50s. As she recounts Bouyer's position: "The theological interpretation he described did not deal with textual details, arbitrarily and fancifully decided upon, but with the great matrix of theological ideas found in Christian doctrine. The corpus of revealed doctrine, articulated by the Church in its creeds, becomes a touchstone against subjectivity and superficiality" (151). For Bouyer, she says, such theological interpretation "depends on the historical-critical method and is complementary to it" (ibid.) because historical-critical research shows that the biblical texts were written in this theological mode, by which they must therefore be interpreted. I am not sure, however, that this point requires a claim about the necessity and priority of historical-critical research, and in this regard I agree with Ayres and Fowl. See also for discussion of the place of historical-critical research, James F. Keating, "The Invincible Allure of the Historical Jesus for Systematic Theology," *Irish Theological Quarterly* 66 (2001): 211–26, whose effort to steer a moderate course between rationalism and fideism would be strengthened by examining further the "rules which normally govern historical inquiry" (215); idem, "Contemporary Epistemology and Theological Application of the Historical Jesus Quest," *Josephinum Journal of Theology* 10 (2003): 343–56, which argues for "postfoundationalism"; and most recently "N. T. Wright and the Necessity of a Historical Apologetic of the Resurrection," *Josephinum Journal of Theology* 12 (2005): 43–56. Keating is certainly correct that historical research into Christianity's origins is appropriate and valuable.

77. Translation from Flannery, *Vatican Council II*, 759.

78. Ibid.

79. Ibid., 757–58.

80. Johnson and Kurz, *The Future of Catholic Biblical Scholarship*, 222; cf. Kurz's earlier work in "narrative criticism": *Reading Luke-Acts: Dynamics of Biblical Narrative* (Louisville: Westminster/John Knox Press, 1993). Kurz refers in particular to the theories of Paul Ricoeur and Marcel Dumais. For the former, see Kevin J. Vanhoozer, *Biblical Narrative in the Philosophy of Paul Ricoeur: A Study in Hermeneutics and Theology* (Cambridge: Cambridge University Press, 1990). For the latter, see Dumais, "L'actualisation de l'Écriture: Fondements

et procédures," *Science et Esprit* 51 (1999): 27–47; idem, "Sens de l'Écriture. Réexamen à la lumière de l'herméneutique philosophique et des approches littéraires récentes," *New Testament Studies* 45 (1999): 310–31. The idea of the "actualization" of Scripture, I think, tends toward making the historical meaning and the theological meaning overly extrinsic in relation to each other.

81. Johnson and Kurz, *The Future of Catholic Biblical Scholarship*, 223.

82. Stephen E. Fowl, "The Role of Authorial Intention in the Theological Interpretation of Scripture," in Green and Turner, *Between Two Horizons* (Grand Rapids, Mich.: Eerdmans, 2000), 71–87; cf. Quentin Skinner, "Motives, Intentions and the Interpretation of Texts," *New Literary History* 3 (1971): 393–408; Mark Brett, "Motives and Intentions in Genesis 1," *Journal of Theological Studies* 42 (1991): 1–16; Kevin J. Vanhoozer, *Is There a Meaning in This Text? The Bible, the Reader, and the Morality of Literary Knowledge* (Grand Rapids, Mich.: Zondervan, 1998). Vanhoozer's work employs speech-act theory in ways that participatory metaphysics complements. For similar use of speech-act theory, see Anthony C. Thiselton's *New Horizons in Hermeneutics: The Theory and Practice of Transforming Biblical Reading* (Grand Rapids, Mich.: Zondervan, 1992); idem, "From Speech Acts to Scripture Acts: The Covenant of Discourse and the Discourse of Covenant," in *After Pentecost: Language and Biblical Interpretation*, ed. C. Bartholomew, C. Greene, and K. Müller (Carlisle: Paternoster, 2001), 1–49. Brevard Childs approves of Thiselton's application of speech-act theory but finds himself in significant disagreement with Nicholas Wolterstorff's use of it in Wolterstorff's *Divine Discourse*: see Childs, "Speech-Act Theory and Biblical Interpretation," *Scottish Journal of Theology* 58 (2005): 375–92. For a critique of speech-act theory in biblical hermeneutics, see Stanley E. Porter, "Hermeneutics, Biblical Interpretation, and Theology: Hunch, Holy Spirit, or Hard Work?" in Marshall, *Beyond the Bible*, 112–18.

83. Olivier Artus sketches a different trajectory: for Artus, *Dei Verbum* takes up the emergent appreciation for historical-critical research in Leo XIII's *Providentissimus Deus* (1893) and Pius XII's *Divino Afflante Spiritu* (1943), and the hermeneutical developments after *Dei Verbum* (1965), especially as regards the reader as co-constituting textual meaning (Gadamer, Ricoeur), are then integrated by the Pontifical Biblical Commission's 1993 *The Interpretation of the Bible in the Church*, which applies the principles of *Dei Verbum*. See Artus, "*Dei Verbum*. L'exégèse catholique entre critique historique et renouveau des sciences bibliques," *Gregorianum* 86 (2005): 76–91. Such a trajectory, I think, makes too little of the patristic-medieval aspects found in *Dei Verbum*.

84. Cf. Hans Frei, "The Encounter of Jesus with the German Academy," app. B to Frei, *Types of Christian Theology*, ed. George Hunsinger and William C. Placher (New Haven: Yale University Press, 1992), 133–46, where he cautions against seeking a resolution "by juxtaposing a 'faith method' and 'historical method,' by trying to unite the Jesus of history with the Christ of faith. Two

methods don't result in one person" (145). In proposing an "integration," I am advocating not two methods but rather the deepening or expanding of our understanding of "historical" (and thus of "critical").

85. For the redaction history of *Dei Verbum*'s prologue, see Jared Wicks, "Pieter Smulders and *Dei Verbum*: 5. A Critical Reception of the Schema *De revelatione* of the Mixed Commission (1963)," *Gregorianum* 86 (2005): 92–134. This article is the fifth in Wicks's series in the *Gregorianum*, beginning in 2001, on Smulders's contributions to *Dei Verbum*.

86. See *Dei Verbum* §3, translation from *Vatican Council II*, vol. 1, *The Conciliar and Post Conciliar Documents*, ed. Austin Flannery, O.P. (Collegeville, Minn.: Liturgical Press, 1992), 751; the Latin reads: "Deus, per Verbum omnia creans (cf. Io 1,3) et conservans, in rebus creatis perenne sui testimonium hominibus praebet (cf. Rm 1, 19–20) et, viam salutis supernae aperire intendens, insuper protoparentibus inde ab initia semetipsum manifestavit" (Tanner, 972).

87. In contrast, Raymond Brown consistently finds historical chasms that need to be bridged by theological/ecclesial engineering. For instance: "If Catholic exegetes are freed from some supposed obligation to find the later custom in the NT and can interpret the first-century evidence for its own worth and not apologetically, we may see how unlikely is the thesis that only those manually ordained by the Twelve or even by the larger group of the apostles celebrated the Eucharist" (Brown, *The Critical Meaning of the Bible* [New York: Paulist Press, 1981], 77).

88. Although on this point, see Stephen E. Fowl, "Could Horace Talk with the Hebrews? Translatability and Moral Disagreement in MacIntyre and Stout," *Journal of Religious Ethics* 19 (1991): 1–20. I agree with Fowl that MacIntyre's claims about, in Fowl's words, "the problems and even the impossibility of translating the language of one tradition into the language of a competing tradition" (1) require nuancing so as to account for evangelization on the basis of persisting areas of agreement. Cf. E. D. Hirsch Jr.'s point, against Gadamer, that the true meaning cannot differ with each interpretation as if interpreters constituted rather than discerned (and thus *participated* in the constitution of) the true meaning: Hirsch, "Meaning and Significance Reinterpreted," *Critical Inquiry* 11 (1984): 202–25, at 212.

89. William S. Babcock, "*Caritas* and Signification in *De doctrina christiana* 1–3," in *De Doctrina Christiana: A Classic of Western Culture*, ed. Duane W. H. Arnold and Pamela Bright (Notre Dame: University of Notre Dame Press, 1995), 145–63, at 154.

90. It should be noted that this point goes beyond Johnson's position that biblical exegesis, including the spiritual senses, must be based in the "literal sense" understood as the narrative meaning, as opposed to the "historical sense." Biblical exegesis should not in Johnson's view be based in the hypothetical reconstructions of what the Bible might originally have meant that constitute

the "historical sense." The "historical sense" remains useful, in his view, as a way of challenging "bad theological claims made on the basis of inadequate history" (Johnson and Kurz, *The Future of Catholic Biblical Scholarship*, 273). I agree with Johnson that while Christianity's claims cannot be severed from history, the reconstructed history is not the history of the gospels: the apostolic witnesses, not academic practitioners of historical-critical reconstruction, must be granted primary ability to proclaim the truth about the history that breaks the boundaries of modern historiography. In this regard Johnson largely follows Frei, and his position is also close to Childs's insistence on canonical reading; his position would be strengthened by identifying the nominalist inheritance within what he calls the "historical sense." Cf. Joel Green's discussion of history and historiography in "In Quest of the Historical: Jesus, the Gospels, and Historicisms Old and New," *Christian Scholar's Review* 27 (1999): 544–60, as well as Joseph Ratzinger's discussion of the *Catechism of the Catholic Church*'s account of Scripture in Ratzinger's *On the Way to Jesus Christ*, trans. Michael J. Miller (German, 2004; San Francisco: Ignatius Press, 2005), 147–53.

91. Johnson and Kurz, *The Future of Catholic Biblical Scholarship*, 279. Johnson and Kurz disagree in this regard. Kurz's position evinces far more understanding of Catholic sexual ethics.

92. Johnson, *The Real Jesus*, 67.

93. These are Johnson's words, with which Kurz agrees: Johnson and Kurz, *The Future of Catholic Biblical Scholarship*, 286; cf. Johnson's discussion of diversity and communion in the early Church, "Koinonia: Diversity and Unity in Early Christianity," *Theology Digest* 46 (1999): 303–13. Cf. Geoffrey Wainwright, "Towards an Ecumenical Hermeneutic: How Can All Christians Read the Scriptures Together?" *Gregorianum* 76 (1995): 639–62. In a manner similar to Johnson and Kurz, Wainwright states that "there could be great ecumenical gain in drawing upon the riches of the hermeneutical Tradition such as they were opened up for us at the beginning of our half-century by Jean Daniélou's patristic *Bible et liturgie* and Henri de Lubac's *Exégèse médiévale*. I do not myself believe that we, in the West, must or can undo modernity, but I consider it possible and desirable that, after passing through the critical centuries, Western Catholics and Protestants should together reach a 'second naïveté' (P. Ricoeur), where we might also meet other Christians with other histories in the faith, whether long or more recent" (647–48). See also the points raised by Brian Daley, S.J., "The *Nouvelle Théologie* and the Patristic Revival: Sources, Symbols and the Science of Theology," *International Journal of Systematic Theology* 7 (2005): 362–82; and Aidan Nichols, O.P., "Thomism and the Nouvelle Théologie," *Thomist* 64 (2000): 1–19.

94. As emphasized by Francis Watson in *Text, Church and World: Biblical Interpretation in Theological Perspective* (Grand Rapids, Mich.: Eerdmans, 1994),

especially in his criticisms of the work of Hans Frei, George Lindbeck, and the "postliberal" school of theology (see especially his introduction to Part II, as well as chaps. 1, 7, and 8). With regard to the problems of postliberalism, which he regards as an improvement over merely historical-critical readings, Watson remarks: "A synchronic reading perspective is more appropriate to the status of the biblical texts as holy scripture than a diachronic one that locates them in the midst of an amorphous mass of uncertain, shifting, competing hypotheses. But a synchronic perspective that understands the text as an aesthetic object, an enclosed and self-contained world, overlooks the fact that the text is also an entity in the public, socio-political domain" (60). The postmodern/postliberal rejection or eschatological deferment of metaphysical and Christian "metanarratives" (foundations) results, at best, in narrative approaches that claim intrasystematic meaning. In Watson's view, for such approaches textuality becomes a covert "metaphysics" that constricts idolatrously the realities being described: "'God" the transcendent signifier who was supposed to provide thought with its transcendent ground, is to be reinscribed as immanent within textuality. He may be disclosed as the product of the futile though inescapable project of logocentrism, or honoured as a very important signifier within local languages; but the result of such an analysis is that the so-called metaphysical attributes of God are covertly transferred to textuality itself. Like God, textuality is unlimited and omnipresent, for there is nothing outside it. Like God, textuality is omnipotent: who can resist its will? Like God, textuality is omniscient, for all possible knowledge is contained within it. Like God, textuality is ultimately incomprehensible, and we can only submit ourselves to what we can never fully understand" (85). Later Watson observes that the epistemological claim that all reality is textually mediated "is not reducible to the ontological claim that there is nothing outside the text" (152). Yet, Watson is noticeably wary of metaphysics, and limits himself to gesturing in metaphysical directions by means of an exegetical account of the biblical creation narrative (on this aspect of Watson's thought, cf. chapters 6 and 7 of Watson's *Text and Truth: Redefining Biblical Theology* [Grand Rapids, Mich.: Eerdmans, 1997], "Creation in the Beginning," 225–75, and "In the Image of God," 277–304). I think that Watson's chapters on creation expose, among other things, that reading the Bible adequately requires a participatory metaphysics of being in order to apprehend the Creator–creature relationship: for a valuable approach to such metaphysics, including a superb critique of Heidegger, see David Bentley Hart, "The Offering of Names: Metaphysics, Nihilism, and Analogy," in *Reason and the Reasons of Faith*, ed. Paul J. Griffiths and Reinhard Hütter (New York: T. & T. Clark, 2005), 255–91. For extended critical engagement with central postmodern thinkers—Deleuze, Derrida, Lyotard, et al.—see Hart's *The Beauty of the Infinite: The Aesthetics of Christian Truth* (Grand Rapids, Mich.: Eerdmans, 2003), as well as Richard Bauckham's brief account of Lyotard's critique of metanarratives, and Bauckham's defense of the Bible as a "meta-narrative," in his "Reading Scripture as a Coherent Story," in Davis and Hays, *The Art of Reading Scripture*, 45–53.

95. Cf. Morna D. Hooker, "The Authority of the Bible: A New Testament Perspective," *Ex Auditu* 19 (2003): 45–64, in which she responds to claims such as the sun going around the earth by arguing that the "authority of the Bible" must be interpreted Christologically.

96. Babcock, "*Caritas* and Signification in *De doctrina christiana* 1–3," 155.

97. See St. Thomas Aquinas, *Summa contra gentiles*, trans. Anton C. Pegis, F. R. S. C. (Notre Dame: University of Notre Dame Press: 1975), Book I, ch. 1, p. 61; cf. Book I, ch. 1: "divine Wisdom testifies that He has assumed flesh and come into the world in order to make the truth known: 'For this I was born, and for this came I into the world, that I should give testimony to the truth' (John 18:37)" (60).

98. Cf. Watson's theses that "Love of neighbour, as understood by Jesus, is a necessary hermeneutical criterion for a Christian interpretation of the Old Testament" and "Since it is grounded in the disclosure of the divine love in the divine-human praxis of Jesus Christ, love for the neighbour is also oriented towards the perfection of community which is the eschatological goal of that praxis" (*Text, Church and World*, 272, 279).

FOUR
Participatory Biblical Exegesis and Human Teachers

1. An earlier version of the first section of this chapter was published in my "The Pontifical Biblical Commission and Aquinas' Exegesis," *Pro Ecclesia* 13 (2004): 25–38.

2. Jeremy Cohen describes the purpose of his *Living Letters of the Law: Ideas of the Jew in Medieval Christianity* (Berkeley: University of California Press, 1999): "In order to meet their particular needs, Christian theology and exegesis created a Jew of their own, and this book investigates the medieval history of such a hermeneutically and doctrinally crafted Jew, from Augustine of Hippo to Thomas Aquinas" (2). These "particular needs" are the understanding of Israel, Jesus Christ, and the Church; from this perspective it may be that Cohen does not give sufficient credit to the purposes of the Christian theologians he treats. This chapter shares the "particular needs" that Cohen describes, but it attempts to describe Jewish biblical exegesis by analyzing the work of Jewish scholars so as to avoid the more sinister implications of "creating" and "crafting" a Jew to be employed in non-Jewish ends.

3. The same question could be asked ecumenically, as regards differences between Catholics and Protestants, for instance.

4. Thus Telford Work, rather than supposing that Christian exegetical practice can be extricated from its relationship with Jewish communal exegetical practice, sees Jesus as obeying, fulfilling, and transforming Israel's "biblical practice" and thereby establishing a communal Christian exegetical practice that requires conversion and formation in Christ (Work, *Living and Active: Scripture in the Economy of Salvation* [Grand Rapids, Mich.: Eerdmans, 2002], 12; cf. *Living and Active*'s chap. 2, esp. 168 f.). Similarly John Webster focuses on the reading of Scripture as an event in the triune God's saving work: Webster, *Holy Scripture: A Dogmatic Sketch* (Cambridge: Cambridge University Press, 2003), 86–93.

5. Pontifical Biblical Commission, "The Jewish People and Their Sacred Scriptures in the Christian Bible" (Vatican City: Libreria Editrice Vaticana, 2002). For the responses, see Henry Wansbrough, "The Jewish People and Its Holy Scripture in the Christian Bible," *Irish Theological Quarterly* 67 (2002): 265–275; Denis Farkasfalvy, O. Cist., "The Pontifical Biblical Commission's Document on Jews and Christians and Their Scriptures: Attempt at an Evaluation," *Communio* 29 (2002): 715–737; and Roch Kereszty, "The Jewish–Christian Dialogue and the Pontifical Biblical Commission's Document on 'The Jewish People and Their Sacred Scriptures in the Christian Bible,'" *Communio* 29 (2002): 738–745. The editor of the *Communio* symposium makes clear that assent is not owed by Catholics to the Pontifical Biblical Commission in the way that it is owed to the Magisterium: "The Pontifical Biblical Commission is not part of the Magisterium of the Bishop of Rome but a consultative body to the Congregation of the Doctrine of the Faith" (714).

6. The relationship of Jewish and Christian communal interpretation, as manifested by St. Paul, has been illumined by Francis Watson, *Paul and the Hermeneutics of Faith* (New York: T. & T. Clark, 2004). See also J. Ross Wagner, *Heralds of the Good News: Isaiah and Paul in Concert in the Letter to the Romans* (Leiden: Brill, 2002). Behind both of these books stands Richard B. Hays's groundbreaking *Echoes of Scripture in the Letters of Paul* (New Haven: Yale University Press, 1989).

7. Wansbrough, "The Jewish People and Its Holy Scripture in the Christian Bible," 265.

8. Ibid., 266.

9. Ibid., 266–67. On intrabiblical exegesis that is participatory in character, see Michael Fishbane, *Biblical Interpretation in Ancient Israel* (Oxford: Oxford University Press, 1985); Hays, *Echoes of Scripture in the Letters of Paul*; Wagner, *Heralds of the Good News*. See also for the issues at stake Richard J. Longenecker, *Biblical Exegesis in the Apostolic Period*, 2d ed. (Grand Rapids, Mich.: Eerdmans, 1999), "Preface to the Second Edition," xiii–xli, esp. his section "Can We Reproduce the Exegesis of the New Testament?" where he argues directly with Hays, who in *Echoes of Scripture in the Letters of Paul* (180–82) criticized

Longenecker's position in the first edition of *Biblical Exegesis in the Apostolic Period* (Grand Rapids, Mich.: Eerdmans, 1975). Hays points out, "Let us not deceive ourselves about this: Paul would flunk our introductory exegesis courses" (181). Taking issue with Longenecker's approach, Hays observes that Longenecker "places Paul on a theological pedestal. We are to believe and 'reproduce' his teachings but not to emulate the freedom with which he reads Scripture. . . . I would contend, however, that the position recommended by Longenecker is inherently unstable: it commits us to a peculiar intellectual schizophrenia in which we arbitrarily grant privileged status to past interpretations that we deem unjustifiable with regard to normal, sober hermeneutical canons. . . . Despite the intended piety of the position, it cuts the lifeline between Paul's time and ours. Ironically, Longenecker's attitude toward the New Testament is formally identical to the view of Scripture that Kugel observes among the rabbis (see pp. 170–71 above): *Scripture belongs to a holy past in which we can no longer presume to participate*" (181, emphasis added). As Hays points out, "Longenecker has circumscribed this freedom for Paul's followers by granting hermeneutical veto power to a modern critical method of which Paul himself was entirely innocent. From the perspective of faith it is not clear why this should be so" (181). See also Hays, "Learning from Paul How to Read Israel's Scripture" and "On the Rebound: A Response to Critiques of *Echoes of Scripture in the Letters of Paul*," in his *The Conversion of the Imagination: Paul as Interpreter of Israel's Scripture* (Grand Rapids, Mich.: Eerdmans, 2005), viii–xvii, 163–89.

10. Wansbrough, "The Jewish People and Its Holy Scripture in the Christian Bible," 268. Wansbrough cites §22, which raises the following questions in light of the Holocaust: "It may be asked whether Christians should be blamed for having monopolised the Jewish Bible and reading there what no Jew has found. Should not Christians henceforth read the Bible as Jews do, in order to show proper respect for its Jewish origins?" The paragraph answers the latter question in the negative, since such a reading would require abandoning faith in Jesus as the Messiah. The paragraph then states: "As regards the first question, the situation is different, for Christians can and ought to admit that the Jewish reading of the Bible is a possible one, in continuity with the Jewish Sacred Scriptures from the Second Temple period, a reading analogous to the Christian reading which developed in parallel fashion. Both readings are bound up with the vision of their respective faiths, of which the readings are the result and expression. Consequently, both are irreducible" (§22). The document's recognition of the Jewish reading as a "possible" one differs somewhat from Wansbrough's claim that both readings are "valid."

11. Pontifical Biblical Commission, "The Jewish People and Their Sacred Scriptures in the Christian Bible," §20. Scholars such as Marc Saperstein and Barry D. Walfish have recently suggested that, for at least some important medieval Jewish exegetes, mystical or typological exegesis "played a

central role in conveying the message that the biblical narratives 'were not merely part of an ancient past, but that they bore a historical message for the present and the future'" (Walfish, "Typology, Narrative, and History: Isaac ben Joseph ha-Kohen on the Book of Ruth," in *With Reverence for the Word: Medieval Scriptural Exegesis in Judaism, Christianity, and Islam*, ed. Jane Dammen McAuliffe, Barry D. Walfish, and Joseph W. Goering [Oxford: Oxford University Press, 2003], 119–32, at 127, quoting Saperstein's "Jewish Typological Exegesis after Nachmanides," *Jewish Studies Quarterly* 1 [1993–94]: 158–70). For positive evaluations of patristic-medieval exegesis, see, e.g., Robert Louis Wilken, "In Defense of Allegory," *Modern Theology* 14 (1998): 197–212; idem, "*In Dominico Eloquio*: Learning the Lord's Style of Language," *Communio* 24 (1997): 846–66; Ignace de la Potterie, "Reading Holy Scripture 'in the Spirit': Is the Patristic Way of Reading the Bible Still Possible Today?" *Communio* 13 (1986): 308–25; idem, "The Spiritual Sense of Scripture," *Communio* 23 (1996): 738–56; R. R. Reno, "Reflections in Aid of Theological Exegesis," in his *The Ruins of the Church* (Grand Rapids, Mich.: Brazos Press, 2002), 165–81; Denis Farkasfalvy, O. Cist., "The Case for Spiritual Exegesis," *Communio* 10 (1983); idem, "In Search of a 'Post-Critical' Method of Biblical Interpretation," *Communio* 13 (1986): 288–307; idem, "A Heritage in Search of Heirs: The Future of Ancient Christian Exegesis," *Communio* 25 (1998): 505–19; David C. Steinmetz, "The Superiority of Precritical Exegesis," *Theology Today* 37 (1980): 27–38; Brian E. Daley, S.J., "Is Patristic Exegesis Still Usable? Reflections on Early Christian Interpretation of the Psalms," *Communio* 29 (2002): 185–216; Chrysogonus Waddell, "A Christological Interpretation of Psalm 1? The Psalter and Christian Prayer," *Communio* 22 (1995): 502–21; Rudolf Voderholzer, *Die Einheit der Schrift und ihr geistiger Sinn. Der Beitrag Henri de Lubacs zur Erforschung von Geschichte und Systematik christlicher Bibelhermeneutik* (Einsiedeln: Johannes Verlag, 1998). Roland Murphy, O. Carm., "Patristic and Medieval Exegesis: Help or Hindrance?" *Catholic Biblical Quarterly* 43 (1981): 505–16, praises some aspects of patristic-medieval commentary on the Song of Songs, but concludes, "If historical-critical methodology is not brought into play, there is nothing to serve as a control on the reading of the text by Christian imagination" (515).

12. Pontifical Biblical Commission, "The Jewish People and Their Sacred Scriptures in the Christian Bible," §20. See also the Pontifical Biblical Commission's 1993 *The Interpretation of the Bible in the Church*, trans. John Kilgallen and Brendan Byrne (Boston: St. Paul Books & Media, 1993), which likewise mentions Aquinas—in contrast to the Fathers—as particularly associated with the literal sense (82); and Joseph Fitzmyer, S.J., *Scripture, the Soul of Theology* (New York: Paulist Press, 1994), 71–72. Cf. in contrast George Lindbeck's and Avery Dulles, S.J.'s comments in the roundtable discussion summarized by Paul Stallsworth in *Biblical Interpretation in Crisis: The Ratzinger*

Conference on Bible and Church, ed. Richard John Neuhaus (Grand Rapids, Mich.: Eerdmans, 1989), 152–55, which display an awareness that Aquinas's understanding of the literal sense belongs to his account of *sacra doctrina,* God's teaching and our participation in it.

13. Pontifical Biblical Commission, "The Jewish People and Their Sacred Scriptures in the Christian Bible," §20.

14. Ibid., Section II. B.

15. Ibid., §23.

16. Wansbrough, "The Jewish People and Its Holy Scripture in the Christian Bible," 272–73. For the need for such an exposition, particularly with regard to John's Gospel, see R. Alan Culpepper, "The Gospel of John as a Threat to Jewish–Christian Relations," in *Overcoming Fear between Jews and Christians,* ed. James H. Charlesworth with Frank X. Blisard and Jerry L. Gorham (New York: Crossroad, 1992), 21–43; Frank J. Matera, "The Future of Catholic Biblical Scholarship: Balance and Proportion," *Nova et Vetera* 4 (2006): 120–32, at 123.

17. Wansbrough, "The Jewish People and Its Holy Scripture in the Christian Bible," 275.

18. Farkasfalvy, "The Pontifical Biblical Commission's Document on Jews and Christians and Their Scriptures," 718–19.

19. Ibid., 720.

20. Ibid., 724–25. Cf. the remark of Joseph Fitzmyer, intending to praise Aquinas: "In effect, Thomas wrote off the three nonliteral senses, the allegorical, moral, and anagogical. While still admitting that there were three other senses, he saw clearly that he was breaking with the tradition that elevated them" (Fitzmyer, "Scripture in the Catholic Tradition," in *Living Traditions of the Bible: Scripture in Jewish, Christian, and Muslim Practice,* ed. James Bowley [St. Louis: Chalice Press, 1999], 145–61, at 154). Fitzmyer goes on to bemoan that fact that despite Aquinas's (alleged) position, and despite the Reformers' opposition to the spiritual senses, the spiritual senses lingered on in Catholic biblical interpretation "precisely because it had been the vogue for so many centuries" (155) until nineteenth-century archeological discoveries brought them to an end.

21. Farkasfalvy, "The Pontifical Biblical Commission's Document on Jews and Christians and Their Scriptures," 727.

22. Ibid., 728.

23. Ibid., 732–33.

24. Kereszty, "The Jewish–Christian Dialogue," 739.

25. Ibid., 740.

26. Ibid., 742.

27. Ibid., 744.

28. Ironically, Christian theologians who reject the biblical Jesus' claim to be the Christ unite themselves with Marcion in his rejection of the Old Testa-

ment as significant for Christian self-understanding. In the Old Testament, there is no promised Christ who would be "king" of the Gentiles but not of the Jews. For further discussion of "fulfillment" as requiring an understanding of covenantal participation, see my *Christ's Fulfillment of Torah and Temple: Salvation according to Thomas Aquinas* (Notre Dame: University of Notre Dame Press, 2002).

29. Robert Grant, in his popular textbook *A Short History of the Interpretation of the Bible*, makes the same mistake in a rhetorically memorable fashion, attributing to Aquinas's *Summa theologiae* I, q. 1, a. 10, ad 1 "theology's declaration of independence from the allegorical method" (Robert M. Grant with David Tracy, *A Short History of the Interpretation of the Bible*, 2d ed. [Philadelphia: Fortress Press, 1984], 90). Grant concludes, "Thomas's love of symbolism is reflected only in his Eucharistic hymns" (91).

30. Cf. the important recent discussion between Gavin D'Costa and John Webster, initiated by D'Costa on the grounds that Webster separates Scripture too sharply from the Church's mediation: D'Costa, "Revelation, Scripture and Tradition: Some Comments on John Webster's Conception of 'Holy Scripture,'" *International Journal of Systematic Theology* 6 (2004): 337–50. In "Purity and Plenitude: Evangelical Reflections on Congar's *Tradition and Traditions*," *International Journal of Systematic Theology* 7 (2005): 399–413—an article that may serve as a response to D'Costa—Webster, while praising Congar's work, cautions against "Congar's folding of scripture into the larger stream of the church's life" (412). For Webster "scripture's task as prophetic and apostolic witness to the divine Word can only be accomplished if it is in some sense an alien element in the church. . . . The sufficiency of scripture (formal and material) [Congar denies formal sufficiency] does not, of course, mean that scripture exists in abstraction from its presence to the church. But what kind of presence? Church and tradition, though they are the 'space' in which scripture is active as sanctified testimony to the *viva vox dei*, do not 'fill out' scripture or make good its insufficiency, any more than the servants of Jesus Christ fill out his lordship. *Sola scriptura* does not extract scripture from Christian history. But it does qualify that history as one which is addressed by an intrusive voice, the voice of the one who awakens the sleepers and raises the dead" (ibid.). But if Scripture is an "alien element," then the Church herself is also "alien" in this sense as the Mystical Body, and not merely a "space." And yet Webster's emphasis on the primacy of *God's* voice is of course correct. As Webster eloquently puts it elsewhere, "the intelligibility of a Christian theology of readers and their acts will depend upon the creation and inhabitation of social spaces in which the hearing of Scripture is practised well. The constellation of dispositions and skills which are deployed by the wise Christian reader cannot be grasped apart from the life and practices of the Christian community, for they are drawn from public stores of accumulated knowledge and experience, and

they take form as ruled behaviour. They are also reinforced by public activities in the church which both appeal to an draw upon a Christian culture of reading. . . . Yet one caveat concerning talk of a Christian culture of reading remains: it is of the greatest importance that in talking of the corporate aspects of Christian reading we do not allow theological language about the church to dissolve into generic language about 'forms of life,' 'sociality, even 'ecclesiality.' Talk of God's action has to be retained as real and operative" (Webster, "Hermeneutics in Modern Theology: Some Doctrinal Reflections," in his *Word and Church: Essays in Christian Dogmatics* [Edinburgh: T. & T. Clark, 2001], 84–85). Cf. with regard to Barth on the Church, Reinhard Hütter, *Evangelische Ethik als kirchliches Zeugnis. Interpretationen zu Schlüsselfragen theologischer Ethik in der Gegenwart* (Neukirchen-Blyn: Neukirchener Verlag, 1993); and Webster's response in *Word and Church*, 213 f.

31. Yosef Hayim Yerushalmi, *Zakhor: Jewish History and Jewish Memory* (Seattle: University of Washington Press, 1996), 89.

32. Francis Watson has observed that for Schleiermacher, Harnack, and Bultmann, and their (conscious and unconscious) followers "the erasure of scriptural texts from both Testaments is motivated by a desire for immediate encounter that seeks to dissolve all forms of textual mediation. Textuality is identified with Jewishness" (Watson, *Text and Truth* [Grand Rapids, Mich.: Eerdmans, 1997], 128). This identification of textuality with a "Jewishness" to be surpassed by Christians contrasts with the patristic-medieval tradition's awareness of the richness of the text as mediating divine *doctrina*, even though of course textuality is not seen as the only mediational reality. See also, for appreciation of this point, David Dawson, *Christian Figural Reading and the Fashioning of Identity* (Los Angeles: University of California, 2002); and Work, *Living and Active*, both cited by Stanley Hauerwas in "The Narrative Turn: Thirty Years Later," in his *Performing the Faith: Bonhoeffer and the Practice of Nonviolence* (Grand Rapids, Mich.: Brazos Press, 2004), 139 n. 6. Hauerwas here warns against "spiritualizing the Bible by failing to see the significance of the bodily character of the text." On the significance of the Bible's sensible character within the broader economy of salvation, see also Charles Morerod, O.P., "Les sens dans la relation de l'homme avec Dieu," *Nova et Vetera* (French) 79 (2004): 7–35.

33. Jon D. Levenson, *The Hebrew Bible, the Old Testament, and Historical Criticism: Jews and Christians in Biblical Studies* (Louisville: Westminster/John Knox Press, 1993), xiv. For a critical reading of this book, see James Barr, *The Concept of Biblical Theology: An Old Testament Perspective* (Minneapolis: Fortress Press, 1999), 291–302; cf. Levenson's able response in his review of this book in *First Things* 100 (February 2000): 59–63.

34. Levenson, *The Hebrew Bible, the Old Testament, and Historical Criticism*, xv. See for a similar understanding of the interplay, in biblical interpretation,

of Christ, the Holy Spirit, and the sacramental dynamism of deification—expressed in the distinctive theological style of Eastern Orthodoxy—the intervention of Melkite Archbishop Neophytos Edelby during the drafting of *Dei Verbum*. An English translation of this intervention is found in "Appendix One: A Neglected Conciliar Intervention," in Gerald O'Collins, S.J., *Retrieving Fundamental Theology: The Three Styles of Contemporary Theology* (New York: Paulist Press, 1993), 174–77. See also Work, *Living and Active*.

35. Levenson, *The Hebrew Bible, the Old Testament, and Historical Criticism*, 3. Levenson compares rabbinic exegesis with Christian exegesis: "A plain-sense exegete *(pashtan)* like Rabbi Samuel ben Meir ('Rashban,' Northern France, twelfth century) could be uncompromising both in his pursuit of the plain sense and in his allegiance to *halakhah* (rabbinic law), which often bases itself on the biblical text in a way that contradicts the *peshat*. He is paralleled by those Christian exegetes who recognized a 'historical sense' to the Old Testament without relinquishing a Christocentric interpretation of it. In both the Jewish and the Christian cases, the unity of the overall religion was maintained, even though it was not seen as operative in all forms of exegesis. There could be concentric circles of context, but the smallest circle, the plain sense, finally yielded to the largest one, the whole tradition, however constituted" (2). Cf. for further discussion of Rashban's exegesis Martin Lockshin, "Rashban as a 'Literary' Exegete," in *With Reverence for the Word: Medieval Scriptural Exegesis in Judaism, Christianity, and Islam*, ed. Jane Dammen McAuliffe, Barry D. Walfish, and Joseph W. Goering (Oxford: Oxford University Press, 2003), 83–91.

36. Levenson, *The Hebrew Bible, the Old Testament, and Historical Criticism*, 5. Among the strongest contemporary advocates for this "Spinozan agenda" is John J. Collins, whose essay "Is a Critical Biblical Theology Possible?" (later collected in Collins, *Encounters with Biblical Theology* [Minneapolis: Fortress Press, 2005]: 11–23) Levenson criticizes in *The Hebrew Bible, the Old Testament, and Historical Criticism*, 106–26. In this essay Collins had concluded, "We return, finally, to our initial questions as to whether a critical biblical theology is possible. The answer evidently depends on the model of theology we are willing to accept. Historical criticism, consistently understood, is not compatible with a confessional theology that is committed to specific doctrines on the basis of faith. It is, however, quite compatible with theology, understood as an open-ended and critical inquiry into the meaning and function of God-language" (22). Such theology, however, could only be about human beings, and not about God at all (not "theology"). In his introduction to *Encounters with Biblical Theology*, Collins defends his views against Levenson's criticisms by observing that "not all traditions are alike. While historical criticism is itself a tradition, it is a tradition of a very different order from religious orthodoxy, as it does not require the a priori acceptance of any particular conclusions. It is neither committed nor opposed in principle to any particular

reconstruction of the history of Israel, or to the unity or divine origin of the Bible. Any position can be defended, so long as its evidence is adduced and arguments are made" (3). But here Collins appears blind to the a priori character of his own acceptance of a solely "linear" theological and metaphysical understanding of historical reality. Within this solely linear worldview, no positions can be defended that involve the real action of a living God. Collins continues: "A confessional approach, such as that advocated by Levenson and many others, wants to privilege certain positions and exempt them from the requirement of supporting arguments, thus in effect taking biblical theology out of the public discussion" (3). It would seem, however, that just such privileging of certain positions, exempted from argumentation, is intrinsic to Collins's understanding of historical reality. If so, then Collins's allegedly neutral "public discussion" profoundly limits the discussion in the name of liberating it from confessional bonds: "One of the great strengths of historical criticism has been that it has created an arena where people with different faith commitments can work together. The bracketing of religious identities and faith commitments has allowed dispassionate assessment of historical and literary questions, even when this might seem subversive to the religious identities in question" (4). The implied message is that scholars who do not bracket their "religious identities and faith commitments" cannot be trusted to pursue truth dialogically. I agree, however, with Collins's view, "At issue here is the nature of the conversation in which we wish to participate" (4). Collins envisions a conversation in which Jews and Christians, as Levenson says, can only participate if they (a priori) accept a reductive understanding of historical reality. Presuming that God's being and action are solely questions of faith, not accessible in any way to rational inquiry, Collins states, "In fact, distinctive articles of faith, such as the question of a divine role in history, cannot ultimately be decided by historical-critical discussion in any case, but there is much that can be discussed about them from a neutral perspective nonetheless" (4). But one wonders what, from this "neutral perspective," could actually be said, since the solely linear-historical perspective rules out truth claims about God. Thus in "Biblical Theology and the History of Israelite Religion," in *Encounters with Biblical Theology*, 24–33, Collins proposes turning Old Testament "biblical theology" into strictly "historical theology," à la Spinoza. Similarly, in "The Politics of Biblical Interpretation" in the same volume, 34–44, Collins distinguishes "between questions of fact and questions of significance" (44), with historical-critical work dealing with fact. The problem here is that God, as creative source and agent of redemption, is excluded, a priori, from the realm of "fact" and relegated entirely to "significance." See also Collins's *The Bible after Babel: Historical Criticism in a Postmodern Age* (Grand Rapids, Mich.: Eerdmans, 2005), which precisely instantiates Babel, since Collins methodologically can conceive of no truly unifying framework for biblical teaching.

37. Levenson, *The Hebrew Bible, the Old Testament, and Historical Criticism*, 10–11. Cf. the "liberal Protestantism" exemplified by Friedrich Schleiermacher, *The Christian Faith*, ed. H. R. Mackintosh and J. S. Stewart (Edinburgh: T. & T. Clark, 1989).

38. Levenson, *The Hebrew Bible, the Old Testament, and Historical Criticism*, 50.

39. Ibid., 50–51.

40. Ibid., 30. Levenson states, "All religious use of past literature is, to some extent, at cross-purposes with historical criticism, if only because the world of the contemporary religious person is not the world of the author. It is a world into which the author's work arrives only after it has been recontextualized through redaction, canonization, and other forms of tradition. Without these recontextualizations it is unavailable. The matrix in which the ancient text speaks to the contemporary community is this larger, anachronizing context" (30). Levenson goes on to point out that this does not mean that religious communities must or should reject historical-critical research, but rather means simply that the interpretive practices of religious communities (including their interpretive assumptions) must go beyond the Spinozist claims adopted by some historical-critical scholars in the interpretive context of the academy. On this point, cf. Hans Frei, "Theology in the University," in Frei, *Types of Christian Theology*, ed. George Hunsinger and William C. Placher (New Haven: Yale University Press, 1992), app. A, 95–132, which explores Schleiermacher's role in founding the University of Berlin. Frei observes: "The tension that Schleiermacher exemplified between theology as *Wissenschaft* and theology as an activity of the Church continued—indeed continues—to haunt both theology itself and theological education" (116).

41. Levenson, *The Hebrew Bible, the Old Testament, and Historical Criticism*, 38. Cf. for further discussion Moshe Halbertal, *People of the Book: Canon, Meaning, and Authority* (Cambridge: Harvard University Press, 1997).

42. Levenson tends to limit the word "historical" to what can be uncovered by historical-critical research (cf. 39), and so would deny that a Christological reading of the Old Testament could be "historical." He certainly would not deny, however, the participatory-historical meanings of revealed realities.

43. Ibid., 46. On the Karaites, cf. Daniel Frank, "Karaite Exegesis," in *Hebrew Bible/Old Testament: The History of Its Interpretation*, vol. I/2, ed. Magne Saebo (Göttingen: Vandenhoeck & Ruprecht, 2000), 110–28; idem, "The Study of Medieval Karaism, 1989–1999," in *Hebrew Scholarship and the Medieval World*, ed. Nicholas De Lange (Cambridge: Cambridge University Press, 2001), 3–22; idem, "Karaite Commentaries on the Song of Songs from Tenth-Century Jerusalem," in *With Reverence for the Word: Medieval Scriptural Exegesis in Judaism, Christianity, and Islam*, ed. Jane Dammen McAuliffe, Barry D. Walfish, and Joseph W. Goering (Oxford: Oxford University Press, 2003), 51–69.

232 — Notes to Page 99

44. As Levenson states, "biblical study in Judaism falls under the category of *talmud tora* (the study of Torah), a sacred and central obligation *(mitsvah)* in the rabbinic universe, but a *mitsvah* that applies to Mishnah, Gemara, medieval rabbinic exegesis, and so on, as well. The traditional Jewish dynamic is quite the opposite of the Protestant, and, unlike the latter, it does not foster an effort to isolate a peculiarly *biblical* theology" (Levenson, *The Hebrew Bible, the Old Testament, and Historical Criticism*, 46).

45. Thus Christians and Jews will disagree about the importance of the "oral Torah of the rabbis," although Christians will find much of value in the oral Torah. Discussing canonical interpretation as regards its potential for uniting Jewish and Christian exegetes, Levenson holds that there is "a broad base for agreement on the meaning of textual units in their most limited literary or historical settings. But when we come to 'the final literary setting' and even more so to 'the context of the canon,' we must part company, for *there is no non-particularistic access to these larger contexts*, and no decision on these issues, even when made for secular purposes, can be neutral between Judaism and Christianity. Jews and Christians can, of course, study each other's Bible and even identify analogically or empathetically with the interpretations that the other's traditional context warrants, growing in discernment and self-understanding as a consequence" (80). Even as regards the "most limited literary or historical setting," the question of history—whether history is providential and thus participatory—may cause disagreements, although less so between practicing Jewish and Christian exegetes. Levenson's balanced approach seems right to me. I have found that Jewish exegetes offer extraordinary insights that, among other things, often recall Christians to a better understanding of Christian faith, just as Levenson suggests one might expect as a fruit of Jews and Christians studying each other's Bible. See also for discussion of Jewish and Christian biblical interpretation Christopher Seitz, "Old Testament or Hebrew Bible? Some Theological Considerations," in his *Word without End: The Old Testament as Abiding Theological Witness* (Grand Rapids, Mich.: Eerdmans, 1998), 61–74; and Joseph T. Lienhard, S.J., *The Bible, the Church, and Authority: The Canon of the Christian Bible in History and Theology* (Collegeville, Minn.: Liturgical Press, 1995), esp. chaps. 1–2.

46. Levenson seems to recognize differences among Christian fulfillment accounts, some of which negate Judaism and others do not, but he is clearly most familiar with the linear-historical supersessionism of classical German historical biblical criticism. Describing the work of Gerhard von Rad, he observes, "Like Hegel, Wellhausen, and Eichrodt, he simply assumed the spiritual necrosis of Judaism after Jesus. After 'the end was reached,' why consider the Jews?" (23). For discussion of supersessionism, see David Novak, "What Does Edith Stein Mean for Jews?" in Novak, *Talking with Christians: Musings of a Jewish Theologian* (Grand Rapids, Mich.: Eerdmans, 2005). Novak observes: "Christian supersessionism need not denigrate Judaism. It can look to the Jew-

ish origins of Christianity happily and still learn of those origins from living Jews, those whom Pope John Paul II likes to call 'our elder brothers.' And Christian supersessionism can still affirm that God has not annulled His everlasting covenant with the Jewish people, neither past nor present nor future. But Jews cannot expect any more than that from Christians, and Christians cannot expect any more than that from yourselves. If Christianity does not regard itself as going beyond Judaism, why should Christians not become Jews? It is always a ready possibility. Where else could you possibly find the Lord God of Israel?" (164).

47. Levenson, *The Hebrew Bible, the Old Testament, and Historical Criticism*, 60.

48. Ibid., 98. As an illustration, Levenson cites a scene from Chaim Potok's brilliant novel, *In the Beginning* (Fawcett, 1986).

49. Levenson, *The Hebrew Bible, the Old Testament, and Historical Criticism*, 86.

50. Ibid., 124.

51. Peter Ochs, "An Introduction to Postcritical Scriptural Interpretation," in *The Return to Scripture in Judaism and Christianity: Essays in Postcritical Scriptural Interpretation*, ed. Peter Ochs (New York: Paulist Press, 1993), 39. For Lindbeck's relation to Ochs's work, cf. George Lindbeck, "Progress in Textual Reasoning: From Vatican II to the Conference at Drew," in *Textual Reasonings: Jewish Philosophy and Text Study at the End of the Twentieth Century*, ed. Peter Ochs and Nancy Levene (Grand Rapids, Mich.: Eerdmans, 2002), 252–58, referring to Ochs's "Talmudic Scholarship as Textual Reasoning: Halivni's Pragmatic Historiography," in Ochs and Levene, *Textual Reasonings*, 120–43. Lindbeck writes, "Under the influence of neo-orthodoxy on the Protestant side and of *la nouvelle theologie* among Roman Catholics, much of David Halivni's approach as recounted by Peter Ochs in this volume was anticipated. It was widely agreed that while historical criticism cannot construct the value-laden (i.e. communally and personally significant) senses of authoritative texts, it can be an important corrective. Liberal ideologues (let's call them 'liberalists') destroy communal faith and practice by limiting the authority of tradition to what passes historical-critical muster, and traditionalists immobilize the faithful by denying historical criticism any role whatsoever, not even a corrective one" (253). For Ochs's project, see also, e.g., his *Peirce, Pragmatism, and the Logic of Scripture* (Cambridge: Cambridge University Press, 1998), esp. 290–325; *Reasoning after Revelation: Dialogues in Postmodern Jewish Philosophy*, ed. Steven Kepnes, Peter Ochs, and Robert Gibbs (Boulder: Westview Press, 1998); Ochs, "A Rabbinic Pragmatism," in *Theology and Dialogue*, ed. Bruce Marshall (Notre Dame: University of Notre Dame Press, 1990); idem, "Postcritical Scriptural Interpretation," in *Torah and Revelation*, ed. Dan Cohn-Sherbok (New York: Edwin Mellen Press, 1992), 51–73; idem, "The Emergence of Postmodern Jewish Theology and Philosophy," in *Reviewing the Covenant: Eugene B. Borowitz*

and the Postmodern Renewal of Jewish Theology, ed. Peter Ochs (Albany: State University of New York Press, 2000), 3–34; idem, "Borowitz and the Postmodern Renewal of Theology," in *Reviewing the Covenant,* 111–44; idem, "Three Postcritical Encounters with the Burning Bush," in *The Theological Interpretation of Scripture: Classic and Contemporary Reading,* ed. Stephen E. Fowl (Oxford: Blackwell, 1997), 129–42; and Ochs's foreword to David Weiss Halivni, *Revelation Restored: Divine Writ and Critical Responses* (Boulder: Westview Press, 1997), xi–xviii. See also Halivni's *Peshat and Derash: Plain and Applied Meaning in Rabbinic Exegesis* (Oxford: Oxford University Press, 1991); both *Revelation Restored* and *Peshat and Derash* envision Ezra as a model of exegetical practice. In the conversation between Robert Gibbs, Steven Kepnes, and Peter Ochs recorded in *Reasoning after Revelation,* Gibbs distinguishes his postmodern Jewish approach from "counterreformational types of traditionalism, like recent attempts by the Catholic Church to reembrace Thomas" (31). When Ochs queries "Isn't such neo-Scholasticism a form of postmodernism?" Gibbs replies, "No, this is antimodernism; like the 1880s and 1890s romantics, this is an attempt to rediscover a monovalent past" (ibid.). Although "modern" and "postmodern" are not sufficient categories either for Aquinas's thought or for contemporary engagements with it, Ochs grasps what is at stake much more clearly than does Gibbs.

52. Ochs, "An Introduction to Postcritical Scriptural Interpretation," 39.

53. Ibid., 40.

54. Ibid., 14.

55. See Max Kadushin, *The Rabbinic Mind,* 3d ed. (New York: Bloch, 1972); as well as Ochs's "Max Kadushin as Rabbinic Pragmatist," in *Understanding the Rabbinic Mind,* ed. Peter Ochs (Atlanta: Scholars Press, 1990), 165–96.

56. Ochs, "An Introduction to Postcritical Scriptural Interpretation," 10.

57. Ibid., 11.

58. Michael Fishbane, *Biblical Interpretation in Ancient Israel* (Oxford: Oxford University Press, 1985), 1.

59. Ibid., 2.

60. Ibid., 543.

61. Michael Fishbane, *The Garments of Torah: Essays in Biblical Hermeneutics* (Bloomington: Indiana University Press, 1989), 4; cf. Fishbane, "'Orally Write Therefore Aurally Right': An Essay on Midrash," in *The Quest for Context and Meaning: Studies in Biblical Intertextuality in Honor of James A. Sanders,* ed. Craig A. Evans and Shemaryahu Talmon (Leiden: Brill, 1997), 531–46.

62. By framing my account of ecclesial scriptural *doctrina* in the context of Jewish–Christian dialogue, I hope to emphasize that Christians cannot displace God's teaching in Israel with other cultural forms that might form a backdrop to the gospel, as seems to be the danger in, e.g., Peter Nyende, "Why Bother with Hebrews? An African Perspective," *Heythrop Journal* 46 (2005): 512–24.

63. These differences cannot be polished over without destroying the New Testament's witness to the coming of Israel's Messiah, the Creator who is now the Redeemer, who accomplishes the salvation of Jews and Gentiles. In the name of Jewish–Christian dialogue, some Christian scholars advocate a two-covenant model that grants that Jesus is not Israel's Messiah, although he is Messiah to the Gentiles. This position, ironically, effectively cuts off the New Testament from the Old. The "newness" of the gospel, similarly, must not be underemphasized as is done, for example, by E. Zenger, *Das Erste Testament. Das jüdische Bibel und die Christen* (Düsseldorf: Patmos Verlag, 1991); and Norbert Lohfink, "Eine Bibel–Zwei Testamente," in *Eine Bibe–Zwei Testamente*, ed. C. Dohmen and T. Söding (Paderborn: Schöningh, 1995); cf. Brevard S. Childs, "The Canon in Recent Biblical Studies: Reflections on an Era," *Pro Ecclesia* 14 (2005): 26–45, at 42. For an exploration of early Christians' use of "new covenant" as a way of understanding Jesus Christ's life, death, and Resurrection, see Scot McKnight, "Covenant and Spirit: The Origins of the New Covenant Hermeneutic," in *The Holy Spirit and Christian Origins: Essays in Honor of James D. G. Dunn*, ed. Graham N. Stanton, Bruce W. Longenecker, and Stephen C. Barton (Grand Rapids, Mich.: Eerdmans, 2004), 41–54. The issues as regards present-day communities of Messianic Jews are also complicated, but the point that cannot be lost is that Jesus Christ, the Messiah of Israel, has established the Church so that all human beings might participate sacramentally in his transformative fulfillment of Israel's Torah. My approach to the concerns raised by Mark S. Kinzer, *Post-Missionary Messianic Judaism: Redefining Christian Engagement with the Jewish People* (Grand Rapids, Mich.: Brazos, 2005); and David J. Rudolph, "Messianic Jews and Christian Theology: Restoring an Historical Voice to the Contemporary Discussion," *Pro Ecclesia* 14 (2005): 58–84, is found in my *Christ's Fulfillment of Torah and Temple*, although further dialogue and discussion is clearly needed.

64. The relationship of Jewish and Christian communal interpretation, as manifested by St. Paul, has been brilliantly illumined by Francis Watson, *Paul and the Hermeneutics of Faith* (New York: T. & T. Clark, 2004). See also Wagner, *Heralds of the Good News*. Behind both of these books stands Richard B. Hays's groundbreaking *Echoes of Scripture in the Letters of Paul*.

65. Pontifical Biblical Commission, "The Jewish People and Their Sacred Scriptures in the Christian Bible," §85.

66. M. Dubois, "Mystical and Realistic Elements in the Exegesis and Hermeneutics of Thomas Aquinas," in *Creative Biblical Exegesis: Christian and Jewish Hermeneutics through the Centuries*, ed. Benjamin Uffenheimer and Henning Graf Reventlow (Sheffield: Sheffield Academic Press, 1988), 53.

67. Pontifical Biblical Commission, "The Jewish People and Their Sacred Scriptures in the Christian Bible," §87.

68. Jon D. Levenson, "The Agenda of *Dabru Emet*," *Review of Rabbinic Judaism* 7 (2004): 1–26, at 12.

69. Ibid., 13. For Christians the Church as the "new Israel" does not negate the covenants that God made with the Jewish people; God does not cease to address these covenantal promises to the Jewish people, who therefore remain the Israel of God, even though the fulfillment of these promises is found in Christ. I have treated these points, in dialogue with Levenson, in *Christ's Fulfillment of Torah and Temple: Salvation according to Thomas Aquinas* (University of Notre Dame: Notre Dame Press, 2002), and *Sacrifice and Community: Jewish Offering and Christian Eucharist* (Oxford: Blackwell, 2005).

70. See, in this vein, Gary A. Anderson's superb essay, combining historical-critical, rabbinic, and patristic insights, "King David and the Psalms of Imprecation," *Pro Ecclesia* 15 (2006): 267–80. Anderson emphasizes the importance of reading the psalms from within the communal life of prayer: "We must not isolate the text of these prayers [the psalms] from the person who prays them. The correlation of person to prayer is not extrinsic to interpretation but absolutely essential" (272). He goes on to say, "If the life of prayer is not merely that of learning words but knowing the occasions on which they are to be used, then the historical critical method will be of limited value. For the data about such mimetic activity is simply not available for historical observation. In short, a prayer is not just a meretricious set of words; it is a script awaiting performance. There is something deeply *mimetic* about the life of prayer. It is not just a question of what is said, but *who* says it and *when*" (279). Anderson's insights here accord with those of the Jewish thinkers we have canvassed. Likewise Anderson approvingly cites Robert Jenson's (Augustinian) argument that "[t]he speaker of the psalms is the *totus Christus*": Jenson, "Hermeneutics and the Life of the Church," in *Reclaiming the Bible for the Church*, ed. Carl Braaten and Robert Jenson (Grand Rapids, Mich.: Eerdmans, 1995), 102 (cited by Anderson, 280 n. 24). See also Anderson's *The Genesis of Perfection* (Louisville: Westminster/John Knox, 2001).

FIVE
Participatory Biblical Exegesis and Ecclesial Authority

1. St. Thomas Aquinas, *Commentary on the Gospel of St. John*, trans. Fabian Larcher, O.P. and James Weisheipl, O.P. (Petersham, Mass.: St. Bede's Publications, 1999), pt. II, ch. 14, lect. 4, §1918 (p. 358).

2. As David S. Yeago reminds us, Hobbes's understanding of Scripture, like Spinoza's, cannot be separated from the failures of ecclesial authority after the Reformation. Yeago remarks, "The modern secularity project was not a demonic upsurge of incomprehensible hostility to the faith; it was in large measure the attempt of decent minds to cope with the chaos public Christianity had wrought in the wake of the Reformation. The incapacity of Christians to live

together in charity in the biblical world subverted the cultural plausibility of that world and motivated the urgency with which the secularist project strove to get the Bible under control. Indeed, precisely in order to liberate their faith from complicity in violence and murder, *Christians* of all ecclesiastical parties took part in the establishment of the secular culture, in which 'religion' would be private, and secular rationality firmly in charge of the public square. The historical-critical movement cannot be understood apart from its ideological roots in secularist thinkers like Hobbes and Spinoza, but scholars in the churches (mostly, but not only, Protestants) took up both the critical challenge and much of the ideological motivation of these great skeptics in the interests of producing a 'purified' Christianity, that is, one that limited its claims to the proper sphere of 'religion,' the moral and spiritual life of the inner person" (Yeago, "Re-Entering the Scriptural World," *Nova et Vetera* 4 [2006]: 159–71, at 167–68).

3. Thomas Hobbes, *Leviathan*, with selected variants from the Latin edition of 1668, ed. Edwin Curley (Indianapolis: Hackett, 1994), 470 (ch. 46, §6, Latin ed.). On Hobbes's viewpoint in its seventeenth-century context, see, e.g., Richard Popkin, *The History of Scepticism: From Savonarola to Bayle*, rev. ed. (Oxford: Oxford University Press, 2003), 189–207. Popkin writes that for Hobbes, "[o]ne should suspend judgment on all knowledge-claims of any import, until they have been vetted politically. . . . So Hobbes, although almost oblivious to his contemporary epistemological sceptics and far more cautious than his contemporary religious ones, did at one point lay the groundwork for a much more dangerous scepticism that makes the sovereign the political arbiter of truth. From arbiter to creator of truth, the modern state then develops its Orwellian character" (206–7). For further discussion, see also Henning Graf Reventlow, "Thomas Hobbes: The Philosophical Presuppositions of His Biblical Criticism," in his *The Authority of the Bible and the Rise of the Modern World*, trans. John Bowden (German, 1980; London: SCM Press, 1984 [English edition contains additional material supplied by the author]), 194–222. Reventlow ties Hobbes's thought to his "royalist system" (221): "he belongs to the group of rationalistic Anglicans who supported the absolutist monarchy and the system of the state church under Charles I, amidst the anti-Roman disposition which this produced, and also continued the antipathy to priests characteristic of Humanism" (220).

4. Hobbes, *Leviathan*, §11 (not in original English version), 470.

5. Ibid., §17, 474.

6. Ibid.

7. Ibid., §18, 474.

8. Ibid., §19, 475.

9. Ibid., §23, 476.

10. Ibid., ch. 42 (original English ed.), §78, 371.

11. Ibid., ch. 41, §5, 330; cf. §3, 329.

12. Ibid., §7, 331.

13. Ibid., ch. 42, §6, 336.

14. Ibid., ch. 41, §3, 328 (not in the Latin ed.).

15. Ibid., ch. 42, §3; cf. ch. 16, §12, 103 (different in the Latin ed.).

16. Hobbes holds that revelation may be "supernatural" in the sense of coming from God, but that it will contain "nothing against natural reason" (ibid., ch. 12, §25, 72). The limits of natural reason are set by Hobbes's materialism.

17. Ibid., ch. 47, §19, 481.

18. Ibid.

19. Ibid., ch. 11, §27, 63.

20. Ibid., ch. 47, §21, 482; cf. ch. 12, §32, 73.

21. Baruch Spinoza, *Theological-Political Treatise* (Gebhart ed., 2d ed.), trans. Samuel Shirley (Indiana: Hackett, 2001), 217. On the impact of Spinoza's biblical hermeneutics, see, e.g., John Webster, "Hermeneutics in Modern Theology: Some Doctrinal Reflections," in Webster, *Word and Church: Essays in Christian Dogmatics* (Edinburgh: T. &. T. Clark, 2001), 47–86, at 55–57; Louis Dupré, *The Enlightenment and the Intellectual Foundations of Modern Culture* (New Haven: Yale University Press, 2004), 231–35; Francis Martin, "Critique historique et enseignement du Nouveau Testament sur l'imitation du Christ," *Revue Thomiste* 93 (1993): 234–62; Murray Rae, *History and Hermeneutics* (Edinburgh: T. & T. Clark, 2005), 7–8. For further context and interpretation, see, e.g., Steven Nadler, *Spinoza's Heresy: Immortality and the Jewish Mind* (Oxford: Oxford University Press, 2001); idem, *Spinoza: A Life* (Cambridge: Cambridge University Press, 1999); Jonathan I. Israel, *Radical Enlightenment: Philosophy and the Making of Modernity 1650–1750* (Oxford: Oxford University Press, 2001); Popkin, *The History of Scepticism*, esp. chaps. 14–15; J. Samuel Preus, *Spinoza and the Irrelevance of Biblical Authority* (Cambridge: Cambridge University Press, 2001); Klaus Scholder, *The Birth of Modern Critical Theology: Origins and Problems of Biblical Criticism in the Seventeenth Century*, trans. John Bowden (German, 1966; Philadelphia: Trinity Press International, 1990).

22. Spinoza, *Theological-Political Treatise*, 153.

23. Ibid., 154.

24. Ibid., 160.

25. Ibid., 161.

26. Ibid.

27. Ibid.

28. Ibid., 162; the footnote by Seymour Feldman to Spinoza's text here points the reader to Spinoza's *Ethics*, where Spinoza denies that God has the attributes of justice or mercy, and denies the value of repentance for sin. For the propositions Spinoza accepts as part of scriptural religion, see also 151.

29. Ibid., 163.

30. Ibid., 165.

31. Ibid., 62, 64 65; cf. for further critique of Maimonides, 100–104.

32. Ibid., 67.

33. Ibid.

34. Ibid., 86.

35. Ibid., 86–87.

36. Ibid., 87.

37. Ibid.

38. Ibid., 89.

39. Cf. ibid., 94–96.

40. Cf. ibid., 96–98.

41. Ibid., 88–90. The continuity of these three rules with non-participatory metaphysical presuppositions, on the one hand, and later full-scale historical-critical exegesis, on the other, should be apparent. Cf. Raymond Brown's representative remark: "Fortunately we live at a time when a considerable degree of objectivity has been reached in biblical scholarship, so that a commentator can profit from the serious work of scholars of all religious communions. What has contributed most in this direction has been the establishment of the clear difference between the thoughts of the various biblical authors (which are the concern of the biblical scholar) and the subsequent use and development of those thoughts in divergent theologies (which are the concern of the theologian). The second point is important, for the majority of those who read Scripture are believers for whom the Bible is more than an interesting witness to past religious phenomena. Nor can it be neglected by the biblical scholar without peril of religious schizophrenia. Nevertheless, as we have come to realize, sincere confessional commitment to a theological position is perfectly consonant with a stubborn refusal to make a biblical text say more than its author meant it to say. There is no reason why scholars of different denominations cannot agree on the literal meaning of Scripture, even though they may disagree on the import of certain passages in the evolution of theology" (Brown, *The Gospel according to John (I–XII)*, vol. 29 of *The Anchor Bible* [New York: Doubleday, 1966], vi). For Brown as for Spinoza, the "literal meaning of Scripture"—its historical meaning, "what it meant"—is objectively accessible because theological and metaphysical presuppositions, while perhaps important, are tangential to the "historical."

42. Spinoza, *Theological-Political Treatise*, 93. Hans Frei proposes that "the notion of a right interpretation of the Bible is itself not meaningless, but it is eschatological. . . . It is a story of constantly varying ideologies; but it is not a story of one thing after another. There are common themes" (Frei, "Some Implications for Biblical Interpretation," in Frei, *Types of Christian Theology*, ed. George Hunsinger and William C. Placher [New Haven: Yale University Press, 1992], 56–69, at 56). In disagreeing about the Magisterium of the Church,

Protestants and Catholics disagree on how "eschatological" applies here. At stake is the degree to which the Church on earth participates in God's *sacra doctrina*. Yet Catholics too would grant that exegetical fullness awaits eternal life. This essay of Frei's contains a discussion of Kant's (followed by Gordon Kaufman) exegetical allegorizing of Christian Scripture, as well as David Tracy's "symbolic-experiential" reading.

43. Spinoza, *Theological-Political Treatise*, 99.

44. Ibid., 99–100.

45. Ibid., 103.

46. Ibid.

47. Ibid., 103–4.

48. An earlier version of this section appears in my "Ecclesial Exegesis and Ecclesial Authority: Childs, Fowl, and Aquinas," *Thomist* 69 (2005): 407–67.

49. Fowl, *Engaging Scripture: A Model for Theological Interpretation* (Oxford: Blackwell, 1998). While I focus on *Engaging Scripture*, many of the key points found in that work also characterize, in less technical form, his co-authored work with L. Gregory Jones, *Reading in Communion: Scripture and Ethics in Christian Life* (Grand Rapids, Mich.: Eerdmans, 1991). For an appreciative reading of Fowl's *Engaging Scripture*, emphasizing that "[r]eading Scripture aright . . . is predicated upon the grace and faithfulness of God" (150), see Rae, *History and Hermeneutics*, chap. 7, 131–52. Rae observes that "nothing seems more likely to misguide our reading than the decision to begin by leaving God out" (150).

50. I cannot fully agree with Francis Watson's view that Childs neglects "the hermeneutical significance of the location of the church within the world," that is to say, "a realistic socio-political orientation" (Watson, *Text, Church and World: Biblical Interpretation in Theological Perspective* [Grand Rapids, Mich.: Eerdmans, 1994], 46). For Watson, Childs's claim that the canon functions harmoniously, rather than conflictually, indicates that Childs's "ideal 'community of faith and practice' is oblivious to the function of the canonical text as a site of ideological conflict. It is alone with the text, free from and untrammelled by historical realities" (44). Watson largely agrees with Childs's description of "the formal outlines of the canonical object, over against an interpretative tradition which has rendered it invisible," but Watson rejects Childs's claims regarding "the *adequacy* and the *sufficiency* of the canon for guidance of the community into the truth" (44). Childs's understanding of "canon" possesses a keen historical sense of rootedness in Luther's Christological reading of the Bible: the canon suffices to guide the community precisely in revealing Christ, and this encounter with Christ forms and guides the community in ways that both sanctify the world and bring the community into conflict with the world. This Lutheran position neither precludes the ecumenical value of canonical biblical interpretation nor implies, as Watson suggests, that the

canon's "truthful witness" is not "given and discovered in the midst and in the depths of the conflict-ridden situations in which it is inevitably entangled" (45), but it does call into question whether Childs's account of the Church is adequate. Granting the Church's role in shaping the biblical canon need not involve supposing the Church to be "over against" the biblical canon. Rather, *participating* in the mediation of God's Word belongs to the very nature of the church as the Body of Christ. See also Childs's *Biblical Theology of the Old and New Testaments: Theological Reflection on the Christian Bible* (Minneapolis: Fortress Press, 1993), 72; as well as Stephen D. Ryan, O.P.'s recent study of the biblical canon in light of contemporary textual criticism: Ryan, "The Text of the Bible and Catholic Biblical Scholarship," *Nova et Vetera* 4 (2006): 132–41.

51. Fowl, *Engaging Scripture*, 3, 25.

52. On the historical development of the discipline of biblical theology, see Childs's *Biblical Theology of the Old and New Testaments*, 3–51, which treats biblical theology's origin in Gabler and Wrede and particularly commends the work of Gerhard Ebeling. For Ebeling see his *Word and Faith*, trans. James W. Leitch (1960; London: SCM Press, 1963). For Gabler see John Sandys-Wunsch and Laurence Eldrege, "J. P. Gabler and the Distinction between Biblical and Dogmatic Theology: Translation, Commentary, and Discussion of His Originality," *Scottish Journal of Theology* 33 (1980): 133–58. See also Fowl, *Engaging Scripture*, 13–31, which surveys the history of biblical theology and critiques the positions of Watson, Childs, and Werner Jeanrond; A. K. M. Adam, *Making Sense of New Testament Theology: "Modern" Problems and Prospects* (Macon, Ga.: Mercer University Press, 1995), 49 ff., in which Adam from a postmodern perspective strives to "direct our attention to the myriad of critical resources that are currently subordinated to history" (209); Ben Ollenburger, "Biblical Theology: Situating the Discipline," in *Understanding the Word: Essays in Honor of Bernhard W. Anderson*, ed. James T. Butler, Edgar W. Conrad, and Ben C. Ollenburger (Sheffield: JSOT Press, 1985), 37–62; Robert Morgan, "Introduction: The Nature of New Testament Theology," in idem, ed., *The Nature of New Testament Theology: The Contribution of William Wrede and Adolf Schlatter* (London: SCM Press, 1973), 1–67; idem, "New Testament Theology," in *Biblical Theology: Problems and Perspectives*, ed. Steven J. Kraftchick, Charles D. Myers Jr., and Ben C. Ollenburger (Nashville: Abingdon Press, 1995), 104–30. See also the essays in *Biblical Theology: Retrospect and Prospect*, ed. Scott J. Hafemann (Downers Grove, Ill.: InterVarsity Press, 2002), esp. Fowl's "The Conceptual Structure of New Testament Theology," 225–36, which emphasizes the Rule of Faith; Richard Schultz, "What Is 'Canonical' about a Canonical Biblical Theology? Genesis as a Case Study of Recent Old Testament Proposals," 83–99; and Christopher Seitz, "Two Testaments and the Failure of One Tradition History," 195–211, which critiques the proposals of Hartmut Gese and Peter Stuhlmacher. For Robert Morgan's efforts to develop a contemporary "New

Testament Theology," proposing that "Christian scripture does not yield a normative theology but suggests a doctrinal [Christological] norm," see his "Can
the Critical Study of Scripture Provide a Doctrinal Norm?" *Journal of Religion*
76 (1996): 206–32; as well as his "Jesus Christ, the Wisdom of God" (2), in
Reading Texts, Seeking Wisdom: Scripture and Theology, ed. David F. Ford and
Graham Stanton (Grand Rapids, Mich.: Eerdmans, 2003), 22–37. Also helpful
for getting one's bearings is John Webster's "Hermeneutics in Modern Theology: Some Doctrinal Reflections," 47–86, esp. his criticism of Jeanrond's *Text
and Interpretation as Categories of Theological Thinking* (Dublin: Gill & Macmillan, 1988); and idem, *Theological Hermeneutics: Development and Significance*
(London: SCM Press, 1994) for privileging hermeneutics over theology. See
also for an overview of New Testament theology especially in the 1990s, Frank
Matera, "New Testament Theology: History, Method, and Identity," *Catholic
Biblical Quarterly* 67 (2005): 1–21.

53. Fowl also wonders what defines a scriptural "voice." Indeed, he would
prefer to avoid altogether imputing human agency to scriptural texts, because
such language tends to blur the reality that texts, including scriptural texts,
require interpreters. See Fowl, *Engaging Scripture*, 27. Fowl remarks later,
"given that the notion of texts having voices is a way of talking about the communities in which these texts are read, then Christians must hold some form
of the view that the proper voice of the Old Testament is heard within those
communities that read the scriptures under the guidance of the Spirit in the
light of the life, death, and resurrection of Jesus. It is not the case that the guild
of professional Old Testament scholars establishes something like the autonomous voice of the Old Testament, which is then related in a complex way
to the autonomous voice of the New Testament (established by professional
New Testament scholars)" (131). He points out in a footnote to this passage,
"I take it that Jews would hold to similar views. That is, the Old Testament
is not really seen as an 'autonomous' voice. Rather it is read in the light of
its subsequent commentaries by those committed to living faithfully (as they
see it) before the God of Israel. As Jon Levenson notes, discussions between
Jews and Christians over the Bible that demand that both Jews and Christians abandon these particular commitments in favor of the commitments of
professional biblical studies are not an exercise in ecumenism. Rather, they
result in the distortion of both traditions" (ibid.). Fowl's distinction between
"supersessionist" and "Marcionite" approaches is helpful in this discussion
(see 129).

54. Like Fowl, Watson questions this aspect of Childs's approach. For the
Christian, Watson suggests, the Old Testament always points beyond itself
to Christ and thus does not possess an autonomous or semi-autonomous voice.
Childs's attempt to separate off such a voice, before attending to the "canonical
context," strikes Watson as a removal of the "single, christological centre as

the object of this discrete witness" (*Text and Truth*, 216). Christopher Seitz responds to Watson on this score in "Christological Interpretation of Texts and Trinitarian Claims to Truth: An Engagement with Francis Watson's *Text and Truth*," *Scottish Journal of Theology* 52 (1999): 209–26, in which Seitz holds that the distinct voice sought by Childs is simply the theology of Israel (e.g., faith in the one God) that remains true in Christ Jesus, and that instructs Christian theology when Christian theology is willing to begin with the Old Testament (seeing there truths of faith) rather than beginning with the New and then facing the problem of what to make of the Old; as Seitz says, "The Old Testament is not a relative with a gas problem, as a former colleague once said, that we must accept and try politely to work around" (226). In a short response to Seitz, Watson suggests that "the differences between us are more apparent than real" (Watson, "The Old Testament as Christian Scripture: A Response to Professor Seitz," *Scottish Journal of Theology* 52 [1999]: 227–32, at 232). The difficulty comes, according to Watson, because Seitz has not fully seen the basis for Watson's critique of Childs. Watson states, "My position is based on a phenomenological description of the structure of the Christian canon, according to which the 'discrete voice' of each of its two major parts can only properly be heard on the assumption of their *interdependence*. . . . To speak of the 'discrete witness' of the Old and New Testaments respectively is to make an important point about the twofoldness, but it tells us nothing about the dialectical unity. If we regard each of the two collections of texts as basically autonomous in relation to the other, it will be difficult to *substantiate* the claim that the God of Israel is the God of Jesus—however emphatically we assert it. The *necessity* of this identification will only be apparent if, without losing their distinctiveness, the Old and New Testaments are seen to be constituted as old and new only in relation to the other and to the definitve disclosure in Jesus of the triune God that both separates and unites them" (227–28). I concur with Watson, and in so doing concur largely also with the points made by Seitz. One should also see Seitz's "We Are Not Prophets or Apostles: The Biblical Theology of B. S. Childs" and "The Changing Face of Old Testament Studies," in Seitz, *Word without End: The Old Testament As Abiding Theological Witness* (Grand Rapids, Mich.: Eerdmans, 1998), 75–82 and 102–9, where he praises Childs's *Biblical Theology of the Old and New Testaments* but expresses concern that Childs's proposals lack both an academic and an ecclesial audience. Here I think Seitz uncovers, probably unconsciously, a problem in Childs's ecclesiology, in which Scripture and the Church tend to stand over against each other rather than participating in each other sacramentally. Seitz offers his own account of Scripture and the Church in "'And without God in the World': A Hermeneutic of Estrangement Overcome," in his *Word without End*, 41–50. He states, "Basic to scripture's very existence is its attachment to a people God has addressed in a privileged way" (49).

55. Fowl, *Engaging Scripture*, 26. See also p. 134, where Fowl, drawing on the work of Richard Hays, argues that "Paul's reading of Abraham's story is not only ecclesiocentric in the sense Hays claims, but that the internal coherence of Paul's reading presupposes and requires that Abraham's story be read within the context of an ecclesia that has experienced the Spirit in the way the Galatians have. Moreover, while Paul insists on the hermeneutical priority of the Galatians' experience of the Spirit, it is an experience interpreted by Paul. The Galatians' Spirit experience is not self-interpreting." Cf. Fowl's "Learning to Narrate Our Lives in Christ," in *Theological Exegesis: Essays in Honor of Brevard S. Childs*, ed. Christopher Seitz and Kathryn Greene-McCreight (Grand Rapids, Mich.: Eerdmans, 1999), 339–54.

56. On the truth sought by allegorical reading, see, e.g., J. Patout Burns, "Delighting the Spirit: Augustine's Practice of Figurative Interpretation," in *De Doctrina Christiana: A Classic of Western Culture*, ed. Duane W. H. Arnold and Pamela Bright (Notre Dame: University of Notre Dame Press, 1995), 182–94. Concerning the "controls" on allegorical reading, see, e.g., Bryan M. Litfin, "The Rule of Faith in Augustine," *Pro Ecclesia* 14 (2005): 85–101; and Joseph T. Lienhard, S.J., *The Bible, the Church, and Authority: The Canon of the Christian Bible in History and Theology* (Collegeville, Minn.: Liturgical Press, 1995), chap. 7; cf. Jaroslav Pelikan, "*Canonica regula*: The Trinitarian Hermeneutics of Augustine," *Proceedings of the Patristic, Medieval and Renaissance Conference* 12–13 (1987–88): 17–29. For Fowl, historical-critical reading, just as much as allegorical reading, methodologically involves practices that lead it away from the actual biblical texts, but the allegiances of the allegorical reading are ecclesial and governed by the Rule of Faith. R. W. L. Moberly holds that the Rule of Faith has often been used "to say what texts 'must' mean on the grounds of post-biblical dogmas, and to attempt to marginalize or silence those who have the courage to show that biblical texts do not necessarily mean what later tradition has thought them to mean," but he nonetheless finds a Rule of Faith necessary for setting "the biblical text within the context of the continuing life of the Christian Church where the one God and humanity are definitively understood in relation to Jesus Christ" (Moberly, *The Bible, Theology, and Faith: A Study of Abraham and Jesus* [Cambridge: Cambridge University Press, 2000], 43; cf. 232–37). He argues that the Rule of Faith works when the Church works (that is, when the Church manifests cruciform charity), and fails when the Church fails.

57. Fowl later points out, in response to the charge that he is advocating an ahistorical reading by rejecting the *necessity* of historical-critical interpretation for the Church, "What is interesting about the argument against ahistorical readings, however, is not so much the chimera it attacks (i.e. historicality), but what it implicitly assumes: When historical critics argue against ahistorical readings they seem to assume that the only alternative is to be a historical

critic" (184). To those who hold that historical-critical interpretation is necessary for the Church because God became man in history, Fowl, following A. K. M. Adam, responds that historical-critical scholarship's value is weakened both by inability to demonstrate much about the historical Jesus, and more importantly by the fact that the mystery of Christ's humanity and divinity, and his theandric acts, exceeds the capacity of historical methodology (185–86).

58. Comparing the community of academic biblical scholarship with the community of the Church, Fowl observes how much formation the academic community requires of its participants. He draws the conclusion that Christian communities should emulate the academic community not by seeking, in general, to become proficient in its methods, but by forming ecclesial readers: "Rather than seeking to become well-versed in the skills, habits, convictions, and practices of professional biblical scholarship so that they can make useful ad hoc judgments about this work, Christians need to become much more well-versed in the skills, habits, convictions, and practices attendant upon Christian interpretation of scripture" (187).

59. Fowl, *Engaging Scripture*, 26.

60. Ibid., 26–27.

61. Ibid., 5.

62. Ibid., 6. For an influential study of ways of understanding and deploying scriptural authority for Christian theology, see David H. Kelsey, *Proving Doctrine: The Uses of Scripture in Modern Theology*, 2d ed. with a new preface (Harrisburg, Pa.: Trinity Press International, 1999), originally published as *The Uses of Scripture in Recent Theology* (Philadelphia: Fortress Press, 1975). Kelsey proposes three basic notions of the authoritative aspect of Scripture: doctrinal-conceptual content, recital-narrative performance, and as mythic-symbolic expression; these correspond roughly to Lindbeck's three modes of theology as sketched in his *The Nature of Doctrine* (Philadelphia: Westminster Press, 1984), namely propositional, cultural-linguistic, and experiential-expressivist. In his new preface Kelsey summarizes his functionalist understanding of scriptural authority: "The argument is: *If* you practice theology in any of these ways, then *de facto* this is what 'the authority of scripture' means practically speaking, i.e., in your practice of doing theology regardless of what your doctrine of scripture may say about scripture's authority *de jure*. However, in my view, the entire analysis falls far short of an adequate argument in support of any one normative, i.e., *de jure*, proposal about scripture's authority for theology" (xiii). The key, I think, consists in adding a rich understanding of *doctrina* and mediation, and thus of the triune God and the Church. Otherwise Kelsey's, and Fowl's, understanding of "the authority of Scripture" tends to downplay the theocentricity of Scripture. "God's teaching" risks being eclipsed by the community's appropriation. Given an adequate understanding of *sacra doctrina*, these two aspects need not be in tension, as I have suggested above.

For an argument that Scripture's authority should be understood as "functional" rather than "content-based," see W. T. Dickens, *Hans Urs von Balthasar's Theological Aesthetics: A Model for Post-Critical Biblical Interpretation* (Notre Dame: University of Notre Dame Press, 2003), 199–205. Dickens disagrees with von Balthasar in this regard, whereas I would agree with von Balthasar. *Doctrina* unites "content-based" and "functional." See also the wonderfully theocentric account of the Bible provided by the Barthian theologian John Webster, in critical discussion with Lindbeck and Frei, in "Hermeneutics in Modern Theology: Some Doctrinal Reflections," 47–86, at 62–63; cf. David Demson, *Hans Frei and Karl Barth: Different Ways of Reading Scripture* (Grand Rapids, Mich.: Eerdmans, 1997).

63. Fowl, *Engaging Scripture*, 7.

64. Ibid., 10; cf. Fowl's chap. 2. This "underdetermined" mode is governed by attention to theological realities. It is not underdetermined in the sense that the Christian could read Scripture any way with equal fruitfulness, but it is underdetermined in the sense that it leaves open various ways of understanding biblical texts. As Fowl explains, "Christians, by virtue of their identity, are required to read scripture theologically. Others may wish to do so, and Christians can certainly benefit from the insights of outsiders who engage scripture theologically. Most obviously, these readings would come from Jews who are reading their scripture theologically, but are not necessarily limited to them. My claims here neither limit the extent of the universal claims Christians want to make, nor seek to eliminate the interpretive practices of others. Christian biblical scholars can in principle engage in the whole panoply of diverse, and irreducibly distinct, interpretive practices characteristic of the profession of biblical scholarship. Neither the profession nor the 'semantic potential' of the Bible requires all critical interpreters to read theologically" (30). In a similar vein, Fowl states in his conclusion that "the ends towards which the church interprets and embodies scripture are simply not those of the profession. As a result, the work of professional biblical scholars must always be appropriated in an ad hoc way, on a case-by-case basis" (183). As I have noted above, Fowl's claims should be moderated by Childs's point (following David Yeago) that "traditional Christian exegesis understood its theological reflection to be responding to the coercion or pressure of the biblical text itself. It was not merely an exercise in seeking self-identity, or in bending an inherited authority to support a sectarian theological agenda" (Childs, "Toward Recovering Theological Exegesis," *Pro Ecclesia* 6 [1997]: 16–26, at 17).

65. Fowl, *Engaging Scripture*, 10.

66. For Fowl's account of this "practical reasoning" of Christian scriptural exegetes (i.e., ideally all Christians), see 194 ff., as well as Fowl's *The Story of Christ in the Ethics of Paul: An Analysis of the Function of the Hymnic Material in the Pauline Corpus* (Sheffield: Sheffield Academic Press, 1991), which deepens

our understanding of what constitutes moral discourse in the Bible by pointing out the relationship between Christology and ethics. See also the valuable insights in this regard of Michael J. Gorman, *Cruciformity: Paul's Narrative Spirituality of the Cross* (Grand Rapids, Mich.: Eerdmans, 2001).

67. Fowl, *Engaging Scripture*, 10.

68. See ibid., 21. Cf. Reinhard Hütter, *Suffering Divine Things: Theology as Church Practice Suffering Divine Things: Theology as Church Practice* (Grand Rapids, Mich.: Eerdmans, 2000), originally published in German in 1997. Naturally Fowl, whose book was published in 1998, does not refer to Hütter.

69. Fowl, *Engaging Scripture*, 20.

70. Ibid.

71. Ibid., 11; cf. Fowl's chap. 3.

72. Ibid., 206.

73. Ibid., 203.

74. This situation is nothing new, although the consumption-driven communications media is largely new. Athanasius, bishop of Alexandria, was seen by Arius and some of the emperors as rigidly ruling out a path chosen by the majority of Christians in many areas. I disagree, therefore, with Francis Watson's application to biblical interpretation of his comparison between monologic and dialogic discourse, the latter representing the eschatological inbreaking of undistorted communication or true interpersonal communion. Watson writes that "the revelation of the eschatological horizon of universally undistorted communication must itself be communicated in a dialogical form rather than imposing itself unilaterally in the form of a monological demand for credence and submission" (Watson, *Text, Church and World*, 123). Ironically, Watson himself issues what might seem to be, in biblical interpretation, a "monological demand for credence and submission" when he rejects 1 Corinthians 14:33–35. He states, "No amount of special pleading can conceal the fact that what occurs here is the violent suppression of dialogue in the name of a truth that is now to be experienced by women in a heteronomous and monological form which undermines their status as persons (for to be a person is to be a dialogue-partner)" (116). For him, persons or churches (one thinks of Roman Catholics and Eastern Orthodox) who defend 1 Corinthians 14:33–35 are engaging in "special pleading" at best and their arguments constitute cooperation in the violent suppression of women's status as persons. This rhetoric is not exactly an invitation to dialogic engagement. This fact suggests that (even for Watson) ecclesial biblical interpretation cannot always be "dialogic" but sometimes must indeed demand a form of "credence and submission" rather than—as Watson defines the "dialogical" vis-à-vis the "monological"—actively promoting further dialogue with "an oppressed or dissident minority" (112). Watson's rejection of 1 Corinthians 14:33–35 also points to further problems with his account of "dialogical" and "monological." Person-constituting "dialogue" with

Christ requires, for Watson, liturgical "speaking in Church," and those who deny this liturgical role to women are supreme instances of the "monological." First, this claim simply ignores the dynamic of sacramental participation, despite Watson's agreement with Jürgen Habermas's critique of "modern philosophy as proceeding from a subjectivity construed in terms of the self-constituting ego" (113). Second, the claim appears to presume that "dialogical" discussion would be ended by the Church's teaching that a doctrine was definitive and unchangeable. The characteristics of fruitful ecclesial dialogue, including what Chesterton calls the "democracy of the dead" who as saints alive in heaven belong even more fully to the Church, are elided. Watson makes similarly tendentious exegetical claims, in my view, in his "Is John's Christology Adoptionist?" in *The Glory of Christ in the New Testament: Studies in Christology*, ed. L. D. Hurst and N. T. Wright (Oxford: Clarendon Press, 1987), 113–24.

75. Corrine Patton observes with reference to the Catholic Church's interpretive judgment that the ordination of women is not possible: "The reality of life within a community of faith, however, is that at points in the community's history, decisions must be made about contemporary church practice and teaching. At those points, when the rubber hits the road, so to speak, fluidity fades into conflict" (Patton, "Canon and Tradition: The Limits of the Old Testament in Scholastic Discussion," in *Theological Exegesis*, ed. Christopher Seitz and Kathryn Greene-McCreight [Grand Rapids, Mich.: Eerdmans, 1999], 75–95, at 95).

76. Fowl, *Engaging Scripture*, 155.

77. Ibid.

78. Ibid.

79. Ibid., 150–51.

80. Ibid., 152–53. In this regard, Fowl agrees with Richard Hays's proposal, in *Echoes of Scripture in the Letters of Paul* (New Haven: Yale University Press, 1989), of three "constraints" (admittedly rather broad and vague) on "interpretive freedom" that characterize well-formed Christian interpreters, Paul and his communities included: "First, no reading can be true if it 'denies the faithfulness of Israel's God to his covenant promises.' Secondly, 'No reading of Scripture can be legitimate if it fails to acknowledge the death and resurrection of Jesus as the climactic manifestation of God's righteousness.' Finally, and most importantly, 'No reading of Scripture can be legitimate, then, if it fails to shape the readers into a community that embodies the love of God as shown forth in Christ'" (153).

81. Fowl, *Engaging Scripture*, 152. The reference is to Hays's *Echoes of Scripture in the Letters of Paul*. As Hays explains in a later essay, he views Paul's "ecclesiocentric" exegesis as emerging from Paul's Christology. Hays states: "My emphasis on the ecclesiocentric character of Paul's hermeneutic is the result of seeking to ask in a disciplined manner, What is Paul actually *doing* with

Scripture when he appeals to it in his arguments? The striking result of such an inquiry is to reveal the relative scarcity of christologically interpreted Old Testament passages in Paul. My explanation for this phenomenon is to propose that Paul's Christological convictions belong to a foundational 'substructure' of his thought; apart from his Christological presuppositions, his ecclesiocentric (or, as I suggested above, *ecclesiotelic*) readings make no sense" (Hays, "On the Rebound: A Response to Critiques of *Echoes of Scripture in the Letters of Paul*," in Hays, *The Conversion of the Imagination: Paul as Interpreter of Israel's Scripture* [Grand Rapids, Mich.: Eerdmans, 2005], 163–89, at 187).

83. Fowl, *Engaging Scripture*, 157.

83. Ibid.

84. Ibid.

85. Ibid.

86. For a discussion of the mystical Body as a visible communion of charitable friendship—a communion sustained, despite human sin, by Christ through the Holy Spirit—see my *Sacrifice and Community: Jewish Offering and Christian Eucharist* (Oxford: Blackwell, 2005), esp. chap. 3. See also Fergus Kerr, O.P., "Charity as Friendship," in *Language, Meaning and God*, ed. Brian Davies, O.P. (London: Geoffrey Chapman, 1987), 1–23; Guy Mansini, O.S.B., "*Similitudo, Communicatio*, and the Friendship of Charity in Aquinas," in *Thomistica. Recherches de théologie ancienne et médiévale*, supp. 1, ed. E. Manning (Leuven: Peeters, 1995), 1–26; James McEvoy, "The Other as Oneself: Friendship and Love in the Thought of St. Thomas Aquinas," in *Thomas Aquinas: Approaches to Truth*, ed. James McEvoy and Michael Dunne (Dublin: Four Courts Press, 2002), 16–37; Anthony Keaty, "Thomas's Authority for Identifying Charity as Friendship: Aristotle or John 15?" *Thomist* 62 (1998): 581–601; Servais Pinckaers, O.P., "Der Sinn für die Freundschaftsliebe als Urtatsache der thomistischen Ethik," in *Sein und Ethos. Untersuchungen zur Grundlegung der Ethik*, ed. P. Engelhardt, O.P. (Mainz: 1960), 228–35.

87. Fowl, *Engaging Scripture*, 159.

88. Ibid., 158.

89. Ibid., 152.

90. Reinhard Hütter, *Bound to Be Free: Evangelical Catholic Engagements in Ecclesiology, Ethics, and Ecumenism* (Grand Rapids, Mich.: Eerdmans, 2004). The question arises, however, as to whether we might be "bound" by an ecclesial falsehood. In this regard, Murray Rae thinks that ecclesial exegesis receives the Spirit's promise that the falsehood will eventually be overcome: "God's calling forth, empowering of, and siding with the tradition does not mean that the tradition is infallible, or that it does not on occasion succumb to error. The promise of the Spirit who will 'guide you into all truth' (John 16.13), however, means, we may faithfully hope, that God will not abandon the Church in its stumbling efforts to bear witness to him, but will, over time, form and reform the Church

in order to safeguard and uphold the truth of the gospel" (Rae, *History and Hermeneutics*, 129). While agreeing with Rae's characterization of the Church's "stumbling efforts," nonetheless one can ask whether Rae's approach suffices to uphold Jesus' promise that "you will know the truth, and the truth will make you free" (Jn 8:32). The particular issue chosen by Fowl, namely the moral status of homosexual acts, exemplifies the difficulty.

91. Fowl, *Engaging Scripture*, 157.

92. Ibid., 156.

93. Ibid., 157.

94. Ibid., 154 and elsewhere. Cf. Fowl and Jones, *Reading in Communion*, 133–35.

95. Fowl, *Engaging Scripture*, chap. 4. I think Fowl is mistaken here. For exegetical arguments against such a reinterpretation, see, e.g., Richard B. Hays, *The Moral Vision of the New Testament: A Contemporary Introduction to New Testament Ethics* (San Francisco: HarperSanFrancisco, 1996), 379–406; Robert A. J. Gagnon, *The Bible and Homosexual Practice: Texts and Hermeneutics* (Nashville: Abingdon Press, 2001); Karl P. Donfried, "Alien Hermeneutics and the Misappropriation of Scripture," in *Reclaiming the Bible for the Church*, ed. Carl E. Braaten and Robert Jenson (Grand Rapids, Mich.: Eerdmans, 1995), 19–45; Christopher R. Seitz, "Scripture and a Three-Legged Stool: Is There a Coherent Account of the Authority of Scripture for Anglicans after Lambeth 1998?" and "Dispirited: Scripture as Rule of Faith and Recent Misuse of the Council of Jerusalem: Text, Spirit, and Word to Culture," in his *Figured Out: Typology and Providence in Christian Scripture* (Louisville: Westminster/John Knox, 2001), 49–68 and 117–29; idem, "Human Sexuality Viewed from the Bible's Understanding of the Human Condition" and "Sexuality and Scripture's Plain Sense: The Christian Community and the Law of God," in his *Word without End*, 263–75 and 319–39. See also *Catechism of the Catholic Church* §§2357–59 in the context of the *Catechism*'s treatment of the sixth commandment. Fowl defends, against Christopher Seitz's "Sexuality and Scripture's Plain Sense," Jeffrey Siker's "How to Decide? Homosexual Christians, the Bible, and Gentile Inclusion," *Theology Today* 51 (1994): 219–34, where Siker argues that the debate over homosexual acts is analogous to the Council of Jerusalem's debate over Gentile inclusion. Fowl's key move is to question "how compatible a static notion of the 'plain sense' of scripture, a plain sense located in the text rather than the believing community, is with Christian theological approaches to the Old Testament" (Fowl, *Engaging Scripture*, 126). This contrast between "in the text" and in "the believing community" risks, I think, a false dichotomy. The danger consists in conceiving of the text as a formless "prime matter" that receives form from the community. Clearly the text is more than this, in part of course because "text" and "community" cannot be separated. Seitz suggests that at stake is whether Scripture mediates, in the Holy Spirit, "God's own

providential ordering" (Seitz, "Introduction," in *Figured Out*, 3–10, at 10), or whether the Holy Spirit is revealing that Scripture itself now stands outside an evolving "providential ordering." On such larger philosophical and theological issues, cf. Graham McAleer's *Ecstatic Morality and Sexual Politics: A Catholic and Antitotalitarian Theory of the Body* (New York: Fordham University Press, 2005).

96. Cf. R.W.L. Moberly's evaluation of *The Postmodern Bible*, ed. Stephen D. Moore et al. (New Haven: Yale University Press, 1995) in Moberly's *The Bible, Theology, and Faith*, 26–37. Moberly shows what happens when interpretation is conceived solely as a power struggle.

97. On this point, see John Webster, *Holy Scripture: A Dogmatic Sketch* (Cambridge: Cambridge University Press, 2003). The nominalist occlusion of participation leads to dichotomies such as the one between "text" and "meaning."

98. Childs largely because (lacking an account of participation) he fears that it limits God's freedom. In this position Childs reflects the influence of Karl Barth among others.

99. Fowl's position risks a danger that, as John Webster points out, afflicts some "accounts of Scripture as the Church's book": "such accounts can sometimes take the form of a highly sophisticated hermeneutical reworking of a Ritschlian social moralism, in which the centre of gravity of a theology of Scripture has shifted away from God's activity toward the uses of the church" (Webster, *Holy Scripture*, 43). On the other hand, Gavin D'Costa has persuasively shown that Webster's *Holy Scripture* would benefit from a deeper theology of the Church. See D'Costa, "Revelation, Scripture and Tradition: Some Comments on John Webster's Conception of 'Holy Scripture,'" *International Journal of Systematic Theology* 6 (2004): 337–50.

100. Cf. Francis J. Moloney, S. D. B., *The Gospel of John* (Collegeville, Minn.: Liturgical Press, 1998), 401–2. For Moloney the Spirit continues Jesus' revelatory presence, and thereby continues to distinguish those who belong to "the world of Jesus" from those who belong to the "world" that rejects the revelatory presence, or truth, of divine love. Love and truth belong solely to what Moloney calls the "realm" or "world" of Jesus, their primary purpose or function seems to be separating this world—instantiated in Moloney's reading in a particular (Johannine) community—from the "world" that is constituted by the rejection of Jesus, that is, the "world" outside the Church's bounds.

101. Fowl, *Engaging Scripture*, 16; cf. Fowl, "The Conceptual Structure of New Testament Theology," 228; cf. Watson, *Text and Truth: Redefining Biblical Theology* (Grand Rapids, Mich.: Eerdmans, 1997), 1–9; Hays, "Response to Robert Wilken, 'In Dominico Eloquio,'" *Communio* 25 (1998): 520–28, at 522, and *The Art of Reading Scripture*, ed. Ellen F. Davis and Richard B. Hays (Grand Rapids, Mich.: Eerdmans, 2003). Fowl blames the "institutional fragmentation"

brought about by increasing specialization and the fact that "[t]o be counted as a professional within each of these disciplines, one has to master such a detailed body of knowledge particular to each field that it is rare to find a scholar in one field whose work is read and used by those in another" ("The Conceptual Structure of New Testament Theology," 229). He argues that the way forward is the ecclesial "rule of faith," with its circularity between the New Testament and Church doctrine. Cf. Robert W. Wall, "Reading the Bible from within Our Traditions: The 'Rule of Faith' in Theological Hermeneutics," in *Between Two Horizons: Spanning New Testament Studies and Systematic Theology,* ed. Joel B. Green and Max Turner (Grand Rapids, Mich.: Eerdmans, 2000), 88–107; as well as Paul M. Blowers, "The *Regula Fidei* and the Narrative Character of Early Christian Faith," *Pro Ecclesia* 6 (1997): 199–228; for Wall's canonical perspective, drawing on both Brevard Childs and James Sanders, see Wall's "Canonical Context and Canonical Conversations," in Green and Turner, *Between Two Horizons,* 165–182; idem, "The Significance of a Canonical Perspective of the Church's Scripture," in *The Canon Debate,* ed. L. M. McDonald and J. A. Sanders (Peabody, Mass.: Hendrickson, 2002), 528–40; as well as Wall's essays in Robert W. Wall and Eugene E. Lemcio, *The New Testament as Canon: A Reader in Canonical Criticism* (Sheffield: JSOT Press, 1992), which applies a canonical perspective to interpretation of various episodes and teachings in the New Testament as well as to contemporary ecumenical discussions.

102. Rather than use endnotes to cite Aquinas's *Commentary on John,* I place the paragraph number from the Marietti edition in parentheses after each quotation. For the English translation of Aquinas's commentary on John 14:15–17, see Aquinas, *Commentary on the Gospel of St. John,* trans. James A. Weisheipl, O.P., and Fabian R. Larcher, O.P., pt. II (Petersham, Mass.: St. Bede's Publications, 1999), ch. 14, lect. 4, 353–59.

103. For an overview of grace in Aquinas's *Commentary on John,* see John R. Sheets, S.J., "The Scriptural Dimension of St. Thomas," *American Ecclesiastical Review* 144 (1961): 154–73. Sheets calls for reading the *Summa* in light of scriptural exegesis in general, and Aquinas's biblical commentaries in particular. Among the theological movements of the twentieth century, Servais Pinckaers, O.P.'s "biblical Thomism" stands out and should be mentioned here as an exemplar, in theology, of the ecclesial biblical exegesis that I describe in this chapter. For its foundations, see also Roger Guindon, O. M. I., "La théologie de saint Thomas d'Aquin dans le rayonnement du 'Prologue' de saint Jean," *Revue de l'Université d'Ottawa* 29 (1959): 5–23 and 121–42; idem, *Béatitude et théologie morale chez saint Thomas d'Aquin* (Ottawa: Editions de l'Université d'Ottawa, 1956); idem, "Le caractè évangelique de la morale de saint Thomas d'Aquin," *Revue de l'Université d'Ottawa* 25 (1955): 145–67; idem, "Le 'De Sermone Domini in monte' de saint Augustin dans l'oeuvre de saint Thomas d'Aquin," *Revue de l'Université d'Ottawa* 28 (1958): 57–85. Cf. Pinckaers's de-

scription of his intellectual formation in his "Dominican Moral Theology in the 20th Century," in *The Pinckaers Reader: Renewing Thomistic Moral Theology*, ed. John Berkman and Craig Steven Titus (Washington, D.C.: Catholic University of America Press, 2005), 73–89, as well as in the same volume Pinckaers's "Scripture and the Renewal of Moral Theology" and "The Sources of the Ethics of St. Thomas Aquinas."

104. Richard B. Hays speaks of a "hermeneutical circle" between the biblical witness that "resurrection-empowered reading occurs primarily in the context of a shared life in community, in the practice of breaking bread together" (cf. Luke 24), and "practices of discipleship and mission": see Hays, "Reading Scripture in Light of the Resurrection," in Davis and Hays, *The Art of Reading Scripture*, 216–38, at 236.

105. Cf. the reflections on biblical interpretation as Christian discipleship in L. Gregory Jones, "Embodying Scripture in the Community of Faith," in Davis and Hays, *The Art of Reading Scripture*, 143–59; Fowl and Jones, *Reading in Communion*. Fowl and Jones owe much to the work of Stanley Hauerwas.

106. Insofar as this self-love is instantiated in a particular political order—for instance in Nazi Germany, or in the "culture of death" marked preeminently by abortion—Christians must oppose the regime or the corrupted aspect of the regime, which has now become the very opposite of *ordo*. Cf. Bernd Wannenwetsch, "You Shall Not Kill—What Does It Take? Why We Need the Other Commandments If We Are to Abstain from Killing," in *I Am the Lord Your God: Christian Reflections on the Ten Commandments*, ed. Carl E. Braaten and Christopher R. Seitz (Grand Rapids, Mich.: Eerdmans, 2005), 148–74, at 171–72; see also idem, "Intrinsically Evil Acts; or: Why Euthanasia and Abortion Cannot Be Justified," in *Ecumenical Ventures in Ethics: Protestants Engage Pope John Paul II's Moral Encyclicals*, ed. Reinhard Hütter and Theodor Dieter (Grand Rapids, Mich.: Eerdmans, 1998), 185–215.

107. See Stanley Hauerwas's sermon "On Being De-Possessed: Or This Is a Hell of a Way to Get Someplace," in his *Unleashing the Scripture: Freeing the Bible from Captivity to America* (Nashville: Abingdon Press, 1993), 105–10.

108. See Richard B. Hays, "Reading Scripture in Light of the Resurrection," 216–38. Hays comments, "When we read Scripture in light of the resurrection, we understand Scripture as testimony to the life-giving power of God. The resurrection of Jesus is not an isolated miracle but a disclosure of God's purpose finally to subdue death and to embrace us within the life of resurrection. 'As all die in Adam, so all will be made alive in Christ' (1 Cor 15:22). For that reason, a hermeneutic responsive to the resurrection can never be a hermeneutic of suspicion toward Scripture's word of promise. The God with whom we have to do is a God who wills life and wholeness for us. If we read the biblical story rightly as a story about this God, we will learn to read it in hopeful trust, open to joyous surprises. We will read with hearts open to the divine

power disclosed in the resurrection—a power that overthrows all human systems of violence and oppression. (See Eph 1:17–23)" (233).

109. Citing Sarah Coakley's "The Resurrection and the 'Spiritual Senses': On Wittgenstein, Epistemology and the Risen Christ," in her *Powers and Submissions* (Oxford: Blackwell, 2002), 130–52, Hays points out that the *sacra doctrina* (as I would put it) of the Cross and Resurrection transforms our understanding: "The Gospel resurrection stories, then, expand our imagination and lead us to discern that God is at work within the sphere of physical time-space reality to transform and restore all things, negating death's power over the body. Our bodies become vehicles and theaters of God's transforming power. That is why the gospel's epistemology [I would add, metaphysics] privileges concreteness and anathematizes all docetism, Neoplatonism, and Kantian epistemological dualism. God the Creator raised Jesus from the dead; therefore, 'flesh is precious'" (Hays, "Reading Scripture in Light of the Resurrection," 236).

110. In this regard some Protestant (and Catholic) scholars do not find Catholic biblical interpretation "critical" enough. If the Catholic exegete holds in faith the teachings of the Church's Magisterium, it would seem that this exegetical a priori prevents the ongoing work of exegesis—and thus the historical particularity of Scripture itself—from truly challenging dogmatic beliefs. For an example of this widespread concern, see George Lindbeck, "The Story-Shaped Church: Critical Exegesis and Theological Interpretation," in *The Theological Interpretation of Scripture: Classic and Contemporary Readings*, ed. Stephen E. Fowl (Oxford: Blackwell, 1997), 39–52; cf. Richard B. Hays, "The Future of *Christian* Biblical Scholarship," *Nova et Vetera* 4 (2006): 95–120, esp. 109, 117.

111. Marion, *God without Being: Hors-Texte*, trans. Thomas A. Carlson (Chicago: University of Chicago Press, 1991 [1982]), 153–56.

112. Fowl and Jones, *Reading in Communion*, 57.

113. Cf. the intriguing study of Charles Kannengiesser, "The Bible in the Arian Crisis," in *The Bible in Greek Christian Antiquity*, ed. and trans. Paul M. Blowers (Notre Dame: University of Notre Dame Press, 1997), 217–28.

114. In this spirit, with reference particularly to the Petrine ministry, Joseph Ratzinger states: "at the inmost core of the new commission, which robs the forces of destruction of their power, is the grace of forgiveness. It constitutes the Church. The Church is founded upon forgiveness. Peter himself is a personal embodiment of this truth, for he is permitted to be the bearer of the keys after having stumbled, confessed and received the grace of pardon. The Church is by nature the home of forgiveness, and it is thus that chaos is banished from within her. She is held together by forgiveness, and Peter is the perpetual living reminder of this reality: she is not a communion of the perfect but a communion of sinners who need and seek forgiveness. Behind the talk of au-

thority, God's power appears as mercy and thus as the foundation stone of the Church; in the background we hear the word of the Lord: 'It is not the healthy who have need of the physician, but those who are ill; I have not come to call the righteous, but sinners' (Mk 2:17)" (Ratzinger, "The Primacy of Peter and the Unity of the Church," in *Called to Communion: Understanding the Church Today*, trans. Adrian Walker from the second German edition [San Francisco: Ignatius Press, 1996], 47–74, at 64–65).

115. Thus I agree with N. T. Wright's conclusion that "the shorthand phrase 'the authority of scripture,' when unpacked, offers a picture of God's sovereign and saving plan for the entire cosmos, dramatically inaugurated by Jesus himself, and now to be implemented through the Spirit-led life of the church *precisely as the scripture-reading community.* . . . Scripture's authority is thus seen to best advantage in its formation of the mind of the church, and its stiffening of our resolve, as we work to implement the resurrection of Jesus, and so to anticipate the day when God will make all things new, and justice, joy and peace will triumph (Ephesians 1:3–23)" (Wright, *The Last Word: Beyond the Bible Wars to a New Understanding of the Authority of Scripture* [New York: HarperSanFrancisco, 2005], 114–15). Wright goes on to suggest that "God's authority exercised through Scripture" is properly honored "by a reading of Scripture that is (a) totally contextual, (b) liturgically grounded, (c) privately studied, (d) refreshed by appropriate scholarship, and (e) taught by the church's accredited leaders" (127). His account of (e) focuses on the need for bishops (in his Anglican communion), and for all "accredited church leaders," to be able to proclaim "the word in the power of the Spirit," rather than leaving the teaching of Scripture to academics (140). True authority is manifested primarily by the power to proclaim the Gospel, and only secondarily by "*legal structures*, important though both church structures and canon law are in their own ways" (140). The question is what Wright means by the "accreditation" of Church leaders. Who accredits them, how do they receive this accreditation, and what does their accredited status mean for the practice of cruciform obedience—surely a prime manifestation of God's transformative authority in the world as cruciform love rather than self-cleaving power—in the Church?

116. Waclaw Swierzawski, "God and the Mystery of His Wisdom in the Pauline Commentaries of Saint Thomas Aquinas," *Divus Thomas* 74 (1971): 500.

Conclusion

1. Reinhard Hütter, "'In.' Some Incipient Reflections on *The Jewish People and Their Sacred Scriptures in the Christian Bible*," *Pro Ecclesia* 13 (2004): 13–24, at 19.

2. Ibid., 21.

3. Brevard Childs, "Toward Recovering Theological Exegesis," *Pro Ecclesia* 6 (1997): 18.

4. Samuel Johnson, "Vanity of an Author's Expectations," in *The Rambler*, selected and introduced by S. C. Roberts (London: J. M. Dent & Sons, 1953), 171. As Johnson also points out: "Of men devoted to literature very few extend their views beyond some particular science, and the greater part seldom inquire, even in their own profession, for any authors but those whom the present mode of study happens to force upon their notice. They desire not to fill their minds with unfashionable knowledge, but contentedly resign to oblivion those books which they now find censured or neglected" ("An Author in Quest of His Own Character," in *The Rambler*, 241–42). For the same theme, applied to all human authors in comparison with the divine Word, see Leonard Boyle, O.P., "St. Thomas Aquinas and the Third Millennium," in *Thomas Aquinas: Approaches to Truth*, ed. James McEvoy and Michael Dunne (Dublin: Four Courts Press, 2002), 38–52.

5. Rahner's general perspective is taken up and developed by Raymond Brown, S.S. in a 1978 address published in *The Critical Meaning of the Bible*, chap. 3: "Scholars against the Church: Fact or Fiction?" 45–63; cf. the essays in Brown, *Biblical Exegesis and Church Doctrine* (New York: Paulist Press, 1985). See also the summary of Rahner's article in Joseph Fitzmyer, S.J., *Scripture, the Soul of Theology* (New York: Paulist Press, 1994), 82–84. Fitzmyer suggests that while Rahner provides good advice, Rahner fails to take it himself: Rahner's *Foundations of Christian Faith: An Introduction to the Idea of Christianity* (New York: Crossroad, 1978) possesses in Fitzmyer's view "a begrudging attitude toward Scripture: unfortunately one has to deal with it, willy nilly" (*Scripture, the Soul of Theology*, 84 n. 49). Cf. Stephen Fowl's point against Francis Watson—a point that in my view does not apply to Watson's project but applies to "systematic theology" as undertaken under the aegis of Kant—"What Watson's whole program seems to presume is that systematic theology has not been subject to the same anti-theological disciplinary forces of the modern university as biblical studies has been" (Fowl, *Engaging Scripture: A Model for Theological Interpretation* [Oxford: Blackwell, 1998], 23).

6. Karl Rahner, S.J., "Exegesis and Dogmatic Theology," in *Dogmatic vs Biblical Theology*, ed. Herbert Vorgrimler (Baltimore: Helicon Press, 1964), 31–65, at 34–35.

7. Ibid., 34.

8. Ibid., 36.

9. Ibid., 45.

10. Ibid., 46.

11. Cf. ibid., 58–59.

12. In Rahner's defense, it will be clear from the historical survey above that, as Denis Farkasfalvy, O. Cist. remarks, "Post-Tridentine exegesis and the theology developed in the interconfessional controversies of the last few centuries were insufficient to handle the challenge which this new era of biblical culture [in the Catholic intellectual world after 1943] presented" (Farkasfalvy, "The Case for Spiritual Exegesis," *Communio* 10 [1983]: 332–50, at 334).

13. Henri de Lubac, S.J., "On an Old Distich: The Doctrine of the 'Fourfold Sense' in Scripture," in de Lubac, *Theological Fragments*, trans. Rebecca Howell Balinski (San Francisco: Ignatius Press, 1989), 109–27 [an article originally published in 1948], at 122; in addition to *Exégèse médiévale*, see also de Lubac's *Scripture in the Tradition*, trans. Luke O'Neill (1968; New York: Crossroad, 2000). For further discussion of de Lubac, see, e.g., Rudolf Voderholzer, *Die Einheit der Schrift und ihr geistiger Sinn. Der Beitrag Henri de Lubacs zur Erforschung von Geschichte und Systematik christlicher Bibelhermeneutik* (Einsiedeln: Johannes Verlag, 1998); Susan K. Wood, *Spiritual Exegesis and the Church in the Theology of Henri de Lubac* (Grand Rapids, Mich.: Eerdmans, 1998); Ignace de la Potterie, "The Spiritual Sense of Scripture," *Communio* 23 (1996): 738–56. Commenting on chapter 6 of de Lubac's *Catholicisme*, de la Potterie writes, "The spiritual interpretation thus bears directly on the events of *history* recounted by the Bible . . . but, as St. Gregory said, this is so because it moves from history to *mystery*, that is, to that which constitutes the *depths* of history. . . . Such a spiritual reading of history is obviously quite different from that practiced by historical-critical exegesis, which is interested only in the superficial and verifiable level of historical facts, and thus remains turned toward the *past*. Spiritual exegesis, on the other hand, has a perspective of 'finality': it points toward the *future*, by seeking to discover the *life* of the great moments of history, the interior *meaning [sens]* of events, which emerges progressively in the posterior tradition" (743–45). Or as de la Potterie puts it further on: "because historical realities are guided by the Spirit, they possess a *depth*, a *hidden* meaning, which is mystery. It is for this reason, Fr. de Lubac said, that we must understand them spiritually. This principle is equally valid for the *events* of history *(gesta)* as for the letter of scripture that recounts them (*littera*, that is, for the literal meaning of the Biblical text). This text, however, is inspired by the Spirit of God" (753). Following de Lubac, de la Potterie calls for both an "'*archeological* interpretation'" and a "'*teleological* interpretation'" (754). De la Potterie's article, which is an overview of de Lubac's work on this topic, responds in particular to Mauro Pesce, who points correctly to "two differing conceptions of historicity, one which seeks only a *scientific history*, and one which seeks to recover a *real history*" (743). The strong affinities between de Lubac's and de la Potterie's approach and my own should be clear. Drawing on A. Russo's *Henri de Lubac. Teologia e dogma nella storia. L'influsso di Blondel* (Rome: Studium, 1990), de la Potterie also helpfully shows the influence

of Maurice Blondel's *Histoire et dogme*, published in 1904, on de Lubac's understanding of history. See Blondel, *The Letter on Apologetics* and *History and Dogma*, trans. Alexander Dru and Illtyd Trethowan (1964; Grand Rapids, Mich.: Eerdmans, 1994).

14. De Lubac, "On an Old Distich," 121.

15. To cite Farkasfalvy again: "while the famous 'ressourcement' (return to the sources) of the French theologians in the fifties meant to re-capture, re-possess and re-evaluate the whole theological tradition of the Church, now in the postconciliar times a certain atrophy in the study of patristic and medieval theology combined with a sudden expansion of the historical-critical investigation of the biblical tradition. As a result, the tools of history and philology acquired an undue pre-potence in the study of the Bible at the expense of theological reflection, not to speak of the fading influence of our Catholic exegetical tradition and of the diminishing role of the documents of the Church's Magisterium" ("The Case for Spiritual Exegesis," 335).

16. De Lubac, "On an Old Distich," 123.

17. Ibid., 117. Farkasfalvy puts it this way: "The treatment of the text as an expression of faith—or the treatment of historical characters, reconstructed from the text, as persons endowed with faith—is still bound to history. The faith of Abraham or of Moses or of Paul, expressed in or reconstructed from relevant texts, is something the believing exegete tries to understand in function not only of his own faith but also of his view of history. Both the subjective faith experience of the exegete, which he supposes to be analogous to what he finds in the text, and the objective (and retrospective) distance characteristic of historical knowledge, are involved. Hence we are still dealing here with a certain kind of literal interpretation. An historical and literal exegesis which also pays attention to the faith experience expressed in the texts is basically still on the level of the 'historia'; however, it has passed beyond the premises of scientific objectivity characteristic of the historical-critical method" ("The Case for Spiritual Exegesis," 344). Farkasfalvy's appeal to an "analogy" between the faith of the exegete and that of scriptural figures indicates his participatory understanding of history as more than a strictly linear set of moments; for Farkasfalvy history is "salvation history" (344–46), in which God calls human beings to "insertion into the community of salvation" (347). At issue is the intelligibility of historical-critical reconstruction's disjuncture between "history alone" and "its meaning and purpose" (346).

18. *Pace* Joseph Fitzmyer, S.J.'s warning that covert fundamentalism includes "those who call for a return to a 'precritical' mode of interpretation, or for a return to a theological interpretation of the Bible. . . . So some Catholic readers of the Bible seek to justify their simplistic reading of the Bible" (Fitzmyer, *Scripture, the Soul of Theology*, 59). Fitzmyer cites Louis Bouyer's article "Liturgie et exégèse spirituelle," *Maison-Dieu* 7 (1946): 27–50, and he

also includes Henri de Lubac, Yves Congar, and Hans Urs von Balthasar in his criticism. See also Fitzmyer's negative response in *Scripture, the Soul of Theology* (90) to Avery Dulles, S.J.'s very mild approbation of the approaches of de Lubac et al. in Dulles's "The Uses of Scripture in Theology," chapter 5 of *The Craft of Theology: From Symbol to System*, new expanded ed. (New York: Crossroad, 1995), 69–85, at 73–74, 85. Similarly Raymond Brown, S.S. already in 1955 warns against Jean Daniélou, S.J.'s approach: see Brown, *The Sensus Plenior of Sacred Scripture* (Baltimore: St. Mary's University, 1955), 81 f., as well as 137–39 regarding Daniélou's and de Lubac's rejection of "sensus plenior" theories. For a more measured perspective on the *Nouvelle théologie*'s efforts to recover patristic-medieval exegesis, see Walter Burghardt, S.J.'s contemporaneous overview, at once appreciative and cautious, of the work on the spiritual senses by de Lubac, Daniélou, and Bouyer in the 1940s: Burghardt, "On Early Christian Exegesis," *Theological Studies* 11 (1950): 78–116; as well as more recently Brian Daley, S.J., "The *Nouvelle Théologie* and the Patristic Revival: Sources, Symbols and the Science of Theology," *International Journal of Systematic Theology* 7 (2005): 362–82. Daley somewhat overlooks the importance of metaphysics for the Fathers as well as the medievals, and as a result separates patristic and medieval theology somewhat too strongly (see 369 f.).

19. De Lubac, "On an Old Distich," 124–25.

20. Maurice Blondel, *The Letter on Apologetics* and *History and Dogma*, 237.

21. De Lubac, "On an Old Distich," 126.

22. For both the contributions and limitations of historical-critical research, see, e.g., N. T. Wright's three groundbreaking volumes *The New Testament and the People of God* (Minneapolis: Fortress Press, 1992); *Jesus and the Victory of God* (Minneapolis: Fortress Press, 1996); and *The Resurrection of the Son of God* (Minneapolis: Fortress Press, 2003). See also Wright's "Jesus and the Identity of God," *Ex Auditu* 14 (1998): 42–56. Helpful critical reviews of Wright's work include Robert H. Gundry's review of *Jesus and the Victory of God*, *Christianity Today* (April 27, 1998): 76–79; Gary A. Anderson's review of *The Resurrection of the Son of God*, *First Things* 137 (November 2003): 51–54; and Douglas Harink's chapter "Israel: 'Who Will Bring Any Charge against God's Elect?'" in his *Paul among the Postliberals: Pauline Theology beyond Christendom and Modernity* (Grand Rapids, Mich.: Brazos Press, 2003), 151–207. Harink points out that Wright has relied too strictly on a linear understanding of history and has thereby fallen into the mistake of reading Paul as a linear supersessionist. As Harink asks, "does Paul employ a linear 'covenantal-historical' narrative in which there is a divinely driven linear movement from Israel, to Christ, to the church, in which historical Israel's role after Christ simply ceases to be of any theological significance, or does Paul display another—I will suggest apocalyptic—way of thinking about

Israel in God's purpose?" (161). For his part, Anderson raises a key concern about the relationship of historical reconstruction to theological penetration. As Wright states in a volume dedicated to scholarly responses to his *Jesus and the Victory of God,* "I want to insist that, a priori, we do not know whether the evangelists got it right or got it wrong and, indeed, that those are not the only alternatives" (Wright, "In Grateful Dialogue: A Response," in *Jesus and the Restoration of Israel: A Critical Assessment of N. T. Wright's* Jesus and the Victory of God, ed. Carey C. Newman [Downers Grove, Ill.: InterVarsity Press, 1999], 246). Wright hopes that his, and others', historical reconstructions will enable "people of our own generation" to "glimpse afresh the 'history-E' [the events in the life of Jesus] that previous 'history-W' [the written narratives of the gospels] was trying to unveil" (247). The problem is twofold: why should bracketing our a priori faith-knowledge enhance our exegetical insight, and what would it mean to classify a contemporary historical reconstruction alongside the inspired historical reconstructions recorded in the gospels? The illumination of our minds by faith lies behind both these issues. See also Luke Timothy Johnson's review of *The New Testament and the People of God*—more critical than I would be—in *Journal of Biblical Literature* 113 (1994): 536–38; and Christopher Seitz's superb "Of Mortal Appearance: The Earthly Jesus and Isaiah as a Type of Christian Scripture," *Ex Auditu* 14 (1998): 31–41, which critically addresses Wright's project as taken up in Wright's essay "The Servant and Jesus: The Relevance of the Colloquy for the Current Quest for Jesus," in *Jesus and the Suffering Servant,* ed. William H. Bellinger and William R. Farmer (Harrisburg, Pa.: Trinity Press International, 1998), 283–99. For Wright's effort to address the issue of supersessionism in the context of demonstrating how theological concerns arise from exegesis, see Wright, "The Letter to the Galatians: Exegesis and Theology," in *Between Two Horizons: Spanning New Testament Studies and Systematic Theology,* ed. Joel B. Green and Max Turner (Grand Rapids, Mich.: Eerdmans, 2000), 205–36. For Wright, the problem with theology is that it continually detaches itself from the particulars of the scriptural narrative and thereby becomes an idealist system from which exegesis requires protection. Here a deeper understanding of *sacra doctrina* and its participatory mediations would be useful.

23. Denis Farkasfalvy states, "The theological content is, however, not outside, nor even beyond the text. It is in the text, except that it remains finally inaccessible for anyone who approaches it without the presuppositions of faith. These presuppositions are themselves in no way alien to the text, yet they are of an order different from scientific thought or literary analysis" (Farkasfalvy, "The Case for Spiritual Exegesis," *Communio* 10 [1983]: 349). The word "text" here could equally be "history." See also R. W. L. Moberly's critique of the positions of James Barr and C. K. Barrett. As Moberly summarizes his find-

ings: "Barr sees the Church and theology as possible and legitimate, yet optional, contexts for the study of the Bible; the Bible can be studied perfectly well on its own. Barrett sees theology and the life of the Church as intrinsic to the study of New Testament theology, yet offers no satisfactory account as to why this should be so. . . . Neither Barr nor Barrett makes explicit that his subject of study—the Bible as Old and New Testaments together or solely the New Testament—is a confessing construct; and so they do not reflect upon what that might entail for their disciplines" (Moberly, *The Bible, Theology, and Faith: A Study of Abraham and Jesus* [Cambridge: Cambridge University Press, 2000], 23; cf. 38).

24. J. Augustine Di Noia, O.P., review of *A Marginal Jew: Rethinking the Historical Jesus*, by John P. Meier, *Pro Ecclesia* 2 (1993): 122–25, at 125; see also the critique of Meier's work offered by Jacob Neusner in his *Rabbinic Literature and the New Testament: What We Cannot Show, We Do Not Know* (Valley Forge, Pa.: Trinity Press International, 1994), chap. 9. Di Noia's excellent critique of Meier's approach makes the case that "the doctrinal tradition, far from obscuring the historical truth about Jesus Christ, in fact provides a privileged access to this truth" (125). Di Noia envisions the integration of historical research with the "so-called 'pre-critical' doctrinal and theological traditions," in which "the doctrinally ruled reading of the Gospels would be understood to have evolved under the guidance of the Holy Spirit, precisely to insure that the full significance of the living Christ would be known, proclaimed and confessed" (125). For similar observations by Di Noia, cf. his "The Church in the Gospel: Catholics and Evangelicals in Conversation," *Pro Ecclesia* 13 (2004): 58–69, at 69.

25. Bockmuehl, "Reason, Wisdom and the Implied Disciple of Scripture," in *Reading Texts, Seeking Wisdom: Scripture and Theology*, ed. David F. Ford and Graham Stanton (Grand Rapids, Mich.: Eerdmans, 2003), 53–68, at 68. The Virgin Mary's "pondering" exhibits the meaning, at the highest level of spiritual and intellectual maturity, of Jesus' striking admonition, "Truly, I say to you, whoever does not receive the kingdom of God like a child shall not enter it" (Lk 18:17). On this attitude and the risk entailed by critical distancing, see John Webster, *Holy Scripture: A Dogmatic Sketch* (Cambridge: Cambridge University Press, 2003), 104–5. Webster notes that "a few years after writing *Act and Being* Bonhoeffer worked out its hermeneutical entailments by urging a childlike naiveté in reading Scripture. Not the least of what may be gleaned from Bonhoeffer is the lesson that reason—including exegetical reason—finds its end, not in subjecting the world to its expert gaze, but in unskilled deference to the divine teacher" (105); cf. Webster, "Reading the Bible: The Example of Barth and Bonhoeffer," in Webster, *Word and Church: Essays in Christian Dogmatics* (Edinburgh: T. &. T. Clark, 2001), 87–110. One might also see Gordon D. Fee's "To What End Exegesis? Reflections on Exegesis and

Spirituality in Philippians 4:10–20," in his *To What End Exegesis? Essays Textual, Exegetical, and Theological* (Grand Rapids, Mich.: Eerdmans, 2001), 276–89. Fee proposes that "the ultimate aim of exegesis is the Spiritual one—to produce in our lives and the lives of others true Spirituality, in which God's people live in faithful fellowship both with one another and with the living God, and thus in keeping with God's purposes in the world" (276). He adds that "the exegesis of the biblical texts belongs primarily in the context of the believing community who are the true heirs of these texts" (ibid.).

WORKS CITED

Abraham, William J. *Canon and Criterion in Christian Theology*. Paperback edition with a new preface. Oxford: Clarendon Press, 2002.

Adam, A. K. M. "Docetism, Käsemann, and Christology: Why Historical Criticism Can't Protect Christological Orthodoxy." *Scottish Journal of Theology* 49 (1996): 391–410.

———. "'He Placed Himself in the Order of Signs': Exegesis Signifying Theology." Forthcoming.

———. *Making Sense of New Testament Theology: "Modern" Problems and Prospects*. Macon, Ga.: Mercer University Press, 1995.

Aguayo, F. Castro. *Relación entre Sagrada Escritura y tradición según la constitución Dei Verbum*. Pamplona: EUNSA, 1987.

Aichele, George, and Gary A. Phillips. "Introduction: Exegesis, Eisegesis, Intergesis." In *Intertextuality and the Bible*, edited by George Aichele and Gary A. Phillips, 7–18. Atlanta: Scholars Press, 1995.

Aichele, George, and Gary A. Phillips, eds. *Intertextuality and the Bible*. Atlanta: Scholars Press, 1995.

Alter, Robert. *The Art of Biblical Narrative*. New York: Basic Books, 1981.

Alter, Robert, and Frank Kermode, eds. *The Literary Guide to the Bible*. Cambridge: Harvard University Press, 1987.

Anderson, Gary A. *The Genesis of Perfection*. Louisville: Westminster/John Knox, 2001.

———. "King David and the Psalms of Imprecation." *Pro Ecclesia* 15 (2006): 267–80.

———. Review of *The Resurrection of the Son of God*, by N. T. Wright. *First Things* 137 (November 2003): 51–54.

Aquinas, Thomas. *Commentary on the Gospel of St. John*. Translated by James A. Weisheipl, O.P., and Fabian R. Larcher, O.P., Part I. Albany: Magi Books, 1980.

————. *Commentary on the Gospel of St. John.* Translated by Fabian Larcher, O.P., and James Weisheipl, O.P. Part II. Petersham, Mass.: St. Bede's Publications, 1999.

————. *On the Power of God: Quaestiones disputatae de potentia dei.* 1932. Reprint, Eugene, Ore.: Wipf & Stock, 2004.

————. *Summa contra gentiles.* Translated by Anton C. Pegis, F. R. S. C. Notre Dame: University of Notre Dame Press, 1975.

————. *Summa theologiae.* English translation, *Summa Theologica.* Translated by the Fathers of the English Dominican Province. Westminster, Md.: Christian Classics, 1981.

————. *Thomas Aquinas: Selected Writings.* Edited and translated by Ralph McInerny. New York: Penguin, 1998.

Arnold, Duane W. H., and Pamela Bright, eds. *De Doctrina Christiana: A Classic of Western Culture.* Notre Dame: University of Notre Dame Press, 1995.

Artus, Olivier. "*Dei Verbum.* L'exégèse catholique entre critique historique et renouveau des sciences bibliques." *Gregorianum* 86 (2005): 76–91.

Athanasius, St. *On the Incarnation.* Crestwood, N.Y.: St. Vladimir's Seminary Press, 1975.

Augustine of Hippo, St. *On Christian Doctrine.* Translated by D. W. Robertson Jr. New York: Macmillan, 1958.

————. *The Trinity.* Translated by Edmund Hill, O.P. Brooklyn: New City Press, 1991.

Ayres, Lewis. *Nicaea and Its Legacy: An Approach to Fourth-Century Trinitarian Theology.* Oxford: Oxford University Press, 2004.

————. "On the Practice and Teaching of Christian Doctrine." *Gregorianum* 80 (1999): 33–94.

Ayres, Lewis, and Stephen E. Fowl. "(Mis)reading the Face of God: *The Interpretation of the Bible in the Church.*" *Theological Studies* 60 (1999): 513–28.

Babcock, William S. "*Caritas* and Signification in *De doctrina christiana* 1–3." In *De Doctrina Christiana: A Classic of Western Culture,* edited by Duane W. H. Arnold and Pamela Bright, 145–63. Notre Dame: University of Notre Dame Press, 1995.

Bakker, Nico T. *History as a Theological Issue.* Leiden: Deo, 2000.

Barr, James. *The Concept of Biblical Theology: An Old Testament Perspective.* Minneapolis: Fortress Press, 1999.

————. *Holy Scripture: Canon, Authority, Criticism.* Philadelphia: Westminster Press, 1983.

Bartholomew, Craig, C. Greene, and K. Müller, eds. *After Pentecost: Language and Biblical Interpretation.* Carlisle: Paternoster, 2001.

Bartholomew, Craig, C. Stephen Evans, Mary Healy, and Murray Rae, eds. *"Behind" the Text: History and Biblical Interpretation.* Grand Rapids, Mich.: Zondervan, 2003.

Bastit, Michel. "Le thomisme est-il un aristotélisme?" *Revue Thomiste* 102 (2001): 101–16.

Bataillon, Louis-Jacques, O.P., "Chronique de doctrines médiévales. Études récentes sur les sermons." *Revue des sciences philosophiques et théologiques* 88 (2004): 789–805.

———. "Early Scholastic and Mendicant Preaching as Exegesis of Scripture." In *Ad litteram: Authoritative Texts and Their Medieval Readers,* edited by Mark D. Jordan and Kent Emery Jr. Notre Dame: University of Notre Dame Press, 1992.

Bauckham, Richard. "Reading Scripture as a Coherent Story." In *The Art of Reading Scripture,* edited by Ellen F. Davis and Richard B. Hays, 38–53. Grand Rapids, Mich.: Eerdmans, 2003.

Bea, Augustinus. *The Word of God and Mankind.* London: 1968.

Bedouelle, Guy, O.P., *Lefèvre d'Étaples et l'Intelligence des Écritures.* Geneva: Librairie Droz, 1976.

Bejczy, Istvan. *Erasmus and the Middle Ages: The Historical Consciousness of a Christian Humanist.* Leiden: Brill, 2001.

Bellinger, William H., and William R. Farmer, eds. *Jesus and the Suffering Servant.* Harrisburg, Pa.: Trinity Press International, 1998.

Betz, John R. "Hamann's London Writings: The Hermeneutics of Trinitarian Condescension." *Pro Ecclesia* 14 (2005): 191–234.

Blankenhorn, Bernhard, O.P. "Balthasar's Method of Divine Naming." *Nova et Vetera* 1 (2003): 245–68.

Blondel, Maurice. *Histoire et dogme.* 1904.

———. *The Letter on Apologetics* and *History and Dogma.* Translated by Alexander Dru and Illtyd Trethowan. 1964. Grand Rapids, Mich.: Eerdmans, 1994.

Blowers, Paul M. "The *Regula Fidei* and the Narrative Character of Early Christian Faith." *Pro Ecclesia* 6 (1997): 199–228.

Blowers, Paul M., Jon D. Levenson, and Robert Wilken, "Interpreting the Bible: Three Views." *First Things* 45 (August/September 1994): 40–46.

Bockmuehl, Markus. "Humpty Dumpty and New Testament Theology." *Theology* 101 (1998): 330–38.

———. "Reason, Wisdom and the Implied Disciple of Scripture." In *Reading Texts, Seeking Wisdom: Scripture and Theology,* edited by David F. Ford and Graham Stanton, 53–68. Grand Rapids, Mich.: Eerdmans, 2003.

———. "'To Be or Not to Be': The Possible Futures of New Testament Scholarship." *Scottish Journal of Theology* 51 (1998): 271–306.

Bonino, Serge-Thomas, O.P., "The Role of the Apostles in the Communication of Revelation according to the *Lectura super Ioannem* of St. Thomas Aquinas." Translated by Teresa Bede and Matthew Levering. In *Reading John with St. Thomas: Theological Exegesis and Speculative Theology,* edited by Michael Dauphinais and Matthew Levering, 318–46. Washington, D.C.: Catholic University of America Press, 2005.

Boss, Marc, Gilles Emery, O.P., and Pierre Gisel, eds., *Postlibéralisme? La théologie de George Lindbeck et sa réception.* Geneva: Labor et Fides, 2004.

Boulnois, Olivier. "Ce dont Dieu n'a pas idée. Problèmes de l'idéalisme médiéval (XIIIe–XIVe siècles)." In *Le contemplateur et les idées: Modèles de la science divine du néoplatonisme au XVIIIe siècle*, edited by Olivier Boulnois, Jacob Schmutz, and Jean-Luc Solère, 45–78. Paris: Vrin, 2002.

———. *Duns Scot. La rigueur de la charité.* Paris: Cerf, 1998.

———. *Être et représentation. Une généalogie de la métaphysique moderne à l'époque de Duns Scot (XIIIe–XIVe siècle).* Paris: Presses Universitaires de France, 1999.

———. "Reading Duns Scotus: From History to Philosophy." *Modern Theology* 21 (2005): 603–7.

Boulnois, Olivier, Jacob Schmutz, and Jean-Luc Solère, eds. *Le contemplateur et les idées: Modèles de la science divine du néoplatonisme au XVIIIe siècle.* Paris: Vrin, 2002.

Bouyer, Louis. "Erasmus in Relation to the Medieval Biblical Tradition." In *The Cambridge History of the Bible*, vol. 2, edited by G.W.H. Lampe, 492–505. Cambridge: Cambridge University Press, 1969.

———. "Liturgie et exégèse spirituelle." *Maison-Dieu* 7 (1946): 27–50.

Bowley, James, ed. *Living Traditions of the Bible: Scripture in Jewish, Christian, and Muslim Practice.* St. Louis: Chalice Press, 1999.

Boyle, John F. "Authorial Intention and the *Divisio textus.*" In *Reading John with St. Thomas Aquinas: Theological Exegesis and Speculative Theology*, edited by Michael Dauphinais and Matthew Levering, 3–8. Washington, D.C.: Catholic University of America Press, 2005.

———. "The Theological Character of the Scholastic 'Division of the Text' with Particular Reference to the Commentaries of Saint Thomas Aquinas." In *With Reverence for the Word: Medieval Scriptural Exegesis in Judaism, Christianity, and Islam*, edited by Jane Dammen McAuliffe, Barry D. Walfish, and Joseph W. Goering, 276–83. Oxford: Oxford University Press, 2003.

Boyle, Leonard, O.P., "St. Thomas Aquinas and the Third Millennium." In *Thomas Aquinas: Approaches to Truth*, edited by James McEvoy and Michael Dunne, 38–52. Dublin: Four Courts Press, 2002.

Boyle, Nicholas. *Sacred and Secular Scriptures: A Catholic Approach to Literature.* Notre Dame: University of Notre Dame Press, 2005.

Braaten, Carl, and Robert Jenson, eds. *Reclaiming the Bible for the Church.* Grand Rapids, Mich.: Eerdmans, 1995.

Braaten, Carl E., and Christopher R. Seitz, eds. *I Am the Lord Your God: Christian Reflections on the Ten Commandments.* Grand Rapids, Mich.: Eerdmans, 2005.

Brett, Mark. "Motives and Intentions in Genesis 1." *Journal of Theological Studies* 42 (1991): 1–16.

Brettler, Marc Zvi. *The Creation of History in Ancient Israel*. London: Routledge, 1995.

———. *How to Read the Bible*. Philadelphia: Jewish Publication Society, 2005.

Brown, Raymond E., S.S. *Biblical Exegesis and Church Doctrine*. New York: Paulist Press, 1985.

———. "The Contribution of Historical Biblical Criticism to Ecumenical Church Discussion." In *Biblical Interpretation in Crisis: The Ratzinger Conference on Bible and Church*, edited by Richard John Neuhaus, 24–49. Grand Rapids, Mich.: Eerdmans, 1989.

———. *The Critical Meaning of the Bible: How a Modern Reading of the Bible Challenges Christians, the Church, and the Churches*. New York: Paulist Press, 1981.

———. *The Gospel according to John (I–XII)*. Vol. 29 of *The Anchor Bible*. New York: Doubleday, 1966.

———. *The* Sensus Plenior *of Sacred Scripture*. Baltimore: St. Mary's University, 1955.

Brueggemann, Walter. "Imagination as a Mode of Fidelity." In *Understanding the Word: Essays in Honor of Bernhard W. Anderson*, edited by James T. Butler, Edgar W. Conrad, and Ben C. Ollenburger, 13–36. Sheffield: JSOT Press, 1985.

———. *Interpretation and Obedience*. Philadelphia: Fortress, 1991.

Buckley, James J., and David S. Yeago, eds. *Knowing the Triune God: The Work of the Spirit in the Practices of the Church*. Grand Rapids, Mich.: Eerdmans, 2001.

Burghardt, Walter, S.J. "On Early Christian Exegesis." *Theological Studies* 11 (1950): 78–116.

Burnett, Richard E. "John Calvin and the *Sensus Literalis*." *Scottish Journal of Theology* 57 (2004): 1–13.

———. *Karl Barth's Theological Exegesis: The Hermeneutical Principles of the* Römerbrief *Period*. Grand Rapids, Mich.: Eerdmans, 2004.

Burns, J. Patout. "Delighting the Spirit: Augustine's Practice of Figurative Interpretation." In *De Doctrina Christiana: A Classic of Western Culture*, edited by Duane W. H. Arnold and Pamela Bright, 182–94. Notre Dame: University of Notre Dame Press, 1995.

Burrell, David B., C.S.C. *Faith and Freedom: An Interfaith Perspective*. Oxford: Blackwell, 2004.

Butler, James T., Edgar W. Conrad, and Ben C. Ollenburger, eds. *Understanding the Word: Essays in Honor of Bernhard W. Anderson*. Sheffield: JSOT Press, 1985.

Butterfield, Herbert. *The Whig Interpretation of History*. New York: W. W. Norton, 1965.

Cahill, Michael. "The History of Exegesis and Our Theological Future." *Theological Studies* 61 (2000): 332–47.

Caldecott, Stratford, ed. *Eternity in Time: Christopher Dawson and the Catholic Idea of History.* New York: T. & T. Clark, 1997.

Carr, Edward Hallett. *What Is History?* New York: Vintage Books, 1961.

Cassirer, Ernst. *The Individual and the Cosmos in Renaissance Philosophy.* Translated by Mario Domandi. 1927. New York: Harper & Row, 1964.

Catechism of the Catholic Church. Translated by United States Catholic Conference. Vatican City: Libreria Editrice Vaticana, 1994.

Cepero, Helen. "Response to Radner." *Ex Auditu* 18 (2002): 171–73.

Cessario, Romanus, O.P. *Introduction to Moral Theology.* Washington, D.C.: Catholic University of America Press, 2001.

————. *A Short History of Thomism.* Washington, D.C.: Catholic University of America Press, 2005.

Chapman, Stephen B. "The Old Testament Canon and Its Authority for the Christian Church." *Ex Auditu* 19 (2003): 125–48.

Charlesworth, James H., with Frank X. Blisard and Jerry L. Gorham, eds. *Overcoming Fear between Jews and Christians.* New York: Crossroad, 1992.

Childs, Brevard S. *Biblical Theology of the Old and New Testaments: Theological Reflection on the Christian Bible.* Minneapolis: Fortress Press, 1993.

————. "The Canon in Recent Biblical Studies: Reflections on an Era." *Pro Ecclesia* 14 (2005): 26–45.

————. "Critique of Recent Intertextual Canonical Interpretations." *Zeitschrift für die alttestamentliche Wissenschaft* 115 (2003): 173–84.

————. "Interpretation in Faith." *Interpretation* 18 (1964): 259–71.

————. *The New Testament as Canon: An Introduction.* London: SCM Press, 1984.

————. "On Reclaiming the Bible for Christian Theology." In *Reclaiming the Bible for the Church,* edited by Carl E. Braaten and Robert Jenson, 1–17. Grand Rapids, Mich.: Eerdmans, 1995.

————. "The Sensus Literalis of Scripture: An Ancient and Modern Problem." In *Beiträge zur Alttestamentlichen Theologie,* edited by Herbert Donner, Robert Hanhart, and Rudolf Smend, 80–93. Göttingen: Vandenhoeck & Ruprecht, 1977.

————. "Speech-Act Theory and Biblical Interpretation." *Scottish Journal of Theology* 58 (2005): 375–92.

————. *The Struggle to Understand Isaiah as Christian Scripture.* Grand Rapids, Mich.: Eerdmans, 2004.

————. "Toward Recovering Theological Exegesis." *Pro Ecclesia* 6 (1997): 16–26.

Clarke, W. Norris, S.J., *The One and the Many: A Contemporary Thomistic Metaphysics.* Notre Dame: University of Notre Dame Press, 2001.

Clines, David J. A., Stephen E. Fowl, and Stanley E. Porter, eds. *The Bible in Three Dimensions.* Sheffield: Sheffield Academic Press, 1990.

Coakley, Sarah. *Powers and Submissions*. Oxford: Blackwell, 2002.

Cohen, Jeremy. *Living Letters of the Law: Ideas of the Jew in Medieval Christianity*. Berkeley: University of California Press, 1999.

Cohn-Sherbok, Dan, ed. *Torah and Revelation*. New York: Edwin Mellen Press, 1992.

Collingwood, R. G. *The Idea of History*. Oxford: Oxford University Press, 1961.

Collins, John J. *The Bible after Babel: Historical Criticism in a Postmodern Age*. Grand Rapids, Mich.: Eerdmans, 2005.

———. *Encounters with Biblical Theology*. Minneapolis: Fortress Press, 2005.

———. "Is a Critical Biblical Theology Possible?" In *Encounters with Biblical Theology* by John J. Collins, 11–23. Minneapolis: Fortress Press, 2005.

Colson, Charles, and Richard John Neuhaus, eds. *Your Word Is Truth: A Project of Evangelicals and Catholics Together*. Grand Rapids, Mich.: Eerdmans, 2002.

Congar, Yves, O.P., *The Meaning of Tradition*. Translated by A. N. Woodrow. 1964. Reprint, with a new foreword by Avery Dulles, S.J., San Francisco: Ignatius Press, 2004.

———. *The Mystery of the Temple or the Manner of God's Presence to His Creatures from Genesis to the Apocalypse*. Translated by Reginald Trevett. London: Burns & Oates, 1962.

Courtenay, William J. "The Bible in the Fourteenth Century: Some Observations." *Church History* 54 (1985): 176–87.

Crehan, F. J., S.J., "The Bible in the Roman Catholic Church from Trent to the Present Day." In *The Cambridge History of the Bible*, vol. 3, *The West from the Reformation to the Present Day*, edited by S. L. Greenslade, 199–237. Cambridge: Cambridge University Press, 1963.

Culpepper, R. Alan. "The Gospel of John as a Threat to Jewish-Christian Relations." In *Overcoming Fear between Jews and Christians*, edited by James H. Charlesworth with Frank X. Blisard and Jerry L. Gorham, 21–43. New York: Crossroad, 1992.

Curtin, T. R. *Historical Criticism and the Theological Interpretation of Scripture: The Catholic Discussion of a Biblical Hermeneutic: 1958–1983*. Rome: Gregorian University, 1987.

Daley, Brian E., S.J., "Is Patristic Exegesis Still Usable? Reflections on Early Christian Interpretation of the Psalms." *Communio* 29 (2002): 185–216.

———. "The *Nouvelle Théologie* and the Patristic Revival: Sources, Symbols and the Science of Theology." *International Journal of Systematic Theology* 7 (2005): 362–82.

Dauphinais, Michael, and Matthew Levering. *Holy People, Holy Land: A Theological Introduction to the Bible*. Grand Rapids, Mich.: Brazos Press, 2005.

Dauphinais, Michael, and Matthew Levering, eds. *Reading John with St. Thomas Aquinas: Theological Exegesis and Speculative Theology*. Washington, D.C.: Catholic University of America Press, 2005.

————. *Wisdom and Holiness, Science and Scholarship: Essays in Honor of Matthew L. Lamb.* Naples, Fla.: Sapientia Press, 2007.

Dauphinais, Michael, Barry David, and Matthew Levering, eds. *Aquinas the Augustinian.* Washington, D.C.: Catholic University of America Press.

Davies, Brian, O.P., ed. *Language, Meaning and God.* London: Geoffrey Chapman, 1987.

Davis, Ellen F. "Teaching the Bible Confessionally in the Church." In *The Art of Reading Scripture*, edited by Ellen F. Davis and Richard B. Hays, 11–12. Grand Rapids, Mich.: Eerdmans, 2003.

Davis, Ellen F., and Richard B. Hays, eds. *The Art of Reading Scripture.* Grand Rapids, Mich.: Eerdmans, 2003.

Davis, Stephen T. "Philosophical Presuppositions and Biblical Exegesis." In *Truth, Religious Dialogue and Dynamic Orthodoxy: Essays on the Work of Brian Hebblethwaite*, edited by Julius J. Lipner, 71–84. London: SCM Press, 2005.

d'Avray, David. *Death and the Prince: Memorial Preaching before 1350.* Oxford: Oxford University Press, 1994.

————. *Medieval Marriage Sermons: Mass Communication in a Culture without Print.* Oxford: Oxford University Press, 2001.

Dawson, David. *Christian Figural Reading and the Fashioning of Identity.* Los Angeles: University of California, 2002.

————. "Figural Reading and the Fashioning of Christian Identity in Boyarin, Auerbach and Frei." *Modern Theology* 14 (1998): 181–96.

D'Costa, Gavin. "Revelation, Scripture and Tradition: Some Comments on John Webster's Conception of 'Holy Scripture.'" *International Journal of Systematic Theology* 6 (2004): 337–50.

de Certeau, Michel. *The Mystic Fable.* Vol. 1, *The Sixteenth and Seventeenth Centuries.* Translated by Michael B. Smith. Chicago: University of Chicago Press, 1992. First published in French (1982).

de la Potterie, Ignace. "Interpretation of Holy Scripture in the Spirit in Which It Was Written." In *Vatican II: Assessment and Perspectives*, vol. 1, ed. René Latourelle, 220–66. New York: Paulist Press, 1988.

————. "Reading Holy Scripture 'in the Spirit': Is the Patristic Way of Reading the Bible Still Possible Today?" *Communio* 13 (1986): 308–25.

————. "The Spiritual Sense of Scripture." *Communio* 23 (1996): 738–56.

de Lubac, Henri, S.J., *Exégèse médiévale: Les quatre sens de l'Écriture.* Seconde partie, II. Paris: Aubier, 1962.

————. *La révélation divine. Commentaire du préambule et du chapitre I de la constitution 'Dei verbum' du Concile Vatican II*, 3d ed. Paris: Éditions du Cerf, 1983.

————. *Scripture in the Tradition.* Translated by Luke O'Neill. 1968. New York: Crossroad, 2000.

————. *The Sources of Revelation.* Translated by Luke O'Neill. New York: Herder, 1968.

————. *Theological Fragments.* Translated by Rebecca Howell Balinski. San Francisco: Ignatius Press, 1989.

de Margerie, Bertrand, S.J. *An Introduction to the History of Exegesis.* Vol. 3, *Saint Augustine.* Translated by Pierre de Fontnouvelle. Petersham, Mass.: Saint Bede's Publications, 1991.

de Toledo, Francisco, S.J., *In Sacrosanctum Ioannis Evangelium Commentarii.* Rome: Iacobum Tornerium, 1588.

de Vio, Tommaso, Cardinal Cajetan, *Opera Omnia, In S. Scripturam Commentarii.*

Demson, David. *Hans Frei and Karl Barth: Different Ways of Reading Scripture.* Grand Rapids, Mich.: Eerdmans, 1997.

Di Noia, J. Augustine, O.P. "The Church in the Gospel: Catholics and Evangelicals in Conversation." *Pro Ecclesia* 13 (2004): 58–69.

————. Review of *A Marginal Jew: Rethinking the Historical Jesus,* by John P. Meier. *Pro Ecclesia* 2 (1993): 122–25.

Dickens, W. T. *Hans Urs von Balthasar's Theological Aesthetics: A Model for Post-Critical Biblical Interpretation.* Notre Dame: University of Notre Dame Press, 2003.

Dionysius the Carthusian. *Opera Omnia.* Edited by the Carthusian Order with the support of Pope Leo XIII, *In Lucam (X–XXI), et Joannem.* Monstolii: Typis Cartusiae S. M. de Pratis, 1901, 339–44.

————. *Spiritual Writings.* Translated by Íde M. Ní Riain. Dublin: Four Courts Press, 2004.

Dodaro, Robert. *Christ and the Just Society in the Thought of Augustine.* Cambridge: Cambridge University Press, 2004.

Dohmen, C., and T. Söding, eds. *Eine Bibel-Zwei Testamente.* Paderborn: Schöningh, 1995.

Domandi, Mario, trans. Introduction to *The Individual and the Cosmos in Renaissance Philosophy,* by Ernst Cassirer. 1927. New York: Harper & Row, 1964.

Donfried, Karl P. "Alien Hermeneutics and the Misappropriation of Scripture." In *Reclaiming the Bible for the Church,* edited by Carl E. Braaten and Robert Jenson, 19–45. Grand Rapids, Mich.: Eerdmans, 1995.

Donner, Herbert, Robert Hanhart, and Rudolf Smend, eds. *Beiträge zur Alttestamentlichen Theologie.* Göttingen: Vandenhoeck & Ruprecht, 1977.

Dorman, Ted M. "The Future of Biblical Theology." In *Biblical Theology: Retrospect and Prospect,* edited by Scott J. Hafemann, 250–63. Downers Grove, Ill.: InterVarsity Press, 2002.

Dubois, M. "Mystical and Realistic Elements in the Exegesis and Hermeneutics of Thomas Aquinas." In *Creative Biblical Exegesis: Christian and Jewish Hermeneutics through the Centuries,* edited by Benjamin Uffenheimer and Henning Graf Reventlow, 39–54. Sheffield: Sheffield Academic Press, 1988.

Duffy, Kevin. "Exegetes and Theologians." *Irish Theological Quarterly* 63 (1998): 219–31.

Dulles, Avery, S.J. *The Craft of Theology: From Symbol to System*. New expanded edition. New York: Crossroad, 1995.

———. "The Interpretation of the Bible in the Church: A Theological Appraisal." In *Kirche sein: nachkonziliare Theologie im Dienst der Kirchenreform*, edited by W. Geerlings and M. Seckler, 29–37. Freiburg: Herder, 1994.

———. "Revelation, Scripture and Tradition." In *Your Word Is Truth: A Project of Evangelicals and Catholics Together*, edited by Charles Colson and Richard John Neuhaus, 35–58. Grand Rapids, Mich.: Eerdmans, 2002.

Dumais, Marcel. "L'actualisation de l'Écriture: Fondements et procédures." *Science et Esprit* 51 (1999): 27–47.

———. "Sens de l'Écriture. Réexamen à la lumière de l'herméneutique philosophique et des approches littéraires récentes." *New Testament Studies* 45 (1999): 310–31.

Dunn, James D. G. "Criteria for a Wise Reading of a Biblical Text." In *Reading Texts, Seeking Wisdom: Scripture and Theology*, edited by David F. Ford and Graham Stanton, 38–52. Grand Rapids, Mich.: Eerdmans, 2003.

———. *A New Perspective on Jesus: What the Quest for the Historical Jesus Missed*. Grand Rapids, Mich.: Baker Academic, 2005.

Dupré, Louis. *The Enlightenment and the Intellectual Foundations of Modern Culture*. New Haven: Yale University Press, 2004.

———. *Passage to Modernity: An Essay in the Hermeneutics of Nature and Culture*. New Haven: Yale University Press, 1993.

Ebeling, Gerhard. *Word and Faith*. Translated by James W. Leitch. 1960. London: SCM Press, 1963.

Eckhart, Meister. *Die Deutschen und Lateinischen Werke*. Edited by Josef Quint. Dritter Band: *Expositio Sancti Evangelii secundum Iohannem*, edited by Karl Christ, Bruno Deder, Joseph Rodj, Heribert Fischer, and Albert Zimmermann. Stuttgart: W. Kohlhammer Verlag, 1953.

Edelby, Melkite Archbishop Neophytos. "A Neglected Conciliar Intervention." In *Retrieving Fundamental Theology: The Three Styles of Contemporary Theology*, by Gerald O'Collins, S.J., 174–77. New York: Paulist Press, 1993.

Elders, Leo J., S.V.D., "Aquinas on Holy Scripture as the Medium of Divine Revelation." In *La doctrine de la révélation divine de saint Thomas d'Aquin*, edited by Leo J. Elders, 132–52. Vatican City: Libreria Editrice Vaticana, 1990.

———. *La doctrine de la révélation divine de saint Thomas d'Aquin*. Vatican City: Libreria Editrice Vaticana, 1990.

Eliade, Mircea. *The Myth of the Eternal Return*. New York: Pantheon Books, 1954.

Elton, G. R. *Return to Essentials: Some Reflections on the Present State of Historical Study*. Cambridge: Cambridge University Press, 1991.

Emery, Gilles, O.P., *La Trinité créatrice*. Paris: Vrin, 1995.

———. "Le propos de la théologie trinitaire spéculative chez saint Thomas d'Aquin." *Nova et Vetera* (French) 79 (2004): 13–43. English trans. in Emery, *Trinity, Church, and the Human Person*, 1–32.

————. "L'intérêt de théologiens catholiques pour la proposition postlibérale de George Lindbeck." In *Postlibéralisme? La théologie de George Lindbeck et sa réception*, edited by Marc Boss, Gilles Emery, O.P., and Pierre Gisel, 39–57. Geneva: Labor et Fides, 2004.

————. "The Personal Mode of Trinitarian Action in Saint Thomas Aquinas." Translated by Matthew Levering. *Thomist* 69 (2005): 31–77.

————. "Thomas d'Aquin postliberal? La lecture de saint Thomas par George Lindbeck." In *Postlibéralisme? La théologie de George Lindbeck et sa réception*, edited by Marc Boss, Gilles Emery, O.P., and Pierre Gisel, 85–111. Geneva: Labor et Fides, 2004. English trans. in Emery, *Trinity, Church, and the Human Person*, 263–90.

————. *Trinity, Church, and the Human Person: Thomistic Essays*. Naples, Fla.: Sapientia Press, 2007.

Engelhardt, P., O.P., ed. *Sein und Ethos. Untersuchungen zur Grundlegung der Ethik*. Mainz: 1960.

Erasmus, Desiderius. *Collected Works of Erasmus: New Testament Scholarship*. Edited by Robert D. Sider. Toronto: University of Toronto Press, 1991.

————. *Opus epistolarum*. Edited by P. S. Allen et al. 1906–57.

————. *Opera Omnia*. Edited by J. Clericus. 1703–6. Reprint, Leiden: 1961–62.

————. *The Praise of Folly*. Translated by Clarence H. Miller. New Haven: Yale University Press, 1979.

Evans, C. Stephen. *The Historical Christ and the Jesus of Faith: The Incarnational Narrative as History*. Oxford: Clarendon Press, 1996.

Evans, Craig A., and Shemaryahu Talmon, eds. *The Quest for Context and Meaning: Studies in Biblical Intertextuality in Honor of James A. Sanders*. Leiden: Brill, 1997.

Farkasfalvy, Denis, O. Cist. "The Case for Spiritual Exegesis." *Communio* 10 (1983): 332–50.

————. "A Heritage in Search of Heirs: The Future of Ancient Christian Exegesis." *Communio* 25 (1998): 505–19.

————. "How to Renew the Theology of Biblical Inspiration?" *Nova et Vetera* 4 (2006): 231–54.

————. "In Search of a 'Post-Critical' Method of Biblical Interpretation." *Communio* 13 (1986): 288–307.

————. "The Pontifical Biblical Commission's Document on Jews and Christians and Their Scriptures: Attempt at an Evaluation." *Communio* 29 (2002): 715–737.

————. "'Prophets and Apostles': The Conjunction of the Two Terms before Irenaeus." In *Texts and Testaments: Critical Essays on the Bible and Early Church*, edited by W. Eugene March, 109–34. San Antonio: Trinity University Press, 1980.

————. "Theology of Scripture in St. Irenaeus." *Revue Bénédictine* 78 (1968): 319–33.

Farkasfalvy, Denis, O. Cist., and William Farmer. *The Formation of the New Testament Canon: An Ecumenical Approach.* New York: Paulist, 1983.

Fee, Gordon D. *God's Empowering Presence: The Holy Spirit in the Letters of Paul.* Peabody, Mass.: Hendrickson, 1994.

———. *To What End Exegesis? Essays Textual, Exegetical, and Theological.* Grand Rapids, Mich.: Eerdmans, 2001.

Feiner, J. "La contribution du secrétariat pour l'unité des chrétiens à la Constitution dogmatique sur la Révélation divine." In *La Révélation divine,* vol. 1, edited by B.-D. Dupuis. Paris: 1968.

Fishbane, Michael. *Biblical Interpretation in Ancient Israel.* Oxford: Oxford University Press, 1985.

———. *The Garments of Torah: Essays in Biblical Hermeneutics.* Bloomington: Indiana University Press, 1989.

———. "'Orally Write Therefore Aurally Right': An Essay on Midrash." In *The Quest for Context and Meaning: Studies in Biblical Intertextuality in Honor of James A. Sanders,* edited by Craig A. Evans and Shemaryahu Talmon, 531–46. Leiden: Brill, 1997.

Fitzmyer, Joseph A., S.J. "The Biblical Commission's Instruction on the Historical Truth of the Gospels." *Theological Studies* 25 (1964): 386–408.

———. "Historical Criticism: Its Role in Biblical Interpretation and Church Life." *Theological Studies* 50 (1989): 244–59.

———. *Scripture and Christology: A Statement of the Biblical Commission with a Commentary.* New York: Paulist Press, 1986.

———. "Scripture in the Catholic Tradition." In *Living Traditions of the Bible: Scripture in Jewish, Christian, and Muslim Practice,* edited by James Bowley, 145–61. St. Louis: Chalice Press, 1999.

———. *Scripture, the Soul of Theology.* New York: Paulist Press, 1994.

Flannery, Austin, O.P. *Vatican Council II.* Vol. 1, *The Conciliar and Post Conciliar Documents.* Rev. ed. Northport, N.Y.: Costello Publishing Company, 1975.

Florovsky, Georges. *Bible, Church, Tradition: An Eastern Orthodox View.* Belmont, Mass.: Nordland Publishing Co., 1972.

Flynn, William T. *Medieval Music as Medieval Exegesis.* Lanham, Md.: Scarecrow Press, 1999.

Fogarty, Gerald P., S.J., *American Catholic Biblical Scholarship: A History from the Early Republic to Vatican II,* with a foreword by Roland Murphy. San Francisco: Harper & Row, 1989.

Foley, Michael P., and Douglas Kries, eds. *Gladly to Learn and Gladly to Teach: Essays on Religion and Political Philosophy in Honor of Ernest L. Fortin, A.A.* Lanham, Md.: Lexington Books, 2002.

Ford, David F. "Jesus Christ, the Wisdom of God (1)." In *Reading Texts, Seeking Wisdom: Scripture and Theology,* edited by David F. Ford and Graham Stanton, 4–21. Grand Rapids, Mich.: Eerdmans, 2003.

Ford, David F., and Graham Stanton, eds. *Reading Texts, Seeking Wisdom: Scripture and Theology.* Grand Rapids, Mich.: Eerdmans, 2003.

Fowl, Stephen E. "The Conceptual Structure of New Testament Theology." In *Biblical Theology: Retrospect and Prospect,* edited by Scott J. Hafemann, 225–36. Downers Grove, Ill.: InterVarsity Press, 2002.

———. "Could Horace Talk with the Hebrews? Translatability and Moral Disagreement in MacIntyre and Stout." *Journal of Religious Ethics* 19 (1991): 1–20.

———. *Engaging Scripture: A Model for Theological Interpretation.* Oxford: Blackwell, 1998.

———. "The Ethics of Interpretation, or What's Left Over after the Elimination of Meaning." In *The Bible in Three Dimensions,* edited by David J. A. Clines, Stephen E. Fowl, and Stanley E. Porter, 379–98. Sheffield: Sheffield Academic Press, 1990.

———. "Learning to Narrate Our Lives in Christ." In *Theological Exegesis: Essays in Honor of Brevard S. Childs,* edited by Christopher Seitz and Kathryn Greene-McCreight, 339–54. Grand Rapids, Mich.: Eerdmans, 1999.

———. "The Role of Authorial Intention in the Theological Interpretation of Scripture." In *Between Two Horizons: Spanning New Testament Studies and Systematic Theology,* edited by Joel B. Green and Max Turner, 71–87. Grand Rapids, Mich.: Eerdmans, 2000.

———. *The Story of Christ in the Ethics of Paul: An Analysis of the Function of the Hymnic Material in the Pauline Corpus.* Sheffield: Sheffield Academic Press, 1991.

———. "Texts Don't Have Ideologies." *Biblical Interpretation* 3 (1995): 15–34.

Fowl, Stephen E., ed. *The Theological Interpretation of Scripture: Classic and Contemporary Reading.* Oxford: Blackwell, 1997.

Fowl, Stephen E., and L. Gregory Jones. *Reading in Communion: Scripture and Ethics in Christian Life.* Grand Rapids, Mich.: Eerdmans, 1991.

Frank, Daniel. "Karaite Commentaries on the Song of Songs from Tenth-Century Jerusalem." In *With Reverence for the Word: Medieval Scriptural Exegesis in Judaism, Christianity, and Islam,* edited by Jane Dammen McAuliffe, Barry D. Walfish, and Joseph W. Goering, 51–69. Oxford: Oxford University Press, 2003.

———. "Karaite Exegesis." In *Hebrew Bible/Old Testament: The History of Its Interpretation.* Vol. I/2, edited by Magne Saebo, 110–28. Göttingen: Vandenhoeck & Ruprecht, 2000.

———. "The Study of Medieval Karaism, 1989–1999." In *Hebrew Scholarship and the Medieval World,* edited by Nicholas De Lange, 3–22. Cambridge: Cambridge University Press, 2001.

Frankemölle, H., and K. Kertelge, eds. *Vom Urchristentum zu Jesus: Für Joachim Gnilka.* Freiburg: Herder, 1989.

Franzini, A. *Tradizione e scrittura. Il contributo del Concilio Vaticano II*. Brescia: 1978.

Frei, Hans W. *The Eclipse of Biblical Narrative: A Study in Eighteenth and Nineteenth Century Hermeneutics*. New Haven: Yale University Press, 1973.

———. *The Identity of Jesus Christ*. Eugene, Ore.: Wipf & Stock Publishers, 1997.

———. "The 'Literal Reading' of Biblical Narrative in the Christian Tradition: Does It Stretch or Will It Break?" In *Theology and Narrative*, edited by George Hunsinger and William C. Placher, 117–52. Oxford: Oxford University Press, 1993.

———. "'Narrative' in Christian and Modern Reading." In *Theology and Dialogue*, edited by Bruce Marshall, 149–63. Notre Dame: University of Notre Dame Press, 1990.

———. *Theology and Narrative*. Edited by George Hunsinger and William C. Placher. Oxford: Oxford University Press, 1993.

———. *Types of Christian Theology*. Edited by George Hunsinger and William C. Placher. New Haven: Yale University Press, 1992.

Funkenstein, Amos. *Theology and the Scientific Imagination from the Middle Ages to the Seventeenth Century*. Princeton: Princeton University Press, 1986.

Gadamer, Hans-Georg. *Reason in the Age of Science*. Cambridge: MIT Press, 1996.

Gaddis, John Lewis. *The Landscape of History: How Historians Map the Past*. Oxford: Oxford University Press, 2002.

Gagnon, Robert A. J. *The Bible and Homosexual Practice: Texts and Hermeneutics*. Nashville: Abingdon Press, 2001.

Gaine, Simon Francis, O.P. *Will There Be Freedom in Heaven? Freedom, Impeccability and Beatitude*. New York: T. & T. Clark, 2003.

Gibson, M. T. "The Place of the *Glossa ordinaria* in Medieval Exegesis." In *Ad Litteram: Authoritative Texts and Their Medieval Readers*, edited by Mark Jordan and Kent Emery Jr., 5–27. Notre Dame: University of Notre Dame Press, 1992.

Gibson, Michael D. "Does Jesus Have a Say in the Kerygma? A Critical Remembrance of Bultmann." *Scottish Journal of Theology* 58 (2005): 83–103.

Gorman, Michael J. *Cruciformity: Paul's Narrative Spirituality of the Cross*. Grand Rapids, Mich.: Eerdmans, 2001.

Grafton, Anthony. *Defenders of the Text: The Traditions of Scholarship in an Age of Science, 1450–1800*. Cambridge: Harvard University Press, 1991.

———. "The Identities of History in Early Modern Europe: Prelude to a Study of the *Artes Historicae*." In *Historia: Empiricism and Erudition in Early Modern Europe*, edited by Gianna Pomata and Nancy G. Siraisi, 41–72. Cambridge: MIT Press, 2005.

Grant, Robert M., with David Tracy. *A Short History of the Interpretation of the Bible*. 2d ed. Philadelphia: Fortress, 1984.

Green, Joel. "In Quest of the Historical: Jesus, the Gospels, and Historicisms Old and New." *Christian Scholar's Review* 27 (1999): 544–60.

———. "Rethinking History (and Theology)." In *Between Two Horizons: Spanning New Testament Studies and Systematic Theology*, edited by Joel B. Green and Max Turner, 237–42. Grand Rapids, Mich.: Eerdmans, 2000.

Green, Joel B., and Max Turner, eds. *Between Two Horizons: Spanning New Testament Studies and Systematic Theology*. Grand Rapids, Mich.: Eerdmans, 2000.

Greenslade, S. L., ed. *The Cambridge History of the Bible*. Vol. 3, *The West from the Reformation to the Present Day*. Cambridge: Cambridge University Press, 1963.

Greer, Rowan. "The Good Shepherd: Canonical Interpretations in the Early Church?" In *Theological Exegesis: Essays in Honor of Brevard S. Childs*, edited by Christopher Seitz and Kathryn Greene-McCreight, 306–30. Grand Rapids, Mich.: Eerdmans, 1999.

Griffiths, Paul J., and Reinhard Hütter, eds. *Reason and the Reasons of Faith*. New York: T. & T. Clark, 2005.

Grillmeier, Alois. "The Divine Inspiration and the Interpretation of Sacred Scripture." In *Commentary on the Documents of Vatican II*. Vol. 3, edited by Herbert Vorgrimler, translated by William Glen-Doepel et al., 199–246. German, 1967. New York: Crossroad, 1989.

Guindon, Roger, O. M. I. *Béatitude et théologie morale chez saint Thomas d'Aquin*. Ottawa: Editions de l'Université d'Ottawa, 1956.

———. "La théologie de saint Thomas d'Aquin dans le rayonnement du 'Prologue' de saint Jean." *Revue de l'Université d'Ottawa* 29 (1959): 5–23 and 121–42.

———. "Le caractè évangelique de la morale de saint Thomas d'Aquin." *Revue de l'Université d'Ottawa* 25 (1955): 145–67.

———. "Le 'De Sermone Domini in monte' de saint Augustin dans l'oeuvre de saint Thomas d'Aquin." *Revue de l'Université d'Ottawa* 28 (1958): 57–85.

Gundry, Robert H. Review of *Jesus and the Victory of God*, by N. T. Wright. *Christianity Today* (April 27, 1998): 76–79.

Gunton, Colin. *Father, Son and Spirit: Essays toward a Fully Trinitarian Theology*. New York: T & T Clark, 2003.

———. "Martin Kähler Revisited: Variations on Hebrews 4:15." *Ex Auditu* 14 (1998): 21–30.

Hackett, Jeremiah, William Murnion, and Carl Still, eds. *Being and Thought in Aquinas*. Binghamton, N.Y.: Global Academic Publishing, 2004.

Hafemann, Scott J., ed. *Biblical Theology: Retrospect and Prospect*. Downers Grove, Ill.: InterVarsity Press, 2002.

Halbertal, Moshe. *People of the Book: Canon, Meaning, and Authority*. Cambridge: Harvard University Press, 1997.

Halivni, David Weiss. *Peshat and Derash: Plain and Applied Meaning in Rabbinic Exegesis.* Oxford: Oxford University Press, 1991.

———. *Revelation Restored: Divine Writ and Critical Responses.* Boulder: Westview Press, 1997.

Halpern, Baruch. *The First Historians: The Hebrew Bible and History.* 1988. University Park, Pa.: Pennsylvania State University Press, 1996.

Hankey, Wayne J. "Aquinas, Pseudo-Denys, Proclus and Isaiah VI.6." *Archives d'histoire doctrinale et littéraire du Moyen Âge* 64 (1997): 59–93.

———. "*Participatio divini luminis,* Aquinas' Doctrine of the Agent Intellect: Our Capacity for Contemplation." *Dionysius* 22 (2004): 149–78.

———. "Radical Orthodoxy's *Poiesis*: Ideological Historiography and Anti-Modern Polemic." *American Catholic Philosophical Quarterly* 80 (2006): 1–21.

———. "Why Philosophy Abides for Aquinas." *Heythrop Journal* 42 (2001): 329–48.

Hankey, Wayne J., and Douglas Hedley, eds. *Deconstructing Radical Orthodoxy: Postmodern Theology, Rhetoric and Truth.* Aldershot: Ashgate, 2005.

Hanvey, James, S.J. "In the Presence of Love: The Pneumatological Realization of the Economy: Yves Congar's *Le Mystère du Temple.*" *International Journal of Systematic Theology* 7 (2005): 383–98.

Harakas, Stanley Samuel. "Doing Theology Today: An Orthodox and Evangelical Dialogue on Theological Method." *Pro Ecclesia* 11 (2002): 435–62.

Harink, Douglas. *Paul among the Postliberals: Pauline Theology beyond Christendom and Modernity.* Grand Rapids, Mich.: Brazos Press, 2003.

Harrisville, Roy A. "The Loss of Biblical Authority and Its Recovery." In *Reclaiming the Bible for the Church,* edited by Carl Braaten and Robert Jenson, 47–61. Grand Rapids, Mich.: Eerdmans, 1995.

———. "What I Believe My Old Schoolmate Is Up To." In *Theological Exegesis: Essays in Honor of Brevard S. Childs,* edited by Christopher Seitz and Kathryn Greene-McCreight, 7–25. Grand Rapids, Mich.: Eerdmans, 1999.

Harrisville, Roy A., and Walter Sundberg. *The Bible in Modern Culture: Theology and Historical-Critical Method from Spinoza to Käsemann.* Grand Rapids, Mich.: Eerdmans, 1995.

Hart, David Bentley. *The Beauty of the Infinite: The Aesthetics of Christian Truth.* Grand Rapids, Mich.: Eerdmans, 2003.

———. *The Doors of the Sea: Where Was God in the Tsunami?* Grand Rapids, Mich.: Eerdmans, 2005.

———. "The Offering of Names: Metaphysics, Nihilism, and Analogy." In *Reason and the Reasons of Faith,* edited by Paul J. Griffiths and Reinhard Hütter, 255–91. New York: T. & T. Clark, 2005.

Hart, Trevor. "Tradition, Authority, and a Christian Approach to the Bible as Scripture." In *Between Two Horizons: Spanning New Testament Studies and*

Systematic Theology, edited by Joel B. Green and Max Turner, 183–204. Grand Rapids, Mich.: Eerdmans, 2000.

Hatina, Thomas R. "Intertextuality and Historical Criticism in New Testament Studies: Is There a Relationship?" *Biblical Interpretation* 7 (1999): 28–43.

Hauerwas, Stanley. *Performing the Faith: Bonhoeffer and the Practice of Nonviolence.* Grand Rapids, Mich.: Brazos Press, 2004.

———. *Unleashing the Scripture: Freeing the Bible from Captivity to America.* Nashville: Abingdon Press, 1993.

Hays, Richard B. *The Conversion of the Imagination: Paul as Interpreter of Israel's Scripture.* Grand Rapids, Mich.: Eerdmans, 2005.

———. *Echoes of Scripture in the Letters of Paul.* New Haven: Yale University Press, 1989.

———. "Faith and History." *First Things* 64 (June/July 1996): 44–46.

———. "The Future of *Christian* Biblical Scholarship." *Nova et Vetera* 4 (2006): 95–120.

———. *The Moral Vision of the New Testament: A Contemporary Introduction to New Testament Ethics.* San Francisco: HarperSanFrancisco, 1996.

———. "Reading Scripture in Light of the Resurrection." In *The Art of Reading Scripture*, edited by Ellen F. Davis and Richard B. Hays, 216–38. Grand Rapids, Mich.: Eerdmans, 2003.

———. "Response to Robert Wilken, 'In Dominico Eloquio.'" *Communio* 25 (1998): 520–28.

Headley, John M. *Tommaso Campanella and the Transformation of the World.* Princeton: Princeton University Press, 1997.

Healy, Mary. "Behind, in Front of . . . or through the Text? The Christological Analogy and the Lost World of Biblical Truth." In *"Behind" the Text: History and Biblical Interpretation*, edited by Craig Bartholomew et al., 181–95. Grand Rapids, Mich.: Zondervan, 2003.

Hengel, Martin. "'Salvation History': The Truth of Scripture and Modern Theology." In *Reading Texts, Seeking Wisdom: Scripture and Theology*, edited by David F. Ford and Graham Stanton, 228–44. Grand Rapids, Mich.: Eerdmans, 2003.

Hercsik, Donath, S.J. "Das Wort Gottes in der nachkonziliaren Kirche und Theologie." *Gregorianum* 86 (2005): 135–62.

Hibbs, Thomas S. *Virtue's Splendor: Wisdom, Prudence, and the Human Good.* New York: Fordham University Press, 2001.

Hirsch, E. D., Jr. "Meaning and Significance Reinterpreted." *Critical Inquiry* 11 (1984): 202–25.

Hobbes, Thomas. *Leviathan.* With selected variants from the Latin edition of 1668. Edited by Edwin Curley. Indianapolis: Hackett, 1994.

Holmes, Jeremy. "Biblical Scholarship New and Old: Learning from the Past." *Nova et Vetera* 1 (2003): 303–20.

Hooker, Morna D. "The Authority of the Bible: A New Testament Perspective." *Ex Auditu* 19 (2003): 45–64.

Hopko, Thomas. "The Church, the Bible, and Dogmatic Theology." In *Reclaiming the Bible for the Church*, edited by Carl Braaten and Robert Jenson, 107–18. Grand Rapids, Mich.: Eerdmans, 1995.

Hunsinger, George, and William C. Placher. *Theology and Narrative*. Oxford: Oxford University Press, 1993.

Hurst, L. D., and N. T. Wright, eds. *The Glory of Christ in the New Testament: Studies in Christology*. Oxford: Clarendon Press, 1987.

Hütter, Reinhard. *Bound to Be Free: Evangelical Catholic Engagements in Ecclesiology, Ethics, and Ecumenism*. Grand Rapids, Mich.: Eerdmans, 2004.

———. *Evangelische Ethik als kirchliches Zeugnis. Interpretationen zu Schlüsselfragen theologischer Ethik in der Gegenwart*. Neukirchen-Blyn: Neukirchener Verlag, 1993.

———. "'In.' Some Incipient Reflections on *The Jewish People and Their Sacred Scriptures in the Christian Bible.*" *Pro Ecclesia* 13 (2004): 13–24.

———. *Suffering Divine Things: Theology as Church Practice Suffering Divine Things: Theology as Church Practice*. German, 1997. Grand Rapids, Mich.: Eerdmans, 2000.

Hütter, Reinhard, and Theodor Dieter, eds. *Ecumenical Ventures in Ethics: Protestants Engage Pope John Paul II's Moral Encyclicals*. Grand Rapids, Mich.: Eerdmans, 1998.

Hyatt, J. Philip, ed. *The Bible in Modern Scholarship*. Nashville: Abingdon Press, 1965.

Ingham, Mary Beth, and Mechthild Dreyer. *The Philosophical Vision of John Duns Scotus*. Washington, D.C.: Catholic University of America Press, 2004.

Israel, Jonathan I. *Radical Enlightenment: Philosophy and the Making of Modernity 1650–1750*. Oxford: Oxford University Press, 2001.

Janz, Paul D. "Radical Orthodoxy and the New Culture of Obscurantism." *Modern Theology* 20 (2004): 362–405.

Jeanrond, Werner. *Text and Interpretation as Categories of Theological Thinking*. Dublin: Gill & Macmillan, 1988.

———. *Theological Hermeneutics: Development and Significance*. London: SCM Press, 1994.

Jenkins, Keith. *On "What Is History?": From Carr and Elton to Rorty and White*. London: Routledge, 1995.

Jennings, Willie James. "Undoing Our Abandonment: Reading Scripture through the Sinlessness of Jesus. A Meditation on Cyril of Alexandria's *On the Unity of Christ.*" *Ex Auditu* 14 (1998): 85–96.

Jenson, Robert W. "The Bible and the Trinity." *Pro Ecclesia* 11 (2002): 329–39.

———. "Hermeneutics and the Life of the Church." In *Reclaiming the Bible for the Church*, edited by Carl Braaten and Robert Jenson, 89–105. Grand Rapids, Mich.: Eerdmans, 1995.

————. "Scripture's Authority in the Church." In *The Art of Reading Scripture*, edited by Ellen F. Davis and Richard B. Hays, 27 37. Grand Rapids, Mich.: Eerdmans, 2003.

————. *Systematic Theology*. Vol. 1, *The Triune God*. Oxford: Oxford University Press, 1997.

St. John of Damascus. *St. John of Damascus: Writings*. Translated by Frederic H. Chase Jr. Washington, D.C.: Catholic University of America Press, 1958.

John Paul II, Pope. *Crossing the Threshold of Hope*. Edited by Vittorio Messori. Translated by Jenny and Martha McPhee. New York: Knopf, 1995.

————. *Fides et Ratio*. 1998.

Johnson, Luke Timothy. "Koinonia: Diversity and Unity in Early Christianity." *Theology Digest* 46 (1999): 303–13.

————. *Living Jesus: Learning the Heart of the Gospel*. New York: Harper-SanFrancisco, 1999.

————. *The Real Jesus: The Misguided Quest for the Historical Jesus and the Truth of the Traditional Gospels*. New York: HarperSanFrancisco, 1996.

————. "Rejoining a Long Conversation." In *The Future of Catholic Biblical Scholarship: A Constructive Conversation*, by Luke Timothy Johnson and William S. Kurz, S.J., 35–63. Grand Rapids, Mich.: Eerdmans, 2002.

————. Review of *The New Testament and the People of God*, by N. T. Wright. *Journal of Biblical Literature* 113 (1994): 536–38.

————. "What's Catholic about Catholic Biblical Scholarship? An Opening Statement." In *The Future of Catholic Biblical Scholarship: A Constructive Conversation* by Luke Timothy Johnson and William S. Kurz, S.J., 3–34. Grand Rapids, Mich.: Eerdmans, 2002.

Johnson, Luke Timothy, and William S. Kurz, S.J. *The Future of Catholic Biblical Scholarship: A Constructive Conversation*. Grand Rapids, Mich.: Eerdmans, 2002.

Johnson, Mark F. "Another Look at the Plurality of the Literal Sense." *Medieval Philosophy and Theology* 2 (1992): 117–41.

Johnson, Samuel. *The Rambler*. Selected and introduced by S. C. Roberts. London: J. M. Dent & Sons, 1953.

Jones, L. Gregory. "Embodying Scripture in the Community of Faith." In *The Art of Reading Scripture*, edited by Ellen F. Davis and Richard B. Hays, 143–59. Grand Rapids, Mich.: Eerdmans, 2003.

Jordan, Mark. "Words and Word: Incarnation and Signification in Augustine's *De Doctrina Christiana*." *Augustinian Studies* 11 (1980): 177–96.

Jordan, Mark, and Kent Emery Jr., eds. *Ad Litteram: Authoritative Texts and Their Medieval Readers*. Notre Dame: University of Notre Dame Press, 1992.

Josipovici, Gabriel. *The Book of God: A Response to the Bible*. New Haven: Yale University Press, 1988.

Kadushin, Max. *The Rabbinic Mind*. 3d ed. New York: Bloch, 1972.

Kannengiesser, Charles. "The Bible in the Arian Crisis." In *The Bible in Greek Christian Antiquity*, edited and translated by Paul M. Blowers, 217–28. Notre Dame: University of Notre Dame Press, 1997.

Kasper, Walter. "Prolegomena zur Erneuerung der geistlichen Schriftauslegung." In *Vom Urchristentum zu Jesus: Für Joachim Gnilka*, edited by H. Frankemölle and K. Kertelge, 508–26. Freiburg: Herder, 1989.

Kavanaugh, Aidan J., O.S.B. "Scriptural Word and Liturgical Worship." In *Reclaiming the Bible for the Church*, edited by Carl Braaten and Robert Jenson, 131–37. Grand Rapids, Mich.: Eerdmans, 1995.

Keating, James F. "Contemporary Epistemology and Theological Application of the Historical Jesus Quest." *Josephinum Journal of Theology* 10 (2003): 343–56.

———. "The Invincible Allure of the Historical Jesus for Systematic Theology." *Irish Theological Quarterly* 66 (2001): 211–26.

———. "N. T. Wright and the Necessity of a Historical Apologetic of the Resurrection." *Josephinum Journal of Theology* 12 (2005): 43–56.

Keaty, Anthony. "Thomas's Authority for Identifying Charity as Friendship: Aristotle or John 15?" *Thomist* 62 (1998): 581–601.

Kelly, Geffrey B., and F. Burton Nelson. "Dietrich Bonhoeffer's Theological Interpretation of Scripture for the Church." *Ex Auditu* 17 (2001): 1–30.

Kelsey, David H. *The Nature of Doctrine*. Philadelphia: Westminster Press, 1984.

———. *Proving Doctrine: The Uses of Scripture in Modern Theology*. 2d ed. with a new preface. Harrisburg, Pa.: Trinity Press International, 1999. Originally published as *The Uses of Scripture in Recent Theology* (Philadelphia: Fortress Press, 1975).

Kent, Bonnie. *Virtues of the Will: The Transformation of Ethics in the Late Thirteenth Century*. Washington, D.C.: Catholic University of America Press, 1995.

Kepnes, Steven, Peter Ochs, and Robert Gibbs, eds. *Reasoning after Revelation: Dialogues in Postmodern Jewish Philosophy*. Boulder: Westview Press, 1998.

Kereszty, Roch. "The Jewish-Christian Dialogue and the Pontifical Biblical Commission's Document on 'The Jewish People and Their Sacred Scriptures in the Christian Bible.'" *Communio* 29 (2002): 738–45.

Kerr, Fergus, O.P. "Charity as Friendship." In *Language, Meaning and God*, edited by Brian Davies, O.P., 1–23. London: Geoffrey Chapman, 1987.

Kienzle, Beverly Mayne, ed. *The Sermon*. Turnhout: Brepols, 2000.

Kinzer, Mark S. *Post-Missionary Messianic Judaism: Redefining Christian Engagement with the Jewish People*. Grand Rapids, Mich.: Brazos, 2005.

Koterski, Joseph W., S.J. "The Doctrine of Participation in Aquinas's *Commentary on St. John*." In *Being and Thought in Aquinas*, edited by Jeremiah Hackett, William Murnion, and Carl Still. Binghamton, N.Y.: Global Academic Publishing, 2004.

Kraftchick, Steven J., Charles D. Myers Jr., and Ben C. Ollenburger, eds. *Biblical Theology: Problems and Perspectives.* Nashville: Abingdon Press, 1995.

Kurz, William S., S.J. "Beyond Historical Criticism: Reading John's Prologue as Catholics." In *The Future of Catholic Biblical Scholarship: A Constructive Conversation,* by Luke Timothy Johnson and William S. Kurz, S.J. , 159—81. Grand Rapids, Mich.: Eerdmans, 2002.

————. *Reading Luke-Acts: Dynamics of Biblical Narrative.* Louisville: Westminster/John Knox Press, 1993.

LaCocque, André, and Paul Ricoeur. *Thinking Biblically: Exegetical and Hermeneutical Studies.* Translated by David Pellauer. Chicago: University of Chicago Press, 1998.

Lagrange, Marie-Joseph, O.P. *Évangile selon saint Jean.* 4th ed. Paris: Librairie Victor Lecoffre, 1927.

————. "L'interprétation de la Sainte Écriture par l'Église." *Revue Biblique* 9 (1900): 135—42.

Lamb, Matthew L. "Eternity and Time." In *Gladly to Learn and Gladly to Teach: Essays on Religion and Political Philosophy in Honor of Ernest L. Fortin, A.A.,* edited by Michael P. Foley and Douglas Kries, 195—214. Lanham, Md.: Lexington Books, 2002.

————. "Nature, History, and Redemption." In *Jesus Crucified and Risen,* edited by William P. Loewe and Vernon J. Gregson, 117—32. Collegeville, Minn.: Liturgical Press, 1998.

————. "The Resurrection and Christian Identity as *Conversatio Dei.*" *Concilium* 249 (1993): 112—23.

————. *Solidarity with Victims: Toward a Theology of Social Transformation.* New York: Crossroad, 1982.

————. *Eternity, Time, and the Life of Wisdom.* Naples, Fla.: Sapientia Press, 2007.

Lampe, G.W. H., ed. *The Cambridge History of the Bible.* Cambridge: Cambridge University Press, 1969.

a Lapide, Cornelius, S.J. *Commentaria in Quatuor Evangelia.* Vol. 4. 3d rev. ed. Paris: Marietti, 1922.

Larraín, Eduardo Pérez-Cotapos. "El valor hermenéutico de la eclesialidad para la interpretación de la Sagrada Escritura." *Teología y Vida* 37 (1996): 169—85.

Lash, Nicholas. *Theology on the Way to Emmaus.* London: SCM Press, 1986.

Latourelle, René, ed. *Vatican II: Assessment and Perspectives.* Vol. 1. New York: Paulist Press, 1988.

Lefèvre d'Etaples, Jacques. *Commentaries on the Four Gospels.* 1521. Lefèvre d'Etaples (also known as Faber Stapulensis)

Leo XIII, Pope. *Providentissimus Deus.* 1893.

Levenson, Jon D. "The Agenda of *Dabru Emet*." *Review of Rabbinic Judaism* 7 (2004): 1–26.

———. *The Hebrew Bible, the Old Testament, and Historical Criticism: Jews and Christians in Biblical Studies.* Louisville: Westminster/John Knox Press, 1993.

———. "Is Brueggemann Really a Pluralist?" *Harvard Theological Review* 93 (2000): 265–94.

———. Review of *The Concept of Biblical Theology: An Old Testament Perspective* by James Barr. *First Things* 100 (February 2000): 59–63.

Levering, Matthew. "Augustine and Aquinas on the Good Shepherd: The Value of an Exegetical Tradition." In *Aquinas the Augustinian*, edited by Michael Dauphinais, Barry David, and Matthew Levering, 205–42. Washington, D.C.: Catholic University of America Press, 2007.

———. *Christ's Fulfillment of Torah and Temple: Salvation according to Thomas Aquinas.* Notre Dame: University of Notre Dame Press, 2002.

———. "Ecclesial Exegesis and Ecclesial Authority: Childs, Fowl, and Aquinas." *Thomist* 69 (2005): 407–67.

———. *Hierarchy and Holiness: Foundations for a Theology of Priesthood.* Chicago: Hillenbrand Books. Forthcoming.

———. "Participation and Exegesis: Response to Catherine Pickstock." *Modern Theology* 21 (2005): 587–601.

———. "The Pontifical Biblical Commission and Aquinas' Exegesis." *Pro Ecclesia* 13 (2004): 25–38.

———. "Principles of Exegesis: Toward a Participatory Biblical Exegesis." *Pro Ecclesia.* Forthcoming.

———. "Reading John with St. Thomas Aquinas." In *Aquinas on Scripture: An Introduction to His Biblical Commentaries*, edited by Thomas Weinandy, O.F.M. Cap., Daniel Keating, and John Yocum, 99–126. New York: T. & T. Clark, 2005.

———. *Sacrifice and Community: Jewish Offering and Christian Eucharist.* Oxford: Blackwell, 2005.

———. *Scripture and Metaphysics: Aquinas and the Renewal of Trinitarian Theology.* Oxford: Blackwell, 2004.

———. "William Abraham and St. Thomas Aquinas." *New Blackfriars* 88 (2007): 46–65.

Levi, Anthony. *Renaissance and Reformation: The Intellectual Genesis.* New Haven: Yale University Press, 2002.

Levi, Antonio. "The Philosophical Category of 'Faith' at the Origins of Modern Scepticism." *Nova et Vetera* 1 (2003): 321–40.

Levine, Joseph M. *The Autonomy of History: Truth and Method from Erasmus to Gibbon.* Chicago: University of Chicago Press, 1999.

Lienhard, Joseph T., S.J. *The Bible, the Church, and Authority: The Canon of the Christian Bible in History and Theology.* Collegeville, Minn.: Liturgical Press, 1995.

Lindbeck, George. *The Nature of Doctrine: Religion and Theology in a Postliberal Age.* Philadelphia: Westminster, 1984.

————. "Progress in Textual Reasoning: From Vatican II to the Conference at Drew." In *Textual Reasonings: Jewish Philosophy and Text Study at the End of the Twentieth Century*, edited by Peter Ochs and Nancy Levene, 252–58. Grand Rapids, Mich.: Eerdmans, 2002.

————. "Scripture, Consensus, and Community." In *Biblical Interpretation in Crisis: The Ratzinger Conference on Bible and Church*, edited by Richard John Neuhaus, 74–101. Grand Rapids, Mich.: Eerdmans, 1989.

————. "The Story-Shaped Church: Critical Exegesis and Theological Interpretation." In *The Theological Interpretation of Scripture: Classic and Contemporary Readings*, edited by Stephen E. Fowl, 39–52. Oxford: Blackwell, 1997.

————. "Two Kinds of Ecumenism: Unitive and Interdenominational." *Gregorianum* 70 (1989): 647–60.

Litfin, Bryan M. "The Rule of Faith in Augustine." *Pro Ecclesia* 14 (2005): 85–101.

Lockshin, Martin. "Rashban as a 'Literary' Exegete." In *With Reverence for the Word: Medieval Scriptural Exegesis in Judaism, Christianity, and Islam*, edited by Jane Dammen McAuliffe, Barry D. Walfish, and Joseph W. Goering, 83–91. Oxford: Oxford University Press, 2003.

Lohfink, Norbert. "Der weiße Fleck in *Dei Verbum*, Artikel 12." *Trierer Theologische Zeitschrift* 101 (1992): 20–35.

————. "Eine Bibel—Zwei Testamente." In *Eine Bibel—Zwei Testamente*, edited by C. Dohmen and T. Söding, 71–81. Paderborn: Schöningh, 1995.

Lonergan, Bernard, S.J. *The Way to Nicea: The Dialectical Development of Trinitarian Theology.* Philadelphia: Westminster Press, 1976.

Long, D. Stephen. "Response to Abraham." *Ex Auditu* 19 (2003): 76–80.

Longenecker, Richard J. *Biblical Exegesis in the Apostolic Period.* 1st ed. Grand Rapids, Mich.: Eerdmans, 1975.

————. *Biblical Exegesis in the Apostolic Period.* 2d ed. Grand Rapids, Mich.: Eerdmans, 1999.

Longenecker, Richard N., ed. *The Challenge of Jesus' Parables.* Grand Rapids, Mich.: Eerdmans, 2000.

Löwith, Karl. *Meaning in History.* Chicago: University of Chicago Press, 1949.

MacIntyre, Alasdair, and Paul Ricoeur. *The Religious Significance of Atheism.* New York: Columbia University Press, 1969.

Maier, Christoph. *Preaching the Crusades: Mendicant Friars and the Cross in the Thirteenth Century.* Cambridge: Cambridge University Press, 1994.

Maldonatus, Joannes, S.J., *Commentarii in Quatuor Evangelistas.* Vol. 2. Edited by Conrad Martin. Moguntiae: Francisci Kirchhemii, 1863.

Maimonides, Moses. *The Guide of the Perplexed.* Translated by Shlomo Pines. Chicago: University of Chicago Press, 1974.

Manent, Pierre. *The City of Man*. Princeton: Princeton University Press, 1998.

Manning, E., ed. *Thomistica. Recherches de théologie ancienne et médiévale.* Supp. 1. Leuven: Peeters, 1995.

Mansini, Guy, O.S.B. "*Similitudo, Communicatio*, and the Friendship of Charity in Aquinas." In *Thomistica. Recherches de théologie ancienne et médiévale*, supp. 1, edited by E. Manning, 1–26. Leuven: Peeters, 1995.

March, W. Eugene, ed. *Texts and Testaments: Critical Essays on the Bible and Early Church*. San Antonio: Trinity University Press, 1980.

Marcel, Gabriel. *The Mystery of Being*. Vol. 1, *Reflection and Mystery*. London: Harvill, 1950.

Marion, Jean-Luc. *God without Being: Hors-Texte*. Translated by Thomas A. Carlson. 1982. Chicago: University of Chicago Press, 1991.

Marshall, Bruce, ed. *Theology and Dialogue*. Notre Dame: University of Notre Dame Press, 1990.

Marshall, I. Howard. *Beyond the Bible: Moving from Scripture to Theology*. Grand Rapids, Mich.: Baker Academic, 2004.

Martin, Francis. "Critique historique et enseignement du Nouveau Testament sur l'imitation du Christ." *Revue Thomiste* 93 (1993): 234–62.

———. "Historical Criticism and New Testament Teaching on the Imitation of Christ." *Anthropotes* 6 (1990): 261–87.

———. "Israel as the Spouse of YHWH: A Story of Sin and Renewed Love." *Anthropotes* 16 (2000): 129–54.

———. "Literary Theory, Philosophy of History and Exegesis." *Thomist* 52 (1988): 575–604.

———. "Revelation as Disclosure: Creation." In *Wisdom and Holiness, Science and Scholarship: Essays in Honor of Matthew L. Lamb*, edited by Michael Dauphinais and Matthew Levering, 205–47. Naples, Fla.: Sapientia Press, 2007.

———. "*Sacra Doctrina* and the Authority of Its *Sacra Scriptura* according to St. Thomas Aquinas." *Pro Ecclesia* 10 (2001): 84–102.

———. *Sacred Scripture: The Disclosure of the Word*. Naples, Fla.: Sapientia Press, 2006.

Matera, Frank J. "The Future of Catholic Biblical Scholarship: Balance and Proportion." *Nova et Vetera* 4 (2006): 120–32.

———. "New Testament Theology: History, Method, and Identity." *Catholic Biblical Quarterly* 67 (2005): 1–21.

Mayeski, Marie Anne. "Quaestio Disputata: Catholic Theology and the History of Exegesis." *Theological Studies* 62 (2001): 140–53.

McAleer, G. J. *Ecstatic Morality and Sexual Politics: A Catholic and Antitotalitarian Theory of the Body*. New York: Fordham University Press, 2005.

McAuliffe, Jane Dammen, Barry D. Walfish, and Joseph W. Goering, eds. *With Reverence for the Word: Medieval Scriptural Exegesis in Judaism, Christianity, and Islam*. Oxford: Oxford University Press, 2003.

McEvoy, James. "The Other as Oneself: Friendship and Love in the Thought of St. Thomas Aquinas." In *Thomas Aquinas: Approaches to Truth*, edited by James McEvoy and Michael Dunne, 16–37. Dublin: Four Courts Press, 2002.

McEvoy, James, and Michael Dunne, eds. *Thomas Aquinas: Approaches to Truth*. Dublin: Four Courts Press, 2002.

McGinn, Bernard. *The Mystical Thought of Meister Eckhart: The Man from Whom God Hid Nothing.* New York: Herder & Herder, 2003.

McGovern, Thomas J. "The Interpretation of Scripture 'in the Spirit': the Edelby Intervention at Vatican II." *Irish Theological Quarterly* 64 (1999): 245–59.

McGrath, Alister. "Reclaiming Our Roots and Vision: Scripture and the Stability of the Christian Church." In *Reclaiming the Bible for the Church*, edited by Carl Braaten and Robert Jenson, 63–88. Grand Rapids, Mich.: Eerdmans, 1995.

McInerny, Ralph, ed. and trans. *Thomas Aquinas: Selected Writings.* New York: Penguin, 1998.

McKnight, Scot. "Covenant and Spirit: The Origins of the New Covenant Hermeneutic." In *The Holy Spirit and Christian Origins: Essays In Honor Of James D. G. Dunn*, edited by Graham N. Stanton, Bruce W. Longenecker, and Stephen C. Barton, 41–54. Grand Rapids, Mich.: Eerdmans, 2004.

Meyer, Ben F. *Reality and Illusion in New Testament Scholarship: A Primer in Critical Realist Hermeneutics.* Collegeville, Minn.: Liturgical Press, 1994.

Michalson, Gordon. *Lessing's "Ugly Ditch": A Study of Theology and History.* Philadelphia: Pennsylvania State University Press, 1985.

Milbank, John. *The Religious Dimension of the Thought of Giambattista Vico.* Part 2, *Language, Law, and History.* Lewiston, N.Y.: Edwin Mellen Press, 1992.

Milbank, John, and Catherine Pickstock. *Truth in Aquinas.* London: Routledge, 2000.

Miner, Robert. *Vico, Genealogist of Modernity.* Notre Dame: University of Notre Dame Press, 2002.

Minnis, A. J. "Material Swords and Literal Lights: The Status of Allegory in William of Ockham's *Breviloquium* on Papal Power." In *With Reverence for the Word: Medieval Scriptural Exegesis in Judaism, Christianity, and Islam*, edited by Jane Dammen McAuliffe, Barry D. Walfish, and Joseph W. Goering, 292–308. Oxford: Oxford University Press, 2003.

Moberly, R. W. L. *The Bible, Theology, and Faith: A Study of Abraham and Jesus.* Cambridge: Cambridge University Press, 2000.

Möhle, Hannes. "Scotus's Theory of Natural Law." In *The Cambridge Companion to Duns Scotus*, edited by Thomas Williams, 312–31. Cambridge: Cambridge University Press, 2003.

Moloney, Francis J., S. D. B., *The Gospel of John.* Collegeville, Minn.: Liturgical Press, 1998.

Momigliano, Arnaldo. *History and the Concepts of Time.* Middletown, Conn.: Wesleyan University Press, 1966.

———. *On Pagans, Jews, and Christians.* Middletown, Conn.: Wesleyan University Press, 1987.

Moore, Stephen D., et al., eds. *The Postmodern Bible.* New Haven: Yale University Press, 1995.

Morerod, Charles, O.P., *Ecumenism and Philosophy.* Translated by Therese Scarpelli. Naples, Fla.: Sapientia Press, 2005.

———. "Les sens dans la relation de l'homme avec Dieu." *Nova et Vetera* 79 (2004): 7–35.

Morgan, Robert. "Can the Critical Study of Scripture Provide a Doctrinal Norm?" *Journal of Religion* 76 (1996): 206–32.

———. "Introduction: The Nature of New Testament Theology." In *The Nature of New Testament Theology: The Contribution of William Wrede and Adolf Schlatter,* edited by Robert Morgan, 1–67. London: SCM Press, 1973.

———. "Jesus Christ, the Wisdom of God." In *Reading Texts, Seeking Wisdom: Scripture and Theology,* edited by David F. Ford and Graham Stanton, 22–37. Grand Rapids, Mich.: Eerdmans, 2003.

———. "New Testament Theology." In *Biblical Theology: Problems and Perspectives,* edited by Steven J. Kraftchick, Charles D. Myers Jr., and Ben C. Ollenburger, 104–30. Nashville: Abingdon Press, 1995.

Morgan, Robert, ed. *The Religion of the Incarnation.* Bristol: Bristol Classical Press, 1989.

Morgan, Robert, ed. and trans. *The Nature of New Testament Theology: The Contribution of William Wrede and Adolf Schlatter.* London: SCM Press, 1973.

Muller, Richard. "Biblical Interpretation in the Era of the Reformation: The View from the Middle Ages." In *Biblical Interpretation in the Era of the Reformation: Essays Presented to David C. Steinmetz,* edited by Richard A. Muller and John L. Thompson, 3–22. Grand Rapids, Mich.: Eerdmans, 1996.

Murphy, Roland, O. Carm. "Patristic and Medieval Exegesis: Help or Hindrance?" *Catholic Biblical Quarterly* 43 (1981): 505–16.

———. "The Song of Songs: Critical Biblical Scholarship vis-à-vis Exegetical Traditions." In *Understanding the Word: Essays in Honor of Bernhard W. Anderson,* edited by James T. Butler, Edgar W. Conrad, and Ben C. Ollenburger, 63–69. Sheffield: JSOT Press, 1985.

———. "What Is Catholic about Catholic Biblical Scholarship?—Revisited." *Biblical Theology Bulletin* 28 (1998): 112–19.

Nadler, Steven. *Spinoza: A Life.* Cambridge: Cambridge University Press, 1999.

———. *Spinoza's Heresy: Immortality and the Jewish Mind.* Oxford: Oxford University Press, 2001.

Natalis, Alexander. *Scripturae Sacrae. Cursus Completus*, vol. 23. Edited by Jacque-Paul Migne. Paris: 1840.

Neuhaus, Richard John, ed. *Biblical Interpretation in Crisis: The Ratzinger Conference on Bible and Church*. Grand Rapids, Mich.: Eerdmans, 1989.

Neusner, Jacob. *Rabbinic Literature and the New Testament: What We Cannot Show, We Do Not Know*. Valley Forge, Pa.: Trinity Press International, 1994.

Newman, Carey C., ed. *Jesus and the Restoration of Israel: A Critical Assessment of N. T. Wright's* Jesus and the Victory of God. Downers Grove, Ill.: Inter-Varsity Press, 1999.

Newman, John Henry. *An Essay on the Development of Christian Doctrine*. Notre Dame: University of Notre Dame Press, 1989.

Nicholas of Lyra. *Bibliorum Sacrorum Tomus Quintus cum Glossa Ordinaria, & Nicolai Lyrani expositionibus, literali & morali: Additionibus insuper & Replicis*. Lugduni: 1545.

Nichols, Aidan, O.P., *Scribe of the Kingdom: Essays on Theology and Culture*. London: Sheed & Ward, 1994.

———. "Thomism and the Nouvelle Théologie." *Thomist* 64 (2000): 1–19.

Novak, David. *Talking with Christians: Musings of a Jewish Theologian*. Grand Rapids, Mich.: Eerdmans, 2005.

Nyende, Peter. "Why Bother with Hebrews? An African Perspective." *Heythrop Journal* 46 (2005): 512–24.

Ochs, Peter. "Borowitz and the Postmodern Renewal of Theology." In *Reviewing the Covenant: Eugene B. Borowitz and the Postmodern Renewal of Jewish Theology*, edited by Peter Ochs, with Eugene B. Borowitz, 111–44. Albany: State University of New York Press, 2000.

———. "The Emergence of Postmodern Jewish Theology and Philosophy." In *Reviewing the Covenant: Eugene B. Borowitz and the Postmodern Renewal of Jewish Theology*, edited by Peter Ochs, 3–34. Albany: State University of New York Press, 2000.

———. Foreword to *Revelation Restored: Divine Writ and Critical Responses* by David Weiss Halivni, xi–xviii. Boulder: Westview Press, 1997.

———. "An Introduction to Postcritical Scriptural Interpretation." In *The Return to Scripture in Judaism and Christianity: Essays in Postcritical Scriptural Interpretation*, edited by Peter Ochs, 3–52. New York: Paulist Press, 1993.

———. "Max Kadushin as Rabbinic Pragmatist." In *Understanding the Rabbinic Mind*, edited by Peter Ochs, 165–96. Atlanta: Scholars Press, 1990.

———. *Peirce, Pragmatism, and the Logic of Scripture*. Cambridge: Cambridge University Press, 1998.

———. "Postcritical Scriptural Interpretation." In *Torah and Revelation*, edited by Dan Cohn-Sherbok, 51–73. New York: Edwin Mellen Press, 1992.

————. "A Rabbinic Pragmatism." In *Theology and Dialogue*, edited by Bruce Marshall, 213–48. Notre Dame: University of Notre Dame Press, 1990.

————. "Talmudic Scholarship as Textual Reasoning: Halivni's Pragmatic Historiography." In *Textual Reasonings: Jewish Philosophy and Text Study at the End of the Twentieth Century*, edited by Peter Ochs and Nancy Levene, 120–43. Grand Rapids, Mich.: Eerdmans, 2002.

————. "Three Postcritical Encounters with the Burning Bush." In *The Theological Interpretation of Scripture*, edited by Stephen E. Fowl, 129–42. Oxford: Blackwell, 1997.

Ochs, Peter, ed. *The Return to Scripture in Judaism and Christianity: Essays in Postcritical Scriptural Interpretation*. New York: Paulist Press, 1993.

Ochs, Peter, ed., with Eugene B. Borowitz. *Reviewing the Covenant: Eugene B. Borowitz and the Postmodern Renewal of Jewish Theology*. Albany: State University of New York Press, 2000.

————, ed. *Understanding the Rabbinic Mind*. Atlanta: Scholars Press, 1990.

Ochs, Peter, and Nancy Levene, eds. *Textual Reasonings: Jewish Philosophy and Text Study at the End of the Twentieth Century*. Grand Rapids, Mich.: Eerdmans, 2002.

O'Collins, Gerald, S.J. *Retrieving Fundamental Theology: The Three Styles of Contemporary Theology*. New York: Paulist Press, 1993.

Olin, John C. *The Catholic Reformation: Savonarola to Ignatius Loyola*. New York: Fordham University Press, 1992.

Ollenburger, Ben C. "Biblical Theology: Situating the Discipline." In *Understanding the Word: Essays in Honor of Bernhard W. Anderson*, edited by James T. Butler, Edgar W. Conrad, and Ben C. Ollenburger, 37–62. Sheffield: JSOT Press, 1985.

————. "What Krister Stendahl 'Meant'—A Normative Critique of 'Descriptive Biblical Theology." *Horizons of Biblical Theology* 8 (1996): 61–98.

Olsen, Glenn W. "Problems with the Contrast between Circular and Linear Concepts of Time in the Interpretation of Ancient and Early Medieval History." *Fides Quarens Intellectum* 1 (2001): 41–65.

Ong, Walter. *Orality and Literacy: The Technologizing of the Word*. 1982. London: Routledge, 1988.

O'Regan, Cyril. "*De Doctrina christiana* and Modern Hermeneutics." In *De Doctrina Christiana: A Classic of Western Culture*, edited by Duane W.H. Arnold and Pamela Bright, 217–44. Notre Dame: University of Notre Dame Press, 1995.

O'Reilly, Terence. Introduction to *Spiritual Writings* by Denis the Carthusian, translated by Íde M. Ní Riain, ix–xiv. Dublin: Four Courts Press, 2004.

Osborne, Thomas M., Jr. *Love of Self and Love of God in Thirteenth-Century Ethics*. Notre Dame: University of Notre Dame Press, 2005.

————. "Ockham as a Divine-Command Theorist." *Religious Studies* 41 (2005): 1–22.

Pabst, Adrian. "De la chrétienté à la modernité? Lecture critique des theses de *Radical Orthodoxy* sur la rupture scotiste et ockhamienne et sur le renouveau de la théologie de saint Thomas d'Aquin." *Revue des sciences théologiques et philosophiques* 86 (2002): 561–99.

Patton, Corrine. "Canon and Tradition: The Limits of the Old Testament in Scholastic Discussion." In *Theological Exegesis*, edited by Christopher Seitz and Kathryn Greene-McCreight, 75–95. Grand Rapids, Mich.: Eerdmans, 1999.

————. Introduction to "Selections from Nicholas of Lyra's *Commentary on Exodus*." Translated by Corrine Patton. In *The Theological Interpretation of Scripture: Classic and Contemporary Readings*, edited by Stephen E. Fowl, 114–19. Oxford: Blackwell, 1997.

Pelikan, Jaroslav. "*Canonica regula*: The Trinitarian Hermeneutics of Augustine." *Proceedings of the Patristic, Medieval and Renaissance Conference* 12–13 (1987–88): 17–29.

Perkins, Pheme. "The Theological Implications of New Testament Pluralism." *Catholic Biblical Quarterly* 50 (1988): 5–23.

Perrier, Emmanuel, O.P. "Duns Scotus Facing Reality: Between Absolute Contingency and Unquestionable Consistency." *Modern Theology* 21 (2005): 619–43.

Pickstock, Catherine. "Duns Scotus: His Historical and Contemporary Significance." *Modern Theology* 21 (2005): 543–74.

Pieper, Josef. *The Truth of All Things*. In Pieper, *Living the Truth*, 11–105. San Francisco: Ignatius Press, 1989.

Pinckaers, Servais, O.P., "Der Sinn für die Freundschaftsliebe als Urtatsache der thomistischen Ethik." In *Sein und Ethos. Untersuchungen zur Grundlegung der Ethik*, edited by P. Engelhardt, O.P. , 228–35. Mainz: 1960.

————. *The Pinckaers Reader: Renewing Thomistic Moral Theology*, edited by John Berkman and Craig Steven Titus, 73–89. Washington, D.C.: Catholic University of America Press, 2005.

————. *The Sources of Christian Ethics*. Translated from the 3d ed. by Mary Thomas Noble, O.P. Washington, D.C.: Catholic University of America Press, 1995.

Pius XII, Pope. Encyclical *Divino Afflante Spiritu*. 1943.

Poffet, Jean-Michel, O.P. *Les chrétiens et la Bible. Les Anciens et les Modernes*. Paris: Cerf, 1998.

Pomata, Gianna, and Nancy G. Siraisi, eds. *Historia: Empiricism and Erudition in Early Modern Europe*. Cambridge: MIT Press, 2005.

Pontifical Biblical Commission. "Bible et christologie" (1984). In *Scripture and Christology: A Statement of the Biblical Commission with a Commentary* by Joseph Fitzmyer, S.J. New York: Paulist Press, 1986.

————. *The Interpretation of the Bible in the Church*. Translated by John Kilgallen and Brendan Byrne. Boston: St. Paul's Books & Media, 1993.

————. "The Jewish People and Their Sacred Scriptures in the Christian Bible." Vatican City: Libreria Editrice Vaticana, 2002.

Popkin, Richard. *The History of Scepticism: From Savonarola to Bayle.* Revised and expanded ed. Oxford: Oxford University Press, 2003.

————. *Isaac La Peyrère, 1596–1676.* Leiden: Brill, 1987.

Porter, Stanley E. "Hermeneutics, Biblical Interpretation, and Theology: Hunch, Holy Spirit, or Hard Work?" in I. Howard Marshall, *Beyond the Bible: Moving from Scripture to Theology,* 112–18. Grand Rapids, Mich.: Baker, 2004.

Potok, Chaim. *In the Beginning.* New York: Fawcett, 1986.

Preus, James Samuel. *From Shadow to Promise: Old Testament Interpretation from Augustine to the Young Luther.* Cambridge: Harvard University Press, 1969.

————. *Spinoza and the Irrelevance of Biblical Authority.* Cambridge: Cambridge University Press, 2001.

Prickett, Stephen. *Words and* The Word: *Language, Poetics and Biblical Interpretation.* Cambridge: Cambridge University Press, 1986.

Prior, Joseph G. *The Historical Critical Method in Catholic Exegesis.* Rome: Editrice Pontificia Univerità Gregoriana, 1999.

Rae, Murray A. *History and Hermeneutics.* Edinburgh: T. & T. Clark, 2005.

Radner, Ephraim. *Hope among the Fragments: The Broken Church and its Engagement with Scripture.* Grand Rapids, Mich.: Brazos, 2004.

————. "Sublimity and Providence: The Spiritual Discipline of Figural Reading." *Ex Auditu* 18 (2002): 155–70.

Rahner, Karl, S.J. "Exegesis and Dogmatic Theology." In *Dogmatic vs Biblical Theology,* edited by Herbert Vorgrimler, 31–65. Baltimore: Helicon Press, 1964.

————. *Foundations of Christian Faith: An Introduction to the Idea of Christianity.* New York: Crossroad, 1978.

Ratzinger, Joseph. "Biblical Interpretation in Crisis: On the Question of the Foundations and Approaches of Exegesis Today." In *Biblical Interpretation in Crisis: The Ratzinger Conference on Bible and Church,* edited by Richard John Neuhaus, 1–23. Grand Rapids, Mich.: Eerdmans, 1989.

————. *Called to Communion: Understanding the Church Today.* Translated by Adrian Walker from the second German ed. San Francisco: Ignatius Press, 1996.

————. *On the Way to Jesus Christ.* Translated by Michael J. Miller. German, 2004. San Francisco: Ignatius Press, 2005.

————. "Origin and Background," commentary on *Dei Verbum.* In *Commentary on the Documents of Vatican II,* vol. 3, edited by Herbert Vorgrimler, translated by William Glen-Doepel et al., 155–66. German, 1967. New York: Crossroad, 1989.

————. Preface to "The Interpretation of the Bible in the Church" by the Pontifical Biblical Commission, translated by John Kilgallen and Brendan Byrne, 27–29. Boston: St. Paul's Books & Media, 1993.

————. "Preface," commentary on *Dei Verbum*. In *Commentary on the Documents of Vatican II*, vol. 3, edited by Herbert Vorgrimler, translated by William Glen-Doepel et al., 167–69. German, 1967. New York: Crossroad, 1989.

————. "Revelation Itself," commentary on chapter 1 of *Dei Verbum*. In *Commentary on the Documents of Vatican II*, vol. 3, edited by Herbert Vorgrimler, translated by William Glen-Doepel et al., 170–80. German, 1967. New York: Crossroad, 1989.

————. "The Transmission of Divine Revelation," commentary on chapter 2 of *Dei Verbum*. In *Commentary on the Documents of Vatican II*, vol. 3, edited by Herbert Vorgrimler, translated by William Glen-Doepel et al., 181–98. German, 1967. New York: Crossroad, 1989.

————. "Sacred Scripture in the Life of the Church," commentary on chapter 6 of *Dei Verbum*. In *Commentary on the Documents of Vatican II*, vol. 3, edited by Herbert Vorgrimler, translated by William Glen-Doepel et al., 262–72. German, 1967. New York: Crossroad, 1989.

Reno, R. R. *The Ruins of the Church*. Grand Rapids, Mich.: Brazos Press, 2002.

Reno, R. R., and John J. O'Keefe. *Sanctified Vision: An Introduction to Early Christian Interpretation of the Bible*. Baltimore: Johns Hopkins, 2005.

Reventlow, Henning Graf. *The Authority of the Bible and the Rise of the Modern World*. Translated by John Bowden. Containing additional material supplied by the author. German, 1980. London: SCM Press, 1984.

Richardson, Alan. "The Rise of Modern Biblical Scholarship and Recent Discussion of the Authority of the Bible." In *The Cambridge History of the Bible: The West from the Reformation to the Present Day*, vol. 3, edited by S. L. Greenslade, 294–338. Cambridge: Cambridge University Press, 1963.

Ricoeur, Paul. "From Interpretation to Translation." In *Thinking Biblically: Exegetical and Hermeneutical Studies* by André LaCocque and Paul Ricoeur, translated by David Pellauer, 331–61. Chicago: University of Chicago Press, 1998.

————. "Thinking Creation." In *Thinking Biblically: Exegetical and Hermeneutical Studies* by André LaCocque and Paul Ricoeur, translated by David Pellauer, 31–67. Chicago: University of Chicago Press, 1998.

————. *Time and Narrative*. 3 vols. Chicago: University of Chicago Press, 1984–88.

Rist, John. *On Inoculating Moral Philosophy against God*. Milwaukee: Marquette University Press, 1999.

————. *Real Ethics: Reconsidering the Foundations of Morality*. Cambridge: Cambridge University Press, 2002.

Rogers, Eugene, Jr. "How the Virtues of the Interpreter Presuppose and Perfect Hermeneutics: The Case of Thomas Aquinas." *Journal of Religion* 76 (1996): 64–81.

Rowe, C. Kavin. "Biblical Pressure and Trinitarian Hermeneutics." *Pro Ecclesia* 11 (2002): 295–312.

—. "The God of Israel and Jesus Christ: Luke, Marcion, and the Unity of the Canon." *Nova et Vetera* 1 (2003): 359–80.

Rowland, Christopher. "An Open Letter to Francis Watson on *Text, Church and World*." *Scottish Journal of Theology* 48 (1995).

Rudolph, David J. "Messianic Jews and Christian Theology: Restoring an Historical Voice to the Contemporary Discussion." *Pro Ecclesia* 14 (2005): 58–84.

Russo, A. *Henri de Lubac. Teologia e dogma nella storia. L'influsso di Blondel.* Rome: Studium, 1990.

Ryan, Stephen D., O.P. "The Text of the Bible and Catholic Biblical Scholarship." *Nova et Vetera* 4 (2006): 132–41.

Sanders, James A. "Canonical Context and Canonical Criticism." *Horizons in Biblical Theology* 2 (1980): 173–97.

—. *From Sacred Story to Sacred Text: Canon as Paradigm.* Philadelphia: Fortress Press, 1987.

Sandys-Wunsch, John, and Laurence Eldrege. "J. P. Gabler and the Distinction between Biblical and Dogmatic Theology: Translation, Commentary, and Discussion of His Originality." *Scottish Journal of Theology* 33 (1980): 133–58.

Saperstein, Marc. "Jewish Typological Exegesis after Nachmanides." *Jewish Studies Quarterly* 1 (1993–94): 158–70.

Schenk, Richard, O.P. "From Providence to Grace: Thomas Aquinas and the Platonisms of the Mid-Thirteenth Century." *Nova et Vetera* 3 (2005): 307–20.

Schindler, David L. "Biotechnology and the Givenness of the Good: Posing Properly the Moral Question Regarding Human Dignity." *Communio* 31 (2004): 612–44.

Schlabach, Gerald W. *For the Joy Set before Us: Augustine and Self-Denying Love.* Notre Dame: University of Notre Dame Press, 2001.

Schlatter, Adolf. "The Theology of the New Testament and Dogmatics" (1909). In *The Nature of New Testament Theology: The Contribution of William Wrede and Adolf Schlatter*, edited and translated by Robert Morgan. London: SCM Press, 1973.

Schleiermacher, Friedrich. *The Christian Faith.* Edited by H. R. Mackintosh and J. S. Stewart. Edinburgh: T. & T. Clark, 1989.

Schmaltz, Tad M. *Radical Cartesianism: The French Reception of Descartes.* Cambridge: Cambridge University Press, 2002.

Schneewind, Jerome B. *The Invention of Autonomy: A History of Modern Moral Philosophy.* Cambridge: Cambridge University Press, 1998.

Schneider, Carolyn. "The Intimate Connection between Christ and Christians in Athanasius." *Scottish Journal of Theology* 58 (2005): 1–12.

Schniedewind, William M. *How the Bible Became a Book: The Textualization of Ancient Israel.* Cambridge: Cambridge University Press, 2004.

Scholder, Klaus. *The Birth of Modern Critical Theology: Origins and Problems of Biblical Criticism in the Seventeenth Century.* Translated by John Bowden. German, 1966. Philadelphia: Trinity Press International, 1990.

Schultz, Richard. "What Is 'Canonical' about a Canonical Biblical Theology? Genesis as a Case Study of Recent Old Testament Proposals." In *Biblical Theology: Retrospect and Prospect,* edited by Scott J. Hafemann, 83–99. Downers Grove, Ill.: InterVarsity Press, 2002.

Seban, Jean-Loup. "From Joseph-Juste Scaliger to Johann Gottfied Eichhorn: The Beginnings of Biblical Criticism." In *Biblical Theology: Problems and Perspectives,* edited by Steven J. Kraftchick, Charles D. Myers Jr., and Ben C. Ollenburger, 28–53. Nashville: Abingdon Press, 1995.

Seitz, Christopher R. "Christological Interpretation of Texts and Trinitarian Claims to Truth: An Engagement with Francis Watson's *Text and Truth.*" *Scottish Journal of Theology* 52 (1999): 209–26.

———. *Figured Out: Typology and Providence in Christian Scripture.* Louisville: Westminster/John Knox, 2001.

———. "Of Mortal Appearance: The Earthly Jesus and Isaiah as a Type of Christian Scripture." *Ex Auditu* 14 (1998): 31–41.

———. "Two Testaments and the Failure of One Tradition History." In *Biblical Theology: Retrospect and Prospect,* edited by Scott J. Hafemann, 195–211. Downers Grove, Ill.: InterVarsity Press, 2002.

———. "What Lesson Will History Teach? The Book of the Twelve as History." In *"Behind" the Text: History and Biblical Interpretation,* edited by Craig Bartholomew et al., 443–67. Grand Rapids, Mich.: Zondervan, 2003.

———. *Word without End: The Old Testament As Abiding Theological Witness.* Grand Rapids, Mich.: Eerdmans, 1998.

Seitz, Christopher, and Kathryn Greene-McCreight, eds. *Theological Exegesis: Essays in Honor of Brevard S. Childs.* Grand Rapids, Mich.: Eerdmans, 1999.

Sheets, John R., S.J. "The Scriptural Dimension of St. Thomas." *American Ecclesiatical Review* 144 (1961): 154–73.

Sherwin, Michael S., O.P. *By Knowledge and By Love: Charity and Knowledge in the Moral Theology of St. Thomas Aquinas.* Washington, D.C.: Catholic University of America Press, 2005.

———. "Christ the Teacher in St. Thomas's *Commentary on the Gospel of John.*" In *Reading John with St. Thomas: Theological Exegesis and Speculative Theology,* edited by Michael Dauphinais and Matthew Levering, 173–93. Washington, D.C.: Catholic University of America Press, 2005.

Siker, Jeffrey. "How to Decide? Homosexual Christians, the Bible, and Gentile Inclusion." *Theology Today* 51 (1994): 219–34.

Sixtus, Bernd. "Bridging the Gap? On Some Suggestions towards Solving the Normative Problem in Ecclesial Exegesis." *Scottish Journal of Theology* 58 (2005): 13–38.

Skinner, Quentin. "Motives, Intentions and the Interpretation of Texts." *New Literary History* 3 (1971): 393–408.

Smith, Jonathan Z. *Drudgery Divine: On the Comparison of Early Christianities and the Religions of Late Antiquity.* Chicago: University of Chicago Press, 1990.

Snodgrass, Klyne R. "From Allegorizing to Allegorizing: A History of the Interpretation of the Parables of Jesus." In *The Challenge of Jesus' Parables*, edited by Richard N. Longenecker, 3–29. Grand Rapids, Mich.: Eerdmans, 2000.

Sorabji, Richard. *Time, Creation, and the Continuum: Theories in Antiquity and the Early Middle Ages.* Ithaca: Cornell University Press, 1983.

Spinoza, Baruch. *Theological-Political Treatise.* Gebhart ed., 2d ed. Translated by Samuel Shirley. Indianapolis: Hackett, 2001.

Stallsworth, Paul. "The Story of an Encounter." In *Biblical Interpretation in Crisis: The Ratzinger Conference on Bible and Church*, edited by Richard John Neuhaus, 102–90. Grand Rapids, Mich.: Eerdmans, 1989.

Stanton, Graham N., Bruce W. Longenecker, and Stephen C. Barton, eds. *The Holy Spirit and Christian Origins: Essays In Honor of James D. G. Dunn.* Grand Rapids, Mich.: Eerdmans, 2004.

Starr, James M. *Sharers in Divine Nature: 2 Pet 1.4 in its Hellenistic Context.* Stockholm: Almqvist & Wiksell, 2000.

Steiner, George. "The Good Books." *Religion and Intellectual Life* 6 (1989): 15–16.

Steinmetz, David C. "The Superiority of Precritical Exegesis." *Theology Today* 37 (1980): 27–38.

———. "Uncovering a Second Narrative: Detective Fiction and the Construction of Historical Method." In *The Art of Reading Scripture*, edited by Ellen F. Davis and Richard B. Hays, 54–65. Grand Rapids, Mich.: Eerdmans, 2003.

Stendahl, Krister. "Biblical Theology." In *The Interpreter's Dictionary of the Bible*," vol. 1, edited by Keith R. Crim and George A. Buttrick. Nashville: Abingdon Press, 1976.

———. "Method in the Study of Biblical Theology." In *The Bible in Modern Scholarship*, edited by J. Philip Hyatt. Nashville: Abingdon Press, 1965.

Stuhlmacher, Peter. *Historical Criticism and Theological Interpretation of Scripture: Toward a Hermeneutics of Consent.* Translated by Roy A. Harrisville. Philadelphia: Fortress Press, 1977.

Sweetman, Robert. "Beryl Smalley, Thomas of Cantimpré, and the Performative Reading of Scripture: A Study in Two *Exempla*." In *With Reverence for the Word: Medieval Scriptural Exegesis in Judaism, Christianity, and Islam*, edited by Jane Dammen McAuliffe, Barry D. Walfish, and Joseph W. Goering, 256–75. Oxford: Oxford University Press, 2003.

Swierzawski, Waclaw. "God and the Mystery of His Wisdom in the Pauline Commentaries of Saint Thomas Aquinas." *Divus Thomas* 74 (1971): 466–500.

Synan, Edward. "The Four 'Senses' and Four Exegetes." In *With Reverence for the Word: Medieval Scriptural Exegesis in Judaism, Christianity, and Islam*, edited by Jane Dammen McAuliffe, Barry D. Walfish, and Joseph W. Goering, 225–36. Oxford: Oxford University Press, 2003.

Tanner, Kathryn. *God and Creation in Christian Theology*. Oxford: Blackwell, 1988.

Tanner, Norman P., S.J. *Decrees of the Ecumenical Councils*. Vol. 2, *Trent–Vatican II*. Washington, D.C.: Georgetown University Press, 1990.

Tavard, George. *Holy Writ or Holy Church: The Crisis of the Protestant Reformation*. New York: Harper & Brothers, 1959.

Taylor, Charles. *Sources of the Self: The Making of Modern Identity*. Cambridge: Harvard University Press, 1989.

Thiselton, Anthony C. "From Speech Acts to Scripture Acts: The Covenant of Discourse and the Discourse of Covenant." In *After Pentecost: Language and Biblical Interpretation*, edited by C. Bartholomew, C. Greene, and K. Müller, 1–49. Carlisle: Paternoster, 2001.

———. *New Horizons in Hermeneutics: The Theory and Practice of Transforming Biblical Reading*. Grand Rapids, Mich.: Zondervan, 1992.

Toner, Christopher. "Angelic Sin in Aquinas and Scotus and the Genesis of Some Central Objections to Contemporary Virtue Ethics." *Thomist* 69 (2005): 79–125.

Topel, John. "Faith, Exegesis, and Theology." *Irish Theological Quarterly* 69 (2004): 337–48.

Torrell, Jean-Pierre, O.P., *Saint Thomas Aquinas*. Vol. 2, *Spiritual Master*. Translated by Robert Royal. Washington, D.C.: Catholic University of America Press, 2003.

Turner, Denys. *The Darkness of God: Negativity in Christian Mysticism*. Cambridge: Cambridge University Press, 1995.

———. *Faith, Reason and the Existence of God*. Cambridge: Cambridge University Press, 2004.

———. "Metaphor, Poetry and Allegory: Erotic Love in the *Sermons on the Song of Songs* of Bernard of Clairvaux." In *Reading Texts, Seeking Wisdom: Scripture and Theology*, edited by David F. Ford and Graham Stanton, 202–16. Grand Rapids, Mich.: Eerdmans, 2003.

Uffenheimer, Benjamin, and Henning Graf Reventlow, eds. *Creative Biblical Exegesis: Christian and Jewish Hermeneutics through the Centuries*. Sheffield: Sheffield Academic Press, 1988.

Valls, Carmen Aparicio. "La tradición según la *Dei Verbum* y su importancia en la teología ecuménica actual." *Gregorianum* 86 (2005): 163–81.

Vanhoozer, Kevin J. *Biblical Narrative in the Philosophy of Paul Ricoeur: A Study in Hermeneutics and Theology.* Cambridge: Cambridge University Press, 1990.

———. *The Drama of Doctrine: A Canonical-Linguistic Approach to Theology.* Louisville: Westminster/John Knox, 2004.

———. *Is There a Meaning in This Text? The Bible, the Reader, and the Morality of Literary Knowledge.* Grand Rapids, Mich.: Zondervan, 1998.

Vatican Council II. *Dei Verbum.* 1965. In *Vatican Council II.* Vol. 1, *The Conciliar and Post Conciliar Documents*, edited by Austin Flannery, O.P., 750–65. Collegeville, Minn.: Liturgical Press, 1992.

Venard, Olivier-Thomas, O.P. "'La Bible en ses Traditions': The New Project of the *École biblique et archéologique française de Jérusalem* Presented as a 'Fourth-Generation' Enterprise." *Nova et Vetera* 4 (2006): 142–59.

Verger, Jacques. "L'exégèse de l'Université." In *Le moyen âge et la Bible*, edited by Pierre Riché and Guy Lobrichon, 199–232. Paris: Beauchesne, 1984.

Voderholzer, Rudolf. *Die Einheit der Schrift und ihr geistiger Sinn. Der Beitrag Henri de Lubacs zur Erforschung von Geschichte und Systematik christlicher Bibelhermeneutik.* Einsiedeln: Johannes Verlag, 1998.

Volf, Miroslav. "Johannine Dualism and Contemporary Pluralism." *Modern Theology* 21 (2005): 189–217.

von Balthasar, Hans Urs. *The Glory of the Lord: A Theological Aesthetics.* Vol. 1, *Seeing the Form.* Translated by from the 2d ed. by Erasmo Leiva-Merikakis. San Francisco: Ignatius Press, 1987.

———. *Theo-Drama: Theological Dramatic Theory.* Vol. 4, *The Action.* Translated by Graham Harrison. German, 1980. San Francisco: Ignatius Press, 1994.

———. *A Theology of History.* New York: Sheed & Ward, 1963.

———. *The Theology of Karl Barth: Exposition and Interpretation.* Translated by Edward T. Oakes, S.J. German, 1951. San Francisco: Ignatius Press, 1992.

Vondey, Wolfgang. "The Holy Spirit and Time in Contemporary Catholic and Protestant Theology." *Scottish Journal of Theology* 58 (2005): 393–409.

Vorgrimler, Herbert, ed. *Commentary on the Documents of Vatican II.* Vol. 3. Translated by William Glen-Doepel et al. German, 1967. New York: Crossroad, 1989.

———. *Dogmatic vs Biblical Theology.* Baltimore: Helicon Press, 1964.

Waddell, Chrysogonus. "A Christological Interpretation of Psalm 1? The Psalter and Christian Prayer." *Communio* 22 (1995): 502–21.

Wagner, J. Ross. *Heralds of the Good News: Isaiah and Paul in Concert in the Letter to the Romans.* Leiden: Brill, 2002.

Wainwright, Geoffrey. "Towards an Ecumenical Hermeneutic: How Can All Christians Read the Scriptures Together?" *Gregorianum* 76 (1995): 639–62.

————. "Psalm 33 Interpreted of the Triune God." *Ex Auditu* 16 (2000): 101–20.

Walfish, Barry D. "Typology, Narrative, and History: Isaac ben Joseph ha-Kohen on the Book of Ruth." In *With Reverence for the Word: Medieval Scriptural Exegesis in Judaism, Christianity, and Islam*, edited by Jane Dammen McAuliffe, Barry D. Walfish, and Joseph W. Goering, 119–32. Oxford: Oxford University Press, 2003.

Walker, Adrian. "Editorial: Fundamentalism and the Catholicity of Truth." *Communio* 29 (2002): 5–27.

Wall, Robert W. "Canonical Context and Canonical Conversations." In *Between Two Horizons: Spanning New Testament Studies and Systematic Theology*, edited by Joel B. Green and Max Turner, 165–82. Grand Rapids, Mich.: Eerdmans, 2000.

————. "Reading the Bible from within Our Traditions: The 'Rule of Faith' in Theological Hermeneutics." In *Between Two Horizons: Spanning New Testament Studies and Systematic Theology*, edited by Joel B. Green and Max Turner, 88–107. Grand Rapids, Mich.: Eerdmans, 2000.

————. "The Significance of a Canonical Perspective of the Church's Scripture." In *The Canon Debate*, edited by L. M. McDonald and J. A. Sanders, 528–40. Peabody, Mass.: Hendrickson, 2002.

Wall, Robert W., and Eugene E. Lemcio. *The New Testament as Canon: A Reader in Canonical Criticism*. Sheffield: JSOT Press, 1992.

Wannenwetsch, Bernd. "Intrinsically Evil Acts; or: Why Euthanasia and Abortion Cannot Be Justified." In *Ecumenical Ventures in Ethics: Protestants Engage Pope John Paul II's Moral Encyclicals*, edited by Reinhard Hütter and Theodor Dieter, 185–215. Grand Rapids, Mich.: Eerdmans, 1998.

————. "You Shall Not Kill—What Does It Take? Why We Need the Other Commandments If We Are to Abstain from Killing." In *I Am the Lord Your God: Christian Reflections on the Ten Commandments*, edited by Carl E. Braaten and Christopher R. Seitz, 148–74. Grand Rapids, Mich.: Eerdmans, 2005.

Wansbrough, Henry. "The Jewish People and its Holy Scripture in the Christian Bible." *Irish Theological Quarterly* 67 (2002): 265–75.

Watson, Francis. "Is John's Christology Adoptionist?" In *The Glory of Christ in the New Testament: Studies in Christology*, edited by L. D. Hurst and N. T. Wright, 113–24. Oxford: Clarendon Press, 1987.

————. "The Old Testament as Christian Scripture: A Response to Professor Seitz." *Scottish Journal of Theology* 52 (1999): 227–32.

————. *Paul and the Hermeneutics of Faith*. New York: T. & T. Clark, 2004.

————. *Text and Truth: Redefining Biblical Theology*. Grand Rapids, Mich.: Eerdmans, 1997.

———. *Text, Church and World: Biblical Interpretation in Theological Perspective.* Grand Rapids, Mich.: Eerdmans, 1994.

Webster, John. *Holy Scripture: A Dogmatic Sketch.* Cambridge: Cambridge University Press, 2003.

———. "Purity and Plenitude: Evangelical Reflections on Congar's *Tradition and Traditions.*" *International Journal of Systematic Theology* 7 (2005): 399–413.

———. *Word and Church: Essays in Christian Dogmatics.* Edinburgh: T. &. T. Clark, 2001.

Weinandy, Thomas, O.F.M. Cap., *Does God Suffer?* Notre Dame: University of Notre Dame Press, 2000.

Weinandy, Thomas, O.F.M. Cap., Daniel Keating, and John Yocum, eds. *Aquinas on Scripture: An Introduction to His Biblical Commentaries.* New York: T. & T. Clark, 2005.

Westermann, Claus. "The Old Testament's Understanding of History in Relation to that of the Enlightenment." In *Understanding the Word: Essays in Honor of Bernhard W. Anderson,* edited by James T. Butler, Edgar W. Conrad, and Ben C. Ollenburger, 207–19. Sheffield: JSOT Press, 1985.

Wicks, Jared. "Pieter Smulders and *Dei Verbum*: 5. A Critical Reception of the Schema *De revelatione* of the Mixed Commission (1963)." *Gregorianum* 86 (2005): 92–134.

Wilken, Robert Louis. "In Defense of Allegory." *Modern Theology* 14 (1998): 197–212.

———. "*In Dominico Eloquio*: Learning the Lord's Style of Language." *Communio* 24 (1997): 846–66.

———. "Wilken's Response to Hays." *Communio* 25 (1998): 529–31.

William of Ockham. *Breviloquium de principatu tyrannico super divina et humana.* Translated by John Kilcullen under the title *A Short Discourse on Tyrannical Government over Things Divine and Human, but Especially over the Empire and Those Subject to the Empire, Usurped by Some Who Are Called Highest Pontiffs,* edited by Arthur Stephen McGrade (Cambridge: Cambridge University Press, 1992).

———. *A Letter to the Friars Minor and Other Writings.* Edited by Arthur Stephen McGrade and John Kilcullen. Translated by John Kilcullen. Cambridge: Cambridge University Press, 1995.

Williams, A. N. "Contemplation: Knowledge of God in Augustine's *De Trinitate.*" In *Knowing the Triune God: The Work of the Spirit in the Practices of the Church,* edited by James J. Buckley and David S. Yeago, 121–46. Grand Rapids, Mich.: Eerdmans, 2001.

Williams, David M. *Receiving the Bible in Faith: Historical and Theological Exegesis.* Washington, D.C.: Catholic University of America Press, 2004.

Williams, J. P. "The Incarnational Apophasis of Maximus the Confessor." *Studia Patristica* 37 (2001): 631–35.

Williams, Rowan. "Historical Criticism and Sacred Text." In *Reading Texts, Seeking Wisdom: Scripture and Theology*, edited by David F. Ford and Graham Stanton, 217–28. Grand Rapids, Mich.: Eerdmans, 2003.

———. "The Incarnation as the Basis of Dogma." In *The Religion of the Incarnation*, edited by Robert Morgan. Bristol: Bristol Classical Press, 1989.

———. *On Christian Theology*. Oxford: Blackwell, 2000.

Williams, Thomas. "The Doctrine of Univocity Is True and Salutary." *Modern Theology* 21 (2005): 575–85.

———. "From Metaethics to Action Theory." In *The Cambridge Companion to Duns Scotus*, edited by Thomas Williams, 332–51. Cambridge: Cambridge University Press, 2003.

Williamson, Peter S. "Catholic Principles for Interpreting Scripture." *Catholic Biblical Quarterly* 65 (2003): 327–49.

———. *Catholic Principles for Interpreting Scripture: A Study of the Pontifical Biblical Commission's* The Interpretation of the Bible in the Church. Rome: Editrice Pontificio Istituto Biblico, 2001.

———. "Catholicism and the Bible: An Interview with Albert Vanhoye." *First Things* 74 (June/July 1997): 35–40.

Wolter, Allan B., O.F.M. "The Unshredded Scotus: A Response to Thomas Williams." *American Catholic Philosophical Quarterly* 77 (2003): 315–56.

Wolter, Allan B., O.F.M., and William A. Frank, eds. *Duns Scotus on the Will and Morality*. Translated by Allan B. Wolter, O.F.M. Washington, D.C.: Catholic University of America Press, 1997.

Wolterstorff, Nicholas. *Divine Discourse: Philosophical Reflections on the Claim That God Speaks*. Cambridge: Cambridge University Press, 1995.

Wood, Susan K. *Spiritual Exegesis and the Church in the Theology of Henri de Lubac*. Grand Rapids, Mich.: Eerdmans, 1998.

Work, Telford. *Living and Active: Scripture in the Economy of Salvation*. Grand Rapids, Mich.: Eerdmans, 2002.

Wright, N. T. "In Grateful Dialogue: A Response." In *Jesus and the Restoration of Israel: A Critical Assessment of N. T. Wright's* Jesus and the Victory of God, edited by Carey C. Newman, 244–79. Downers Grove, Ill.: InterVarsity Press, 1999.

———. "Jesus and the Identity of God." *Ex Auditu* 14 (1998): 42–56.

———. *Jesus and the Victory of God*. Minneapolis: Fortress Press, 1996.

———. *The Last Word: Beyond the Bible Wars to a New Understanding of the Authority of Scripture*. New York: HarperSanFrancisco, 2005.

———. "The Letter to the Galatians: Exegesis and Theology." In *Between Two Horizons: Spanning New Testament Studies and Systematic Theology*, edited by Joel B. Green and Max Turner, 205–36. Grand Rapids, Mich.: Eerdmans, 2000.

———. *The New Testament and the People of God*. Minneapolis: Fortress Press, 1992.

————. *The Resurrection of the Son of God*. Minneapolis: Fortress Press, 2003.

————. "The Servant and Jesus: The Relevance of the Colloquy for the Current Quest for Jesus." In *Jesus and the Suffering Servant*, edited by William II. Bellinger and William R. Farmer, 283–99. Harrisburg, Pa.: Trinity Press International, 1998.

Yeago, David S. "The New Testament and Nicene Dogma." *Pro Ecclesia 3* (1994): 152–64.

————. "Re-Entering the Scriptural World." *Nova et Vetera* 4 (2006): 159–71.

Yerushalmi, Yosef Hayim. *Zakhor: Jewish History and Jewish Memory*. Seattle: University of Washington Press, 1996.

Young, Frances. *Virtuoso Theology: The Bible and Interpretation*. 1993. Eugene, Ore.: Wipf & Stock, 2002.

Zenger, E. *Das Erste Testament. Das jüdische Bibel und die Christen*. Düsseldorf: Patmos Verlag, 1991.

Zimmermann, Jens. *Recovering Theological Hermeneutics: An Incarnational-Trinitarian Theory of Interpretation*. Grand Rapids, Mich.: Baker, 2004.

INDEX

Abraham, 123
Adam, 32, 123
Adam, A. K. M., 206
Al-Ghazali, 152
Albert the Great, 37
allegory, 119, 123, 183
Alter, Robert, 201
Ambrose, 50, 52
analogy, 19
Anderson, Gary A., 236
anti-Judaism, 92, 94–95
anti-Semitism, 92, 94, 104
Aquaviva, Claudius, 50
Aquinas, Thomas, 10, 11, 19, 22,
    25–34, 37, 48, 54, 57, 61, 64,
    70–77, 80–81, 86, 89, 92–93,
    96, 103–4, 107, 132–38,
    144–45, 147–48, 161, 186,
    188, 226
Arias, Benito, 50
Aristotelian, 19
Aristotle, 108–9, 112
Arius, 139
Athanasius, 139, 203
Augustine, 21, 28, 42, 46, 50, 54–56,
    59, 64–71, 73, 77, 81, 86–87,
    89, 102, 137, 183, 204–5
authority, 109–10, 124–28, 237

autonomy, 14, 20, 27, 128
Ayres, Lewis, 185, 217

Babcock, William, 87, 89
baptism, 129
Barr, James, 46, 189–91
Barth, Karl, 12, 163
Baumgarten, Sigmund Jakob, 21
beatific vision, 45
Bede, 50
biblical theology, 119
biblical Thomism, 252
Blondel, Maurice, 145
Bockmuehl, Markus, 147–48,
    199–200
Bonaventure, 37
Boulnois, Olivier, 19–20
Bouyer, Louis, 46
Brett, Mark, 86
Brown, Raymond, 58–61, 196–99,
    202, 219, 239
Brueggemann, Walter, 209–10
Buddha, Gautama, 103
Burrell, David B., 170

Cajetan, Thomas de Vio, Cardinal,
    47–49, 52
Calvin, John, 190–91

MATTHEW LEVERING

is associate professor of theology at
Ave Maria University. He has published numerous books,
including *Christ's Fulfillment of Torah and Temple:
Salvation according to Thomas Aquinas*
(University of Notre Dame Press, 2002).